Discovering Computers

Technology in a World of Computers, Mobile Devices, and the Internet

ESSENTIALS ENHANCED

Discovering Computers

Technology in a World of Computers, Mobile Devices, and the Internet

ESSENTIALS ENHANCED

Misty E. Vermaat
Susan L. Sebok
Steven M. Freund

Jennifer T. Campbell
Mark Frydenberg, Bentley University

Shelly Cashman Series®

 CENGAGE
Learning·

Australia • Brazil • Japan • Korea • Mexico • Singapore • Spain • United Kingdom • United States

CENGAGE
Learning

Discovering Computers: Technology in a World of Computers, Mobile Devices, and the Internet, Essentials Enhanced
Misty E. Vermaat
Susan L. Sebok
Steven M. Freund
Jennifer T. Campbell
Mark Frydenberg

Product Director: Kathleen McMahon

Product Team Manager: Donna Gridley

Senior Content Developer: Emma Newsom

Associate Content Developer: Crystal Parenteau

Marketing Managers: Kristie Clark, Gretchen Swann

Marketing Coordinator: Elizabeth Murphy

Manufacturing Planner: Julio Esperas

Senior Content Project Manager: Matthew Hutchinson

Development Editor: Lyn Markowicz

Researcher: F. William Vermaat

Management Services: PreMediaGlobal

Interior Designer: Joel Sadagursky

Art Director: Cheryl Pearl, GEX

Text Design: Joel Sadagursky

Cover Design: Lisa Kuhn, Curio Press, LLC

Cover Photos: Tom Kates Photography

Illustrator: PreMedialGlobal

Compositor: PreMedialGlobal

Printer: RRD Menasha

Library of Congress Control Number: 2014930132

ISBN-13: 978-1-285-84553-1

ISBN-10: 1-285-84553-6

Course Technology
20 Channel Center Street
Boston, MA 02210
USA

Cengage Learning is a leading provider of customized learning solutions with office locations around the globe, including Singapore, the United Kingdom, Australia, Mexico, Brazil and Japan. Locate your local office at:
international.cengage.com/region

Cengage Learning products are represented in Canada by Nelson Education, Ltd.

Visit our Web site **www.cengage.com/ct/shellycashman**

Purchase any of our products at your local college bookstore or at our preferred online store at **www.cengagebrain.com**

Printed in the United States of America
1 2 3 4 5 6 19 18 17 16 15 14

Discovering Computers Essentials Enhanced

Technology in a World of Computers, Mobile Devices, and the Internet

Table of Contents at a Glance

Discovering Computers Essentials Enhanced
Technology in a World of Computers, Mobile Devices, and the Internet

Table of Contents

CHAPTER **3**

Evaluating the Possibilities 103

CHAPTER **4**

Using Software at Work, School, and Home 151

CHAPTER **5**

Identifying Threats, Issues, and Defenses 201

Preface

The Shelly Cashman Series® offers the finest textbooks in computer education. We are proud of the fact that the previous seventeen editions of this textbook have been the most widely used in computer education. With this edition of *Discovering Computers,* Essentials Enhanced we have implemented significant improvements based on current computer trends and comments made by instructors and students. *Discovering Computers: Technology in a World of Computers, Mobile Devices, and the Internet,* Essentials Enhanced continues with the innovation, quality, and reliability you have come to expect from the Shelly Cashman Series.

In *Discovering Computers: Technology in a World of Computers, Mobile Devices, and the Internet,* Essentials Enhanced you will find an educationally sound, highly visual, interactive, and easy-to-follow pedagogy that, with the help of animated figures, relevant video, and interactive activities in the e-book, presents an in-depth treatment of introductory computer subjects. Students will finish the course with a solid understanding of computers, how to use computers, and how to access information on the Web.

Objectives of this Text, e-Book, and CourseMate Web Site

Discovering Computers: Technology in a World of Computers, Mobile Devices, and the Internet, Essentials Enhanced is intended

for use as a stand-alone solution or in combination with an applications, Internet, or programming textbook in a full-semester introductory computer course. No experience with computers is assumed. The objectives of this offering are to:

- Present the most-up-to-date technology in an ever-changing discipline
- Give students an in-depth understanding of why computers are essential in business and society
- Teach the fundamentals of and terms associated with computers and mobile devices, the Internet, programs and apps, and digital safety and security
- Present the material in a visually appealing, interactive, and exciting manner that motivates students to learn
- Provide exercises, lab assignments, and interactive learning activities that allow students to learn by actually using the computer, mobile devices and the Internet
- Present strategies for purchasing desktop computers, mobile computers, and mobile devices
- Provide alternative learning techniques and reinforcement via the Web
- Offer distance-education providers a textbook with a meaningful and exercise-rich digital learning experience

Hallmarks of Discovering Computers

To date, more than six million students have learned about computers using *Discovering Computers*. With the Web integration and interactivity, streaming up-to-date audio and video, extraordinary step-by-step visual drawings and photographs, unparalleled currency, and the Shelly and Cashman touch, this book will make your computer concepts course exciting and dynamic. Hallmarks of Shelly Cashman Series *Discovering Computers* include:

A Proven Pedagogy

Careful explanations of complex concepts, educationally-sound elements, and reinforcement highlight this proven method of presentation.

A Visually Appealing Book that Maintains Student Interest

The latest technology, pictures, drawings, and text are combined artfully to produce a visually appealing and

easy-to-understand book. Many of the figures include a step-by-step presentation, which simplifies the more complex computer concepts. Pictures and drawings reflect the latest trends in computer technology. This combination of pictures, step-by-step drawings, and easy-to-read text layout sets the standard for computer textbook design.

Latest Technologies and Terms

The technologies and terms your students see in *Discovering Computers* are those they will encounter when they start using computers. Only the latest application software is shown throughout the book.

Web Integrated

This book uses the Web as a major learning tool. The purpose of integrating the Web into the book is to (1) offer students additional information and currency

Distinguishing Features

Discovering Computers: Technology in a World of Computers, Mobile Devices, and the Internet Essentials Enhanced includes a variety of compelling features, certain to engage and challenge students, making learning with *Discovering Computers* Essentials Enhanced an enriched experience. These compelling features include:

NEW!

- **Focus On.** New Focus On features present practical information on purchasing and troubleshooting your technology devices, jump starting your career, and also provide hands on workbook opportunities for content reinforcement.
- **Strong Content.** Based on market research and in-depth assessment of organization and each chapter's content, Discovering Computers has been restructured and reorganized to improve retention of material and promote transference of knowledge. The text's visually engaging presentation showcases current technology as well as course fundamentals in order to reinforce classroom and real world applications.
- **Balanced Presentation.** The print book provides students only with what they really need to know to be successful digital citizens in the classroom and beyond. The media-rich ebook addresses timely content, such

as statistics, trends, prices, models, and expands on the print, with content appropriate for Computing majors. Students and instructors can choose to utilize this digital-only content, empowering each to fit the content to their specific needs and goals for the course.

- **Thematic Approach.** Chapter boxes, marginal elements, and accompanying digital-only content are linked by common themes to facilitate class discussions and help students make connections. These connections shed light on the integral role technology plays in business and society.
- **Media Engagement.** Enrichment content is available only in the e-book to enhance student knowledge and understanding through links to content and interactive media embedded at locations most appropriate for learning. Developed by the authors, activities providing deeper understanding and encourage learning by doing as well as offer practical skill development.
- **Reinforcement and Support.** End-of-chapter student assignments, along with the accompanying CourseMate web site, offer students an exceptional learning solution in addition to significant practice opportunities in the form of study guide materials, flash cards, practice tests and critical thinking opportunities.

on important topics; (2) use its interactive capabilities to offer creative reinforcement and online quizzes; (3) make available alternative learning techniques with Web-based learning games, practice tests, and interactive labs; (4) underscore the relevance of the Web as a basic information tool that can be used in all facets of society; (5) introduce students to doing research on the Web; and (6) offer instructors the opportunity to organize and administer their traditional campus-based or distance-education-based courses on the Web using various learning management systems.

Extensive End-of-Chapter Student Assignments

A notable strength of *Discovering Computers* is the extensive student assignments and activities at the end of each chapter. Well-structured student assignments can make the difference between students merely participating in a class and students

retaining the information they learn. End-of-chapter student assignments include the following:

- Study Guide exercises reinforce material for the exams
- Key Terms pages review chapter terms
- Checkpoint exercises test knowledge of chapter concepts
- How To — Your Turn exercises require that students learn new practical skills
- Problem Solving exercises require that students seek solutions to practical technology problems
- Internet Research exercises require that students search for information on the web
- Critical Thinking exercises challenge student assessment and decision-making skills
- Beyond the Book exercises expand understanding of chapter animations, boxes, figures, mini features, social media posts, and third-party links and videos through thought-provoking questions

Instructor Resources

The Instructor Resources include both teaching and testing aids.

Instructor's Manual Includes lecture notes summarizing the chapter sections, figures and boxed elements found in every chapter, teacher tips, classroom activities, lab activities, and quick quizzes in Microsoft Word files.

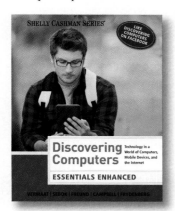

Syllabus Easily customizable sample syllabi that cover policies, assignments, exams, and other course information.

Figure Files Illustrations for every figure in the textbook in electronic form. Figures are provided both with and without callouts.

Solutions to Exercises Includes solutions for all end-of-chapter student assignments.

PowerPoint Presentations — Course Presenter A one-click-per-slide presentation system that provides PowerPoint slides for every subject in each chapter. Course Presenter provides consistent coverage for multiple lecturers.

Test Bank & Test Engine Test banks include 220 questions for every chapter, featuring objective-based and critical thinking question types, and including page number references and figure references, when appropriate. Also included is the test engine, ExamView, the ultimate tool for your objective-based testing needs.

Printed Test Bank A Rich Text Format (.rtf) version of the test bank that you can print.

Test Out/Final Exam Objective-based exam that can be used to test students out of your course, or as a final examination.

Pretest/Posttest Carefully prepared tests that can be used at the beginning and the end of the semester to measure student progress.

Computer Concepts CourseMate

The Computer Concepts CourseMate for *Discovering Computers* is the most expansive digital site for any computer concepts text in the market today! The content in the CourseMate solution is integrated into each page of the text, giving students easy access to current information on important topics, reinforcements activities, and alternative learning techniques. Integrating the Computer Concepts CourseMate into the classroom keeps today's students engaged and involved in the learning experience.

These interactive activities are captured within the CourseMate EngagementTracker, making it easy to assess students' retention of concepts.

MindTap

Typical courses often require students to juggle a variety of print and digital resources, as well as an array of platforms, access codes, logins, and homework systems. Now all of those resources are available in one personal learning experience called Mind Tap. Mind Tap is a cloud-based, interactive, customizable, and complete online course. More than an e-book, and different than a learning management system, each Mind Tap course is built upon authoritative Cengage learning content, accessible anytime, anywhere, with support soon available on a variety of mobile devices. The customizable learning path includes core text, activities, videos, reading, quizzing, reference materials, and social engagement that increases student engagement, improves understanding, and reinforces concepts.

Contact Us

Colleges, Universities, Continuing Education Departments, Post-Secondary Vocational Schools, Career Colleges, Business, Industry, Government, Trade, Retailer, Wholesaler, Library, and Resellers
Call Cengage Learning at 800-354-9706

K-12 Schools, Secondary Vocational Schools, Adult Education, and School Districts
Call Cengage Learning at 800-354-9706

In Canada
Call Nelson Cengage Learning at 800-268-2222

Anywhere
www.cengage.com/coursetechnology

Visual Walkthrough of the Book

Current. Relevant. Innovative.
Teaching the Significance of Today's Digital World.

Chapter Opener
Chapter Opening Objectives familiarize students with the material in each chapter.

Initial Chapter Figure
The first figure in each chapter provides an engaging overview of the major purpose of the chapter.

Consider This
features provide readers with critical thinking opportunities.

How To
features enable readers to learn new practical skills

Interactive e-Book Activity Icon
Several elements in each chapter are interactive learning activities in the e-book and are identified by this icon or by blue text.

Mini Feature
throughout the text explore various real world topics to deepen concept understanding.

Secure IT
features allow students to broaden their knowledge with details regarding security issues they will face.

Now You Know
feature provides assessment opportunity and integrates directly to chapter learning objectives to assess learning outcomes.

By The Way (BTW)
marginal elements assist readers in broadening their knowledge.

Ethics and Issues

boxes raise controversial, computer-related topics, challenging readers to carefully consider general concerns of computers in society.

Chapter Summary

allows another review of materials presented in the chapter to reinforce learning and provide additional self assessment opportunities.

Technology @ Work

features put chapter information to practical use and provide context within students' lives

End-of-Chapter Student Assignments

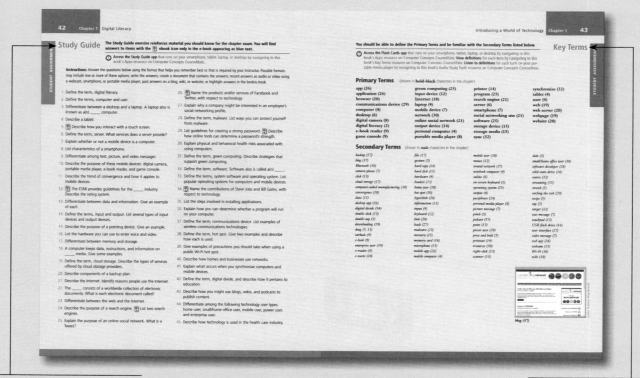

Study Guide

materials reinforce chapter content while **Study Guide mobile app** provides practice opportunities on the go.

Key Terms

Before taking a test, use the Key Terms page as a checklist of terms to know.

Checkpoint

Use these pages of multiple-choice, true/false, matching, and short answer exercises to reinforce understanding of the topics presented in the chapter.

STUDENT ASSIGNMENTS

How To: Your Turn

activities enable readers to learn
and to reinforce new practical
skills with personally meaningful
and applicable exercies.

STUDENT ASSIGNMENTS

Problem Solving

Personal activities call on students to relate concepts to their own lives.

[Screenshot of page 50]

50 Chapter 1 Digital Literacy

STUDENT ASSIGNMENTS

Problem Solving

The Problem Solving exercises extend your knowledge of chapter concepts by seeking solutions to practical problems with technology that you may encounter at home, school, or work. The Collaboration exercise should be completed with a team.

Challenge yourself with additional Problem Solving exercises by navigating to this book's Problem Solving resource on Computer Concepts CourseMate.

Instructions: You often can solve problems with technology in multiple ways. Determine a solution to the problems in these exercises by using one or more resources available to you (such as a computer or mobile device, articles on the web or in print, blogs, podcasts, videos, television, user guides, other individuals, electronics or computer stores, etc.). Describe your solution, along with the resource(s) used, in the format requested by your instructor (brief report, presentation, discussion, blog post, video, or other means).

Personal

1. **Shopping for Software** You are shopping for software that will assist you with your home's interior design. The package for the program you would like to purchase states that it was designed for the most recent version of Windows, but an older version is installed on your computer. How can you determine whether the program will run on your computer?

2. **Bad Directions** You are driving to your friend's house and are using your smartphone for directions. While approaching your destination, you realize that your smartphone app instructed you to turn the wrong way on your friend's street. How could this have happened?

3. **Bank Account Postings** While reviewing your checking account balance online, you notice that debit card purchases have not posted to your account for the past several days. Because you use online banking to balance your account, you become concerned about your unknown account balance. What steps will you take to correct this situation?

4. **Inaccessible Media** You insert a memory card with digital photos from your most recent family vacation and discover that your computer will not read the memory card. What might be wrong?

5. **Problematic Camera** After charging your digital camera battery overnight, you insert the battery and turn on the camera only to find that it is reporting a low battery. Seconds later, the camera shuts off automatically. What might be wrong?

Professional

6. **Discarding Old Computer Equipment** Your company has given you a new laptop to replace your current, outdated desktop. Because of the negative environmental impact of discarding the old computer in the trash, your supervisor asked you to suggest options for its disposal. How will you respond?

7. **Dead Battery** While traveling for business, you realize that you forgot to bring the battery charger for your laptop. Knowing that you need to use the laptop to give a presentation tomorrow, what steps will you take tonight to make sure you have enough battery power?

8. **Software Installation** You are attempting to install a program on your office computer. After inserting the installation disc and specifying that you would like to begin the installation, your computer appears to begin installing the program. Halfway through the installation process, an error message appears stating that you must have administrative privileges to perform the installation. Why were you not informed immediately upon beginning the installation? What are your next steps?

9. **Incorrect Sign-In Credentials** Upon returning to the office from a well-deserved two-week vacation, you turn on your computer. When you enter your user name and password, an error message appears stating that your password is incorrect. What are your next steps?

10. **Synchronization Error** You added appointments to the calendar on your computer, but these appointments are not synchronizing with your smartphone. Your calendar has synchronized with your smartphone in the past, but it has stopped working without explanation. What are your next steps?

Collaboration

11. **Technology in Health Care** Your dentist is moving from a shared office so that he can open his own practice. He mentioned that he would like to use technology in his office that not will only improve the patient experience, but also make his job easier. Form a team of three people to determine the types of technology your dentist can use in his new office. One team member should research ways that technology can help improve patient check-in and billing. Another team member should research the types of technology your dentist can use while he is working with patients, and the third team member should research any additional technology that can be used in the office to improve the patient experience. Compile your findings in a report and submit it to your instructor.

Internet Research

Internet Research exercises require follow-up research on the Web and suggest writing a short article or presenting the findings of the research to the class.

[Screenshot of page 48]

48 Chapter 1 Digital Literacy

STUDENT ASSIGNMENTS

Internet Research

The Internet Research exercises broaden your understanding of chapter concepts by requiring that you search for information on the web.

Instructions: Use a search engine or another search tool to locate the information requested or answers to questions presented in the exercises. Describe your findings, along with the search term(s) you used and your web source(s), in the format requested by your instructor (brief report, presentation, discussion, blog post, video, or other means).

1 Making Use of the Web
Search Engines and Research
Sixty percent of all American adults use a search engine every day, according to Pew Internet, and they generally are pleased with the outcome of their research experience. In How To 1-2 and 1-3 on pages 20 and 21 in this chapter, you learned to use a browser to display a webpage and to perform a basic web search.

Using these skills, find the answers to the following questions. (1) Visit the Pew Internet website and locate the latest Search Engine Use report. What are three of the users' positive search experiences? Which search engine is the most popular among the people surveyed? When was the survey conducted, and how many adults were surveyed? (2) Visit the CNET website and read at least three reviews of products. Create a table listing the product name, price, editors' and users' ratings, and "bottom line" summary. (3) Use a search engine or research website to locate articles about banning mobile devices in schools. What policies have schools created in lieu of a total ban on this technology? How have schools integrated mobile devices in the classroom as a vehicle to enhance learning?

2 Social Media
Historians place the birth of online social networking with the BBS (Bulletin Board System), where users communicated with a central computer and sent messages to other BBS members and also downloaded files and games. The next phase of social networking evolved when CompuServe, AOL (America Online), and Prodigy were among the services linking people with similar interests. Today's social networks share

many of the same basic principles by allowing members to communicate common interests, play games, and share photos, videos, and music. Some of these social networking sites are for personal use, while others are for entrepreneurs, business owners, and professionals to share job-related topics.

Compare the features of the top personal social networks, and create a table listing the number of active members in the United States and worldwide, the number of years the sites have existed, the more popular features, and the amount of content, such as photos, news stories, and links, that is shared each month. What types of advertisements are featured in each of these sites? Which sites are marketed toward younger and older users? Then, research the social networks used for business. How does their content differ from that found on the personal social networks? How many companies use these sites as a recruiting tool? How many native languages are supported? How are professionals using these websites to find potential clients and business partners?

3 Search Sleuth
(1) Which magazine introduced the first microcomputer kit for the MITS Altair in its January 1975 issue? (2) Which company sold the TRS-80, one of the more popular personal computers introduced in 1977? (3) What material did Douglas Engelbart use to create the first mouse? (4) What is the code name for the 12 engineers who developed the IBM PC? (5) Who received the first text message in 1992? What was the content of this message? (6) Which company developed the first digital camera? How many pounds did this camera weigh? (7) What is the title of Stephen King's e-book that was released in 2000? (8) In which year did Amazon.com report that for the first time sales of e-books exceeded the sales of hardcover books? (9) What is the name of the keyboard developed in the 1930s with a layout designed to maximize efficiency and reduce hand stress? (10) When did the first USB flash drive appear on the retail market? Which company developed this storage medium?

Critical Thinking
activities provide opportunities for creative solutions to these thought-provoking activities presented in each chapter. The Critical Thinking exercises are constructed for class discussion, presentation, and independent research. The Collaboration exercise is designed for a team environment.

STUDENT ASSIGNMENTS

Beyond the Book
exercises expand student understanding by allowing research and supported learning opportunities.

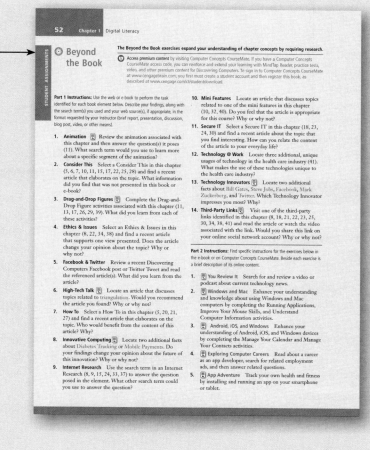

Visual Walkthrough of the Computer Concepts CourseMate for Discovering Computers

Interactive. Current. Engaging.
Your Interactive Guide to the Digital World!

Introduce the most current technology into the classroom with the Computer Concepts CourseMate for Discovering Computers. An integrated e-book and a wide range of online learning games, quizzes, practice tests, videos, and Web links expand on the topics covered in the text with hands-on reinforcement. The Pointer Icon integrated into each page of the text illustrates when to access the CourseMate Web site and quickly shows students the connection between the text and the digital solution.

Who Wants to Be a Computer Genius?

The Who Wants to Be a Computer Genius? learning game allows students to quiz themselves on chapter content within a dynamic and entertaining game scenario. Question results are provided instantly so that students quickly see which concepts they understand and which concepts they need to study. Page remediation is included with question results so students know exactly where in the text to find the information they need.

EngagementTracker

EngagementTracker makes assessing students easy by tracking student progress on the interactive activities. Clear and visual reports illustrate the class progress as a whole.

Wheel of Terms

Wheel of Terms is an interactive study tool for learning the Key Terms in each chapter. This learning game presents students with a short definition of one of the chapter's Key Terms and prompts them to type the correct term as the answer.

Online Content

SAM: Skills Assessment Manager

Get your students workplace-ready with SAM, the market-leading proficiency-based assessment and training solution for Microsoft Office! SAM's active, hands-on environment helps students master Microsoft Office skills and computer concepts that are essential to academic and career success, delivering the most comprehensive online learning solution for your course!

Through skill-based assessments, interactive trainings, business-centric projects, and comprehensive remediation, SAM engages students in mastering the latest Microsoft Office programs on their own, giving instructors more time to focus on teaching. Computer concepts labs supplement instruction of important technology-related topics and issues through engaging simulations and interactive, auto-graded assessments. With enhancements including streamlined course setup, more robust grading and reporting features, and the integration of fully interactive MindTap Readers containing Cengage Learning's premier textbook content, SAM provides the best teaching and learning solution for your course.

Learn Online

CengageBrain.com is the premier destination for purchasing or renting Cengage Learning textbooks, eBooks, eChapters, and study tools at a significant discount (eBooks up to 50% off Print). In addition, CengageBrain.com provides direct access to all digital products including eBooks, eChapters and digital solutions (i.e., CourseMate and SAM) regardless of where purchased. The following are some examples of what is available for this product on www.cengagebrain.com.

MindLinks

MindLinks is a new Cengage Learning Service designed to provide the best possible user experience and facilitate the highest levels of learning retention and outcomes, enabled through a deep integration of Cengage Learning's

digital suite into an instructor's Learning Management System (LMS). MindLinks works on any LMS that supports the IMS Basic LTI open standard. Advanced features, including gradebook exchange, are the result of active, enhanced LTI collaborations with industry-leading LMS partners to drive the evolving technology standards forward.

CourseCasts Learning on the Go

Always available. . . always relevant.

Our fast-paced world is driven by technology. You know because you are an active participant — always on the go, always keeping up with technological trends, and always learning new ways to embrace technology to power your life. Let CourseCasts, hosted by Ken Baldauf of Florida State University, be your guide to weekly updates in this ever-changing space. These timely, relevant podcasts are produced weekly and are available for download at http://coursecasts.course.com or directly from iTunes (search by CourseCasts). CourseCasts are a perfect solution to getting students (and even instructors) to learn on the go!

CourseNotes — Technology in a Flash!

Course Technology's CourseNotes are six-panel quick reference cards that reinforce the most important and widely used features of a software application in a visual and user-friendly format. CourseNotes serve as a great reference tool during and after the student completes the course. CourseNotes are available for software applications, such as Microsoft Office 2013, Word 2013, PowerPoint 2013, Excel 2013, Access 2013, and Windows 8. Topic-based CourseNotes are available for Best Practices in Social Networking, Hot Topics in Technology, and Web 2.0. Visit www.cengage.com/ct/coursenotes to learn more!

About Our Covers

The Shelly Cashman Series is continually updating our approach and content to reflect the way today's students learn and experience new technology. This focus on student success is reflected on our covers, which feature real students from the University of Rhode Island using the Shelly Cashman Series in their courses, and reflect the varied ages and backgrounds of the students learning with our books. When you use the Shelly Cashman Series, you can be assured that you are learning computer skills using the most effective courseware available.

Discovering Computers

Technology in a World of Computers, Mobile Devices, and the Internet

ESSENTIALS ENHANCED

Purchasing the Right Computer

As a student in a technology course, you might be thinking of purchasing a desktop, laptop, or tablet to help you with this course and future courses in your academic career. In addition to the information in this feature, consider speaking with your instructors, as well as an academic advisor, to see if they have any specific recommendations for computers or mobile devices you might use in the courses you plan to take. If your academic institution has a store that sells computers, it also might have specific computer or mobile device recommendations. Make sure the computer or mobile device you purchase is capable of running the software that you will need for your classes.

Note: This Focus On section uses a variety of terms that are described throughout this book. These terms also are defined in the index at the back of this book. If you need additional information about a particular topic, refer to the appropriate chapter in this book.

Step 1: Choose the Computer Type

Desktops, laptops, and tablets each serve a different purpose. It is important that you choose the type of computer or mobile device best suited to your needs. This section briefly describes and identifies some of the pros and cons associated with each type of device. See Chapter 3 for a more thorough discussion of computer types.

Desktops

A **desktop** is a computer designed to be in a stationary location, where all of its components fit on or under a desk or table (Figure A). Users who may prefer desktops include those with basic home or office computing needs who do not require the portability of a mobile computer or those with high-end computing needs, such as 3-D gaming or HD video editing.

Figure A   Two different types of desktops.

⚙ PROS

- Often more powerful than laptops and tablets
- Can connect to a large monitor
- Contain several different types of ports or multiple duplicate ports
- Can accommodate more types of external devices than laptops and tablets (i.e., keyboard, mouse, microphone, monitor, printer, scanner, webcam, speakers, etc.)
- Often support more memory and hard drive capacity than laptops and tablets
- Support programs and apps specifically designed for desktops and laptops
- Relatively easy for a user to upgrade and repair

⚙ CONS

- Are not portable
- Require several external, separate components, such as a keyboard, mouse, speakers, and sometimes the monitor
- High-end models can be more expensive than laptops and tablets
- Cannot run apps designed for mobile device operating systems, such as Android and iOS

Laptops

A **laptop** is a thin, lightweight mobile computer with a screen in its lid and a keyboard in its base (Figure B). Users who need or want to be able carry a computer from place to place may choose a laptop.

Figure B Two different types of laptops.
© Sergey Peterman / Shutterstock. com; © iStockphoto / Skip Odonnell

traditional laptop

ultrathin laptop

⚙ PROS

- Portable
- Use less electricity than a desktop
- Contain a battery that can last at least several hours without being plugged in to an external power source
- Often more powerful than a tablet
- Contain several different types of ports
- All required components housed in a single unit (i.e., compact keyboard, touchpad, screen, speakers, etc.)
- Can support more types of external devices than tablets (i.e., full-sized keyboard, mouse, microphone, monitor, printer, scanner, webcam, speakers, etc.)
- Support programs and apps specifically designed for desktops and laptops
- Can connect to a large monitor

CONS

- Might not be as powerful as high-end desktops
- May not support as much memory and hard drive space as desktops
- Contain fewer ports than desktops
- May support fewer external devices than desktops
- Not as easy for a user to upgrade or repair as desktops
- May not be as portable as tablets

Tablets

A **tablet** is a thin, lightweight mobile computer that has a touch screen (Figure C). Users who do not need the power of a laptop but require a portable computer for basic tasks may choose a tablet.

slate tablet in stand

convertible tablet

Figure C Two different types of tablets.
© iStockphoto / Pedro Castellano; Courtesy of Lenovo

PROS

- More portable than laptops
- Lightweight (most tablets weigh less than two pounds)
- Use less electricity than a desktop
- Battery life often is superior to laptops
- All required components housed in a single unit (touch screen, speakers, etc.)
- Use thousands of free and fee-based apps
- Often are easier to use than desktops and laptops
- Built-in memory card slots can increase storage capacity

CONS

- Not as powerful as desktops and laptops
- Hardware cannot be upgraded
- Typically do not support the same types of apps as desktops and laptops
- Have limited multitasking capabilities
- More susceptible to damage because they frequently are moved from place to place
- Because a touch screen is the primary form of input, it may be difficult to type large amounts of text on a tablet (unless an external keyboard is connected)
- Lack surface to rest wrists and arms, so ergonomic problems may develop

Most students will find that a desktop or laptop is most suitable for their coursework or for gaming. In addition, they might choose a tablet to carry with them at other times because tablets are ideal for everyday tasks, such as searching the web, checking email messages, participating in video calls, and reading e-books.

Step 2: Choose the Operating System

An **operating system** is software (a program) that coordinates all the activities among computer components. Multiple operating systems exist for each type of device (Table 1). Deciding which operating system is best for you will be the next step in determining the specific brand of computer that ultimately meets your needs. Certain courses may require specific applications (apps), and those applications may be available only on a specific operating system. For example, a course that teaches digital media might require an application that is available only for Mac OS. Table 2 illustrates the various categories of programs and apps. This section outlines the more common operating systems for each type of device. See Chapter 4 for a more thorough discussion of an operating system.

Table 1	Examples of Operating Systems by Category
Category	**Name**
Desktop	Windows
	OS X
	UNIX
	Linux
	Chrome OS
Mobile	Google Android
	Apple iOS
	Windows Phone

Table 2	Categories of Programs and Apps	
Category	**Sample Applications**	**Sample Uses**
Communications	Browser	Access and view webpages.
	Email	Send and receive messages.
	VoIP	Speak to other users over the Internet.
	FTP	Transfer items to and from other computers on the Internet.
Graphics and Media	Photo Editing	Modify digital photos, i.e., crop, remove red-eye, etc.
	Video and Audio Editing	Modify recorded movie clips, add music, etc.
	Media Player	View images, listen to audio/music, watch videos.
Personal Interest	Travel, Mapping, and Navigation	View maps, obtain route directions, locate points of interest.
	Reference	Look up material in dictionaries, encyclopedias, etc.
	Educational	Learn through tutors and prepare for tests.
	Entertainment	Receive entertainment news alerts, check movie times and reviews, play games.

Categories of Programs and Apps

Category	Sample Applications	Sample Uses
Productivity	Word Processing	Create letters, reports, and other documents.
	Presentation	Create visual aids for presentations.
	Schedule and Contact Management	Organize appointments and contact lists.
	Personal Finance	Balance a checkbook, pay bills, and track income and expenses.
Security	Antivirus	Protect a computer against viruses.
	Personal Firewall	Detect and protect against unauthorized intrusions.
	Spyware, Adware, and other Malware Removers	Detect and delete spyware, adware, and other malware.

© Cengage Learning; Courtesy of NCH Software, Source: Apple Inc.; Source: Google Inc.; Courtesy of AVG Technologies

Desktops and Laptops

The two primary operating systems available on desktops and laptops are Windows (shown in Figure D) and Mac OS (shown in Figure E on the next page). While other operating systems, such as UNIX, Linux, and ChromeOS also are available, Windows and Mac OS are the most common. Some computers can run multiple operating systems. For example, Apple computers can run Windows and Linux in addition to Mac OS. Windows and Mac OS each offer a unique user experience, and the best way to determine which one you are most comfortable with is to try using each one. Most stores that sell desktops and laptops will have some working models that you can evaluate. Make sure the operating system you decide to use also is capable of running the programs and apps required for your courses.

Figure D Windows operating system.

Source: Microsoft

Figure E   Mac OS operating system.
Source: Apple Inc.

Tablets

Tablets often include one of three operating systems: Android (Figure F), iOS (Figure G), or Windows (Figure H). While Android and iOS are the most popular operating systems on tablets, the Windows operating system is increasing in popularity. Determine the types of apps you wish to use on the tablet and then determine which operating systems support those apps.

If you want your tablet to synchronize seamlessly with other computers and devices, such as a desktop, laptop, or smartphone, consider an operating system that is compatible with your other computer or device. For example, if you have an Android phone, you might prefer the Android operating system for your tablet. If you use an iPhone or iPod Touch, you might prefer the iOS operating system for your tablet.

Figure F   Tablet running the Android operating system.
iStockphoto/ Petko Danov

Figure G   Tablet running the iOS operating system.
iStockphoto/ Hocus Focus Studio

Step 3: Choose Configuration Options

The final step in choosing the best desktop, laptop, or tablet to meet your needs is to choose the specific configuration details. For example, you may have to choose the size of the display, amount of memory, storage capacity, and processor speed.

Display Screen Size

Display screens for computers are available in a variety of sizes (Figure I). Desktops often use a monitor as their display, with the size of screens on these monitors ranging from 13 inches to more than 30 inches. A laptop's screen typically can range from 11 to 17 inches, and a tablet's screen generally is between 7 and 10 inches. If you purchase a laptop or tablet, a smaller screen size will make the device lighter and more portable. For example, laptops with screens exceeding 15 inches typically are much heavier, which makes them less convenient to transport.

If you primarily will be sending and receiving email messages, creating and editing documents using a word processing app, and browsing the Internet, a device with a smaller screen should meet your needs. If you require a larger screen to work with large documents or display multiple windows simultaneously, or if you want to experience less eyestrain with the contents appearing larger on the screen, consider a desktop or laptop display with a larger screen size. If you require touch functionality (and the operating system you plan to use supports it), purchase a screen that supports touch input. In addition, if you decide to purchase a desktop or laptop, you usually can connect a second monitor.

monitor display

laptop display

digital camera display

Memory

The amount of memory (RAM) installed in your desktop, laptop, or tablet will help determine the types of programs and apps that can run on the computer, as well as how many programs and apps can run simultaneously (Figure J). If you are purchasing a desktop or laptop, review the system requirements for the programs and apps you plan to use, and make sure to purchase a computer with enough memory to meet those system requirements. For example, if the operating system you plan to use requires at least 4 GB (gigabytes) of memory, and you plan to use a word processing app that requires 4 GB of memory, you should purchase a desktop or laptop with at least 8 GB of memory. It is recommended that you purchase a computer with slightly more memory than you need at the present time. This enables you to use multiple programs and apps simultaneously and also accommodates programs and apps you might install and use at a later time.

Figure J   Memory modules contain memory chips.
mycola/ Shutterstock.com; TerryM/ Shutterstock.com

Storage Capacity

Desktops, laptops, and tablets are available with various storage capacities (Figure K). The higher the storage capacity, the more data and information you can keep on the computer or device. To determine the ideal storage capacity, add together the amount of storage space required for all the programs and apps you want to use. In addition, estimate the amount of space you might need to store the files you create. If you are planning to store digital media such as audio, photos, and videos, make sure the storage device has sufficient space for those files as well. Try not to purchase a device with exactly the amount of storage space you anticipate needing. Always purchase more than you need so that you do not risk running out of space.

Processor Speed

If you are purchasing a desktop or laptop, you probably will have to determine the processor that will best meet your needs. Many different brands and models of processors are available (Figure L). Review the system requirements for the programs and apps you want to run to determine the processor best suited to your needs. Because a variety of brands and models of processors exist, you may find it difficult to decide which one to purchase. When you are shopping for your desktop, laptop, or tablet, ask a sales associate to explain the differences among the various processors so that you can make an informed decision.

Figure K   Two different types of storage devices.
Andresr/ Shutterstock.com;
roadk/Shutterstock.com

video card

Figure L   Processor that might be found in a computer or device.
RAW_group/iStockphoto.com

Digital Literacy

Introducing a World of Technology

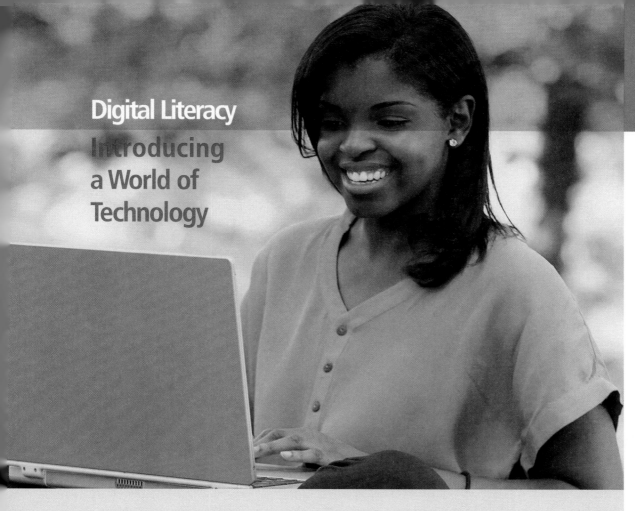

Technology provides access to the digital world around you.

"I use computers, mobile devices, and the Internet to do homework, look up information, check email, play games, post updates, talk to friends, upload photos, sync music, and so much more! So, why am I in this class? What more could I possibly learn?"

True, you may be familiar with some of the material in this chapter, but do you know . . .

When to use a swipe and a pinch?

How to ease eyestrain while working on a computer or mobile device?

Why some educators shun some wikis as valid sources of research?

Who helped build the first desktop and was on the cover of *Time* by age 26?

How to use a public Wi-Fi hot spot safely?

What steps occur after you place an online order?

How a GPS knows where you are all the time?

When you would use a blog and a wiki?

Which features make your kitchen appliances smart?

How the health care industry relies on computers, mobile devices, and related technologies?

Which health and fitness apps would fit your lifestyle best?

Why some of the text in this book is blue?

How to sign up for Computer Concepts CourseMate?

Why you should 'like' the Discovering Computers page on Facebook and 'follow' it on Twitter?

For these answers and to discover much more information essential to this course, read this chapter and visit the associated Computer Concepts CourseMate at www.cengagebrain.com.

✔ Objectives

After completing this chapter, you will be able to:

1 Differentiate among laptops, tablets, desktops, and servers

2 Describe the purpose and uses of smartphones, digital cameras, portable media players, e-book readers, and game devices

3 Describe the relationship between data and information

4 Briefly explain various input options (keyboards, pointing devices, voice and video input, and scanners), output options (printers, displays, and speakers), and storage options (hard disks, solid-state drives, USB flash drives, memory cards, optical discs, and cloud storage)

5 Differentiate the Internet from the web, and describe the relationship among the web, webpages, websites, and web servers

6 Explain the purpose of a browser, a search engine, and an online social network

7 Briefly describe digital security risks associated with viruses and other malware, privacy, your health, and the environment

8 Differentiate between an operating system and applications

9 Differentiate between wired and wireless network technologies, and identify reasons individuals and businesses use networks

10 Discuss how society uses technology in education, retail, finance, entertainment, health care, travel, government, science, publishing, and manufacturing

11 Identify technology used by home users, small office/home office users, mobile users, power users, and enterprise users

A World of Technology

In the course of a day, you may . . . complete a homework assignment and watch a streaming video on your laptop, flip through news headlines and refill a prescription on your tablet, search for directions and the local weather forecast on your smartphone, book a flight and create a shipping label using your office computer, and listen to your favorite songs on a portable media player. These and many other technologies are an integral part of everyday life: at school, at home, and at work (Figure 1-1).

Technology can enable you to more efficiently and effectively access and search for information; share personal ideas, photos, and videos with friends, family, and others; communicate with and meet other people; manage finances; shop for goods and services; play games or access other sources of entertainment; keep your life and activities organized; and complete business activities.

Because technology changes, you must keep up with the changes to remain digitally literate. **Digital literacy** involves having a current knowledge and understanding of computers, mobile devices, the Internet, and related technologies. This book presents the knowledge you need to be digitally literate today.

As you read this first chapter, keep in mind it is an overview. Most of the terms and concepts introduced in this chapter will be discussed in more depth later in the book.

Figure 1-1 Technology is an integral part of life at school, home, and work.

© iStockphoto / BlueJeanImages; © iStockphoto / elkor; © iStockphoto / svetikd; © Avava / Dreamstime.com; © Zai Aragon / Shutterstock.com

Computers

A **computer** is an electronic device, operating under the control of instructions stored in its own memory, that can accept data (*input*), process the data according to specified rules, produce information (*output*), and store the information for future use. Computers contain many electric, electronic, and mechanical components known as *hardware*.

Electronic components in computers process data using instructions, which are the steps that tell the computer how to perform a particular task. A collection of related instructions organized for a common purpose is referred to as software or a program. Using software, you can complete a variety of activities, such as search for information, type a paper, balance a budget, create a presentation, or play a game.

One popular category of computer is the personal computer. A **personal computer** (PC) is a computer that can perform all of its input, processing, output, and storage activities by itself and is intended to be used by one person at a time. Most personal computers today also can communicate with other computers and devices.

Types of personal computers include laptops, tablets, and desktops, with the first two sometimes called mobile computers. A *mobile computer* is a portable personal computer, designed so that a user can carry it from place to place. A **user** is anyone who interacts with a computer or mobile device, or utilizes the information it generates.

Figure 1-2   A typical laptop has a keyboard in the base and a screen in the lid, with the lid attaching to the base with hinges.
© iStockphoto / Stephen Krow

Laptops

A **laptop**, also called a *notebook computer*, is a thin, lightweight mobile computer with a screen in its lid and a keyboard in its base (Figure 1-2). Designed to fit on your lap and for easy transport, laptops weigh up to 10 pounds (varying by manufacturer and specifications). A laptop that is less than one inch thick and weighs about 3 pounds or less sometimes is referred to as an ultrathin laptop. Most laptops can operate on batteries or a power supply or both.

Tablets

Usually smaller than a laptop but larger than a phone, a **tablet** is a thin, lighterweight mobile computer that has a touch screen (read How To 1-1 for ways to interact with a touch screen). A popular style of tablet is the slate, which does not contain a physical keyboard (Figure 1-3). Like laptops, tablets run on batteries or a power supply or both; however, batteries in a tablet typically last longer than those in laptops.

Figure 1-3   A slate tablet.
© iStockphoto / franckreporter

CONSIDER THIS ———————————————————————————————————————

If the slate tablet has no keyboard, how do you type on it?

You can use your fingers to press keys on a keyboard that appears on the screen, called an *on-screen keyboard,* or you can purchase a separate physical keyboard that attaches to or wirelessly communicates with the tablet.

 HOW TO 1-1 ———————————————————————————————————————

Interact with a Touch Screen

You usually can interact with a touch screen using gestures. A *gesture* is a motion you make on a touch screen with the tip of one or more fingers or your hand. Touch screens are convenient because they do not require a separate device for input. Tablets and smartphones typically have touch screens.

The table below presents common ways to interact with a touch screen.

Touch Screen Gestures

Motion	Description	Common Uses
Tap	Quickly touch and release one finger one time.	Activate a link (built-in connection) Press a button Run a program or app
Double-tap	Quickly touch and release one finger two times.	Run a program or app Zoom in (show a smaller area on the screen, so that contents appear larger) at the location of the double-tap
Press and hold	Press and hold one finger to cause an action to occur, or until an action occurs.	Display a shortcut menu (immediate access to allowable actions) Activate a mode enabling you to move an item with one finger to a new location
Drag, or *slide*	Press and hold one finger on an object and then move the finger to the new location.	Move an item around the screen Scroll
Swipe	Press and hold one finger and then move the finger horizontally or vertically on the screen.	Scroll Display a bar that contains commands on an edge of the screen
Stretch	Move two fingers apart.	Zoom in (show a smaller area on the screen, so that contents appear larger)
Pinch	Move two fingers together.	Zoom out (show a larger area on the screen, so that contents appear smaller)

 In addition to the motions listed in the table, what other motions do you think a touch screen should support?

© Cengage Learning

Desktops

A **desktop**, or desktop computer, is a personal computer designed to be in a stationary location, where all of its components fit on or under a desk or table. On many desktops, the screen is housed in a device that is separate from a tower, which is a case that contains the processing circuitry (Figure 1-4a). Other desktops, sometimes called all-in-one desktops, do not contain a tower and instead use the same case to house the screen and the processing circuitry (Figure 1-4b). Some screens for desktops support touch.

(b)

all-in-one desktop

(a)

Figure 1-4 Some desktops have a separate tower; others do not.
© iStockphoto / Oleksiy Mark; Source: Microsoft; © iStockphoto / hocus-focus; Apple, Inc.

 CONSIDER THIS

Which type of computer — laptop, tablet, or desktop — is best?
It depends on your needs. Because laptops can be as powerful as the average desktop, more people today choose laptops over desktops so that they have the added benefit of portability. Tablets are ideal for those not needing the power of a laptop or for searching for information, communicating with others, and taking notes in lectures, at meetings, conferences, and other forums where a laptop is not practical.

---

screen

keyboard

Figure 1-5 A server provides services to other computers or devices on a network.
© iStockphoto / alxpin

Servers

A **server** is a computer dedicated to providing one or more services to other computers or devices on a network. A network is a collection of computers and devices connected together, often wirelessly. Services provided by servers include storing content and controlling access to hardware, software, and other resources on a network.

A server can support from two to several thousand connected computers and devices at the same time. Servers are available in a variety of sizes and types for both small and large business applications (Figure 1-5). Smaller applications, such as at home, sometimes use a high-end desktop as a server. Larger corporate, government, and Internet applications use powerful, expensive servers to support their daily operations.

Mobile and Game Devices

A **mobile device** is a computing device small enough to hold in your hand. Because of their reduced size, the screens on mobile devices are small — often between 3 and 5 inches.

Some mobile devices are Internet capable, meaning that they can connect to the Internet wirelessly. You often can exchange information between the Internet and a mobile device or between a computer or network and a mobile device. Popular types of mobile devices are smartphones, digital cameras, portable media players, and e-book readers.

 CONSIDER THIS

Are mobile devices computers?
The mobile devices discussed in this section can be categorized as computers because they operate under the control of instructions stored in their own memory, can accept data, process the data according to specified rules, produce or display information, and store the information for future use.

Smartphones

A **smartphone** is an Internet-capable phone that usually also includes a calendar, an appointment book, an address book, a calculator, a notepad, games, and several other apps (which are programs on a smartphone). Smartphones typically communicate wirelessly with other devices or computers. With several smartphone models, you also can listen to music and take photos.

Many smartphones have touch screens. Instead of or in addition to a touch screen, some smartphones have a built-in mini keyboard on the front of the phone or a keyboard that slides in and out from behind the phone (Figure 1-6). Others have keypads that contain both numbers and letters.

mini keyboard

touch screen

slide out keyboard

Figure 1-6   Smartphones may have a touch screen and/or a mini keyboard or slide out keyboard.
© iStockphoto / Cagri Özgür; © iStockphoto / serts; © iStockphoto / Oleksiy Mark

Instead of calling someone's phone to talk, you can send messages to others by pressing images on an on-screen keyboard, keys on the mini keyboard, or buttons on the phone's keypad. Three popular types of messages that you can send with smartphones include text messages, picture messages, and video messages.

- A *text message* is a short note, typically fewer than 300 characters, sent to or from a smartphone or other mobile device.
- A *picture message* is a photo or other image, sometimes along with sound and text, sent to or from a smartphone or other mobile device. A phone that can send picture messages sometimes is called a *camera phone*.
- A *video message* is a short video clip, usually about 30 seconds, sent to or from a smartphone or other mobile device.

Read Ethics & Issues 1-1 on the next page to consider whether sending text messages affects writing skills.

 BTW

Messaging Services
Providers of wireless communications services may charge additional fees for sending text, picture, or video messages, depending on the service plan.

ETHICS & ISSUES 1-1

Do Text Messages Affect Writing Skills?

When you send text messages, the goal is to communicate the most amount of information using the fewest words and characters. This type of rapid-fire communications places a higher priority on brevity and speed than spelling, capitalization, and punctuation. Educators wonder about the effect that text messages might have on the writing habits and grammar skills of today's students. Their use of text acronyms such as LOL (laugh out loud) and text abbreviations that include numbers, such as gr8 (for great) or 2 (for to, too, or two), is working its way into their formal writing. While adults also use text acronyms and abbreviations, the concern is

that teens and young adults use them so often before developing formal writing skills. The result could be students who are less able to use formal language when needed.

Research indicates that the more text messages students send, the more likely it is that they may have difficulty with formal writing. On the positive side, by reducing a message to as few words as possible, students learn to present the most important content first, without rambling or exaggeration. The downside is this can lead to short, choppy sentences that do not connect with each other and a lack of supporting details, which are essential in formal writing. Other positives are that students are writing more than ever, and that this

type of writing can be considered a form of journaling, or recording of thoughts, activities, and opinions. Some educators argue that rather than worrying about the writing style that students use in their text messages, they should focus on helping students distinguish between formal and informal communications, and what is appropriate in each.

Does the use of text messages make students less likely to perform well in formal writing assignments? Why or why not? Should teachers allow students to use text acronyms and abbreviations in formal writing? Why or why not? Do text messages have any positive impact on communications skills? Why or why not?

Digital Cameras

A **digital camera** is a device that allows you to take photos and store the photographed images digitally (Figure 1-7). While many digital cameras look like a traditional camera, some are built into smartphones and other mobile devices.

Internet Research

What is a digital SLR camera?

Search for: digital slr camera introduction

Digital cameras typically allow you to review, and sometimes modify, images while they are in the camera. You also can transfer images from a digital camera to a computer, so that you can review, modify, share, organize, or print the images. Digital cameras often can connect to or communicate wirelessly with a computer, a printer, or the Internet, enabling you to access the photos on the camera without using a cable. Some also can record videos. Many digital devices, such as smartphones and tablets, include an integrated digital camera.

Figure 1-7 With a digital camera, you can view photographed images immediately through a small screen on the camera to see if the photo is worth keeping.
© iStockphoto / Oktay Ortakcioglu; © iStockphoto / Oktay Ortakcioglu; © Louis Bourgeois / Shutterstock.com

Portable Media Players

Internet Research

What are popular portable media players?

Search for: portable media players

A **portable media player**, sometimes called a *personal media player*, is a mobile device on which you can store, organize, and play or view digital media (Figure 1-8). Digital media includes music, photos, and videos. Portable media players enable you to listen to music, view photos, and watch videos, movies, and television shows. With most, you transfer the digital media from a computer (or the Internet, if the device is Internet capable) to the portable media player.

earbuds

Figure 1-8 Portable media players, such as the iPod shown here, typically include a set of earbuds.
© iStockphoto / Sebastien Cote

Portable media players usually include a set of *earbuds*, which are small speakers that rest inside each ear canal. Some portable media player models have a touch screen, while others have a pad that you operate with a thumb or finger, so that you can navigate through digital media, adjust volume, and customize settings. Some portable media players also offer a calendar, address book, games, and other apps (discussed later in this chapter).

E-Book Readers

An **e-book reader** (short for electronic book reader), or *e-reader*, is a mobile device that is used primarily for reading e-books (Figure 1-9). An *e-book*, or digital book, is an electronic version of a printed book, readable on computers and other digital devices. In addition to books, you typically can purchase and read other forms of digital media such as newspapers and magazines.

Most e-book reader models have a touch screen, and some are Internet capable. These devices usually are smaller than tablets but larger than smartphones.

Figure 1-9   An e-book reader.
© iStockphoto / Michael Bodmann

Game Devices

A **game console** is a mobile computing device designed for single-player or multiplayer video games. Gamers often connect the game console to a television so that they can view their gameplay on the television's screen (Figure 1-10). Many game console models are Internet capable and also allow you to listen to music and watch movies or view photos. Typically weighing between three and eleven pounds, the compact size of game consoles makes them easy to use at home, in the car, in a hotel, or any location that has an electrical outlet and a television screen.

A handheld game device is small enough to fit in one hand, making it more portable than the game console. Because of their reduced size, the screens are small — similar in size to some smartphone screens. Some handheld game device models are Internet capable and also can communicate wirelessly with other similar devices for multiplayer gaming.

game console

handheld game device

Figure 1-10   Game consoles often connect to a television; handheld game devices contain a built-in screen.
© iStockphoto / Gene Chutka; © Barone Firenze / Shutterstock.com

✷ **CONSIDER THIS** ────────────────────────────────

Are digital cameras, portable media players, e-book readers, and handheld game devices becoming obsolete because more and more smartphones and tablets include their functionality?

True, many smartphones and tablets enable you to take and store photos; store, organize, and play or view your digital media; read e-books; and play games. This trend of computers and devices with technologies that overlap, called *convergence,* means that consumers may need fewer devices for the functionality that they require.

Still, consumers often purchase separate stand-alone devices (i.e., a separate digital camera, portable media player, etc.) for a variety of reasons. The stand-alone device (i.e., a digital camera) may have more features and functionality than the combined device offers (i.e., a smartphone). You might want to be able to use both devices at the same time, for example, send text messages on the phone while reading a book on an e-book reader. Or, you might want protection if your combined device (i.e., smartphone) breaks. For example, you still can listen to music on a portable media player if your smartphone becomes nonfunctional.

 MINI FEATURE 1-1 ──────────────────────────

Living Digitally – Gaming

Video gamers spend billions of dollars each year making the most of their downtime with game consoles and devices. With outstanding 3-D graphics and challenging gameplay, nearly three-fourths of U.S. households own game hardware and software/apps. The popularity is due, in large part, to the social aspect of gathering families and friends to play together as a group or online with each other and those around the world.

Game Accessories and Input Techniques

The more popular game consoles work with a wide variety of accessories and input techniques for directing movements and actions of on-screen players and objects, some of which are described below and shown in the images to the left:

- **Gamepads:** Holding the gamepad with both hands, press buttons with your thumbs or move sticks in various directions to trigger events.

- **Air gestures:** Moving your body or a handheld device in predetermined directions through the air, you may need at least six feet of open space to accommodate your motions.

- **Voice commands:** Speaking instructions toward the game console, ensure no background noise is in the room, or use a headset.

- **Fitness accessories:** Working with fitness accessories, such as balance boards and resistance bands, you can make fitness fun and functional.

Games

Gamers have several options available for purchasing games for game consoles. They can (1) purchase or rent discs or other media that contain games; (2) download games, or transfer them from online stores, to a game console; or (3) sign up for cloud gaming services that stream games, or transfer games on demand.

For tablets and smartphones, you can download games from an app store to your mobile computer or device. Games are the most popular downloaded app category. Two of the major factors for this attractiveness are price, for many of the games can be downloaded at no or little cost, and impressive, fast graphics that draw users into the action.

The wide variety of categories offers a gaming experience for practically everyone. Numerous games are available in each genre (some of these games are shown on the next page).

- **Action and adventure:** Characters move through their world by running, jumping, and climbing in an attempt to reach the next level of play and eventually defeat a villain or rescue a prisoner.

- **Education:** Engaging and entertaining puzzles and problems present practical instruction and possible assessment to teach skills and concepts that are applicable in real-world circumstances.

- **Music and fitness:** Individuals and groups improve their physical and mental fitness while engaging in athletic competitions, aerobics, dance, and yoga.

- **Puzzle and strategy:** Players use their skills and intelligence to solve problems, generally with the goal of moving objects to create a pattern.

- **Racing and sports:** Athletes and drivers strive to complete a course or to cross a finish line in record time.

- **Role-playing:** Gamers assume the role of a character and experience adventures while on a major quest.

- **Simulation:** Players control an activity in a simulated situation, such as piloting an airplane or playing an instrument in a rock band.

The Entertainment Software Rating Board (ESRB) assigns ratings to provide guidance of a game's age-appropriateness and content.

※ The number of hours spent playing games has increased steadily each year, and the tablet and smartphone industry is partly responsible for this rise in popularity. Is game playing advantageous to society? What are the advantages of playing games, and do they outweigh the disadvantages?

© iStockphoto / Ivan Vasilev

Data and Information

Computers process data (input) into information (output) and often store the data and resulting information for future use. *Data* is a collection of unprocessed items, which can include text, numbers, images, audio, and video. *Information* conveys meaning to users. Both business and home users can make well-informed decisions because they have instant access to information from anywhere in the world.

Many daily activities either involve the use of or depend on information from a computer. For example, as shown in Figure 1-11, computers process several data items to print information in the form of a cash register receipt.

 CONSIDER THIS

Can you give another example of data and its corresponding information?
Your name, address, term, course names, course sections, course grades, and course credits all represent data that is processed to generate your semester grade report. Other information on the grade report includes results of calculations such as total semester hours, grade point average, and total credits.

BTW
Links to Media
When you see the 📱 e-book icon in this book, it means you can tap or click corresponding material in the Discovering Computers e-book for related interactive content, such as viewing an animation, interacting with a figure, visiting a website, or watching a video.

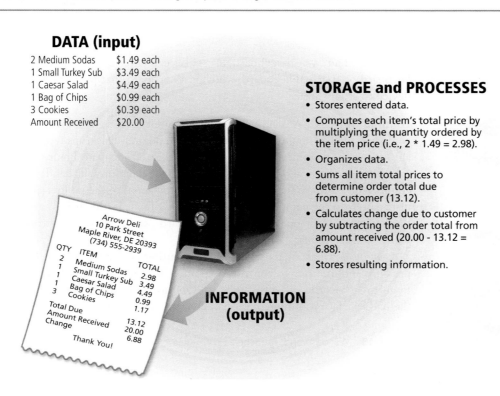

DATA (input)

2 Medium Sodas	$1.49 each
1 Small Turkey Sub	$3.49 each
1 Caesar Salad	$4.49 each
1 Bag of Chips	$0.99 each
3 Cookies	$0.39 each
Amount Received	$20.00

STORAGE and PROCESSES

- Stores entered data.
- Computes each item's total price by multiplying the quantity ordered by the item price (i.e., 2 * 1.49 = 2.98).
- Organizes data.
- Sums all item total prices to determine order total due from customer (13.12).
- Calculates change due to customer by subtracting the order total from amount received (20.00 - 13.12 = 6.88).
- Stores resulting information.

INFORMATION (output)

Arrow Deli
10 Park Street
Maple River, DE 20393
(734) 555-2939

QTY	ITEM	TOTAL
2	Medium Sodas	2.98
1	Small Turkey Sub	3.49
1	Caesar Salad	4.49
1	Bag of Chips	0.99
3	Cookies	1.17

Total Due   13.12
Amount Received 20.00
Change   6.88

Thank You!

Figure 1-11
A computer processes data into information. In this simplified example, the item ordered, item price, quantity ordered, and amount received all represent data (input). The computer processes the data to produce the cash register receipt (information, or output).
© Cengage Learning;
© iStockphoto / Norman Chan

Input

Users have a variety of input options for entering data into a computer, many of which involve using an input device. An **input device** is any hardware component that allows you to enter data and instructions into a computer or mobile device. The following sections discuss common input methods.

desktop keyboard

laptop keyboard

Keyboards A *keyboard* contains keys you press to enter data and instructions into a computer or mobile device (Figure 1-12). All desktop keyboards have a typing area that includes letters of the alphabet, numbers, punctuation marks, and other basic keys. Some users prefer a wireless keyboard because it eliminates the clutter of a cord.

Keyboards for desktops contain more keys than keyboards for mobile computers and devices. To provide the same functionality as a desktop keyboard, many of the keys on mobile computers and devices serve two or three purposes. On a laptop, for example, you often use the same keys to type numbers and to show various areas on a screen, switching a key's purpose by pressing a separate key first.

Figure 1-12 Users have a variety of keyboard options.
© skyfotostock / Shutterstock.com;
© Africa Studio / Shutterstock.com;
© iStockphoto / kycstudio;
© iStockphoto / MorePixels;
Courtesy of Virtek, Inc.

on-screen keyboard

mini keyboard

virtual keyboard

Instead of a physical keyboard, users also can enter data via an on-screen keyboard or a virtual keyboard, which is a keyboard that projects from a device to a flat surface.

Pointing Devices A pointing device is an input device that allows a user to control a small symbol on a screen, called the pointer. Desktops typically use a mouse as their pointing device, and laptops use a touchpad (Figure 1-13).

A *mouse* is a pointing device that fits under the palm of your hand comfortably. With the mouse, you control movement of the pointer and send instructions to the computer or mobile device. Table 1-1 identifies some of the common mouse operations. Like keyboards, some users prefer working with a wireless mouse.

A *touchpad* is a small, flat, rectangular pointing device that is sensitive to pressure and motion. To control the pointer with a touchpad, slide your fingertip across the surface of the pad. On most touchpads, you also can tap the pad's surface to imitate mouse operations such as clicking.

mouse

touchpad

Figure 1-13 A mouse and a touchpad.
© iStockphoto / PhotoTalk; © iStockphoto / Michael Bodmann

Table 1-1   Mouse Operations

Operation	Description	Common Uses
Point	Move the mouse until the pointer is positioned on the item of choice.	Position the pointer on the screen.
Click	Press and release the primary mouse button, which usually is the left mouse button.	Select or deselect items on the screen or start a program or feature.
Right-click	Press and release the secondary mouse button, which usually is the right mouse button.	Display a shortcut menu.
Double-click	Quickly press and release the primary mouse button twice without moving the mouse.	Start a program or program feature.
Drag	Point to an item, hold down the primary mouse button, move the item to the desired location on the screen, and then release the mouse button.	Move an object from one location to another or draw pictures.

Voice and Video Input   Some mobile devices and computers enable you to speak data instructions using voice input and to capture live full-motion images using video input. With your smartphone, for example, you may be able to use your voice to send a text message, schedule an appointment, and dial a phone number. Or, you may opt for video calling instead of a traditional phone call, so that you and the person you called can see each other as you chat on a computer or mobile device. As in this example, video input usually works in conjunction with voice input. For voice input, you use a microphone, and for video input you use a webcam (Figure 1-14).

Figure 1-14   You can speak instructions into a microphone or wireless headset and capture live video on a webcam for a video call.
© iStockphoto / Stephen Krow; © iStockphoto / pierrephoto; © iStockphoto / Suprijono Suharjoto

A *microphone* is an input device that enables you to speak into a computer or mobile device. Many computers and most mobile devices contain built-in microphones. You also can talk into a *headset*, which contains both a microphone and a speaker. Many headsets can communicate wirelessly with the computer or mobile device. A *webcam* is a digital video camera that allows you to capture video and usually audio input for your computer or mobile device.

Scanners   A *scanner* is a light-sensing input device that converts printed text and images into a form the computer can process (Figure 1-15). A popular type of scanner works in a manner similar to a copy machine, except that instead of creating a paper copy of the document or photo, it stores the scanned document or photo electronically.

Figure 1-15   A scanner.
© iStockphoto / Edgaras Marozas

Output

Users have a variety of output options to convey text, graphics, audio, and video — many of which involve using an output device. An **output device** is any hardware component that conveys information from a computer or mobile device to one or more people. The following sections discuss common output methods.

Printers A **printer** is an output device that produces text and graphics on a physical medium such as paper. Printed content sometimes is referred to as a *hard copy* or *printout*. Most printers today print text and graphics in both black-and-white and color on a variety of paper types (Figure 1-16). Some printer models also can print lab-quality photos. A variety of printers support wireless printing, where a computer or other device communicates wirelessly with the printer.

Figure 1-16 A printer can produce a variety of printed output.

Courtesy of Epson America, Inc.; © designsstock / Shutterstock.com; © iStockphoto / Henrik Jonsson; © maigi / Shutterstock.com

Displays A display is an output device that visually conveys text, graphics, and video information. Displays consist of a screen and the components that produce the information on the screen. The display for a desktop typically is a monitor, which is a separate, physical device. Mobile computers and devices typically integrate the display in their same physical case (Figure 1-17). Some displays have touch screens.

smartphone display

digital camera display

tablet display

laptop display

monitor display

Figure 1-17 Displays vary depending on the computer or mobile device.

© iStockphoto / Sebastien Cote; © David Lentz / Photos.com; © Dmitry Rukhlenko / Photos.com; © Mrallen / Dreamstime.com; © Pakhnyushcha / Shutterstock.com

✳ **CONSIDER THIS** ──────────────────────────

What can you do to ease eyestrain while using a computer or mobile device?
Position the display about 20 degrees below eye level. Clean the screen regularly. Blink your eyes every five seconds. Adjust the room lighting. Face into an open space beyond the screen. Use larger fonts or zoom the display. Take an eye break every 30 minutes. If you wear glasses, ask your doctor about computer glasses.

──

Speakers   Speakers allow you to hear audio, that is, music, voice, and other sounds. Most personal computers and mobile devices have a small internal speaker. Many users attach higher-quality speakers to their computers and mobile devices, including game consoles.

So that only you can hear sound, you can listen through earbuds (shown in Figure 1-8 on page 8) or headphones, which cover or are placed outside of the ear (Figure 1-18). Both earbuds and headphones usually include noise-cancelling technology to reduce the interference of sounds from the surrounding environment. To eliminate the clutter of cords, users can opt for wireless speakers or wireless headphones.

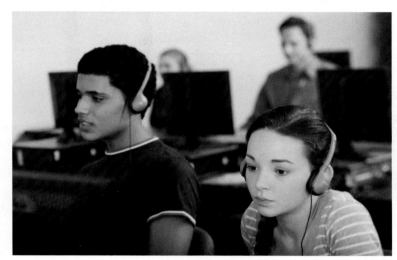

Figure 1-18   In a crowded environment where speakers are not practical, users can wear headphones to hear music, voice, and other sounds.
© iStockphoto / Photo_Alto

Memory and Storage

Memory consists of electronic components that store instructions waiting to be executed and the data needed by those instructions. Although some forms of memory are permanent, most memory keeps data and instructions temporarily, which means its contents are erased when the computer is shut off.

Storage, by contrast, holds data, instructions, and information for future use. For example, computers can store hundreds or millions of student names and addresses permanently. A computer keeps data, instructions, and information on **storage media**. Examples of storage media are hard disks, solid-state drives, USB flash drives, memory cards, and optical discs. The amount of storage for each type of storage media varies, but hard disks, solid-state drives, and optical discs usually hold more than USB flash drives and memory cards. Some storage media are portable, meaning you can remove the medium from one computer and carry it to another computer.

A **storage device** records (writes) and/or retrieves (reads) items to and from storage media. Storage devices often also function as a source of input and output because they transfer items from storage to memory and vice versa. Drives and readers/writers, which are types of storage devices, accept a specific kind of storage media. For example, a DVD drive (storage device) accepts a DVD (storage media).

Hard Disks   A *hard disk* is a storage device that contains one or more inflexible, circular platters that use magnetic particles to store data, instructions, and information. The entire device is enclosed in an airtight, sealed case to protect it from contamination. Desktops and laptops often contain at least one hard disk that is mounted inside the computer's case, called a fixed disk because this hard disk is not portable (Figure 1-19a on the next page).

 BTW
Disk vs. Disc
The spelling, disk, is used for hard disks and other magnetic media, and disc is used for CDs, DVDs, and other optical media.

Figure 1-19   A fixed disk is mounted inside a laptop's case; an external hard disk is a separate, freestanding device.
© iStockphoto / Brian Balster; © iStockphoto / murat sarica

hard disk is positioned in base of laptop

(a)

External hard disks are separate, portable, freestanding hard disks that usually connect to the computer with a cable (Figure 1-19b).

external hard disk connected to laptop

(b)

hard disk contains moving parts

SSD contains no moving parts

Figure 1-20   A solid-state drive (SSD) is about the same size as a laptop hard disk.
© iStockphoto / Ludovit Repko

Solid-State Drives   A *solid-state drive* (SSD) is a storage device that typically uses flash memory to store data, instructions, and information. Flash memory contains no moving parts, making it more durable and shock resistant than other types of media. For this reason, some manufacturers are using SSDs instead of hard disks in their desktops, laptops, and tablets (Figure 1-20).

USB Flash Drives   A *USB flash drive* is a portable flash memory storage device that you plug in a USB port, which is a special, easily accessible opening on a computer or mobile device (Figure 1-21). USB flash drives are convenient for mobile users because they are small and lightweight enough to be transported on a keychain or in a pocket.

Memory Cards   A *memory card* is removable flash memory, usually no bigger than 1.5 inches in height or width, that you insert in and remove from a slot in a computer, mobile device, or card reader/writer (Figure 1-22). With a card reader/writer, you can transfer the stored items, such as digital photos, from a memory card to a computer or printer that does not have a built-in card slot.

USB flash drive

USB port

Figure 1-21   You insert a USB flash drive in a USB port on a computer.
© Pakhnyushcha / Shutterstock.com

Figure 1-22
Computers and mobile devices use a variety of styles of memory cards to store documents, photos, and other items.
© Verisakeet / Fotolia;
© Sonar / Fotolia;
© Xuejun li / Fotolia;
© uwimages / Fotolia

memory card in computer

memory card in digital camera

memory card in phone

memory card in card reader/writer, which is attached to computer

Optical Discs   An optical disc is a type of storage media that consists of a flat, round, portable metal disc made of metal, plastic, and lacquer that is written and read by a laser. CDs (compact discs) and DVDs (digital versatile discs) are two types of optical discs (Figure 1-23).

Figure 1-23   You can insert a DVD in a DVD drive on a computer.
© iStockphoto / Hanquan Chen

 CONSIDER THIS ───────────────────────────────

What is the general use for each type of storage media?
Hard disks and SSDs store software and all types of user files. A *file* is a named collection of stored data, instructions, or information and can contain text, images, audio, and video. Memory cards and USB flash drives store files you intend to transport from one location to another, such as a homework assignment or photos. Optical discs generally store software, photos, movies, and music.

Cloud Storage   Instead of storing data, instructions, and information locally on a hard disk or other media, you can opt for cloud storage. *Cloud storage* is an Internet service that provides storage to computer users (Figure 1-24).

Types of services offered by cloud storage providers vary. Some provide storage for specific types of media, such as photos, whereas others store any content and provide backup services. A *backup* is a duplicate of content on a storage medium that you can use in case the original is lost, damaged, or destroyed. Read Secure IT 1-1 on the next page for suggestions for backing up your computers and mobile devices.

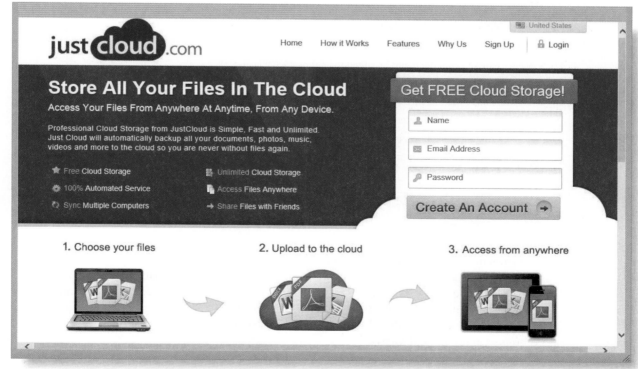

Figure 1-24   JustCloud is an example of a website that provides cloud storage solutions to home and business users.
Source: JustCloud.com

SECURE IT 1-1

Backing Up Computers and Mobile Devices

Many factors, including power outages and hardware failure, can cause loss of data, instructions, or information on a computer or mobile device. To protect against loss, you should back up the contents of storage media regularly. Backing up can provide peace of mind and save hours of work attempting to recover important material in the event of loss.

A backup plan for computers could include the following:

- Use a backup program, either included with your computer's operating system or one that you purchased separately, to copy the contents of your entire hard disk to a separate device.

- Regularly copy music, photos, videos, documents, and other important items to a USB flash drive, external hard disk, or DVD.

- Subscribe to a cloud storage provider.

- Schedule your files to be backed up regularly.

Backup plans for mobile devices are less specific. Apps for backing up your smartphone or tablet's content are available. You also can back up a mobile device to your computer's hard disk using synchronization software that runs on your computer (synchronization software is discussed later in this chapter). Some mobile device manufacturers, such as Apple, provide cloud storage solutions to owners of their devices. Other services allow subscribers to use a friend's computer as a backup storage location.

Overall, the best advice is to back up often using a variety of methods.

 Do you back up files regularly? If not, why not? What would you do if you had no backup and then discovered that your computer or mobile device had failed?

cloud storage provider

Courtesy of Western Digital Corporation; © iStockphoto / Stephen Krow; © Cengage Learning

---

 NOW YOU KNOW

Be sure you understand the material presented in the sections titled Computers, Mobile and Game Devices, and Data and Information, as it relates to the chapter objectives.
You now should know . . .

- Which type of computer might be suited to your needs (Objective 1)

- Why you would use a smartphone, digital camera, portable media player, and an e-book reader, and which game software/apps you find interesting (Objective 2)

- How to recognize the difference between data and information (Objective 3)

- When you might use the various methods of input, output, and storage (Objective 4)

Quiz Yourself Online: Check your knowledge of related content by navigating to this book's Quiz Yourself resource on Computer Concepts CourseMate and then tapping or clicking Objectives 1–4.

The Internet

The **Internet** is a worldwide collection of computer networks that connects millions of businesses, government agencies, educational institutions, and individuals (Figure 1-25). The Internet provides society with access to global information and instant communications.

Businesses, called Internet service providers (ISPs), offer users and organizations access to the Internet free or for a fee. By subscribing to an ISP, you can connect to the Internet through your computers and mobile devices.

Today, more than two billion home and business users around the world access a variety of services on the Internet. The World Wide Web is one of the more widely used Internet services. Other popular services include email, instant messaging, VoIP, and FTP (all discussed later in this chapter).

 BTW

Web vs. Internet
The terms, web and Internet, should not be used interchangeably. The web is a service of the Internet.

Figure 1-25 The Internet is the largest computer network, connecting millions of computers and devices around the world.
© Cengage Learning; © Mmaxer / Shutterstock.com; © Alfonso de Tomas /Shutterstock.com; © SSSCCC / Shutterstock.com; © iStockphoto / Petar Chernaev; © amfoto / Shutterstock.com; © iStockphoto / Oleksiy Mark; © iStockphoto / Oleksiy Mark; © iStockphoto / sweetym; Source: Microsoft; © Oleksiy Mark / Shutterstock.com; Source: Cengage Learning; © iStockphoto / Stephen Krow; © Cengage Learning; © iStockphoto / Skip O'Donnell;Source: Apple Inc; © iStockphoto / Skip O'Donnell; Source: Nutrition Blog Network; © iStockphoto / Ayaaz Rattansi; Source: Microsoft; © Oleksiy Mark / Shutterstock.com; Source: Microsoft; © Cengage Learning;

The World Wide Web

The World Wide Web (or web, for short) is a global library of information available to anyone connected to the Internet. People around the world access the web to accomplish a variety of online tasks, including:

- Search for information
- Conduct research
- Communicate with and meet other people
- Share information, photos, and videos with others
- Access news, weather, and sports
- Participate in online training
- Shop for goods and services
- Play games with others
- Download or listen to music
- Watch videos
- Download or read books

The **web** consists of a worldwide collection of electronic documents. Each electronic document on the web is called a **webpage**, which can contain text, graphics, audio, and video (Figure 1-26).

BTW

Downloading
Downloading is the process of transferring content from a server on the Internet to a computer or mobile device.

Figure 1-26 Webpages, such as the one shown here, can display text, graphics, audio, and video on a computer or mobile device. Pointing to a link on the screen typically changes the shape of the pointer to a small hand with a pointing index finger.
Source: WTMJ

Webpages often contain links. A *link*, short for *hyperlink*, is a built-in connection to other documents, graphics, audio files, videos, webpages, or websites. To activate an item associated with a link, you tap or click the link. In Figure 1-26 on the previous page, for example, tapping or clicking the audio link connects to a live radio show so that you can hear the broadcast. A text link often changes color after you tap or click it to remind you visually that you previously have visited the webpage or downloaded the content associated with the link.

Links allow you to obtain information in a nonlinear way. That is, instead of accessing topics in a specified order, you move directly to a topic of interest. Some people use the phrase *surfing the web* to refer to the activity of using links to explore the web.

A **website** is a collection of related webpages, which are stored on a web server. A **web server** is a computer that delivers requested webpages to your computer or mobile device.

Web Browsing

A **browser** is software that enables users with an Internet connection to access and view webpages on a computer or mobile device. Some widely used browsers include Internet Explorer, Firefox, Safari, and Google Chrome. Read How To 1-2 for instructions about using a browser to display a webpage on a computer or mobile device.

HOW TO 1-2

Use a Browser to Display a Webpage
The following steps describe how to use a browser to display a webpage on a computer or mobile device:

1. Run the browser. (For instructions on running programs and apps, see How To 1-4 and How To 1-5 on page 27.)

2. If necessary, tap or click the address bar to select it and any previously displayed web address it may contain. (A web address is a unique address that identifies a webpage.)

3. In the address bar, type the web address of the webpage you want to visit and then press the ENTER key or tap or click the Go (or similar) button to display the webpage. For example, www.cengagebrain.com is a valid web address, which displays the CengageBrain webpage shown in the figure below. (Chapter 2 discusses the components of a web address in more detail.)

4. If necessary, scroll to view the entire webpage. You can scroll either by sliding your finger across a touch screen or by using a pointing device, such as a mouse, to drag the scroll bar.

5. Tap or click links on the webpage to navigate to the link's destination.

What should you do if the web address you enter does not display a webpage or you receive an error message?

Source: Cengage Learning

Web Searching

A primary reason that people use the web is to search for specific information, including text, photos, music, and videos. The first step in successful searching is to identify the main idea or concept in the topic about which you are seeking information. Determine any synonyms, alternate spellings, or variant word forms for the topic. Then, use a search engine, such as Google, to help you locate the information. A **search engine** is software that finds websites, webpages, images, videos, news, maps, and other information related to a specific topic. Read How To 1-3 for instructions about how to perform a basic web search using a search engine on a computer or mobile device.

 HOW TO 1-3

Perform a Basic Web Search
The following steps describe how to use a search engine on a computer or mobile device to perform a basic web search:

1. Run a browser. (For instructions on running programs and apps, see How To 1-4 and How To 1-5 on page 27.)

2. If the browser does not contain a separate Search box near the address bar, display the search engine's webpage on the screen by entering its web address in the address bar. For example, you could type google.com to display the Google search engine, bing.com to display the Bing search engine, or yahoo.com to display the Yahoo! search engine.

3. Tap or click the Search box and then type the desired search text in the Search box. The more descriptive the search text, the easier it will be to locate the desired search results. As the figure shows, the search engine may provide search text suggestions as you type search text in the Search box.

4. To display search results based on your typed search text, press the ENTER key or tap or click the Search button. To display search results based on one of the suggestions provided by the search engine, tap or click the desired search text suggestion.

5. Scroll through the search results and then tap or click a search result to display the corresponding webpage.

6. To return to the search results, tap or click the Back button in your browser, which typically looks like a left-pointing arrow.

What search text would you enter to locate the admission criteria for your school?

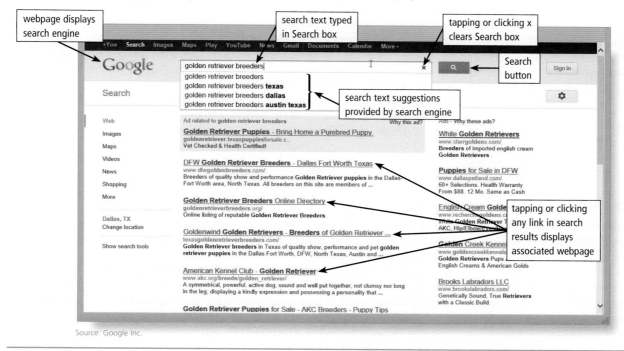

webpage displays search engine

search text typed in Search box

tapping or clicking x clears Search box

Search button

search text suggestions provided by search engine

tapping or clicking any link in search results displays associated webpage

Source: Google Inc.

Online Social Networks

An **online social network**, also called a **social networking site**, is a website that encourages members in its online community to share their interests, ideas, stories, photos, music, and videos with other registered users (Figure 1-27 on the next page). Popular social networking sites include Facebook, Twitter, and LinkedIn.

Some social networking sites have no specialized audience; others are more focused. A photo sharing site, for example, is a specific type of social networking site that allows users to create an online photo album and store and share their digital photos. Similarly, a video sharing site is a type of social networking site that enables users to store and share their personal videos.

 BTW

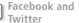 Facebook and Twitter
Technology Innovators:
You should be familiar with Facebook, Mark Zuckerberg, and Twitter.

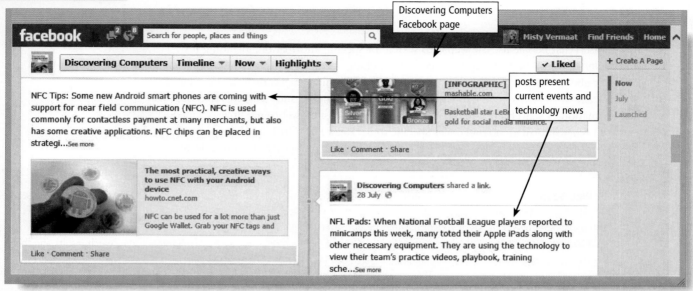

Discovering Computers Facebook page

posts present current events and technology news

Figure 1-27 When Facebook users 'like' this Discovering Computers Facebook page, the posts shown here appear on their own personal pages. As a student in this class, you should 'like' the Discovering Computers page so that you easily can keep up to date with relevant technology changes and events in the computing industry. If you do not have a Facebook account, use a search engine to search for the text, discovering computers facebook, to display the page in a browser.
Source: Facebook

 BTW

Blogs
Posts on Twitter also form a blog, because of its journal format with the most recent entry at the top.

 CONSIDER THIS

How do Facebook, Twitter, and LinkedIn differ?
With Facebook, you share messages, interests, activities, events, photos, and other personal information — called posts — with family and friends. You also can 'like' pages of celebrities, companies, products, etc., so that posts on these pages appear on your Facebook page. With Twitter, you 'follow' people, companies, and organizations in which you have an interest. Twitter enables you to stay current with the daily activities of those you are following via their Tweets, which are short posts (messages) that Tweeters broadcast for all their followers.

On LinkedIn, you share professional interests, education, and employment history, and add colleagues or coworkers to your list of contacts. You can include recommendations from people who know you professionally. Many employers post jobs using LinkedIn and consider information in your profile as your online resume.

Read Ethics & Issues 1-2 to consider whether employees should be held accountable for their social networking posts.

ETHICS & ISSUES 1-2

Should Employees Be Held Accountable for Their Social Networking Posts?
Companies no longer solely rely on a resume and interview to consider you as a potential employee. At a minimum, the hiring manager may search the web to find out any information readily available about you. This includes your use of social networking or blogging sites, such as Facebook or Twitter. Once employed, your manager still may track and review your online presence. You might believe your posts and photos should be your own business. Some companies, however, feel that what you say and do online, as well as what others say about you, could reflect poorly on them and, thus, should affect your employment. These companies are worried not only about their reputations but also

potential red flags. For example, companies may be on the lookout for employees who discuss company sales activity on their blogs, gripe about their managers on Twitter, or have Facebook photos that show them taking part in unethical, illegal, or unsavory activities.

Social network-related firings have made headlines. Two examples include a CFO (chief financial officer) fired for blogging details about his publicly traded company and a teacher fired for making disparaging remarks on her Facebook page about students and their parents. Accessing an employee's or a potential employee's social networking profile also could have consequences for the company. For example, if a company realizes that a person is a member of a minority group or has a disability, the company could face

discrimination charges if it does not hire or later fires the employee. Debate regarding what falls under free speech is ongoing. Remember that what you post online is not deleted easily. Whether or not you currently are searching for a job, online posts you make now can damage your future employment opportunities.

What are the results when you search for yourself online? What steps can you take to clean up and protect your online reputation? Would you share social networking accounts or passwords with an employer or potential employer? Why or why not? Should companies be allowed to view and monitor employees' accounts? Why or why not?

Internet Communications

The web is only one of the services on the Internet. Some of the other services on the Internet facilitate communications among users:

- Email allows you to send messages to and receive messages and files from other users via a computer network.
- With instant messaging (IM), you can have a real-time typed conversation with another connected user (real-time means that both of you are online at the same time).
- VoIP enables users to speak to other users over the Internet.
- With FTP, users can transfer items to and from other computers on the Internet.

Digital Security and Safety

People rely on computers to create, store, and manage their information. To safeguard this information, it is important that users protect their computers and mobile devices. Users also should be aware of health risks and environmental issues associated with using computers and mobile devices.

Viruses and Other Malware

Malware, short for malicious software, is software that acts without a user's knowledge and deliberately alters the computer's and mobile device's operations. Examples of malware include viruses, worms, trojan horses, rootkits, spyware, adware, and zombies. Each of these types of malware attacks your computer or mobile device differently. Some are harmless pranks that temporarily freeze, play sounds, or display messages on your computer or mobile device. Others destroy or corrupt data, instructions, and information stored on the infected computer or mobile device. If you notice any unusual changes in the performance of your computer or mobile device, it may be infected with malware. Read Secure IT 1-2 for ways to protect computers from viruses and other malware.

BTW

Malware
A leading maker of security software claims its software blocked more than five billion malware attacks in a single year.

 SECURE IT 1-2

Protection from Viruses and Other Malware

Although it is impossible to ensure a virus or malware never will attack a computer, you can take steps to protect your computer by following these practices:

- **Use virus protection software.** Install a reputable antivirus program and then scan the entire computer to be certain it is free of viruses and other malware. Update the antivirus program and the virus signatures (known specific patterns of viruses) regularly.

- **Use a firewall.** Set up a hardware firewall or install a software firewall that protects your network's resources from outside intrusions.

- **Be suspicious of all unsolicited email attachments.** Never open an email attachment unless you are expecting it *and* it is from a trusted source. When

in doubt, ask the sender to confirm the attachment is legitimate before you open it. Delete or quarantine flagged attachments immediately.

- **Disconnect your computer from the Internet.** If you do not need Internet access, disconnect the computer from the Internet. Some security experts recommend disconnecting from the computer network before opening email attachments.

- **Download software with caution.** Download programs or apps only from websites you trust, especially those with music and movie sharing software.

- **Close spyware windows.** If you suspect a pop-up window (rectangular area that suddenly appears on your screen) may be spyware, close the window. Never click an Agree or OK button in a suspicious window.

- **Before using any removable media, scan it for malware.** Follow this procedure even for shrink-wrapped software from major developers. Some commercial software has been infected and distributed to unsuspecting users. Never start a computer with removable media inserted in the computer unless you are certain the media are uninfected.

- **Keep current.** Install the latest updates for your computer software. Stay informed about new virus alerts and virus hoaxes.

- **Back up regularly.** In the event your computer becomes unusable due to a virus attack or other malware, you will be able to restore operations if you have a clean (uninfected) backup.

✳ What precautions do you take to prevent viruses and other malware from infecting your computer? What new steps will you take to attempt to protect your computer?

Privacy

Nearly every life event is stored in a computer somewhere . . . in medical records, credit reports, tax records, etc. In many instances, where personal and confidential records were not protected properly, individuals have found their privacy violated and identities stolen. Some techniques you can use to protect yourself from identity theft include shredding financial documents before discarding them, never tapping or clicking links in unsolicited email messages, and enrolling in a credit monitoring service.

Adults, teens, and children around the world are using online social networks to share their photos, videos, journals, music, and other personal information publicly. Some of these unsuspecting, innocent computer users have fallen victim to crimes committed by dangerous strangers. Protect yourself and your dependents from these criminals by being cautious in email messages and on websites. For example, do not share information that would allow others to identify or locate you and do not disclose identification numbers, user names, passwords, or other personal security details. A user name is a unique combination of characters, such as letters of the alphabet or numbers, that identifies one specific user. A password is a private combination of characters associated with a user name. Read Secure IT 1-3 for tips on creating strong passwords.

Internet Research

What are other techniques that deter identity theft?

Search for: prevent identity theft

SECURE IT 1-3

Creating Strong Passwords

A good password is easy for you to remember but difficult for criminals and password-breaking software to guess. Use these guidelines to create effective, strong passwords:

- **Personal information:** Avoid using any part of your first or last name, your family members' names, phone number, street address, license plate number, Social Security number, or birth date.
- **Length:** Use at least eight characters.
- **Difficulty:** Use a variety of uppercase and lowercase letters, numbers, punctuation, and symbols. Select characters located on different parts of the keyboard, not the ones you commonly use or that are

adjacent to each other. Criminals use software that converts common words to symbols, so changing the word, two, to the numeral, 2, or the word, and, to the ampersand symbol, &, is not likely to foil a thief.

- **Modify:** Change the password frequently, at least every three months.
- **Variation:** Do not use the same password for all accounts. Once criminals have stolen a password, they attempt to use that password for other accounts they find on your computer or mobile device, especially banking websites.
- **Passphrase:** A *passphrase*, which is similar to a password, consists of several words separated by spaces. Security experts

recommend misspelling a few of the words and adding several numerals. For example, the phrase, "Create a strong password," could become the passphrase, "Creaet a strang pasword42."

- **Common sequences:** Avoid numbers or letters in easily recognized patterns, such as "asdfjkl;," "12345678," "09870987," or "abcdefg." Also, do not spell words backwards or use common abbreviations.
- **Test:** Use online tools to evaluate password strength.

❈ How strong are your passwords? How will you modify your passwords using some of these guidelines?

Health Concerns

Prolonged or improper computer use can lead to injuries or disorders of the hands, wrists, elbows, eyes, neck, and back. Computer users can protect themselves from these health risks through proper workplace design, good posture while at the computer, and appropriately spaced work breaks.

Two behavioral health risks are technology addiction and technology overload. Technology addiction occurs when someone becomes obsessed with using technology. Individuals suffering from technology overload feel distressed when deprived of computers and mobile devices. Once recognized, both technology addiction and technology overload are treatable disorders.

Environmental Issues

Manufacturing processes for computers and mobile devices along with *e-waste*, or discarded computers and mobile devices, are depleting natural resources and polluting the environment. When computers and mobile devices are stored in basements or other locations, disposed in landfills, or burned in incinerators, they can release toxic materials and potentially dangerous levels of lead, mercury, and flame retardants.

Green computing involves reducing the electricity consumed and environmental waste generated when using a computer. Strategies that support green computing include recycling, using energy efficient hardware and energy saving features, regulating manufacturing processes, extending the life of computers, and immediately donating or properly disposing of replaced computers. When you purchase a new computer, some retailers offer to dispose of your old computer properly. To learn more about green computing, complete the Green Computing exercise in the Internet Research section of the student assignments in each chapter of this book.

 CONSIDER THIS ———————————————————————

How can you contribute to green computing?
Some habits you can alter that will help reduce the environmental impact of computing include the following:

1. Do not leave a computer or device running overnight.
2. Turn off your monitor, printer, and other devices when you are not using them.
3. Use energy efficient hardware.
4. Use paperless methods to communicate.
5. Recycle paper and buy recycled paper.
6. Recycle toner, computers, mobile devices, printers, and other devices.
7. Telecommute.
8. Use videoconferencing and VoIP for meetings.

BTW

Bill Gates and Steve Jobs

Technology Innovators: You should be familiar with Bill Gates (Microsoft's founder) and Steve Jobs (Apple's cofounder).

Programs and Apps

Software, also called a **program**, consists of a series of related instructions, organized for a common purpose, that tells the computer what tasks to perform and how to perform them.

Two categories of software are system software and application software. System software consists of the programs that control or maintain the operations of the computer and its devices. Operating systems are a widely recognized example of system software. Other types of system software, sometimes called tools, enable you to perform maintenance-type tasks usually related to managing devices, media, and programs used by computers and mobile devices. The next sections discuss operating systems and application software.

Operating Systems

An *operating system* is a set of programs that coordinates all the activities among computer or mobile device hardware. It provides a means for users to communicate with the computer or mobile device and other software. Many of today's computers and mobile devices use a version of Microsoft's Windows, Apple's Mac OS, Apple's iOS, or Google's Android (Figure 1-28).

To use application software, your computer or mobile device must be running an operating system.

Figure 1-28 Shown here are the Mac OS and Windows operating systems for personal computers and the Android and iOS operating systems for smartphones. You interact with these operating system interfaces by tapping or clicking their icons or tiles.
Source: Apple Inc.; Apple Inc.; Google Inc.; Microsoft.

Applications

Application software, usually simply called an **application** (or **app** for short), consists of programs designed to make users more productive and/or assist them with personal tasks. Browsers, discussed in an earlier section, are an example of an application that enables users with an Internet connection to access and view webpages. Table 1-2 identifies the categories of applications with samples of ones commonly used in each category.

Applications include programs stored on a computer, as well as those on a mobile device or delivered to your device over the Internet. The term, *desktop app*, often is used to describe applications stored on a computer. The term, *web app* is an application stored on a web server that you access through a browser. A *mobile app* is an application you download from a mobile device's application store or other location on the Internet to a smartphone or other mobile device. Some applications are available as both a web app and a mobile app. For practice working with web apps and mobile apps, see the exercises called App Adventure on the Beyond the Book student assignment page in each chapter of this book.

Table 1-2 Categories of Applications

Category	Sample Applications	Sample Uses
Productivity	Word Processing	Create letters, reports, and other documents.
	Presentation	Create visual aids for presentations.
	Schedule and Contact Management	Organize appointments and contact lists.
	Personal Finance	Balance checkbook, pay bills, and track income and expenses.
Graphics and Media	Photo Editing	Modify digital photos, i.e., crop, remove red-eye, etc.
	Video and Audio Editing	Modify recorded movie clips, add music, etc.
	Media Player	View images, listen to audio/music, watch videos.
Personal Interest	Travel, Mapping, and Navigation	View maps, obtain route directions, locate points of interest.
	Reference	Look up material in dictionaries, encyclopedias, etc.
	Educational	Learn through tutors and prepare for tests.
	Entertainment	Receive entertainment news alerts, check movie times and reviews, play games.
Communications	Browser	Access and view webpages.
	Email	Send and receive messages.
	VoIP	Speak to other users over the Internet.
	FTP	Transfer items to and from other computers on the Internet.
Security	Antivirus	Protect a computer against viruses.
	Personal Firewall	Detect and protect against unauthorized intrusions.
	Spyware, Adware, and other Malware Removers	Detect and delete spyware, adware, and other malware.

Installing and Running Applications

Installing software is the process of setting up software to work with a computer, printer, and other hardware. When you buy a computer, it usually has some software such as an operating system preinstalled on its hard disk so that you can use the computer the first time you turn it on. Installed operating systems often include other programs such as a browser, media player, and calculator. To use additional desktop apps on a computer, you usually need to install the software. Mobile apps typically install automatically after you transfer the app's files to your device from its website. You usually do not need to install web apps before you can run them.

Once installed, you can run an application so that you can interact with it. When you instruct a computer or mobile device to run an application, the computer or mobile device *loads* its software, which means the application is copied from storage to memory. Once in memory, the computer or mobile device can carry out, or execute, the instructions in the application so that you can use it.

You interact with a program or application through its user interface. The *user interface* controls how you enter data and instructions and how information is displayed on the screen. Often, you work with icons or tiles (shown in Figure 1-28 on page 25), which are miniature images that link to programs, media, documents, or other objects. Read How To 1-4 for instructions about installing, running, and exiting applications; and read How To 1-5 for instructions about locating, installing, and running mobile apps.

 HOW TO 1-4

Install, Run, and Exit an Application

The following steps describe how to install, run, and exit an application on a computer.

Locate the Application
- Locate the application to install. Applications are available from retail stores, websites, and from other services such as Apple's App Store or Google Play.

Download and/or Install the Application
- If you are installing an application from physical media such as a CD or DVD, insert the media in your computer. If the installation does not start automatically, locate the installation program on the media and then double-tap or double-click the installation program.

- If the application is available from a website or online store, download the application to your computer. Once the download is complete, if the installation does not start automatically, locate and then double-tap or double-click the downloaded file to begin the installation.

Run the Application
- You have various options for running an application:
  - Tap or click the application's tile or double-tap or double-click the application's icon in the desktop.
  - Display a list of all applications on your computer and then tap or click the icon representing the application to run (some computers may require

you to double-tap or double-click the icon).
  - Use the search feature in the operating system to locate the newly installed application and then tap or click the search result to run the application.

Exit the Application
- Locate and tap or click an Exit or Close button or an Exit or Close command, which often can be found on an application's File menu.

- Locate and tap or click the Close button on the application's title bar (horizontal space at top of window).

☀ If you run a second application without first exiting the one you are using, how can you return to the first application?

 HOW TO 1-5

Locate, Install, and Run a Mobile App

The following steps describe how to locate, install, and run an app on a mobile device:

1. Navigate to the online store for your device. Common stores used to obtain apps include Apple's App Store and Google Play.
2. Use the search feature to browse for the type of app you would like to download

and install. If the app is not free, follow the payment instructions.
3. Tap or click the appropriate button to download the desired app. Depending on your device, you may need to enter additional information, such as a password, to download the app. Once the app downloads, it should install automatically.

4. Locate the app's icon on your device and then tap or click the icon to run the app. Depending on the app, you may have to create a profile, which contains personal data about a user, or enter your email address.

☀ After installing an app on your device, what are some locations you might look to find the new app's icon or tile?

✲ CONSIDER THIS

How do you know if a program will run on your computer?
When you buy a computer, the box, the manufacturer's website, or the order summary will list the computer's specifications. Similarly, when you buy software, the software box or the product's website will list specifications and minimum requirements for memory, speed, and more. Your computer's specifications should be the same as or greater than the software specifications. Ensure the software will run on your computer before making a purchase, because many retailers will not allow you to return software.

Developing Programs and Apps

A *software developer*, sometimes called an application developer or computer programmer, is someone who develops programs and apps or writes the instructions that direct the computer or mobile device to process data into information. When writing instructions, a developer must be sure the program or app works properly so that the computer or mobile device generates the desired results. Complex programs can require thousands to millions of instructions.

Software developers use a programming language or program development tool to create computer programs and apps. Popular programming languages include C++, Java, JavaScript, Visual C#, and Visual Basic. Figure 1-29 shows some of the Visual Basic instructions a programmer may write to create a simple payroll program.

Figure 1-29
A developer writes instructions using Visual Basic (a) to create the Payroll Information window shown here (b).
© Cengage Learning

NOW YOU KNOW

Be sure you understand the material presented in the sections titled The Internet, Digital Security and Safety, and Programs and Apps, as it relates to the chapter objectives.
You now should know . . .

- Why webpages use links (Objective 5)

- How you could use a browser to display a webpage and how to perform a basic web search (Objective 6)

- What risks you are exposed to as a result of your technology use and how you can minimize those risks (Objective 7)

- How to recognize an operating system and which programs and apps you might find useful (Objective 8)

 Quiz Yourself Online: Check your knowledge of related content by navigating to this book's Quiz Yourself resource on Computer Concepts CourseMate and then tapping or clicking Objectives 5–8.

Communications and Networks

Communications technologies are everywhere. Many require that you subscribe to an Internet service provider. With others, an organization such as a business or school provides communications services to employees, students, or customers.

In the course of a day, it is likely you use, or use information generated by, one or more of the communications technologies in Table 1-3.

Table 1-3 Uses of Communications Technologies	
Type	**Brief Description**
Chat rooms	Real-time typed conversation among two or more people on a computers or mobile devices connected to a network
Email	Transmission of messages and files via a computer network
Fax	Transmission and receipt of documents over telephone lines
FTP	Permits users to transfer files to and from servers on the Internet
GPS	Navigation system that assists users with determining their location, ascertaining directions, and more
Instant messaging	Real-time typed conversation with another connected user where you also can exchange photos, videos, and other content
Internet	Worldwide collection of networks that links millions of businesses, government agencies, educational institutions, and individuals
Newsgroups	Online areas in which users have written discussions about a particular subject
RSS	Specification that enables web content to be distributed to subscribers
Videoconference	Real-time meeting between two or more geographically separated people who use a network to transmit audio and video
Voice mail	Allows users to leave a voice message for one or more people
VoIP	Conversation that takes place over the Internet using a telephone connected to a computer, mobile device, or other device
Wireless Internet access points	Enables users with computers and mobile devices to connect to the Internet wirelessly
Wireless messaging services	Send and receive wireless messages to and from smartphones, mobile phones, handheld game devices, and other mobile devices using text messaging and picture/video messaging

© Cengage Learning

Wired and Wireless Communications

Computer communications describes a process in which two or more computers or devices transfer (send and receive) data, instructions, and information over transmission media via a communications device(s).
A **communications device** is hardware capable of transferring items from computers and devices to transmission media and vice versa. Examples of communications devices are modems, wireless access points, and routers. As shown in Figure 1-30, some communications involve cables and wires; others are sent wirelessly through the air.

Figure 1-30 Modems, wireless access points, and routers are examples of communications devices that enable communications between computers/mobile devices and the Internet. Notice that some computers and devices communicate via wires and others communicate wirelessly.

Wired communications often use some form of telephone wiring, coaxial cable, or fiber-optic cables to send communications signals. The wiring or cables typically are used within buildings or underground between buildings.

Because it is more convenient than installing wires and cables, many users opt for wireless communications, which sends signals through the air or space. Examples of wireless communications technologies include Wi-Fi, Bluetooth, and cellular radio:

BTW
Wireless Communications
Innovative Computing: You should be familiar with innovative uses of technology related to wireless communications.

- *Wi-Fi* uses radio signals to provide high-speed Internet and network connections to computers and devices capable of communicating via Wi-Fi. Most computers and many mobile devices, such as smartphones and portable media players, can connect to a Wi-Fi network.
- *Bluetooth* uses short-range radio signals to enable Bluetooth-enabled computers and devices to communicate with each other. For example, Bluetooth headsets allow you to connect a Bluetooth-enabled phone to a headset wirelessly.
- Cellular radio uses the cellular network to enable high-speed Internet connections to devices with built-in compatible technology, such as smartphones. Cellular network providers use the categories 3G, 4G, and 5G to denote cellular transmission speeds, with 5G being the fastest.

Wi-Fi and Bluetooth are both hot spot technologies. A *hot spot* is a wireless network that provides Internet connections to mobile computers and devices. Wi-Fi hot spots provide wireless network connections to users in public locations such as airports and airplanes, train stations, hotels, convention centers, schools, campgrounds, marinas, shopping malls, bookstores, libraries, restaurants, coffee shops, and more. Bluetooth hot spots provide location-based services, such as sending coupons or menus, to users whose Bluetooth-enabled devices enter the coverage range. Read Secure IT 1-4 for tips on protecting your personal data while using a public hot spot.

SECURE IT 1-4

Using Public Wi-Fi Hot Spots Safely

Connecting wirelessly to a public hot spot at your local coffee shop or at the airport can be convenient and practical. Using this free service can be risky, however, because cybercriminals lurk in these areas hoping to gain access to confidential information on your computer or mobile device. Follow these guidelines for a safer browsing experience:

- **Avoid typing passwords and financial information.** Identity thieves are on the lookout for people who sign in to accounts, enter their credit card account numbers in shopping websites, or conduct online banking transactions. If you must type this personal information, be certain the web address begins with "https," not "http." If the web address

changes to "http," sign out of (end your Internet session) immediately.

- **Sign out of websites.** When finished using an account, sign out of it and close the window.
- **Disable your wireless connection.** If you have finished working online but still need to use the computer, disconnect from the wireless connection.
- **Do not leave the computer unattended.** It may seem obvious, but always stay with your computer or mobile device. Turning your back to talk with a friend or to refill your coffee gives thieves a few seconds to steal sensitive information that may be displayed on the screen.
- **Beware of over-the-shoulder snoopers.** The person sitting behind you

may be watching or using a camera phone to record your keystrokes, read your email messages and social networking posts, and view your photos and videos.

✹ How will you apply these precautions the next time you use a public Wi-Fi hot spot? Should businesses post signs alerting customers about Wi-Fi security issues?

© DeiMosz / Shutterstock.com

Networks

A **network** is a collection of computers and devices connected together, often wirelessly, via communications devices and transmission media. Networks allow computers to share *resources*, such as hardware, software, data, and information. Sharing resources saves time and money. In many networks, one or more computers act as a server. The server controls access to the resources on a network. The other computers on the network, each called a client, request resources from the server (Figure 1-31). The major differences between the server and client computers are that the server typically has more power, more storage space, and expanded communications capabilities.

BTW
The Internet
The world's largest computer network is the Internet.

Figure 1-31 A server manages the resources on a network, and clients access the resources on the server. This network enables three separate computers to share the same printer, one wirelessly.

Many homes and most businesses and schools network their computers and devices. Most allow users to connect their computers wirelessly to the network. Users often are required to sign in to, or log on, a network, which means they enter a user name and password (or other credentials) to access the network and its resources.

Home Networks   Home networks save the home user money and provide many conveniences. Each networked computer or mobile device on a home network has the following capabilities:

- Connect to the Internet at the same time
- Share a single high-speed Internet connection
- Access photos, music, videos, and other content on computers and devices throughout the house
- Share devices such as a printer, scanner, or external hard disk
- Play multiplayer games with players on other computers and mobile devices in the house
- Connect game consoles to the Internet
- Subscribe to and use VoIP

Home networks usually are small, existing within a single structure, and use wireless technologies such as those shown in Figure 1-30 on page 29. You do not need extensive knowledge of networks to set up a home network. You will need a communications device, such as a router, which usually includes setup instructions. Most operating systems also provide tools enabling you easily to connect all the computers and devices in your house.

Business Networks   Business and school networks can be small, such as in a room or building, or widespread, connecting computers and devices across a city, country, or the globe. Some reasons that businesses network their computers and devices together include the following:

- **Facilitate communications.** Using a network, employees and customers communicate efficiently and easily via email, instant messaging, blogs, online social networks, video calls, online meetings, video conferencing, VoIP, wireless messaging services, and more.
- **Share hardware.** In a networked environment, each computer on the network can access the hardware on the network, instead of providing each user with the same piece of hardware. For example, computer and mobile device users can access the laser printer on the network, as they need it.
- **Share data, information, and software.** In a networked environment, any authorized computer user can access data, information, and software stored on other computers on the network. A large company, for example, might have a database of customer information that any authorized user can access.

MINI FEATURE 1-2

Living Digitally: Staying in Sync

If you use multiple computers and mobile devices throughout the day, keeping track of common files may be difficult. For example, each morning, you may begin the day by checking your appointment calendar on your computer. That same calendar appears on your smartphone, so that you can view your schedule throughout the day. You may, however, add, change, or delete appointments using the smartphone, so when you return home you will need to update the calendar on your computer to reflect these edits. When you **synchronize**, or **sync**, computers and mobile devices, you match the files in two or more locations with each other, as shown in the figure below. Along with appointments, other commonly synced files from a smartphone are photos, email messages, music, apps, contacts, calendars, and ringtones.

Syncing can be a one-way or a two-way process. With a one-way sync, also called mirroring, you add, change, or delete files in a destination location, called the *target,* without altering the same files in the original location, called the *source*. For example, you may have a large collection of music stored on your computer at home (the source), and you often copy some of these songs to your mobile device (the target). If you add or delete songs from your computer, you also will want to add or change these songs on your mobile device. If, however, you add or change the songs on your mobile device, you would not want to make these changes on your computer.

In two-way sync, any change made in one location also is made in any other sync location. For example, you and your friends may be working together to create one document reflecting your combined ideas. This document could be stored on a network or on cloud storage on the Internet. Your collaboration efforts should reflect the latest edits each person has made to the file.

You can use wired or wireless methods to sync. In a wired setup, cables connect one device to another, which allows for reliable data transfer. While wireless syncing offers convenience and automation, possible issues include battery drain and low signal strength when the devices are not close to each other. Strategies for keeping your files in sync include the following:

- **Use a cable and software.** Syncing photos from a camera or a smartphone to a computer frees up memory on the mobile device and creates a backup of these files. You easily can transfer photos using a data sync cable and synchronization software. Be certain not to disconnect the mobile device from the computer until the sync is complete. You also can copy your photos and documents from the computer to a smartphone, an external hard disk, a USB flash drive, or some other portable storage device.

- **Use cloud storage.** Cloud storage can provide a convenient method of syncing files stored on multiple computers and accessing them from most devices with Internet access. Several cloud storage providers offer a small amount of storage space at no cost and additional storage for a nominal fee per month or per year. Each provider has specific features, but most allow users to share files with other users, preview file contents, set passwords, and control who has permission to edit the files.

- **Use web apps.** By using web apps for email, contacts, and calendars, your information is stored online, so that it is accessible anywhere you have an Internet connection, and can sync with multiple devices.

✹ Synchronization is an effective method of organizing and sharing common files. What files have you synced, such as photos, music, and email? Which sync method did you use?

© iStockphoto /123render; Source: Microsoft; © iStockphoto / Moncherie; © iStockphoto / Ivan Stevanovic; Courtesy of Western Digital Corporation

Uses of Technology in Society

Technology has changed society today as much as the industrial revolution changed society in the eighteenth and nineteenth centuries. People interact directly with technology in fields such as education, government, finance, retail, entertainment, health care, travel, science, publishing, and manufacturing.

Education

Educators and teaching institutions use technology to assist with education. Most equip labs and classrooms with computers. Some even provide computers to students. Many require students to have a mobile computer or mobile device to access the school's network or Internet wirelessly, or to access digital-only content provided by a textbook publisher. To promote education by computer, vendors often offer substantial student discounts on hardware and software.

Educators may use an interactive whiteboard, which is a touch-sensitive device resembling a dry-erase board, that displays images on a connected computer screen (Figure 1-32). They also may use a course management system, sometimes called a learning management system, which is software that contains tools for class preparation, distribution, and management. For example, through the course management system, students access course materials, grades, assessments, and a variety of collaboration tools. Read Ethics & Issues 1-3 on the next page to consider issues related to schools integrating technology into the classroom.

Many schools offer distance learning classes, where the delivery of education occurs at one place while the learning occurs at other locations. Distance learning courses provide time, distance, and place advantages for students who live far from a campus or work full time. A few schools offer entire degrees online. National and international companies offer distance learning training because it eliminates the costs of airfare, hotels, and meals for centralized training sessions.

 BTW

Technology @ Work
For more information about how technology is used in a variety of fields, read the Technology @ Work feature at the end of each chapter in this book.

 Internet Research

How do educators use iTunes U?

Search for: itunes u

Figure 1-32   Teachers and students can write directly on an interactive whiteboard.

Used with permission of SMART Technologies ULC (www.smarttech.com). SMART Board and the SMART logo are trademarks of SMART Technologies ULC and may be registered in the European Union, Canada, the United States and other countries.

✸ ETHICS & ISSUES 1-3

Does Technology Create a Divide between the More and Less Fortunate?

A teacher assigns a research paper that requires students to read several articles on the web. A school requires that all students type papers on a computer and submit the papers using email. While these may be valid ways to integrate technology in a curriculum or to help instructors manage their classroom, they assume all students have ample access to technology outside of school. School districts that assume all students have computers at home place less fortunate students at a further disadvantage. These students may have to stay after school to use a computer or study at the local library to access the Internet. Students at school districts in

disadvantaged areas may fall further behind if the school is unable to provide access to the technology taken for granted at other schools, including interactive whiteboards and dedicated technology specialists. These discrepancies are known collectively as the *digital divide*, a term used to illustrate the gap between those with and without access to technology.

With the recent widespread growth of mobile device users, some aspects of the digital divide are closing. Students can email and do research on Internet-capable mobile devices, as well as access education-related apps. Mobile device capabilities, however, are limited. You cannot use a mobile device to write a research paper, prepare a resume, or submit a college application. Some companies

and organizations are trying to provide better access. One cable company provides low-cost Internet access to families who receive free or reduced school lunches. Schools can apply for technology grants to purchase classroom computers. These grants may be able to provide access to students, but if no one can teach the students or their teachers how to use the technology, it may not solve the problem.

Is it the school's responsibility to provide an even playing field regarding technology access? Why or why not? Should schools be allowed to require students to use technology? Why or why not? What steps can society take to narrow the digital divide?

Government

Most government offices have websites to provide citizens with up-to-date information. People in the United States access government websites to view census data, file taxes, apply for permits and licenses, pay parking tickets, buy stamps, report crimes, apply for financial aid, and renew vehicle registrations and driver's licenses.

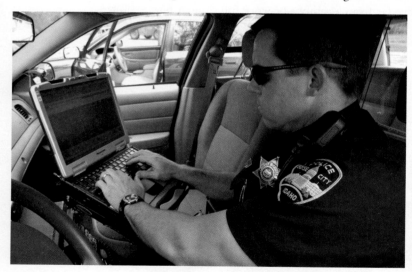

Figure 1-33 Law enforcement officials have in-vehicle computers and mobile devices to access emergency, missing person, and criminal records in computer networks in local, state, and federal agencies.

© David R. Frazier Photolibrary, Inc. / Alamy

Employees of government agencies use computers as part of their daily routine. North American 911 call centers use computers to dispatch calls for fire, police, and medical assistance. Military and other agency officials use the U.S. Department of Homeland Security's network of information about domestic security threats to help protect against terrorist attacks. Law enforcement officers have online access to the FBI's National Crime Information Center (NCIC) through in-vehicle laptops, fingerprint readers, and mobile devices (Figure 1-33). The NCIC contains more than 15 million missing persons and criminal records, including names, fingerprints, parole/probation records, mug shots, and other information.

Finance

Many people and companies use online banking or finance software to pay bills, track personal income and expenses, manage investments, and evaluate financial plans. The difference between using a financial institutions' website versus finance software on your computer is that all your account information is stored on the bank's computer instead of your computer. The advantage is you can access your financial records from anywhere in the world.

Investors often use online investing to buy and sell stocks and bonds — without using a broker. With online investing, the transaction fee for each trade usually is much less than when trading through a broker.

Retail

You can purchase just about any product or service on the web, including groceries, flowers, books, computers and mobile devices, music, movies, airline tickets, and concert tickets. To purchase from an online retailer, a customer visits the business's storefront, which contains product descriptions, images, and a shopping cart. The shopping cart allows the customer to collect purchases. When ready to complete the sale, the customer enters personal data and the method of payment, which should be through a secure Internet connection. Figure 1-34 illustrates the steps involved when a customer purchases from an online retailer.

Many mobile apps make your shopping experience more convenient. Some enable you to manage rewards, use coupons, locate stores, or pay for goods and services directly from your phone or other mobile device. Other mobile apps will check a product's price and availability at stores in your local area or online.

 BTW
Mobile Payments
Innovative Computing: You should be familiar with innovative uses of technology related to mobile payments.

Purchasing from an Online Retailer

Step 1
The customer displays the online retailer's storefront.

Step 2
The customer collects purchases in a shopping cart.

Step 3
The customer enters payment information on a secure website. The online retailer sends financial information to a bank.

Step 5
The online retailer's web server sends confirmation to the customer, processes the order, and then sends it to the fulfillment center.

Step 4
The bank performs security checks and sends authorization back to the online retailer.

Step 6
The fulfillment center packages the order, prepares it for shipment, and then sends a report to the server where records are updated.

Step 7
While the order travels to the customer, shipping information is posted on the web.

Step 8
The order is delivered to the customer, who may be required to sign a handheld computer or document to acknowledge receipt.

Figure 1-34 This figure shows the steps involved when a customer purchases from an online retailer.
© Comstock Images / Photos.com; © iStockphoto / Mark Evans; © iStockphoto / AndyL; © iStockphoto / Mlenny Photography; © Oleksiy Mark / Photos.com; © Oleksiy Mark / Shutterstock.com.; © iStockphoto / Ed Hidden; © iStockphoto / Oksana Perkins; © Bill Aron / PhotoEdit; © Cengage Learning

Entertainment

You can use computers and mobile devices to listen to audio clips or live audio; watch video clips, television shows, or live performances and events; read a book, magazine, or newspaper; and play a myriad of games individually or with others. In some cases, you download the media from the web to a computer or mobile device so that you can watch, listen to, view, or play later. Some websites support *streaming*, where you access the media content while it downloads. For example, radio and television broadcasts often use streaming media to broadcast music, interviews, talk shows, sporting events, news, and other segments so that you can listen to the audio or view the video as it downloads to your computer. You also can create videos, take photos, or record audio and upload (transfer) your media content to the web to share with others, such as on an online social network.

✳ **CONSIDER THIS** ———————————————

Can I make copies of songs or other media that I have purchased and downloaded from a legitimate website, such as iTunes?

You typically can make a copy as a personal backup, but you cannot share the copy with others in any format unless you have legal permission from the copyright owner to do so. That is, you cannot give someone a CD copy, nor can you share a digital file by posting it on the web or emailing it.

Health Care

Nearly every area of health care today uses computers. Whether you are visiting a family doctor for a regular checkup, having lab work or an outpatient test, filling a prescription, or being rushed in for emergency surgery, the medical staff around you will be using computers for various purposes:

- Hospitals and doctors use computers and mobile devices to maintain and access patient records.
- Computers and mobile devices monitor patients' vital signs in hospital rooms and at home; patients use computers to manage health conditions, such as diabetes.
- Robots deliver medication to nurses' stations in hospitals.
- Computers and computerized devices assist doctors, nurses, and technicians with medical tests (Figure 1-35).
- Doctors use the web and medical software to assist with researching and diagnosing health conditions.
- Doctors use email, text messaging, and other communications services to correspond with patients.

Figure 1-35 Doctors, nurses, technicians, and other medical staff use computers and computerized devices to assist with medical tests.
© Jupiterimages / Photos.com

- Patients use computers and mobile devices to refill prescriptions, and pharmacists use computers to file insurance claims and provide customers with vital information about their medications.
- Surgeons implant computerized devices, such as pacemakers, that allow patients to live longer.
- Surgeons use computer-controlled devices to provide them with greater precision during operations, such as for laser eye surgery and robot-assisted heart surgery.

Travel

Whether traveling by car or plane, your goal is to arrive safely at your destination. As you make the journey, you may interact with a navigation system or GPS, which uses satellite signals to determine a geographic location. GPS technology also assists people with creating maps, determining the best route between two points, locating a lost person or stolen object, monitoring a person's or object's movement, determining altitude, calculating speed, and finding points of interest. Vehicles manufactured today typically include some type of onboard navigation system (Figure 1-36). Many mobile devices such as smartphones also have built-in navigation systems.

Figure 1-36 Many vehicles include an onboard navigation system.
© kaczor58 / Shutterstock.com

In preparing for a trip, you may need to reserve a car, hotel, or flight. Many websites offer these services to the public where you can search for and compare flights and prices, order airline tickets, or reserve a rental car. You also can print driving directions and maps from the web.

Science

All branches of science, from biology to astronomy to meteorology, use computers to assist them with collecting, analyzing, and modeling data. Scientists also use the Internet to communicate with colleagues around the world. Breakthroughs in surgery, medicine, and treatments often result from scientists' use of computers. Tiny computers now imitate functions of the central nervous system, retina of the eye, and cochlea of the ear. A cochlear implant allows a deaf person to listen. Electrodes implanted in the brain stop tremors associated with Parkinson's disease.

A *neural network* is a system that attempts to imitate the behavior of the human brain. Scientists create neural networks by connecting thousands of processors together much like the neurons in the brain are connected. The capability of a personal computer to recognize spoken words is a direct result of scientific experimentation with neural networks.

Publishing

Many publishers of books, magazines, newspapers, music, film, and video make their works available online. Organizations and individuals publish their thoughts and ideas using a blog, podcast, or wiki.

- A *blog* is an informal website consisting of time-stamped articles (posts) in a diary or journal format, usually listed in reverse chronological order (Figure 1-37). Posts can contain text, photos, links, and more. As others read articles in your blog, you can enable them to reply with their own thoughts. A blog that contains video is called a video blog.
- Podcasts are a popular way to distribute audio or video on the web. A *podcast* is recorded media that users can download or stream to a computer or portable media player. Examples of podcasts include lectures, political messages, radio shows, and commentaries. Podcasters register their podcasts so that subscribers can select content to automatically download when they are connected.

blog posts

Figure 1-37 Any group or individual can create a blog, so that they can share thoughts and ideas.
Source: Nutrition Blog Network

- A *wiki* is a collaborative website that allows users to create, add to, modify, or delete the content via their browser. Many wikis are open to modification by the general public. The difference between a wiki and a blog is that users cannot modify original posts made by a blogger. Read Ethics & Issues 1-4 for an issue related to using wikis as a source for research.

✹ ETHICS & ISSUES 1-4

Should Wikis Be Allowed as Valid Sources for Academic Research?

As wikis have grown in number, size, and popularity, many educators and librarians have shunned the sites as valid sources of research. While some wikis are tightly controlled with a limited number of contributors and expert editors, these usually focus on narrowly defined, specialized topics. Most large online wikis, such as Wikipedia, often involve thousands of editors, many of whom remain anonymous.

Critics of wikis cite the lack of certified academic credentials by the editors, as well as political or gender bias by contributors. Wikis also are subject to vandalism. Vandals' motives vary; some enter false information to discredit the wiki, and others for humorous results. On occasion, rival political factions have falsified or embellished wiki entries in an attempt to give their candidate an advantage. Some wiki supporters argue that most wikis provide adequate controls to correct false or misleading content quickly and to punish those who submit it. One popular wiki now requires an experienced editor to verify changes made to certain types of articles. Other wiki protection methods include locking articles from editing, creating a list of recently edited articles, enabling readers to report vandalism, and allowing people to be notified about changes to a wiki page that they have edited or that is about them. Some proponents propose that people should use wikis as a starting point for researching a fact, but that they should verify the fact using traditional sources.

Should instructors allow wikis as valid sources for academic research? Why or why not? Would you submit a paper to your instructor that cites a wiki as a source? Why or why not? What policies might wikis enforce that could garner more confidence from the public? If a wiki provided verification of the credentials of the author, would you trust the wiki more? Why or why not?

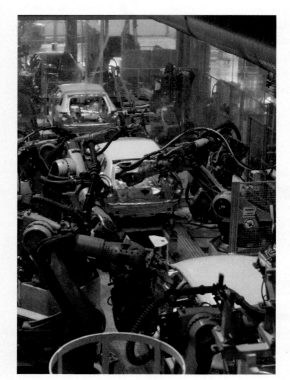

Figure 1-38 Automotive factories use industrial robots to weld car bodies.
© Small Town Studio / Shutterstock.com

Manufacturing

Computer-aided manufacturing (CAM) refers to the use of computers to assist with manufacturing processes such as fabrication and assembly. Industries use CAM to reduce product development costs, shorten a product's time to market, and stay ahead of the competition. Often, robots carry out processes in a CAM environment. CAM is used by a variety of industries, including oil drilling, power generation, food production, and automobile manufacturing. Automobile plants, for example, have an entire line of industrial robots that assemble a car (Figure 1-38).

Special computers on the shop floor record actual labor, material, machine, and computer time used to manufacture a particular product. The computers process this data and automatically update inventory, production, payroll, and accounting records on the company's network.

Technology Users

Every day, people around the world use various technologies at home, at work, and at school. Depending on the hardware, software, and communications requirements, these users generally can be classified in one of five categories. Keep in mind that a single user may fall into more than one category.

- A *home user* is any person who spends time using technology at home. Parents, children, teenagers, grandparents, singles, couples, etc., are all examples of home users.
- A *small/home office user* includes employees of companies with fewer than 50 employees, as well as the self-employed who work from home. Small offices include local law practices, accounting offices, travel agencies, and florists.
- A *mobile user* includes any person who works with computers or mobile devices while away from a main office, home, or school. Examples of mobile users are sales representatives, real estate agents, insurance agents, meter readers, package delivery people, journalists, consultants, and students.

- A *power user* is a user who requires the capabilities of a powerful computer. Examples of power users include engineers, scientists, architects, desktop publishers, and graphic artists.
- An enterprise has hundreds or thousands of employees or customers who work in or do business with offices across a region, the country, or the world. Each employee or customer who uses computers, mobile devices, and other technology in the enterprise is an *enterprise user*.

Table 1-4 illustrates the range of hardware, programs/apps, and communications forms used in each of these categories.

Table 1-4 Categories of Users

User	Sample Hardware	Sample Desktop Apps	Sample Mobile or Web Apps	Forms of Communications
All Users	– Smartphone – Digital camera – Printer	– Word processing – Schedule and contact management – Browser – Security	– Alarm clock – Calculator – News, weather, sports – Reference – Finance	– Email – Online social networks – Blogs
Home User	– Desktop or laptop – Portable media player and earbuds – Game console – E-book reader – Webcam – Headset	– Personal finance – Photo and video editing – Media player – Educational – Entertainment	– Banking – Travel – Mapping – Navigation – Health and fitness – Retail – Media sharing – Educational	– Instant messaging – VoIP
Small/Home Office User	– Desktop(s) or laptop(s) – Server – Webcam – Scanner	– Spreadsheet – Database – Accounting	– Travel – Mapping	– Instant messaging – VoIP – FTP
Mobile User	– Laptop or tablet – Video projector – Wireless headset	– Note taking – Presentation – Educational – Entertainment	– Travel – Mapping – Navigation – Retail – Educational	
Power User	– Desktop – Scanner	– Desktop publishing – Multimedia authoring – Computer-aided design – Photo, audio, video editing		– FTP – Videoconferencing
Enterprise User	– Server – Desktop(s) or laptop(s) – Industry-specific handheld computer – Webcam – Scanner	– Spreadsheet – Database – Accounting	– Travel – Mapping – Navigation	– Instant messaging – VoIP – FTP – Videoconferencing

✦ MINI FEATURE 1-3

Living Digitally: Digital Home

Technology has made homes efficient, safe, and entertaining. Although computers are found throughout today's home, the concept of home automation can be traced back to 1898 when Nikola Tesla invented the first remote control.

Home Automation

New home builders and existing homeowners are integrating features that automate a wide variety of tasks, save time and money, and enhance the overall at-home environment.

- **Lighting:** Controlling lighting is one of the more common uses of technology in the home. Remotes turn light fixtures on and off, motion sensors turn on lights when a car or a visitor approaches the driveway or walkway, and light sensors brighten or dim lighting based on outdoor conditions.

- **Thermostats:** Programmable thermostats adjust to seasonal needs and can be set to control temperatures in individual rooms. Homeowners can use their smartphones to monitor heating and cooling systems, adjust temperatures, and manage energy consumption.

- **Appliances:** Smart appliances, such as dishwashers, can be programmed to run at nonpeak electrical times. Coffeemakers can turn on at set times and shut off if an overheating coffeepot has been left on accidentally. Refrigerators can track expiration dates and create shopping lists.

- **Security:** Alarm system networks monitor many areas of the home. They can detect break-ins at doors, glass breakage, and heat from fires. Surveillance cameras keep a watchful eye on the outside premises and on interior rooms; homeowners can view the images on televisions and computers within the house or on a webpage when they are away from home, as shown in the figure to the left. The security systems can send text and email messages to alert a homeowner when someone has entered or left the home.

- **Vacuums:** Vacuum systems can clean rugs and floors automatically. Sensors prevent the cleaning unit from falling down stairs or bumping into walls. When the cleaning process is complete, the unit returns to the charging station.

Home Entertainment

Televisions have become devices that allow you to do much more than watch a movie or weekly program. By connecting televisions to the Internet and subscribing to online services, users can encounter a wide variety of entertaining options.

- **Gaming:** Although many games are played using a controller, several systems operate by allowing the player to be the controller. Arcade, strategy, and adventure games can be played individually, with a group, or with online friends. Fitness fans can experience a full body workout with yoga sessions, fitness bands, and weights, and new songs, workouts, and difficulty levels.

- **Streaming and sharing content:** Users instantly can watch streaming HD (high-definition) movies, television programs, and sports. They also can connect their tablets and smartphones to share content, including photos and music, chat face-to-face, and update their social networking status.

- **Remotes:** Choosing, configuring, and using remote controls for a home entertainment system can require some time and patience. Although universal remotes are popular choices, many people are turning to using their smartphones and tablets to control all the devices in the room. As shown in the figure below, users enjoy the convenience of customizing apps to operate their television, DVD player, and speakers and to perform other functions anywhere in the home.

✹ How has your life become more efficient, safe, and enjoyable by using home automation and entertainment features?

NOW YOU KNOW

Be sure you understand the material presented in the sections titled Communications and Networks, Uses of Technology in Society, and Technology Users, as it relates to the chapter objectives.
You now should know...

- When you might use wired and wireless communications, and why you would use a network (Objective 9)

- How you would use technology in education, government, finance, retail, entertainment, health care, travel, science, publishing, and manufacturing (Objective 10)

- What types of hardware, software, and communications you could use at home, school, and work (Objective 11)

Quiz Yourself Online: Check your knowledge of related content by navigating to this book's Quiz Yourself resource on Computer Concepts CourseMate and then tapping or clicking Objectives 9–11.

Chapter Summary

Chapter 1 introduced you to basic computer concepts. You learned about laptops, tablets, desktops, servers, smartphones, digital cameras, portable media players, e-book readers, and game devices. The chapter introduced various methods for input, output, memory, and storage. It discussed the Internet, browsing and searching the web, and online social networks. Next, the chapter introduced digital security and safety risks and precautions, along with various types of programs, applications, communications, and networks. The many different uses of technology applications in society also were presented, along with types of users.

This chapter is an overview. Many of the terms and concepts introduced will be discussed further in later chapters.

Test your knowledge of chapter material by accessing the Study Guide, Flash Cards, and Practice Test apps that run on your smartphone, tablet, laptop, or desktop.

TECHNOLOGY @ WORK

Health Care

During an intramural volleyball game, you suffer an injury that requires a trip to an emergency room, which is extremely crowded. Upon check-in, the employee at the front desk uses a computer to record your personal data and symptoms. She also uses the computer to verify that your insurance coverage is current and informs you of your co-payment amount. After waiting several minutes, a triage nurse takes your temperature and blood pressure and then asks a series of questions about your symptoms. The nurse also records this data in a tablet and asks you to remain in the waiting room until someone from the radiology department is available to perform a CT scan. The radiology department is located in a different area of the hospital, so the technicians watch a computer screen that displays a list of patients who currently are waiting for their services.

About 30 minutes later, a technician calls your name and escorts you to the radiology department for your CT scan. As she is performing the scan, a computer records the images that later will be reviewed by a physician. When the CT scan is complete, you return to the waiting room until a physician reviews the results. Once he receives the results and reviews them, a hospital employee takes you to a consultation room.

The physician informs you that other than a few bumps and bruises, he believes that you have sustained no permanent damage and prescribes medication to help ease the pain. He then returns to a computer at the nurses' station and adds his diagnosis to the database that stores your medical records. He also sends your prescription electronically to the hospital's pharmacy. Once discharged, you visit the cashier to pay the bill. You then use a tablet to sign an electronic version of your discharge paperwork so that the hospital can store it electronically. The hospital bills your insurance company electronically. If you owe a balance after the insurance company pays its portion, a computer at the hospital will generate a bill that will be mailed to you. After purchasing your medication and leaving the hospital, you realize that despite the hospital being busy, computers decreased the time of your visit by automating processes that otherwise would have been performed manually and reduced possible errors by storing all of your personal information centrally.

How else might computers and technology be used in the health care industry?

© Steve Cole / Photos.com

STUDENT ASSIGNMENTS

Study Guide

The Study Guide exercise reinforces material you should know for the chapter exam. You will find answers to items with the e-book icon only in the e-book appearing as blue text.

Access the Study Guide app that runs on your smartphone, tablet, laptop, or desktop by navigating to this book's Apps resource on Computer Concepts CourseMate.

Instructions: Answer the questions below using the format that helps you remember best or that is required by your instructor. Possible formats may include one or more of these options: write the answers; create a document that contains the answers; record answers as audio or video using a webcam, smartphone, or portable media player; post answers on a blog, wiki, or website; or highlight answers in the book/e-book.

1. Define the term, digital literacy.

2. Define the terms, computer and user.

3. Differentiate between a desktop and a laptop. A laptop also is known as a(n) _____ computer.

4. Describe a tablet.

5. Describe how you interact with a touch screen.

6. Define the term, server. What services does a server provide?

7. Explain whether or not a mobile device is a computer.

8. List characteristics of a smartphone.

9. Differentiate among text, picture, and video messages.

10. Describe the purpose of these mobile devices: digital camera, portable media player, e-book reader, and game console.

11. Describe the trend of convergence and how it applies to mobile devices.

12. The ESRB provides guidelines for the _____ industry. Describe the rating system.

13. Differentiate between data and information. Give an example of each.

14. Define the terms, input and output. List several types of input devices and output devices.

15. Describe the purpose of a pointing device. Give an example.

16. List the hardware you can use to enter voice and video.

17. Differentiate between memory and storage.

18. A computer keeps data, instructions, and information on _____ media. Give some examples.

19. Define the term, cloud storage. Describe the types of services offered by cloud storage providers.

20. Describe components of a backup plan.

21. Describe the Internet. Identify reasons people use the Internet.

22. The _____ consists of a worldwide collection of electronic documents. What is each electronic document called?

23. Differentiate between the web and the Internet.

24. Describe the purpose of a search engine. List two search engines.

25. Explain the purpose of an online social network. What is a Tweet?

26. Name the products and/or services of Facebook and Twitter, with respect to technology.

27. Explain why a company might be interested in an employee's social networking profile.

28. Define the term, malware. List ways you can protect yourself from malware.

29. List guidelines for creating a strong password. Describe how online tools can determine a password's strength.

30. Explain physical and behavioral health risks associated with using computers.

31. Define the term, green computing. Describe strategies that support green computing.

32. Define the term, software. Software also is called a(n) _____.

33. Define the terms, system software and operating system. List popular operating systems for computers and mobile devices.

34. Name the contributions of Steve Jobs and Bill Gates, with respect to technology.

35. List the steps involved in installing applications.

36. Explain how you can determine whether a program will run on your computer.

37. Define the term, communications device. List examples of wireless communications technologies.

38. Define the term, hot spot. Give two examples and describe how each is used.

39. Give examples of precautions you should take when using a public Wi-Fi hot spot.

40. Describe how homes and businesses use networks.

41. Explain what occurs when you synchronize computers and mobile devices.

42. Define the term, digital divide, and describe how it pertains to education.

43. Describe how you might use blogs, wikis, and podcasts to publish content.

44. Differentiate among the following technology user types: home user, small/home office user, mobile user, power user, and enterprise user.

45. Describe how technology is used in the health care industry.

You should be able to define the Primary Terms and be familiar with the Secondary Terms listed below.

Key Terms

 Access the Flash Cards app that runs on your smartphone, tablet, laptop, or desktop by navigating to this book's Apps resource on Computer Concepts CourseMate. **View definitions** for each term by navigating to this book's Key Terms resource on Computer Concepts CourseMate. **Listen to definitions** for each term on your portable media player by navigating to this book's Audio Study Tools resource on Computer Concepts CourseMate.

Primary Terms   (shown in **bold-black** characters in the chapter)

app (26)	green computing (25)	printer (14)	synchronize (32)
application (26)	input device (12)	program (25)	tablet (4)
browser (20)	Internet (18)	search engine (21)	user (4)
communications device (29)	laptop (4)	server (6)	web (19)
computer (4)	mobile device (7)	smartphone (7)	web server (20)
desktop (6)	network (30)	social networking site (21)	webpage (19)
digital camera (8)	online social network (21)	software (25)	website (20)
digital literacy (2)	output device (14)	storage device (15)	
e-book reader (9)	personal computer (4)	storage media (15)	
game console (9)	portable media player (8)	sync (32)	

Secondary Terms   (shown in *italic* characters in the chapter)

backup (17)	*file (17)*	*mobile user (38)*	*slide (5)*
blog (37)	*gesture (5)*	*mouse (12)*	*small/home office user (38)*
Bluetooth (30)	*hard copy (14)*	*neural network (37)*	*software developer (28)*
camera phone (7)	*hard disk (15)*	*notebook computer (4)*	*solid-state drive (16)*
click (13)	*hardware (4)*	*online (6)*	*source (32)*
cloud storage (17)	*headset (13)*	*on-screen keyboard (5)*	*streaming (35)*
computer-aided manufacturing (38)	*home user (38)*	*operating system (25)*	*stretch (5)*
convergence (10)	*hot spot (30)*	*output (4)*	*surfing the web (20)*
data (11)	*hyperlink (20)*	*passphrase (24)*	*swipe (5)*
desktop app (26)	*information (11)*	*personal media player (8)*	*tap (5)*
digital divide (34)	*input (4)*	*picture message (7)*	*target (32)*
double-click (13)	*keyboard (12)*	*pinch (5)*	*text message (7)*
double-tap (5)	*link (20)*	*podcast (37)*	*touchpad (12)*
downloading (19)	*loads (27)*	*point (13)*	*USB flash drive (16)*
drag (5, 13)	*malware (23)*	*power user (39)*	*user interface (27)*
earbuds (9)	*memory (15)*	*press and hold (5)*	*video message (7)*
e-book (9)	*memory card (16)*	*printout (14)*	*web app (26)*
enterprise user (39)	*microphone (13)*	*resources (30)*	*webcam (13)*
e-reader (9)	*mobile app (26)*	*right-click (13)*	*Wi-Fi (30)*
e-waste (24)	*mobile computer (4)*	*scanner (13)*	*wiki (38)*

blog (37)

Checkpoint

The Checkpoint exercises test your knowledge of the chapter concepts. The page number containing the answer appears in parentheses after each exercise. The Consider This exercises challenge your understanding of chapter concepts.

Complete the Checkpoint exercises interactively by navigating to this book's Checkpoint resource on Computer Concepts CourseMate. **Access the Test Prep app** that runs on your smartphone, tablet, laptop, or desktop by navigating to this book's Apps resource on Computer Concepts CourseMate. After successfully completing the self-assessment through the Test Prep app, **take the Practice Test** by navigating to this book's Practice Test resource on Computer Concepts Coursemate.

True/False   Mark T for True and F for False.

_____ 1. Electronic components in computers process data using instructions, which are the steps that tell the computer how to perform a particular task. (4)

_____ 2. Screens for desktops cannot yet support touch. (6)

_____ 3. Smaller applications, such as at home, typically use a powerful, expensive server to support their daily operations. (6)

_____ 4. Smartphones typically communicate wirelessly with other devices or computers. (7)

_____ 5. Data conveys meaning to users, and information is a collection of unprocessed items, which can include text, numbers, images, audio, and video. (11)

_____ 6. As widespread as computers appear to be, most daily activities do not involve the use of or depend on information from them. (11)

_____ 7. A scanner is a light-sensing output device. (13)

_____ 8. Because it contains moving parts, flash memory is less durable and shock resistant than other types of media. (16)

_____ 9. The terms, web and Internet, are interchangeable. (18)

_____ 10. One way to protect your computer from malware is to scan any removable media before using it. (23)

_____ 11. Operating systems are a widely recognized example of system software. (25)

_____ 12. You usually do not need to install web apps before you can run them. (27)

Multiple Choice   Select the best answer.

1. A(n) _____ is any hardware component that allows you to enter data and instructions into a computer or mobile device. (12)
   a. output device   c. input device
   b. communications device d. display

2. Which of the following is *not* an example of an output device? (13)
   a. scanner   c. display
   b. printer   d. speaker

3. _____ consists of electronic components that store instructions waiting to be executed and the data needed by those instructions. (15)
   a. Storage   c. Solid-state drives
   b. Cloud storage d. Memory

4. A(n) _____ is removable flash memory, usually no bigger than 1.5 inches in height or width, that you insert in and remove from a slot in a computer, mobile device, or card reader/writer. (16)
   a. memory card   c. solid-state drive (SSD)
   b. USB flash drive d. optical disc

5. A computer that delivers requested webpages to your computer or mobile device is a(n) _____. (20)
   a. VoIP computer c. FTP device
   b. web server   d. hard disk

6. _____ software consists of programs designed to make users more productive and/or assist them with personal tasks. (26)
   a. System   c. Operating system
   b. Application   d. Gaming

7. _____ uses the cellular network to enable high-speed Internet connections to devices with built-in compatible technology, such as smart phones. (30)
   a. Cellular radio c. Wi-Fi
   b. Bluetooth   d. Hot spot

8. A(n) _____ is a collaborative website that allows users to create, add to, modify, or delete the content via their browser. (38)
   a. podcast c. online social network
   b. blog   d. wiki

Checkpoint

Matching   Match the terms with their definitions.

_____ 1. laptop (4)

_____ 2. server (6)

_____ 3. picture message (7)

_____ 4. convergence (10)

_____ 5. touchpad (12)

_____ 6. storage device (15)

_____ 7. hard disk (15)

_____ 8. file (17)

_____ 9. software (25)

_____ 10. operating system (25)

a. term that describes the trend of computers and devices with technologies that overlap

b. storage device that contains one or more inflexible, circular platters that use magnetic particles to store data, instructions, and information

c. thin, lightweight mobile computer with a screen in its lid and a keyboard in its base

d. small, flat, rectangular pointing device that is sensitive to pressure and motion

e. set of programs that coordinates all the activities among computer or mobile device hardware

f. named collection of stored data, instructions, or information

g. a photo or other image, sometimes along with sound and text, sent to or from a smartphone or mobile device

h. series of related instructions, organized for a common purpose, that tells the computer what tasks to perform and how to perform them

i. computer that is dedicated to providing one or more services to other computers or devices on a network

j. component that records and/or retrieves items to and from storage media

Short Answer   Write a brief answer to each of the following questions.

1. Define an online social network. (21) Differentiate among Facebook, Twitter, and LinkedIn. (22)

2. Name several different types of malware. (23) List steps you can take to protect your computer from malware and viruses. (23)

3. What is a passphrase? (24) List the guidelines you should use when creating strong passwords. (24)

4. Define green computing. (25) List steps you can take to contribute to green computing. (25)

5. Define application software. (26) Differentiate among desktop apps, web apps, and mobile apps. (26)

✳ Consider This   Answer the following questions in the format specified by your instructor.

1. Answer the critical thinking questions posed at the end of these elements in this chapter: Ethics & Issues (8, 22, 34, 38), How To (5, 20, 21, 27, 27), Mini Features (10, 32, 40), Secure IT (18, 23, 24, 30), and Technology @ Work (41).

2. What does it mean to be digitally literate, and why is it important? (2)

3. 📑 What are the different touch screen gestures and the actions they may cause to occur? (5)

4. Can a smartphone replace the need for a desktop or laptop? Why or why not? What tasks would be more difficult to accomplish on a smartphone? (7)

5. What types of keyboards are available for smartphones and tablets? (5, 7)

6. In what circumstances is it appropriate or inappropriate to use text acronyms and abbreviations? (8)

7. Do video calls and web conferencing replace the need for face-to-face meetings? Why or why not? (13)

8. Are USB flash drives an appropriate method of backing up data and files? Why or why not? (16)

9. When is it better to use email instead of IM? (23)

10. How do you know if you are addicted to computers or suffer from technology overload? (24)

11. Why is green computing important? (25)

12. What is the difference between system and application software? (25)

13. 📑 How does the cellular transmission speed change from 3G, 4G, and 5G? (30)

14. When should you use a one-way sync or a two-way sync? (32)

15. What types of websites are legitimate sources of streaming video? (35)

✷ How To: Your Turn

The How To: Your Turn exercises present general guidelines for fundamental skills when using a computer or mobile device and then require that you determine how to apply these general guidelines to a specific program or situation.

Instructions: You often can complete tasks using technology in multiple ways. Figure out how to perform the tasks described in these exercises by using one or more resources available to you (such as a computer or mobile device, articles on the web or in print, online or program help, user guides, blogs, podcasts, videos, other individuals, trial and error, etc.). Summarize your 'how to' steps, along with the resource(s) used, in the format requested by your instructor (brief report, presentation, discussion, blog post, video, or other means).

❶ Use Computer Concepts CourseMate

Computer Concepts CourseMate provides access to multiple resources to supplement the concepts and skills you are learning in this text. The following steps guide you through the process of signing in to Computer Concepts CourseMate, navigating the website, and accessing various resources.

a. Run your browser and then navigate to www.cengagebrain.com.

b. Sign in with your CourseMate user name and password. If you do not have a user name, tap or click the link to sign up and then follow the instructions to obtain an account.

c. If necessary, add this textbook to your CourseMate account.

d. Tap or click the link to access Computer Concepts CourseMate.

e. Select the desired chapter.

f. Tap or click the resource you want to use.

g. When you are finished viewing the first resource, tap or click the next resource you want to use.

h. Sign out of your CourseMate account when you are finished viewing available resources.

Exercises

1. Summarize the process you use to sign in to your Computer Concepts CourseMate account.

2. Describe each Computer Concepts CourseMate resource available for this book and for each chapter.

3. Which resources on Computer Concepts CourseMate do you feel will best help you reinforce the chapter content? Why?

❷ Create a Facebook Account, Find the Discovering Computers Facebook Page, and Like It

The Discovering Computers Facebook page contains links to current events and other technology news, as well as relating the link to content in this book. The following steps guide you through the process of signing up for a Facebook account, navigating to the Discovering Computers Facebook page, and liking the page.

a. Run your browser and then navigate to www.facebook.com.

b. Follow the steps on the Facebook webpage to sign up for a new account. If you already have an account, enter your login information and log into your Facebook account.

c. Search for the Discovering Computers Facebook page using the search text, Discovering Computers.

d. Select the Discovering Computers Product/Service in the search results.

e. Click the Like button to like the page.

f. If your screen displays a Subscribe button, click it to see information from the Discovering Computers Facebook page in your news feed.

g. View the posts and click links on the page that are of interest to you.

h. When you are finished, sign out of Facebook.

Exercises

1. Summarize the process you use to sign up for or sign in to your Facebook account.

2. Which links on the Discovering Computers Facebook page are of interest to you? Why?

3. Browse Facebook and find at least three other Facebook pages that are of interest to you. Which pages have you found, and why do you like them?

Source: Facebook

❸ Create a Twitter Account, Find the Discovering Computers Twitter Account, and Follow It

The Discovering Computers Twitter account contains links to current events and other technology news, as well as how it relates to the content in this textbook. The following steps guide you through the process of signing up for a Twitter account, navigating to the Discovering Computers Twitter account, and following it.

a. Run your browser and then navigate to www.twitter.com.

How To: Your Turn ☀

b. Follow the steps on the Twitter webpage to sign up for a new account. If you already have an account, enter your sign-in information and sign in to your Twitter account.

c. Search for the Discovering Computers Twitter account using the search text, DiscoveringComp.

d. Select the Shelly Cashman @DiscoveringComp in the search results.

e. Click the Follow button to follow the account.

f. View the posts and click links on the page that are of interest to you.

g. When you are finished, sign out of Twitter.

Exercises

1. Summarize the process you use to sign up for or sign in to your Twitter account.

2. How is the Discovering Computers Twitter account similar to the Discovering Computers Facebook page? How are they different?

3. Browse Twitter and find at least three other Twitter accounts to follow. Which ones have you found, and why do you like them?

4 **Sign Up for a Microsoft Account**

A Microsoft account provides access to resources on several Microsoft websites. These websites include access to resources such as a free email account, cloud storage, a location to store information about your contacts, and an online calendar. You will need a Microsoft account to complete some of the exercises in this book. The following steps guide you through the process of signing up for a Microsoft account.

a. Run a browser and navigate to www.outlook.com.

b. Click the link and follow the on-screen instructions to sign up for a free Microsoft account.

c. Browse the resources available to you in your Microsoft account.

d. If approved by your instructor, compose and send a new email message to your instructor stating that you have signed up for a Microsoft account successfully.

e. Add your instructor's contact information. Next, add contact information for at least three additional people.

f. Add your birthday to the calendar.

g. Edit your Microsoft account profile to add additional contact and work information.

Exercises

1. If necessary, navigate to and view your new outlook.com email account. What are some ways to prevent junk email using the mail settings? What is junk email?

2. What is SkyDrive? How much space do you have available on SkyDrive to post files?

3. How can you see yourself using the various features in your newly created Microsoft account?

5 **Connect to a Wireless Network**

Wireless networks are available in many homes and businesses. Connecting to a wireless network can provide you with high-speed access to the Internet and other network resources. The following steps guide you through the process of connecting to a wireless network from a computer or mobile device.

a. If necessary, turn on your computer or mobile device and make sure wireless functionality is enabled.

b. Obtain the name of the wireless network to which you want to connect. *Note: You should connect only to wireless networks for which you have permission.*

c. On your computer or mobile device, view the list of available wireless networks.

d. Select the wireless network to which you want to connect.

e. If necessary, enter the requested security information, such as an encryption key or a password.

f. Run your browser to test your connection to the wireless network.

Exercises

1. Why should you not connect to a wireless network unless you have permission?

2. What is the name of the wireless network to which you connected?

3. Why might you connect to a wireless network on your smartphone instead of using your mobile data plan?

© Cengage Learning; © iStockphoto / Petar Chernaev; © iStockphoto / Oleksiy Mark; © Courtesy of Verizon Wireless; © topseller / Shutterstock.com; © alexmisu / Shutterstock.com; © Pablo Eder / Shutterstock.com; © iStockphoto / 123render; Source: Microsoft

✳ Internet Research

The Internet Research exercises broaden your understanding of chapter concepts by requiring that you search for information on the web.

Instructions: Use a search engine or another search tool to locate the information requested or answers to questions presented in the exercises. Describe your findings, along with the search term(s) you used and your web source(s), in the format requested by your instructor (brief report, presentation, discussion, blog post, video, or other means).

① Making Use of the Web
Search Engines and Research

Sixty percent of all American adults use a search engine every day, according to Pew Internet, and they generally are pleased with the outcome of their research experience. In How To 1-2 and 1-3 on pages 20 and 21 in this chapter, you learned to use a browser to display a webpage and to perform a basic web search.

Using these skills, find the answers to the following questions. (1) Visit the Pew Internet website and locate the latest Search Engine Use report. What are three of the users' positive search experiences? Which search engine is the most popular among the people surveyed? When was the survey conducted, and how many adults were surveyed? (2) Visit the CNET website and read at least three reviews of products. Create a table listing the product name, price, editors' and users' ratings, and "bottom line" summary. (3) Use a search engine or research website to locate articles about banning mobile devices in schools. What policies have schools created in lieu of a total ban on this technology? How have schools integrated mobile devices in the classroom as a vehicle to enhance learning?

many of the same basic principles by allowing members to communicate common interests, play games, and share photos, videos, and music. Some of these social networking sites are for personal use, while others are for entrepreneurs, business owners, and professionals to share job-related topics.

Compare the features of the top personal social networks, and create a table listing the number of active members in the United States and worldwide, the number of years the sites have existed, the more popular features, and the amount of content, such as photos, news stories, and links, that is shared each month. What types of advertisements are featured in each of these sites? Which sites are marketed toward younger and older users? Then, research the social networks used for business. How does their content differ from that found on the personal social networks? How many companies use these sites as a recruiting tool? How many native languages are supported? How are professionals using these websites to find potential clients and business partners?

③ Search Sleuth

(1) Which magazine introduced the first microcomputer kit for the MITS Altair in its January 1975 issue? (2) Which company sold the TRS-80, one of the more popular personal computers introduced in 1977? (3) What material did Douglas Engelbart use to create the first mouse? (4) What is the code name for the 12 engineers who developed the IBM PC? (5) Who received the first text message in 1992? What was the content of this message? (6) Which company developed the first digital camera? How many pounds did this camera weigh? (7) What is the title of Stephen King's e-book that was released in 2000? (8) In which year did Amazon.com report that for the first time sales of e-books exceeded the sales of hardcover books? (9) What is the name of the keyboard developed in the 1930s with a layout designed to maximize efficiency and reduce hand stress? (10) When did the first USB flash drive appear on the retail market? Which company developed this storage medium?

Source: Microsoft

② Social Media

Historians place the birth of online social networking with the BBS (Bulletin Board System), where users communicated with a central computer and sent messages to other BBS members and also downloaded files and games. The next phase of social networking evolved when CompuServe, AOL (America Online), and Prodigy were among the services linking people with similar interests. Today's social networks share

Internet Research ✹

4 Green Computing

The average American household has 24 electronic products, according to the Consumer Electronics Association. When these devices, such as televisions, computers, and mobile devices become outdated or inoperable, the owner is left with the challenge of disposing or donating them. Many options exist to prevent these electronics from being discarded in landfills and, in turn, producing toxic waste. The United States Environmental Protection Agency (EPA) lists many eCycling resources on its website, including information about locations to donate or recycle electronics, answers to common questions about electronic waste, and regional and state eCycling programs. Visit the EPA site and read about recycling electronics. What toxic substances are found in computer components? Most major computer manufacturers provide recycling services. Identify which companies provide this service and how donations are made. For example, do users mail their electronics, drop them off at a store, or arrange for pickup?

The Electronics TakeBack Coalition encourages consumer electronics manufacturers to take responsibility for the entire life cycle of their products, from manufacture to disposal. Visit the Electronics TakeBack website and read what actions consumers can take to buy and dispose of their products responsibly and to urge companies to practice safe and environmentally friendly policies. Find a computer or phone recycling center in your area and then use an online mapping app (such as Google or Bing Maps) to find directions to these locations. In addition, many nonprofit organizations accept donations of electronic equipment, including computers. Locate several of these organizations and determine which devices they accept as donations. Some electronics retailers will accept used equipment and also sponsor recycling events. Which of these stores are near your residence? What products will they accept?

5 Security

Secure IT 1-1 on page 18 discusses the benefits of creating a backup plan for computers and mobile devices. One backup method is subscribing to a cloud storage provider. Consumer subscriptions to cloud storage services are experiencing double-digit growth each year, with an estimated 1.3 billion users predicted by 2017. Amazon, Google, Microsoft, and Apple are among the many companies offering cloud storage services.

Locate information about two of these services and review the features. Then, locate at least two independent cloud service providers, such as JustCloud, and read about accounts. How much free storage is available? What is the charge for additional storage? Are both limited and unlimited storage plans available? What is the maximum individual file size allowed? What methods do these companies take to secure the files? For example, how do they check the authenticity of the person signing in to the account? How do they monitor suspicious activity? Do they allow users to review all the sign-ins within a set period of time? Do they require account holders to modify their passwords occasionally? Is live customer support available 24 hours each day at no charge? In which country is the company and server located?

Source: JustCloud, Inc.

6 Ethics in Action

The Internet has increased the ease with which students can plagiarize material for research paper assignments. In an attempt to detect plagiarized material, teachers and students are using online services to check for original writing and offer feedback on methods of rewriting and citing sources correctly. For example, Turnitin and WriteCheck both use the same database of millions of student papers and billions of websites to compare phrases. Many other plagiarism checking services exist, and their cost, features, and reliability vary widely.

Visit the Turnitin and WriteCheck sites and then summarize of how these services are used. Compare these services with at least one other service. What are the fees to use these websites? How accurate are the results? How large are the databases of online and offline publications and papers? What features, such as allowing multiple resubmissions and grammar checking, do they offer? What types of reports are generated that give feedback and show plagiarized sources? What help and support are available? In general, how prevalent is plagiarism on your campus? What is your schools' official policy on disciplining students who submit plagiarized papers? Does your school have an honor code?

✺ Problem Solving

The Problem Solving exercises extend your knowledge of chapter concepts by seeking solutions to practical problems with technology that you may encounter at home, school, or work. The Collaboration exercise should be completed with a team.

⊠ Challenge yourself with additional Problem Solving exercises by navigating to this book's Problem Solving resource on Computer Concepts CourseMate.

Instructions: You often can solve problems with technology in multiple ways. Determine a solution to the problems in these exercises by using one or more resources available to you (such as a computer or mobile device, articles on the web or in print, blogs, podcasts, videos, television, user guides, other individuals, electronics or computer stores, etc.). Describe your solution, along with the resource(s) used, in the format requested by your instructor (brief report, presentation, discussion, blog post, video, or other means).

Personal

1. **Shopping for Software**   You are shopping for software that will assist you with your home's interior design. The package for the program you would like to purchase states that it was designed for the most recent version of Windows, but an older version is installed on your computer. How can you determine whether the program will run on your computer?

2. **Bad Directions**   You are driving to your friend's house and are using your smartphone for directions. While approaching your destination, you realize that your smartphone app instructed you to turn the wrong way on your friend's street. How could this have happened?

3. **Bank Account Postings**   While reviewing your checking account balance online, you notice that debit card purchases have not posted to your account for the past several days. Because you use online banking to balance your account, you become concerned about your unknown account balance. What steps will you take to correct this situation?

4. **Inaccessible Media**   You insert a memory card with digital photos from your most recent family vacation and discover that your computer will not read the memory card. What might be wrong?

5. **Problematic Camera**   After charging your digital camera battery overnight, you insert the battery and turn on the camera only to find that it is reporting a low battery. Seconds later, the camera shuts off automatically. What might be wrong?

Professional

6. **Discarding Old Computer Equipment**   Your company has given you a new laptop to replace your current, outdated desktop. Because of the negative environmental impact of discarding the old computer in the trash, your supervisor asked you to suggest options for its disposal. How will you respond?

7. **Dead Battery**   While traveling for business, you realize that you forgot to bring the battery charger for your laptop. Knowing that you need to use the laptop to give a presentation tomorrow, what steps will you take tonight to make sure you have enough battery power?

8. **Software Installation**   You are attempting to install a program on your office computer. After inserting the installation disc and specifying that you would like to begin the installation, your computer appears to begin installing the program. Halfway through the installation process, an error message appears stating that you must have administrative privileges to perform the installation. Why were you not informed immediately upon beginning the installation? What are your next steps?

9. **Incorrect Sign-In Credentials**   Upon returning to the office from a well-deserved two-week vacation, you turn on your computer. When you enter your user name and password, an error message appears stating that your password is incorrect. What are your next steps?

10. **Synchronization Error**   You added appointments to the calendar on your computer, but these appointments are not synchronizing with your smartphone. Your calendar has synchronized with your smartphone in the past, but it has stopped working without explanation. What are your next steps?

Collaboration

11. **Technology in Health Care**   Your dentist is moving from a shared office so that he can open his own practice. He mentioned that he would like to use technology in his office that not will only improve the patient experience, but also make his job easier. Form a team of three people to determine the types of technology your dentist can use in his new office. One team member should research ways that technology can help improve patient check-in and billing. Another team member should research the types of technology your dentist can use while he is working with patients, and the third team member should research any additional technology that can be used in the office to improve the patient experience. Compile your findings in a report and submit it to your instructor.

© iStockphoto / Oleksiy Mark

The Critical Thinking exercises challenge your assessment and decision-making skills by presenting real-world situations associated with chapter concepts. The Collaboration exercise should be completed with a team.

Critical Thinking ✸

Challenge yourself additional Critical Thinking exercises by navigating to this book's Critical Thinking resource on Computer Concepts CourseMate.

Instructions: Evaluate the situations below, using personal experiences and one or more resources available to you (such as articles on the web or in print, blogs, podcasts, videos, television, user guides, other individuals, electronics or computer stores, etc.). Perform the tasks requested in each exercise and share your deliverables in the format requested by your instructor (brief report, presentation, discussion, blog post, video, or other means).

1. Class Discussion

Reactions to Software Problems   Everyone who uses computers and mobile devices has experienced problems with software, including operating systems, desktop apps, web apps, and mobile apps. Problems range from not being able to install or download the program or app to a computer or mobile device, to a program or an app producing unanticipated results. Depending on the situation, these problems can result in user stress. Many people believe reactions to software problems tend to be more extreme than reactions to problems with other tools. Evaluate situations in which you have seen people react to program and app problems on their computers and mobile devices. Discuss how these users can reduce their frustration when dealing with such problems. Have you ever been frustrated by problems with a program or an app? How did you react? What did you do to solve the problem?

2. Research and Share

Energy Efficiency   Increases in energy prices lead many individuals to look at purchasing energy-efficient computers. Energy-efficient computers often look and perform similarly to equivalent computers that use more energy. Find two computers of identical configuration, where the only difference is energy consumption. How much energy does the energy-efficient computer save? Are energy-efficient computers more or less expensive? Will the difference in cost (if any) affect your purchasing decision? How else might you be able to

change your computer to save energy? Use the web to locate articles that recommend energy efficient products and that provide tips about additional ways to save energy. Compile your findings and then share them with the class.

3. Case Study

Farmers' Market   You are the new manager for a group of organic farmers who have a weekly market in season. The previous manager tracked all of the data on paper. You realize that using technology will increase your efficiency and enable you to communicate better with the board of directors, vendors, and customers. At the board's next meeting, you will share ideas of how you will use technology. Before the meeting, you compile the following: differences between input and output, a list of the types of data you can use as input, and a list of the types of information you can produce as output. You include the types of computers, mobile devices, and other technologies you will use to enter data and produce the information. Incorporate your own experiences and user reviews of the devices. Compile your findings.

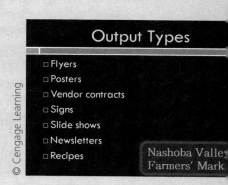

Collaboration

4. **Recommending Technology Solutions**   People use computers and mobile devices in a variety of fields, including travel, manufacturing, and more. Although the way people use computers and mobile devices varies, each use involves hardware, programs and apps, and some type of communications method, such as the Internet or cellular network. Form a three-member team and choose a field in which you all are interested. Assign one member to investigate hardware, another to investigate programs and apps, and the third member to investigate communications methods used in the field. Locate user reviews and articles by industry experts. Each team member should develop a list of related items that may be used. After the investigation, create a hypothetical business or organization in the field. Recommend specific hardware, programs or apps, and communications capabilities that would be best for the network or organization. Include comparisons of specific items, as well as costs. Be sure to summarize your investigations, describe the hypothetical business or organization, and outline and support your recommendations.

✱ Beyond the Book

The Beyond the Book exercises expand your understanding of chapter concepts by requiring research.

Access premium content by visiting Computer Concepts CourseMate. If you have a Computer Concepts CourseMate access code, you can reinforce and extend your learning with MindTap Reader, practice tests, video, and other premium content for Discovering Computers. To sign in to Computer Concepts CourseMate at www.cengagebrain.com, you first must create a student account and then register this book, as described at www.cengage.com/ct/studentdownload.

Part 1 Instructions: Use the web or e-book to perform the task identified for each book element below. Describe your findings, along with the search term(s) you used and your web source(s), if appropriate, in the format requested by your instructor (brief report, presentation, discussion, blog post, video, or other means).

1. **Animation** 📱 Review the animation associated with this chapter and then answer the question(s) it poses (11). What search term would you use to learn more about a specific segment of the animation?

2. **Consider This** Select a Consider This in this chapter (5, 6, 7, 10, 11, 15, 17, 22, 25, 28) and find a recent article that elaborates on the topic. What information did you find that was not presented in this book or e-book?

3. **Drag-and-Drop Figures** 📱 Complete the Drag-and-Drop Figure activities associated with this chapter (11, 13, 17, 26, 29, 39). What did you learn from each of these activities?

4. **Ethics & Issues** Select an Ethics & Issues in this chapter (8, 22, 34, 38) and find a recent article that supports one view presented. Does the article change your opinion about the topic? Why or why not?

5. **Facebook & Twitter** Review a recent Discovering Computers Facebook post or Twitter Tweet and read the referenced article(s). What did you learn from the article?

6. **High-Tech Talk** 📱 Locate an article that discusses topics related to triangulation. Would you recommend the article you found? Why or why not?

7. **How To** Select a How To in this chapter (5, 20, 21, 27) and find a recent article that elaborates on the topic. Who would benefit from the content of this article? Why?

8. **Innovative Computing** 📱 Locate two additional facts about Diabetes Tracking or Mobile Payments. Do your findings change your opinion about the future of this innovation? Why or why not?

9. **Internet Research** Use the search term in an Internet Research (8, 9, 15, 24, 33, 37) to answer the question posed in the element. What other search term could you use to answer the question?

10. **Mini Features** Locate an article that discusses topics related to one of the mini features in this chapter (10, 32, 40). Do you feel that the article is appropriate for this course? Why or why not?

11. **Secure IT** Select a Secure IT in this chapter (18, 23, 24, 30) and find a recent article about the topic that you find interesting. How can you relate the content of the article to your everyday life?

12. **Technology @ Work** Locate three additional, unique usages of technology in the health care industry (41). What makes the use of these technologies unique to the health care industry?

13. **Technology Innovators** 📱 Locate two additional facts about Bill Gates, Steve Jobs, Facebook, Mark Zuckerberg, and Twitter. Which Technology Innovator impresses you most? Why?

14. **Third-Party Links** 📱 Visit one of the third-party links identified in this chapter (8, 18, 21, 22, 23, 25, 30, 34, 38, 41) and read the article or watch the video associated with the link. Would you share this link on your online social network account? Why or why not?

Part 2 Instructions: Find specific instructions for the exercises below in the e-book or on Computer Concepts CourseMate. Beside each exercise is a brief description of its online content.

1. 📱 **You Review It** Search for and review a video or podcast about current technology news.

2. 📱 **Windows and Mac** Enhance your understanding and knowledge about using Windows and Mac computers by completing the Running Applications, Improve Your Mouse Skills, and Understand Computer Information activities.

3. 📱 **Android, iOS, and Windows** Enhance your understanding of Android, iOS, and Windows devices by completing the Manage Your Calendar and Manage Your Contacts activities.

4. 📱 **Exploring Computer Careers** Read about a career as an app developer, search for related employment ads, and then answer related questions.

5. 📱 **App Adventure** Track your own health and fitness by installing and running an app on your smartphone or tablet.

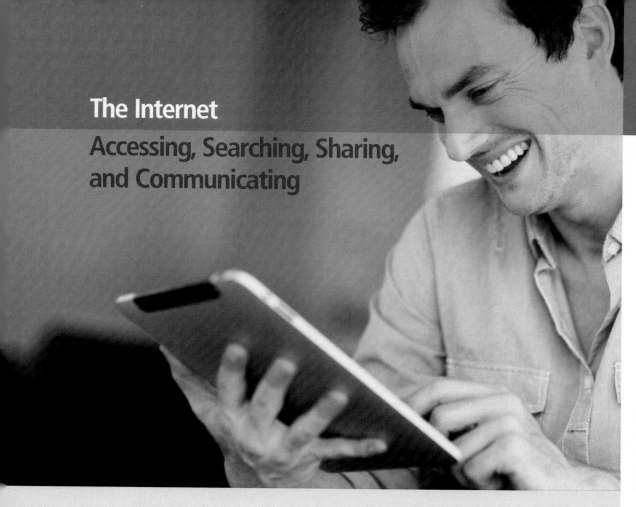

The Internet
Accessing, Searching, Sharing, and Communicating

You can access the Internet using a variety of computers and devices.

"I use the Internet and web to shop for bargains, browse Google for all sorts of information, manage my fantasy sports teams, download music, check email on my phone, and so much more! What more could I gain from using the Internet?"

True, you may be familiar with some of the material in this chapter, but do you know …

How to protect yourself from identity theft?

How you can write search text to improve results of web searches?

Why some smartphones include GPS receivers?

How to check the speed of your Internet connection?

When you would use a hashtag?

How to search for a job online?

Who created the web and why?

How to create a blog?

How devices on the Internet locate each other?

Why you would want accounts on multiple social networking sites?

What you can do to combat cyberbullying?

Which email app is best suited to your needs?

How the transportation industry relies on computers, mobile devices, and related technologies?

What wording you should avoid in online communications?

How you can publish a webpage?

For these answers and to discover much more information essential to this course, read this chapter and visit the associated Computer Concepts CourseMate at www.cengagebrain.com.

✔ Objectives

After completing this chapter, you will be able to:

1 Discuss the evolution of the Internet
2 Briefly describe various broadband Internet connections
3 Describe the purpose of an IP address and its relationship to a domain name
4 Describe features of browsers and identify the components of a web address
5 Describe ways to enter effective search text
6 Explain benefits and risks of using social networking sites
7 Describe uses of various types of websites: search engines; online social networks; informational; media sharing and bookmarking; news, weather, sports, and other mass media; educational; business, governmental, and organizational; blogs; wikis; health and science; entertainment; financial; travel and mapping; shopping and auctions; careers and employment; e-commerce; and portals
8 Identify and briefly describe the steps required for web publishing
9 Explain how the web uses graphics, animation, audio, video, and virtual reality
10 Explain how email, email lists, instant messaging, chat rooms, discussion forums, VoIP, and FTP work
11 Identify the rules of netiquette

The Internet

One of the major reasons business, home, and other users purchase computers and mobile devices is for Internet access. The **Internet** is a worldwide collection of networks that connects millions of businesses, government agencies, educational institutions, and individuals. Each of the networks on the Internet provides resources that add to the abundance of goods, services, and information accessible via the Internet.

Today, billions of home and business users around the world access a variety of services on the Internet using computers and mobile devices. The web, email, and VoIP are three of the more widely used Internet services (Figure 2-1). Other Internet services include instant messaging, chat rooms, discussion forums, and FTP. To enhance your understanding of Internet services, the chapter begins by discussing the history of the Internet and how the Internet works and then explains each of these services.

Evolution of the Internet

The Internet has its roots in a networking project started by the Pentagon's Advanced Research Projects Agency (ARPA), an agency of the U.S. Department of Defense. ARPA's goal was to build a network that (1) allowed scientists at different physical locations to share information and work together on military and scientific projects and (2) could function even if part of the network were disabled or destroyed by a disaster such as a nuclear attack. That network, called *ARPANET*, became functional in September 1969, linking scientific and academic researchers across the United States.

The original ARPANET consisted of four main computers, one each located at the University of California at Los Angeles, the University of California at Santa Barbara, the Stanford Research Institute, and the University of Utah. Each of these computers served as a host on the network. A *host*, more commonly known today as a server, is any computer that provides services and connections to other computers on a network. Hosts often use high-speed communications to transfer data and messages over a network. By 1984, ARPANET had more than 1,000 individual computers linked as hosts. Today, millions of hosts connect to this network, which now is known as the Internet.

access information

send email

converse with others

Figure 2-1 People around the world use the Internet in daily activities, such as accessing information, sending email messages, and conversing with others from their computers and mobile devices.

The Internet consists of many local, regional, national, and international networks. Both public and private organizations own networks on the Internet. These networks, along with phone companies, cable and satellite companies, and the government, all contribute toward the internal structure of the Internet.

 CONSIDER THIS ───────────────────────────────────────

Who owns the Internet?

Internet Research

How can you learn more about the World Wide Web Consortium?

Search for: w3c

No single person, company, institution, or government agency owns the Internet. Each organization on the Internet is responsible only for maintaining its own network.

The World Wide Web Consortium (*W3C*), however, oversees research and sets standards and guidelines for many areas of the Internet. The mission of the W3C is to ensure the continued growth of the web. Nearly 400 organizations from around the world are members of the W3C, advising, defining standards, and addressing other issues.

Connecting to the Internet

Users can connect their computers and mobile devices to the Internet through wired or wireless technology and then access its services free or for a fee. With wired connections, a computer or device physically attaches via a cable or wire to a communications device, such as a modem, that transmits data and other items over transmission media to the Internet. For wireless connections, many mobile computers and devices include the necessary built-in technology so that they can transmit data and other items wirelessly. Computers without this capability can use a wireless modem or other communications device that enables wireless connectivity. A *wireless modem*, for example, uses the cellular radio network to provide Internet connections. Figure 2-2 shows examples of modems. The wireless modem shown in the figure is known as a *dongle*, which is a small device that connects to a computer.

Today, users often connect to the Internet via *broadband* Internet service because of its fast data transfer speeds and its always-on connection. Through broadband Internet service, users can download webpages quickly, play online games, communicate in real time with others, and more. Table 2-1 shows examples of popular wired and wireless broadband Internet service technologies for home and small business users.

Figure 2-2   Using a modem is one way to connect computers and mobile devices to the Internet.

Table 2-1   Popular Broadband Internet Service Technologies

	Technology	Description
Wired	Cable Internet service	Provides high-speed Internet access through the cable television network via a cable modem
	DSL (digital subscriber line)	Provides high-speed Internet connections through the telephone network via a DSL modem
	Fiber to the Premises (FTTP)	Uses fiber-optic cable to provide high-speed Internet access via a modem
Wireless	Wi-Fi (wireless fidelity)	Uses radio signals to provide high-speed Internet connections to computers and devices with built-in Wi-Fi capability or a communications device that enables Wi-Fi connectivity
	Mobile broadband	Offers high-speed Internet connections over the cellular radio network to computers and devices with built-in compatible technology (such as 3G, 4G, or 5G) or a wireless modem or other communications device
	Fixed wireless	Provides high-speed Internet connections using a dish-shaped antenna on a building, such as a house or business, to communicate with a tower location via radio signals
	Satellite Internet service	Provides high-speed Internet connections via satellite to a satellite dish that communicates with a satellite modem

© Cengage Learning

Employees and students typically connect their computers and mobile devices to the Internet wirelessly through a business or school network, which, in turn, usually connects to a very high-speed Internet service. When away from the office, home, or school, mobile users access the Internet using a variety of Internet services. Some use a **cybercafé**, or Internet café, which is a location that provides computers with Internet access, usually for a fee. Cybercafés exist in cities around the world. Hotels and airports often provide wired or wireless Internet connections as a free service to travelers.

Many public locations, such as airports, hotels, schools, shopping malls, coffee shops, and city parks are Wi-Fi hot spots. Recall that a *hot spot* is a wireless network that provides Internet connections to mobile computers and devices. Although most hot spots enable unrestricted or open access, some require that users agree to terms of service, obtain a password (for example, from the hotel's front desk), or perform some other action in order to connect to the Internet.

Home and small business users can share and provide wireless Internet connections by creating their own Wi-Fi hot spot through a communications device in the home or business that is connected to broadband Internet service. Instead of a stationary Wi-Fi hot spot, some users opt to create mobile hot spots through mobile broadband Internet service via a separate communications device or a tethered Internet-capable device (Figure 2-3). *Tethering* transforms

Internet Research

What is a MiFi device?

Search for: what is mifi

communications device

tethered smartphone

mobile broadband Internet service

Internet

mobile hot spot

Figure 2-3   You can create a mobile hot spot using a communications device or by tethering a smartphone.

Courtesy of Verizon Wireless
© figarro / Can Stock Photo;
© iStockphoto / Dane Wirtzfeld;
© amfoto / Shutterstock.com;
© Alex Staroseltsev / Shutterstock.com; Source: Microsoft; © Cengage Learning

a smartphone or Internet-capable tablet into a portable communications device that shares its Internet access with other computers and devices wirelessly. Users typically pay additional fees for mobile hot spot and tethering services.

 CONSIDER THIS ――――――――――――――――――――――――――――――

Does everyone use broadband Internet?
No. Some home users connect computers to the Internet via slower-speed dial-up access because of its lower cost or because broadband access is not available where they live. *Dial-up access* takes place when a modem in a computer connects to the Internet via a standard telephone line that transmits data and information using an analog (continuous wave pattern) signal.

Internet Service Providers

An **Internet service provider** (**ISP**), sometimes called an Internet access provider, is a business that provides individuals and organizations access to the Internet free or for a fee. ISPs often charge a fixed amount for an Internet connection, offering customers a variety of plans based on desired speeds, bandwidth, and services. In addition to Internet access, ISPs typically include services such as news, weather, financial data, games, travel guides, email, instant messaging, photo communities, and online storage.

Bandwidth represents the amount of data that travels over a network. A higher bandwidth means more data transmits. Data sizes typically are stated in terms of megabytes and gigabytes. A *megabyte* (*MB*) is equal to approximately one million characters, and a *gigabyte* (*GB*) is equal to approximately one billion characters. Table 2-2 shows approximate data usage for various Internet activities.

Wi-Fi networks often provide free Internet access, while some charge a daily or per use fee. Instead of locating a hot spot, some users prefer to subscribe to a mobile service provider, such as Verizon Wireless, so that they can access the Internet wherever they have mobile phone access. A *mobile service provider*, sometimes called a wireless data provider, is an ISP that offers wireless Internet access to computers and mobile devices with the necessary built-in wireless capability (such as Wi-Fi), wireless modems, or other communications devices that enable wireless connectivity. An antenna on or built into the computer or device, wireless modem, or communications device typically sends signals through the airwaves to communicate with a mobile service provider.

BTW

Byte
A byte is the basic storage unit on a computer or mobile device and represents a single character.

Internet Research

Can I check the speed of my Internet connection?

Search for: internet speed test

Table 2-2 Data Usage Examples

Activity	Quantity	Approximate Data Usage
Send and receive email messages (with no attachments)	100 messages	3–6 MB
Post on social networking sites	100 posts	0.75–1 GB
Send and receive email messages (with attachments)	100 messages	0.75–1 GB
Visit webpages	200 visits	1 GB
Talk with others using VoIP (without video)	1 hour	1.25 GB
Upload or download photos	10 photos	1.5 GB
Listen to streaming music	1 hour	1–2 GB
Play online games	1 hour	1.75 GB
Watch smaller, standard-quality streaming video	1 hour	2–5 GB
Download apps, games, music, e-books	25 downloads	3 GB
Talk with others using VoIP (with video)	1 hour	5–7.5 GB
Watch HD streaming video	1 hour	5–20 GB

© Cengage Learning

How Data and Information Travel the Internet

Computers connected to the Internet work together to transfer data and information around the world using servers and clients and various wired and wireless transmission media. On the Internet, your computer is a client that can access data, information, and services on a variety of servers. Wired transmission media used includes phone line, coaxial cable, and fiber-optic cable. Wireless transmission media includes radio waves and satellite signals.

The inner structure of the Internet works much like a transportation system. Just as interstate highways connect major cities and carry the bulk of the automotive traffic across the country, several main transmission media carry the heaviest amount of *traffic*, or communications activity, on the Internet. These major carriers of network traffic are known collectively as the *Internet backbone*.

In the United States, the transmission media that make up the Internet backbone exchange data and information at several different major cities across the country. That is, they transfer data and information from one network to another until reaching the final destination (Figure 2-4).

BTW

DNS Servers and IPv6
High-Tech Talk: DNS servers work with the IPv4 and IPv6 addressing schemes to locate computers and devices on the Internet.

How a Home User's Request for a Webpage Might Travel the Internet Using Cable Internet Service

Step 1
You send a request to the Internet. For example, you enter the web address of a webpage you want to visit in the address bar of your browser.

Step 2
A cable modem transfers the computer's digital signals to the cable television line in your house.

Step 3
Your request (digital signals) travels through cable television lines to a central cable system, which is shared by up to 500 homes in a neighborhood.

Step 4
The central cable system sends your request over high-speed fiber-optic lines to the cable operator, who often also is the ISP.

Step 5
The ISP routes your request through the Internet backbone to the destination server (in this example, the server that contains the requested webpage).

Step 6
The server retrieves the requested webpage and sends it back through the Internet backbone to your computer.

Figure 2-4   This figure shows how a home user's request for eBay's webpage might travel the Internet using cable Internet service.
© romakoma / Shutterstock.com; © Pablo Eder / Shutterstock.com; © dotshock / Shutterstock.com; © TonyV3112 / Shutterstock.com; Donna Cox and Robert Patterson, courtesy of the National Center for Supercomputing Applications (NCSA) and the Board of Trustees of the University of Illinois; © iStockphoto / luismmolina; Source: eBay

Domain Names and IP Addresses

The Internet relies on an addressing system much like the postal service to send data and information to a computer or device at a specific destination. An **IP address**, short for Internet Protocol address, is a sequence of numbers that uniquely identifies the location of each computer or device connected to the Internet.

The Internet uses two IP addressing schemes: IPv4 and IPv6. Due to the growth of the Internet, the original scheme, IPv4, began dwindling in availability. To rectify the problem, the IPv6 scheme lengthened the addresses, which increased the available number of IP addresses exponentially. Because all-numeric IP addresses are difficult to remember and use, the Internet supports domain names. A **domain name** is a text-based name that corresponds to the IP address of a server that hosts a website (Figure 2-5). A domain name is part of the web address that you type in a browser's address bar to access a website.

Figure 2-5 The IPv4 and IPv6 addresses, along with the domain name for Google's website.
© Cengage Learning

IPv4 address	→ 72.14.207.99
IPv6 address	→ 2001:4860:4860::8844
Domain name	→ google.com

top-level domain

Table 2-3	Popular TLDs
TLD	**Intended Purpose**
.com	Commercial organizations, businesses, and companies
.edu	Educational institutions
.gov	Government agencies
.mil	Military organizations
.net	Network providers or commercial companies
.org	Nonprofit organizations

© Cengage Learning

The suffix of the domain name, called the *top-level domain* (*TLD*), identifies the type of organization associated with the domain. In Figure 2-5, for example, the .com is the TLD. Table 2-3 lists some of the more popular TLDs. The organization that approves and controls TLDs is called *ICANN* (pronounced EYE-can), which stands for Internet Corporation for Assigned Names and Numbers. For websites outside the United States, the suffix of the domain name may include a country code TLD (*ccTLD*), which is a two-letter country code, such as au for Australia. For example, www.philips.com.au is the domain name for Philips Australia.

 CONSIDER THIS

How can you secure a domain name?
Individuals and companies register domain names so that people can find their websites easily using a browser. You register a domain name through a registrar, which is an organization that sells and manages domain names. Before purchasing a domain name, you must confirm that it is available, select your desired TLD, and specify the length of time for which you want to reserve the name. Read Ethics & Issues 2-1 to consider issues related to rights of domain names.

 ETHICS & ISSUES 2-1

Who Has Rights to a Domain Name?
You learn from a registrar that a domain name containing your company name is not available. When you enter the web address in a browser, however, a webpage appears indicating that the domain name is available for purchase, likely by a cybersquatter. Cybersquatters buy and register unused or lapsed domain names so that they can profit from selling them. Cybersquatters sometimes will sell you the domain name, but some take advantage of people trying to reach a more popular website and redirect to a website for their own business.

Website owners periodically must renew domain name registrations. Cybersquatters look for out-of-date registrations and buy them so that the original website owner must buy them back. Cybersquatters may purchase domain names with common words, alternate spellings of trademarked terms, or celebrity names. For example, Google won a case that awarded them the rights to more than 750 domain names that included the word, google.

More than 10 years ago, lawmakers enacted the *Anticybersquatting Consumer Protection Act* (ACPA). The ACPA's goal is to protect trademark owners from being forced to pay a cybersquatter for a domain name that includes their trademark. To win a case against a cybersquatter, you must prove that the cybersquatter acted in bad faith, meaning they tried knowingly to profit from purchasing a domain name with a trademarked term.

Should cybersquatters be prosecuted? Why or why not? Does a large company have the right to sue a smaller company in order to purchase their domain? How should companies protect their brands when registering for domain names?

The *domain name system* (*DNS*) is the method that the Internet uses to store domain names and their corresponding IP addresses. When you enter a domain name (i.e., google.com) in a browser, a DNS server translates the domain name to its associated IP address so that the request can be routed to the correct computer (Figure 2-6). A *DNS server* is a server on the Internet that usually is associated with an ISP.

How a Browser Displays a Requested Webpage

Step 1
Run the browser and enter the web address in the browser's address bar.

web address contains domain name

Step 2
The browser communicates with a DNS server maintained by your ISP or another provider. The DNS server looks up the domain name portion of the web address, finds its associated IP address, and then sends the IP address to your computer or mobile device.

Step 3
The browser uses the IP address to contact the web server at the specified IP address to request the content of the desired webpage. The web server fulfills the user's request by sending the desired content to the user's browser, which formats the page for display on the screen.

72.14.207.99
2001:4860:4860::8844

Figure 2-6 This figure shows how a user's entered domain name (google.com) uses a DNS server to display a webpage (Google, in this case).
Source: Apple Inc.; © Cengage Learning; © Cengage Learning; © Sashkin / Shutterstock.com; Source: Google Inc.

The World Wide Web

While the Internet was developed in the late 1960s, the World Wide Web emerged in the early 1990s. Since then, it has grown phenomenally to become one of the more widely used services on the Internet.

Recall that the **World Wide Web** (**WWW**), or **web**, consists of a worldwide collection of electronic documents. Each electronic document on the web is called a **webpage**, which can contain text, graphics, animation, audio, and video. Some webpages are static (fixed); others are dynamic (changing). Visitors to a *static webpage* all see the same content. With a *dynamic webpage*, by contrast, visitors can customize some or all of the viewed content, such as desired stock quotes, weather for a region, or ticket availability for flights. The time required to download a webpage varies depending on the speed of your Internet connection and the amount of graphics and other media involved.

A **website** is a collection of related webpages and associated items, such as documents and pictures, stored on a web server. A **web server** is a computer that delivers requested webpages to your computer or mobile device. The same web server can store multiple websites.

 BTW

Tim-Berners Lee
Technology Innovator:
You should be familiar with Tim Berners-Lee (creator of the World Wide Web).

As web technologies matured in the mid-2000s, industry experts introduced the term *Web 2.0* to refer to websites that provide a means for users to share personal information (such as online social networks), allow users to modify website content (such as wikis), and provide applications through a browser (such as web apps).

Browsing and Navigating the Web

Recall from Chapter 1 that a **browser** is an application that enables users with an Internet connection to access and view webpages on a computer or mobile device. Internet-capable mobile devices such as smartphones use a special type of browser, called a *mobile browser*, which is designed for their smaller screens and limited computing power. Many websites can detect if you are accessing their content on a mobile device (Figure 2-7).

When you run a browser, it may retrieve and display a starting webpage, sometimes called a home page. The initial home page that is displayed is specified in the browser. You can change your browser's home page at any time through its settings, options, or similar commands.

Another use of the term, **home page**, refers to the first page that is displayed on a website. Similar to a book cover or a table of contents, a website's home page provides information about its purpose and content. Many websites allow you to personalize the home page so that it contains areas of interest to you.

Desktop browsers typically support **tabbed browsing**, where the top of the browser shows a tab (similar to a file folder tab) for each webpage you display (shown in Figure 2-7). To move from one displayed webpage to another, you tap or click the tab in the browser. Tabbed browsing allows users to have multiple home pages that automatically are displayed when the browser runs. You also can organize tabs in a group, called a tab group, and save the group as a favorite, so that at any time you can display all tabs at once.

Because some websites attempt to track your browsing habits or gather personal information, current browsers usually include a feature that allows you to disable and/or more tightly control the dissemination of your browsing habits and personal information. Read Secure IT 2-1 for safe browsing tips.

Internet Research

How do I change my browser's home page?

Search for: change browser home page

 SECURE IT 2-1

Safe Browsing Techniques

Browsing the web resembles crossing a busy street: you need to exercise caution and look carefully for unexpected traffic. Cybercriminals are on the lookout to prey upon unsuspecting users, so you should follow these guidelines when browsing:

- **Verify the website is safe.** Type the website address of your email, banking, social networking, and other personal accounts directly in a browser; never visit these websites merely by tapping or clicking links found in email messages. Before you sign in, double-check the web address to verify it is correct. Most browsers change the color of the address bar to verify the website is legitimate. Also, check that the web address begins with https instead of the less secure http, and look for a closed padlock symbol beside it.

- **Clear your browsing history.** A copy of every website you visit is stored in the browser's *cache* (pronounced cash) folder. If you perform online banking or view your credit card transactions, the cache could contain personal information such as passwords and account numbers. You can specify to clear cache automatically each time you close a browser.

- **Use a phishing filter.** *Phishing* is a scam in which a perpetrator attempts to obtain your personal and/or financial information. Many browsers include a *phishing filter*, which is a program that warns or blocks you from potentially fraudulent or suspicious websites.

- **Enable a pop-up blocker.** Malicious software creators can develop a *pop-up ad*, which is an Internet advertisement that suddenly appears in a new window on top of a webpage displayed in a browser. A **pop-up blocker** is a filtering program that stops pop-up ads from displaying on webpages. Many browsers include a pop-up blocker. You also can download pop-up blockers from the web at no cost.

- **Browse anonymously.** To protect your online identity, use a *proxy server*, which is another computer that screens all your incoming and outgoing messages. The proxy server will prevent your browsing history, passwords, user names, and other personal information from being revealed.

☀ What pop-ups have you encountered while browsing? What new techniques will you use to browse the web safely?

Figure 2-7 Many websites, such as the Centers for Disease Control and Prevention shown here, provide a mobile version that is designed specifically for display on a mobile browser.
Source: Centers for Disease Control and Prevention

⭐ MINI FEATURE 2-1

Browsers

The decision of which browser to use is a topic of discussion among computer experts and novices alike. All browsers can retrieve and display webpages, but their features and ease of use vary.

Configuring Options

Users can customize some settings to improve their browsing experience, such as those listed below.

- **Favorites**, also called *bookmarks*, are links to preferred websites. When you add a website to the list of favorites, you can visit that website simply by tapping or clicking its name in a list instead of typing its web address. Favorites can be organized into folders, alphabetized, and sorted by date or how frequently you view the websites.

- Security features, such as filters and secure connections, help protect you from fraudulent and malicious websites that might attempt to steal your identity and personal information. These features also can block websites you do not want to display and can instruct the browser to save passwords.

- Privacy features help prevent thieves from accessing information about your browsing history, such as websites you have visited, data about your browsing session, and content you have seen on specific webpages.

Obtaining Browsers

A browser often is included in the operating system of a computer or mobile device. For example, many computer manufacturers include Internet Explorer when they install Windows and include Safari when they install Mac OS. To locate a particular browser, you can visit the software developer's website and download the program at no cost. Several browsers also are available at shareware websites. Keep your browser up to date to prevent security holes. You can set your browser to perform updates automatically.

Making a Decision

Selecting the best browser for your needs involves some careful thought. You may decide to install several and then use each one for specific needs. Perform some research to compare browsers and then consider the following factors:

- How old is your computer or mobile device? A newer browser may not work properly on older hardware.

- How much memory is in your computer or mobile device? Some browsers work best with a lot of memory.

- Which platform are you using? Some browsers are available for specific operating systems.

- What do you want the browser to do? Some browsers are best suited for performing simple searches while others excel when running media-laden websites.

continued on next page

Chrome

Firefox

Internet Explorer

Safari

Opera

Source: Google Inc; Mozilla
Foundation; Microsoft; Apple Inc;
Opera Software

continued from previous page

Specific Browsers

- **Chrome:** Google's Chrome is one of the newer browser offerings, first released in 2008. This free browser is available for Windows and Mac OS and must be downloaded and installed. It includes a large number of security features. Chrome has independent tabbed browsing; if one tab develops a problem, the other tabs continue to function.

- **Firefox:** Developed by the Mozilla Corporation for computers running Windows, Mac OS, and Linux, Firefox is recognized for its extensive array of plug-ins (discussed later in the chapter). This free general-purpose browser was first released in 2004 and must be downloaded and installed. It has enhanced privacy and security features, a spelling checker, tabbed browsing, and a password manager.

- **Internet Explorer:** Microsoft's free browser, Internet Explorer, is available primarily for Microsoft Windows and comes preinstalled. First released in 1995, the browser features the capability to rearrange tabs, protection against phishing and malware, and settings to delete information about searches performed and webpages visited.

- **Safari:** Preinstalled on Apple computers and mobile devices, Safari has been the default browser for Mac OS since 2003 and is relatively new to Windows. The browser is recognized for its sleek design, built-in sharing with online social networks, fast performance, parental controls, and ease of use.

- **Opera:** This second-oldest browser is free, fast, and small. Used on both computers and mobile devices, Opera must be downloaded and installed. It began as a research project in Norway in 1994 and introduced several features found on most of today's browsers.

Mobile Browsers

Many browsers are included by default with some mobile devices and smartphones. Their features vary greatly. Some allow users to zoom and use keyboard shortcuts with most websites, while others display only websites optimized for mobile devices. The more popular mobile browsers are Opera Mini, Safari, Google Android's browser, Google Chrome, Firefox Mobile, and Internet Explorer Mobile.

 Which browser or browsers have you used? Why did you use that browser? Would you consider using another browser? Why or why not?

Web Addresses

A webpage has a unique address, called a **web address** or *URL* (Uniform Resource Locator). For example, the web address of http://www.nps.gov identifies the U.S. Department of the Interior National Park Service home page. A browser retrieves a webpage using its web address.

If you know the address of a webpage, you can type it in the address bar in of the browser. For example, if you type the address http://www.nps.gov/history/places.htm in the address bar and then press the ENTER key or tap or click the Search, Go, or similar button, the browser downloads and displays the webpage shown in Figure 2-8. The path, history/places.htm, in this web address identifies a webpage that is specified in a file named places.htm, which is located in a folder named history on the server that hosts the nps.gov website. When you enter this web address, after obtaining the IP address for the nps.gov domain name, the browser sends a request to the web server to retrieve the webpage named places.htm, and delivers it to your browser to be displayed.

A web address consists of a protocol, domain name, and sometimes the host name, path to a specific webpage, or file name of the webpage. The *http*, which stands for Hypertext Transfer Protocol, is a set of rules that defines how webpages transfer on the Internet. Many web addresses begin with http:// as the protocol. The text between the protocol and the domain name, called the host name, identifies the type of Internet server. The www, for example, indicates a web server.

✹ CONSIDER THIS

Do you need to type the protocol and host name in a web address?
Many browsers and websites do not require that you enter the http:// or the host name (www) in the web address. For example, you could enter nps.gov instead of http://www.nps.gov. As you begin typing a web address or if you enter an incorrect web address, browsers often display a list of similar addresses or related websites from which you can select.

Figure 2-8   After entering http://www.nps.gov/history/places.htm in the address bar and then pressing the ENTER key or tapping or clicking the Search, Go, or similar button in a browser, the U.S. Department of the Interior National Park Service home page shown here is displayed.
Source: National Park Service U.S. Department of the Interior

Web Feeds   When you enter a web address in a browser, you request, or *pull*, information from a web server. Another way users can pull content is by subscribing to a *web feed*, which contains content that has changed on a website. Mass media, blogs, and online social networks often provide web feeds, saving users the time spent checking the websites for updated content. Websites that use web feeds usually display a feed icon (Figure 2-9). Most browsers contain the capability to read web feeds. *RSS*, which stands for Really Simple Syndication, and *Atom* are popular specifications used to distribute content, such as web feeds, to subscribers. A feed reader, sometimes called an aggregator, is a type of software for computers and mobile devices that reads a user's specified web feeds and collects their most recent content.

Figure 2-9   Websites commonly use this symbol to indicate you can subscribe to their web feed.
Source: Mozilla Foundation

Web Apps and Mobile Apps

Recall from Chapter 1 that a *web app* is an application stored on a web server that you access through a browser. Users typically interact with web apps directly at a website, sometimes referred to as the host. Web app hosts usually provide storage for users' data and information on their servers, known as *cloud storage*.

Many web app hosts provide free access to their software, such as the Word Web App shown in Figure 2-10 on the next page. Others offer part of their web app free and charge for access to a more comprehensive program. Many include advertisements in the free version and charge for an advertisement-free version. Some allow you to use the web app free and pay a fee when a certain action occurs. For example, you can prepare your tax return free, but if you elect to print it or file it electronically, you pay a minimal fee.

A *mobile app* is an application you download from a mobile device's app store or other location on the Internet to a smartphone or other mobile device. Mobile apps often take advantage of features of the device, such as touch screens, digital cameras, microphones, and embedded GPS receivers, to enable you to enter and capture data.

browser window

cloud storage

Word Web App

Riley Clarke
8982 West Condor Avenue, Donner, OH 44772
804-555-2982 (home); 804-555-0291 (cell)
E-mail: rclarke@worldview.net

Objective | To obtain a full-time veterinary technician position with a veterinary

Figure 2-10 Through a browser, you can create documents using the Word Web App and save them on cloud storage, which in this case is Microsoft's SkyDrive.
Source: Microsoft Corporation

Web apps and mobile apps often work together. You might have an account on a website, such as a banking app, that you access from a desktop or laptop. The website may provide a mobile app that you install on a smartphone so that you can access the same information from a mobile device. Because the data and information for each app is stored on cloud storage, all data is synchronized and accessible from anywhere you have an Internet connection, regardless of the computer or device used. The functionality of the app across computers and devices generally is the same, although the mobile app sometimes has fewer features. Some tasks may be easier to accomplish on one device or the other. For example, if a lot of typing is required, you may opt to use the web app on a laptop so that you can use a standard keyboard.

Internet Research
What are popular mobile apps?
Search for: top mobile apps

CONSIDER THIS

What are GPS receivers?

GPS (global positioning system) is a navigation system that consists of one or more earth-based receivers that accept and analyze signals sent by satellites in order to determine the receiver's geographic location. A *GPS receiver* is a handheld, mountable, or embedded device that contains an antenna, a radio receiver, and a processor. Most smartphones include embedded GPS receivers so that users can determine their location, obtain directions, and locate points of interest. Read Ethics & Issues 2-2 to consider issues related to apps that track your location.

ETHICS & ISSUES 2-2

Should Apps Be Allowed to Track Your Location?

When you download an app to your smartphone, you unintentionally may be allowing the app to send personal data. Apps can transmit your location, as well as the time you spend using the app. Apps also can collect personal information, including gender and birth year, if you access the app through an online social network profile. Although apps often present an option to review their security policies, some track user data without permission. Further, the

U.S. Circuit Court of Appeals ruled that police can track GPS signals without a warrant or probable cause, meaning that the government can track activities without permission or knowledge.

If you search for driving directions, coupons, or restaurant tips based on your current location or past activities, you might be using apps that openly use this type of tracking. For example, a check in app posts your location to online social networks, and another app enables you to locate friends by tracking their Bluetooth signals. Even when

you opt to share data, use of these types of apps is not without risk. When people use location-tracking apps, for instance, they run the risk of someone stalking or robbing them.

Do you have an expectation of privacy when you download an app? Should the police be allowed to track GPS data without warrants? Why or why not? Would you use apps that post your location to your online social network profile or otherwise alert others of your whereabouts? Why or why not?

NOW YOU KNOW ─────────────────────────────

Be sure you understand the material presented in the sections titled The Internet, Connecting to the Internet, and The World Wide Web, as it relates to the chapter objectives.
You now should know…

- Why you interact with hosts and networks on the Internet (Objective 1)

- Which broadband Internet service and ISP is best suited to your needs (Objective 2)

- How your browser works with domain names and IP addresses when you enter a web address (Objectives 3 and 4)

- Which browser(s) you would use and why (Objective 4)

 Quiz Yourself Online: Check your knowledge of related content by navigating to this book's Quiz Yourself resource on Computer Concepts CourseMate and then tapping or clicking Objectives 1–4.

Types of Websites

The web contains several types of websites: search engines; online social networks; informational; media sharing and bookmarking; news, weather, sports, and other mass media; educational; business, governmental, and organizational; blogs; wikis; health and science; entertainment; financial; travel and mapping; shopping and auctions; careers and employment; e-commerce; and portals. Many websites fall into more than one of these types. All of these websites can be accessed from computers or mobile devices but often are formatted differently and may have fewer features on mobile devices.

Search Engines

A web **search engine** is software that finds websites, webpages, images, videos, news, maps, and other information related to a specific topic. Thousands of search engines are available. Some search engines, such as Bing, Google, and Yahoo!, are helpful in locating information on the web for which you do not know an exact web address or are not seeking a specific website. Those that work with GPS devices or services are location based, meaning they display results related to the device's current geographical position. For example, your smartphone may be able to display all gas stations within a certain distance of your current location. Some search engines restrict searches to a specific type of information, such as jobs or recipes.

Search engines typically allow you to search for one or more of the following items:

- Images: photos, diagrams, and drawings
- Videos: home videos, music videos, television programs, and movie clips
- Maps: maps of a business or address, or driving directions to a destination
- Audio: music, songs, recordings, and sounds
- Publications: news articles, journals, and books
- People or Businesses: addresses and telephone numbers
- Blogs: specific opinions and ideas of others

Search engines require that you enter a word or phrase, called *search text*, to describe the item you want to find. Search text can be broad, such as spring break destinations, or more specific, such as Walt Disney World. If you misspell search text, search engines may correct the misspelling or identify alternative search text. Some also provide suggested search text, links, and/or images as you type your search text.

Depending on your search text, search engines may respond with thousands to billions of search results, sometimes called *hits*. The content of the search results varies depending on the type of information you are seeking and your search text. Some search results contain links to webpages or articles; others are media, such as images or videos. Most search engines sequence the search results based on how close the words in the search text are to one another in the titles and descriptions of the results. Thus, the first few links probably contain more relevant information.

 BTW
Yahoo! and Google
Technology Innovators: You should be familiar with Yahoo! and Google.

 Internet Research
What is a natural language search engine?
Search for: natural language search

 Internet Research
What is a search engine spider?
Search for: search engine spider

If you enter a phrase with spaces between the words in search text, most search engines display results that include all of the keywords. Because keywords describe content, search results exclude articles, conjunctions, and other similar words (e.g., to, the, and). Table 2-4 lists some operators you can use in search text to refine searches. Instead of working with operators to refine search text, many search engines provide an advanced search feature or search tools that assist with limiting search results based on items such as date, TLD, language, etc.

Table 2-4   Search Engine Operators

Operator	Description	Examples	Explanation
Space or +	Display search results that include specific words.	art + music art music	Results have both words, art and music, in any order.
OR	Display search results that include only one word from a list.	dog OR puppy	Results have either the word, dog, or the word, puppy.
		dog OR puppy OR canine	Results have the word, dog, or the word, puppy, or the word, canine.
( )	Combine search results that include specific words with those that include only one word from a list.	Kalamazoo Michigan (pizza OR subs)	Results include both words, Kalamazoo Michigan, and either the word, pizza, or the word, subs.
−	Exclude a word from search results.	automobile −convertible	Results include the word, automobile, but do not include the word, convertible.
" "	Search for an exact phrase in a certain order.	"19th century literature"	Results include the exact phrase, 19th century literature.
*	Substitute characters in place of the asterisk.	writer*	Results include any word that begins with the text, writer (e.g., writer, writers, writer's)

© Cengage Learning

✹ CONSIDER THIS

How can you improve search results?
You may find that many items listed in the search results have little or no bearing on the item you are seeking. You can eliminate superfluous items in search results by carefully crafting search text and use search operators to limit search results. Other techniques you can use to improve your searches include the following:

• Use specific nouns.
• Put the most important terms first in the search text.
• List all possible spellings, for example, email, e-mail.
• Before using a search engine, read its Help information.
• If the search is unsuccessful with one search engine, try another.

Subject Directories   A *subject directory* classifies webpages in an organized set of categories, such as sports or shopping, and related subcategories. A subject directory provides categorized lists of links arranged by subject. Using a subject directory, you locate a particular topic by tapping or clicking links through different levels, moving from the general to the specific. A disadvantage with a subject directory is that users sometimes have difficulty deciding which categories to choose as they work through the menus of links presented.

Online Social Networks

Recall from Chapter 1 that an **online social network**, or **social networking site**, is a website that encourages members in its online community to share their interests, ideas, stories, photos, music, and videos with other registered users. Some social networking sites also enable users to communicate through text, voice, and video chat, and play games together online. You interact with a social networking site through a browser or mobile app on your computer or mobile device.

MINI FEATURE 2-2

Social Networking Sites

People you know through personal and professional circles form your social networks. You share common interests, work or spend leisure time together, and know many of one another's friends. Social networking sites allow you to manage your social networks online.

Your account on a social networking site includes profile information, such as your name, location, photos, and personal and professional interests. You might create accounts on a variety of social networking sites to better separate your personal and professional activities. Social networking sites allow you to view the profiles of other users and designate them as your *friends* or contacts. Some social networking sites, such as Facebook and LinkedIn, require friends to confirm a friendship, while others, such as Twitter and Google+ allow users to follow one another without confirmation.

You can expand your own online social network by viewing your friends' friends and then, in turn, designating some of them as your friends. Friends of your friends and their friends form your *extended contacts*.

- Extended contacts on a personal social networking site such as Facebook can introduce you to others at your college or from your hometown, connect you with long-distance friends or relatives, or enable you to stay in touch with those who have interests similar to yours.

- Extended contacts on a professional social networking site such as LinkedIn can introduce you to people who work at companies where you might be seeking employment. You can share employment history and skills in your profile, enabling potential employers who look at your profile to learn about your specific skills.

Read Secure IT 2-2 on the next page for tips about securing your privacy when using social networking sites.

Personal Uses

Many people use social networking sites to share photos and videos, personal greetings, or status updates. A *status update* informs friends about what you are doing. Watching television becomes a social activity as broadcasts encourage viewers to share comments on Twitter or Facebook.

You can *like*, or recommend, online content as a way to share interests with your friends. Your activity updates appear on a designated activity stream, often called a *timeline* or *wall*, which is associated with your account. Activity updates from your friends often appear on a separate page associated with your account, often called a *news feed*.

Many mobile devices have GPS capabilities. Accessing a social networking site with a GPS-enabled device allows you to *check in* at a location, which reveals your location as part of a status update. Mobile social networking apps can share your location with friends, find others nearby, and alert you to promotional deals from local businesses.

Check In button

Business Uses

Businesses use social networking sites to connect with their customers, provide promotional offers, and offer targeted advertising. For example, users who recommend online content about travel services may see travel-related advertising on their social networking site's webpage.

Businesses also use data from social networking sites to better connect with and understand customers. They can review comments from customers about their experiences using companies' products or services. Monitoring these feeds continuously gives companies immediate feedback from customers.

Nonprofit organizations use social networking sites to promote activities and causes, accept donations, and allow volunteers to contact one another online.

✹ Do the benefits of using social networking sites outweigh the risks? Why or why not? Does your answer differ based on whether it is personal or business use?

Source: © iStockphoto / SchulteProductions; © iStockphoto / Slobodan Vasic; © iStockphoto / Gonzalo Andres Aragon Orejuela

SECURE IT 2-2

Privacy and Security Risks with Online Social Networks

Social networking sites can be excellent places to share messages, photos, and videos. They can, however, be risky places to divulge personal information. Follow these tips to help protect against thieves who are following the traffic and attempting to invade private facets of your life.

- **Choose friends carefully.** You may receive a friend request that appears to be from someone you know. In reality, this message may originate from an identity thief who created a fake profile in an attempt to obtain your personal information. Confirm with the sender that the request is legitimate.

- **Limit friends.** While many online social networks encourage the practice, do not try to gather too many friends in your social network. Some experts believe that a functional online social network should not exceed 150 people. Occasionally review what your friends are posting about you.

- **Prohibit email address book scans.** Online social networks occasionally ask users to enter their email address and password to determine if their friends also are members of the network. In turn, the network obtains access to contacts in your address book and can send spam (unsolicited email messages) to your friends.

- **Divulge only relevant information.** Write details about yourself that are relevant to the reasons you are participating in an online social network. When posting information, be aware that the message may be accessible publicly and associated with your identity permanently. Do not post anything you would not want to be made public.

- **Be leery of urgent requests for help.** Avoid responding to emergency pleas for financial assistance from alleged family members. In addition, do not reply to messages concerning lotteries you did not enter and fabulous deals that sound too good to be true.

- **Read the privacy policy.** Evaluate the website's privacy policy, which describes how it uses your personal information. For example, if you watch a video while signed in to your account, an external website or app may have access to this information and post this activity as an entry in both your activity stream and your friends' news feeds.

- **Manage your profile.** Check for privacy settings, usually found on the Settings or Options tabs, to set permissions so that you can control who can review your profile and photos, determine how people can search for you and make comments, and if desired, block certain people from viewing your page.

Should social networking sites do a better job of telling their users what information is safe or unsafe to share? What role should parents play in overseeing their child's involvement in social networking sites?

Informational

An informational website contains factual information. Examples include libraries, encyclopedias, dictionaries, directories, guides (Figure 2-11), and other types of reference. You can find guides on numerous topics such as health and medicine, research paper documentation styles, and grammar rules. Many of the other types of websites identified in this section also are used to look up information.

Media Sharing and Bookmarking Sites

A *media sharing site* is a website that enables members to manage and share media such as photos, videos, and music. These websites are sometimes called photo sharing sites, video sharing sites (Figure 2-12), and music sharing sites, respectively. Media sharing sites, which

Figure 2-11 You can look up first aid treatments on a medical website, such as WebMD, shown here formatted for display on a mobile device.
Source: WebMD, LLC

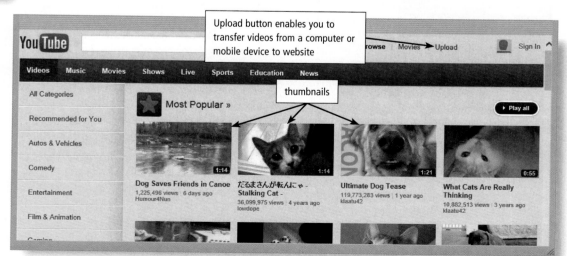

Figure 2-12 YouTube is an example of a video sharing site. You tap or click the thumbnail to view the video.
Source: YouTube, Inc.

may be free or charge a fee, provide a quick and efficient way to upload, organize, store, share, and download media.

 CONSIDER THIS ───

Why would you use a media sharing site instead of a social networking site?
If you simply want to post photos, videos, or music to share with others and do not require the full functionality of an online social network, consider using a media sharing site. Before you allow someone to take your photo or record video of you, however, remember that the photo or video may end up on a media sharing site. These photos or videos may be accessible publicly and associated with your identity for a long time. Also, once posted, you may be giving up certain rights to the media. Further, do not post photos or videos that are protected by copyright.

A *bookmarking site* is a website that enables members to organize, tag, and share links to media and other online content. A *tag* is a short descriptive label that you assign to webpages, photos, videos, blog posts, email messages, and other digital content so that it is easier locate at a later time. Many websites and web apps support tagging, which enables users to organize their online content.

BTW
Pinterest and Delicious
Innovative Computing:
You should be familiar
with the bookmarking
sites, Pinterest and
Delicious.

News, Weather, Sports, and Other Mass Media

News, weather, sports, and other mass media websites contain newsworthy material, including stories and articles relating to current events, life, money, politics, weather (Figure 2-13), and sports. You often can customize these websites so that you can receive local news or news about specific topics. Some provide a means to send you alerts, such as weather updates or sporting event scores, via text or email messages.

Newsprint on the web is not replacing the newspaper but enhancing it and reaching different populations. Although some exist solely online, many magazines and newspapers sponsor websites that provide summaries of printed articles, as well as articles not included in the printed versions. Newspapers, magazines, and television and radio stations often have corresponding news, weather, or sports websites and mobile apps.

Figure 2-13 Forecasts, radar, and other weather conditions are available on the WEATHER webpage on USA TODAY's website.
Source: Gannett

Educational

An educational website offers exciting, challenging avenues for formal and informal teaching and learning. The web contains thousands of tutorials from learning how to fly airplanes to learning how to cook a meal. For a more structured learning experience, companies provide online training to employees, and colleges offer online classes and degrees. Instructors often use the web to enhance classroom teaching by publishing course materials, grades, and other pertinent class information.

Business, Governmental, and Organizational

A business website contains content that increases brand awareness, provides company background or other information, and/or promotes or sells products or services. Nearly every enterprise has a business website. Examples include Allstate Insurance Company, Dell Inc., General Motors Corporation, Kraft Foods Inc., and Walt Disney Company.

Most United States government agencies have websites providing citizens with information, such as census data, or assistance, such as filing taxes (Figure 2-14). Many other types of organizations use the web for a variety of reasons. For example, nonprofit organizations raise funds for a cause and advocacy groups present their views or opinions.

Figure 2-14
Government agencies, such as the IRS webpage shown here, have websites providing assistance and information to citizens.
Source: IRS

Discovering Computers Twitter feed

Tweets present current events and technology news

search for related posts by entering a hashtag

Figure 2-15 When Twitter users 'follow' this Discovering Computers feed, Tweets such as those shown here appear on their own personal accounts. As a student in this class, you should 'follow' @DiscoveringComp so that you easily can keep current with relevant technology changes and events in the computing industry.
Source: Twitter

Blogs

As described in Chapter 1, a **blog** (short for weblog) is an informal website consisting of time-stamped articles, or posts, in a diary or journal format, usually listed in reverse chronological order. The term *blogosphere* refers to the worldwide collection of blogs. A blog that contains video sometimes is called a video blog, or vlog. A *microblog* allows users to publish short messages usually between 100 and 200 characters, for others to read. The collection of a user's Tweets, or posts on Twitter, for example, forms a microblog (Figure 2-15).

✻ CONSIDER THIS

How can you locate Tweets about certain topics?
When searching Twitter, you can use hashtags to find related posts. A *hashtag*, which consists of a number sign (#) followed by a keyword, describes and categorizes a Tweet. Similarly, you can tag any word(s) in your Tweets by typing it as a hashtag, such as #election.

Similar to an editorial section in a newspaper, blogs reflect the interests, opinions, and personalities of the author, called the **blogger**, and sometimes website visitors. Blogs have become an important means of worldwide communications. Businesses create blogs to communicate with employees, customers, and vendors. They may post announcements of new information on a corporate blog. Teachers create blogs to collaborate with other teachers and students. Home users create blogs to share aspects of their personal lives with family, friends, and others.

Wikis

Whereas blogs are a tool for publishing and sharing messages, wikis enable users to organize, edit, and share information. A **wiki** is a collaborative website that allows users to create, add, modify, or delete the website content via a browser. Wikis can include articles, documents, photos, or videos. Some wikis are public, accessible to everyone (Figure 2-16). Others are private so that content is accessible only to certain individuals or groups. Many companies, for example, set up wikis for employees to collaborate on projects or access information, procedures, and documents.

Contributors to a wiki typically register before they can edit content or add comments. Wikis usually collect edits on a webpage so that someone can review them for accuracy. Unregistered users typically can review the content but cannot edit it or add comments.

🔅 **Internet Research**

Have errors been found in Wikipedia?

Search for: wikipedia factual errors

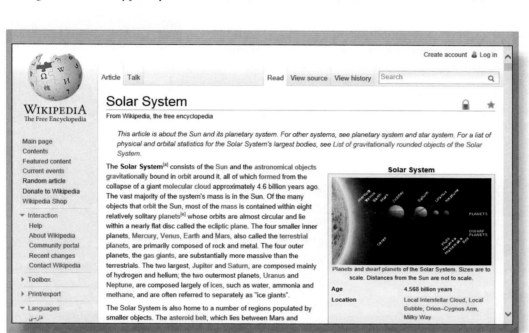

Figure 2-16   Wikipedia is a popular public wiki.
Source: Wikimedia Foundation

Health and Science

Many websites provide up-to-date medical, fitness, nutrition, or exercise information for public access. Some offer the capability of listening to health-related seminars and discussions. Consumers, however, should verify the online information they read with a personal physician. Health service organizations store your personal health history, including prescriptions, lab test results, doctor visits, allergies, and immunizations. Doctors use the web to assist with researching and diagnosing health conditions.

Several websites contain information about space exploration, astronomy, physics, earth sciences, microgravity, robotics, and other branches of science. Scientists use online social networks to collaborate on the web. Nonprofit science organizations use the web to seek public donations to support research.

Entertainment

Entertainment is a growing part of the web's future. An entertainment website offers music, videos, shows, performances, events, sports, games, and more in an interactive and engaging environment. Many entertainment websites support streaming media. **Streaming** is the process of transferring data in a continuous and even flow, which allows users to access and use a file while it is transmitting. You can listen to streaming audio or watch streaming video, such as a live performance or broadcast, as it downloads to your computer, mobile device, or an Internet-connected television.

Sophisticated entertainment websites often partner with other technologies. For example, you can cast your vote about a topic on a television show via your phone or online social network account.

Financial

Online banking and online trading enable users to access their financial records from anywhere in the world, as long as they have an Internet connection. Using online banking, users can access accounts, pay bills, transfer funds, calculate mortgage payments, and manage other financial activities from their computer or mobile device (Figure 2-17). With online trading, users can invest in stocks, options, bonds, treasuries, certificates of deposit, money market accounts, annuities, mutual funds, and so on, without using a broker. Read Secure IT 2-3 for tips about protecting your bank accounts and other personal information from identity theft.

Figure 2-17 Many banks, such as Busey shown here, provide mobile versions of their online banking website so that users can manage financial accounts from their smartphones.
Source: First Busey Corporation

 SECURE IT 2-3

Protecting Yourself from Identity Theft

More than eight million U.S. households are victims of identity theft each year, with the unauthorized use of an existing credit card accounting for much of the growing problem. The National Crime Victimization Survey reports that household identity theft losses amount to more than $13 billion each year, and that figure does not account for the aggravation and time required to repair the accounts. Practice these techniques to thwart attempts to steal your personal data:

- Do not tap or click links in or reply to spam for any reason.

- Install a personal firewall (software that protects network resources from outside intrusions).

- Clear or disable web cookies (small text files that web servers store on a computer) in your browser. This action might prevent some cookie-based websites from functioning, but you will be able to decide which cookies to accept or reject.

- Turn off file and printer sharing on your Internet connection.

- Set up a free email account. Use this email address for merchant forms.

- Sign up for email filtering through your ISP or use an anti-spam program.

- Shred financial documents before you discard them.

- Provide only the required information on website forms.

- Public computers are notorious for running *keyloggers*, which record keystrokes in a hidden file, and other tracking software. Avoid checking your email or performing banking activities at these computers. If you must use a public computer for critical activities, be certain to sign out of any password-protected website and to clear the browser's cache.

- Request a free copy of your medical records each year from the Medical Information Bureau.

- Obtain your credit report once a year from each of the three major credit reporting agencies and correct any errors. Enroll in a credit monitoring service.

- Request, in writing, to be removed from mailing lists.

- Place your phone number on the National Do Not Call Registry.

- Avoid shopping club and buyer cards.

- Do not write your phone number on charge or credit receipts. Ask merchants not to write this number or any other personal information, especially your Social Security Number and driver's license number, on the back of your personal checks.

- Do not preprint your phone number or Social Security Number on personal checks.

- Fill in only the required information on rebate, warranty, and registration forms.

- Learn how to block your phone number from displaying on the receiver's system.

If your identity has been stolen, immediately change any passwords that may have been compromised. If you have disclosed your debit or credit card numbers, contact your financial institutions. You also should visit the Federal Trade Commission website or call the FTC help line.

✳ Do you know anyone who has been a victim of identity theft? What steps will you take to protect your identity using some of these guidelines?

Travel and Mapping

Travel websites, sometimes called online travel agencies, enable users to reserve a flight, hotel, or vehicle. On these websites, you can read travel reviews, search for and compare flights and prices, order airline tickets, book a room, or reserve a rental car.

Several mapping web apps, sometimes called web maps, exist that enable you to display up-to-date maps by searching for an address, postal code, telephone number, or point of interest (such as an airport, lodging, or historical site). The maps can be displayed in a variety of views, including terrain, aerial, maps, streets, buildings, traffic, and weather. These websites also provide directions when a user enters a starting and destination point (Figure 2-18). Many work with GPS to determine where a user is located, eliminating the need for a user to enter the starting point and enabling the website to recommend nearby points of interest.

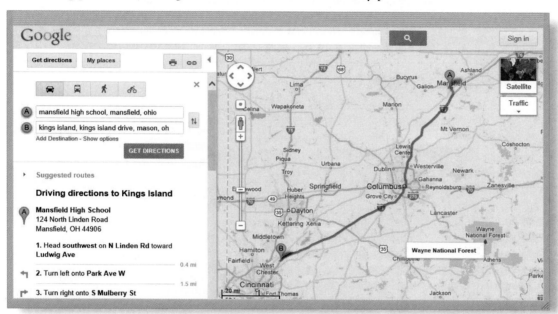

Figure 2-18 Using mapping web apps, such as Google Maps shown here, you can obtain driving directions from one destination to another.
Source: Google Inc.

Shopping and Auctions

You can purchase just about any product or service on the web, a process that sometimes is called *e-retail* (short for electronic retail). To purchase online, the customer visits the business's *electronic storefront*, which contains product descriptions, images, and a shopping cart (Figure 2-19).

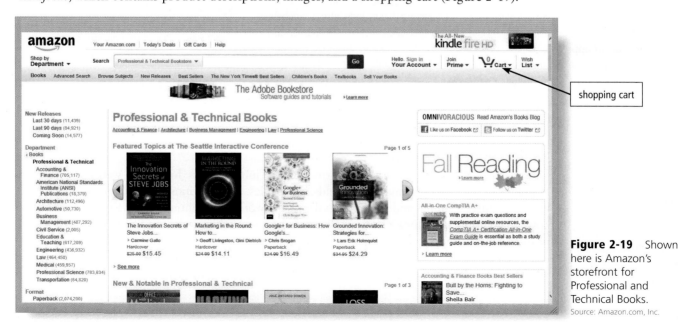

shopping cart

Figure 2-19 Shown here is Amazon's storefront for Professional and Technical Books.
Source: Amazon.com, Inc.

The *shopping cart* allows the customer to collect purchases. When ready to complete the sale, the customer enters personal data and the method of payment, which should be through a secure Internet connection.

With an **online auction**, users bid on an item being sold by someone else. The highest bidder at the end of the bidding period purchases the item. eBay is one of the more popular online auction websites.

 CONSIDER THIS

Is it safe to enter financial information online?

As an alternative to entering credit card, bank account, or other financial information online, some shopping and auction websites allow consumers to use an online payment service such as PayPal. To use an online payment service, you create an account that is linked to your credit card or funds at a financial institution. When you make a purchase, you use your online payment service account, which transfers money for you without revealing your financial information. Read Secure IT 2-4 for additional tips to help you shop safely online.

 SECURE IT 2-4

 Shopping Safely Online

Browsing electronic storefronts and making online purchases can be convenient and economical, but the experience can be a disaster if you encounter unscrupulous vendors. These tips can help you enjoy a safe and productive online shopping trip.

- **Read customer reviews.** Shoppers frequently post comments about merchandise quality, pricing, and shipping. Their evaluations may help you decide whether a company is legitimate. Be aware, however, that the Federal Trade Commission has sued companies for posting false positive reviews and that some companies remove negative comments. Make it a habit to rate merchants as often as possible so that others can learn from your experiences.

- **Look for seals of approval.** Online businesses can display seals if they have met rigorous standards. Some unscrupulous

Source: TRUSTe

Source: Better Business Bureau

merchants, however, will place the seals on their websites even if they have not been approved. To check a seal's legitimacy, click the logo and be certain you are directed to the issuing agency's website.

- **Create a strong password and password questions.** If the merchant requires you to create a user name and password, be certain to develop a long, complex password with at least eight characters that include letters, numbers, and special characters. The website also may ask for answers to security questions; if so, do not supply information that hackers could locate easily, such as your

high school, place of birth, or family member or pet names.

- **Check website details.** Locate the business's privacy policy to learn how your information will be stored. Also, look for phone numbers, physical addresses, and email addresses to contact the vendor if questions arise about damaged goods or billing discrepancies.

- **Beware of requests to supply further information.** After you have placed an order, you may receive an email message asking you to confirm the transaction or to supply additional account information. A reputable business will not solicit these requests, so do not reply to the message.

 Have you made online purchases? If so, have you followed the precautions listed here? How will you change your activities the next time you shop online?

Careers and Employment

You can search the web for career information and job openings. Job search websites list thousands of openings in hundreds of fields, companies, and locations. This information may include required training and education, salary data, working conditions, job descriptions, and more. In addition, many organizations advertise careers on their websites. Read How To 2-1 for instructions about how to use a job search website.

When a company contacts you for an interview, learn as much about the company and the industry as possible before the interview. Many have websites with detailed company profiles.

🌸 **HOW TO 2-1** ——————————————————————————————

Search for a Job Online

If you know the company for which you would like to work, you may be able to visit that company's website and search for a webpage with current job postings. If you would like to search for openings in multiple companies, consider using a job search website. The following steps describe how to search for a job online using a job search website.

1. Run a browser.
2. Use a search engine to locate a job search website and then navigate to the website.

3. Many job search websites allow you to search for jobs by criteria, such as keyword, category, or location. If you are searching for a job in a specific field, enter relevant keyword(s) (i.e., loan officer) or select an appropriate category (i.e., finance). To limit your search results to a specific geographical area, specify a location (i.e., Seattle).
4. Some websites allow you to search for jobs based on additional criteria, such as company, salary, job type, education, and experience. To specify these additional criteria, tap or click a link to perform an advanced search.

5. After entering the job search criteria, start the search by tapping or clicking a Search button (or similar feature on the website).
6. When the search results appear, scroll through the results. To find out more about a particular job, you may be able to tap or click the job listing.
7. If desired, follow the instructions in the job listing to apply for the job.

🌼 Which keywords would you use on a job search website to search for a job in your desired field?

Source: Monster

E-Commerce

E-commerce, short for electronic commerce, is a business transaction that occurs over an electronic network such as the Internet. Anyone with access to a computer or mobile device, an Internet connection, and a means to pay for purchased goods or services can participate in e-commerce. Some people use the term *m-commerce* (mobile commerce) to identify e-commerce that takes place using mobile devices. Popular uses of e-commerce by consumers include shopping and auctions, finance, travel, entertainment, and health.

Three types of e-commerce are business-to-consumer, consumer-to-consumer, and business-to-business.

- *Business-to-consumer (B2C) e-commerce* consists of the sale of goods and services to the general public, such as at a shopping website.
- *Consumer-to-consumer (C2C) e-commerce* occurs when one consumer sells directly to another, such as in an online auction.
- *Business-to-business (B2B) e-commerce* occurs when businesses provide goods and services to other businesses, such as online advertising, recruiting, credit, sales, market research, technical support, and training.

Portals

A **portal** is a website that offers a variety of Internet services from a single, convenient location (Figure 2-20). A wireless portal is a portal designed for Internet-capable mobile devices. Most portals offer these free services: search engine; news, sports, and weather; web publishing; reference tools such as yellow pages, stock quotes, and maps; shopping; and email and other communications services.

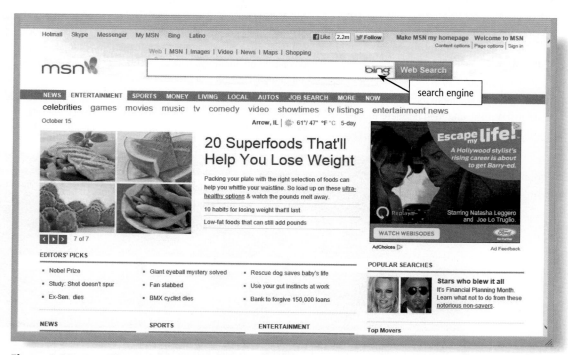

Figure 2-20 Portals, such as MSN, offer a variety of Internet services from a single location.
Source: Microsoft

※ **CONSIDER THIS**

Can you assume that content on a website is correct and accurate?
No. Any person, company, or organization can publish a webpage on the Internet. No one oversees the content of these webpages.
  Use the criteria below to evaluate a website or webpage before relying on its content.
- Affiliation: A reputable institution should support the website without bias in the information.
- Audience: The website should be written at an appropriate level.
- Authority: The website should list the author and the appropriate credentials.
- Content: The website should be well organized and the links should work.
- Currency: The information on the webpage should be current.
- Design: The pages at the website should download quickly, be visually pleasing, and easy to navigate.
- Objectivity: The website should contain little advertising and be free of preconceptions.

Web Publishing

By creating their own websites, businesses and individuals can convey information to billions of people. The content of the webpages ranges from news stories to product information to blogs. **Web publishing** is the development and maintenance of websites. To develop a website, you do not have to be a computer programmer. For the small business or home user, web publishing is fairly easy as long as you have the proper tools.

The five major steps in web publishing are as follows:

1. **Plan the website.** Identify the purpose of the website and the characteristics of the people you want to visit the website. Determine ways to differentiate your website from other similar ones. Decide how visitors will navigate the website.
2. **Design the website.** Design the appearance and layout of elements on the website. Decide colors and formats. Determine content for links, text, graphics, animation, audio, video, virtual reality, and blogs. To complete this step, you may need specific hardware such as a digital camera, webcam, video camera, scanner, and/or audio recorder. You also may need software that enables you to create images or edit photos, audio, and video.
3. **Create the website.** To create a website, you have several options:
   a. Use the features of a word processing program that enable you to create basic webpages from documents containing text and graphics.
   b. Use a *content management system*, which is a program that assists you with creating, editing, and hosting content on a website.
   c. Use website authoring software to create more sophisticated websites that include text, graphics, animation, audio, video, special effects, and links.
   d. More advanced users create sophisticated websites by using a special type of software, called a text editor, to enter codes that instruct the browser how to display the text, images, and links on a webpage.
   e. For advanced features such as managing users, passwords, chat rooms, and email, you may need to purchase specialized website management software.
4. **Host the website.** Options for transferring the webpages from your computer to a web server include the following:
   a. Many ISPs offer their customers storage space on a web server.
   b. Content management systems usually include hosting services for free or a fee.
   c. A *web hosting service* provides storage space on a web server for a reasonable monthly fee. To help others locate your webpage, register your web address with various search engines to ensure your website appears in the search results.
5. **Maintain the website.** Visit the website regularly to ensure its contents are current and all links work properly.

 NOW YOU KNOW _____

Be sure you understand the material presented in the section titled Types of Websites as it relates to the chapter objectives.
You now should know…

- How to enter search text and improve your search results (Objective 5)
- How you can benefit from social networking sites (Objective 6)
- When you would use specific types of websites (Objective 7)
- How you can publish your own website (Objective 8)

 Quiz Yourself Online: Check your knowledge of related content by navigating to this book's Quiz Yourself resource on Computer Concepts CourseMate and then tapping or clicking Objectives 5–8.

Media on the Web

Most webpages include more than just formatted text and links. The more exciting webpages use *multimedia*, which refers to any application that combines text with media. Media includes graphics, animation, audio, video, and/or virtual reality. The sections that follow discuss how the web uses these types of media. Read Ethics & Issues 2-3 on the next page to consider issues related to website accessibility for everyone.

ETHICS & ISSUES 2-3

Should Websites Be Required to Meet Accessibility Guidelines?

The W3C (World Wide Web Consortium) publishes accessibility guidelines for websites. The W3C first published the guidelines in 1999 and updates them periodically. Website designers use the guidelines to increase access for all users, including those with poor eyesight or color blindness; tremors and loss of muscle control; hearing loss; seizure disorders, which may be affected by flashing effects; and other disabilities, including dyslexia. The W3C urges website designers to provide alternate text for audio or visual content, include features that allow objects to be activated and understood using a variety of input and output devices, and make the user interface easy to navigate using screen readers or other adaptive technologies.

Several web design programs include built-in tools that web designers use to find potential issues. Companies also employ user testing, or they hire experts to review and test a website for potential issues. Many websites, including several for disability organizations, fail to comply with the standards. Users who cannot access a website's features can bring a lawsuit against the website owners. Many organizations lack the funding necessary to review, test, and rework their website to meet the accessibility standards.

Should the government require that all websites meet the W3C accessibility guidelines? Why or why not? Do websites hosted by disability organizations have a moral obligation to meet the guidelines? Why? What can be done to encourage people and organizations to make their websites more accessible?

Graphics

A **graphic** is a visual representation of nontext information, such as a drawing, chart, or photo. Many webpages use colorful graphics to convey messages (Figure 2-21). Some websites use thumbnails on their pages because graphics can be time-consuming to display. A *thumbnail* is a small version of a larger object that you usually can tap or click to display a larger image or object.

The web often uses infographics to present concepts, products, and news. An *infographic* (short for information graphic) is a visual representation of data or information, designed to

Figure 2-21 Many webpages use colorful graphics to convey messages. For example, the variety of colors, images, shapes, and thumbnails on the San Diego Zoo webpage visually separate and draw attention to areas of the webpage, making the webpage more dynamic and enticing.
Source: Zoological Society of San Diego

communicate quickly, simplify complex concepts, or present patterns or trends (Figure 2-22). Many forms of infographics exist: maps, signs, charts, and diagrams.

Of the graphics formats for displaying images on the web (Table 2-5), the JPEG and PNG formats are more common. *JPEG* (pronounced JAY-peg) is a compressed graphics format that attempts to reach a balance between image quality and file size. With JPG files, the more compressed the file, the smaller the image and the lower the quality. *PNG* (pronounced ping) is a patent-free compressed graphics format that restores all image details when the file is viewed. That is, the PNG format does not lose image quality during compression.

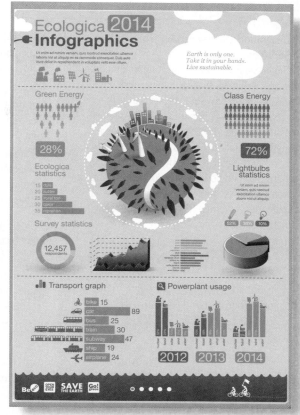

Figure 2-22 An infographic presents complex concepts at a glance.
© radoma / Shutterstock.com

Table 2-5 Graphics Formats Used on the Web

Abbreviation	Name	Uses
BMP	Bitmap	Desktop backgrounds Scanned images
GIF	Graphics Interchange Format	Images with few colors Simple diagrams Shapes
JPEG	Joint Photographic Experts Group	Digital camera photos Game screenshots Movie still shots
PNG	Portable Network Graphics	Comic-style drawings Line art Web graphics
TIFF	Tagged Image File Format	Photos used in printing industry

© Cengage Learning

✳ **CONSIDER THIS**

What is a PDF file?
PDF, which stands for Portable Document Format, is an electronic image format by Adobe Systems that mirrors the appearance of an original document. Users can view a PDF without needing the software that originally created the document.

Animation Many webpages use *animation*, which is the appearance of motion created by displaying a series of still images in sequence. For example, text that animates by scrolling across the screen can serve as a ticker to display stock updates, news, sports scores, weather, or other information. Web-based games often use animation.

Audio

On the web, you can listen to audio clips and live audio. *Audio* includes music, speech, or any other sound. Simple applications consist of individual audio files available for download to a computer or device. Once downloaded, you can play (listen to) the content of these files. Read How To 2-2 on the next page for instructions about downloading digital media from online services. Other applications use streaming audio so that you can listen to the audio while it downloads.

HOW TO 2-2

Download Digital Media from Online Services

Online services make various forms of digital media available, such as books, music, movies, and apps. You typically can use a program, such as iTunes, or an app, such as the Google Play Store, to access digital media. Digital media also may be available from these services' websites. The following steps describe how to download digital media from online services when you know the name or keyword(s) for the digital media you want to find.

1. On your computer or mobile device, run the program or app from which the digital media is available. If a program or app is not accessible easily, navigate to the online service using your browser.

2. Enter the name or keyword(s) in the Search box.

3. Tap or click the Search button to perform the search.

4. Navigate through the search results and then tap or click the search result for the item you want to download.

5. Locate and then tap or click the Download button or link to download the digital media to your computer or mobile device.

The following steps describe how to browse for and download digital media.

1. On your computer or mobile device, run the program or app from which the digital media is available. If a program or app is not accessible easily, navigate to the online service using your browser.

2. Tap or click the category corresponding to the type of digital media you want to browse. Common categories include music, movies, books, and apps.

3. Browse the items in the category.

4. When you find an item you want to download, tap or click the item to display additional information.

5. Look for and then tap or click the Download button or link to download the digital media to your computer or mobile device.

✺ In addition to the online services listed in this box, what are three additional resources from which you can download digital media?

Audio files are compressed to reduce their file sizes. For example, the *MP3* format reduces an audio file to about one-tenth its original size, while preserving much of the original quality of the sound.

To listen to an audio file on your computer, you need special software called a *media player*. Most current operating systems contain a media player; for example, the Windows operating system includes Windows Media Player. Some audio files, however, might require you to download a media player. Media players available for download include iTunes (Figure 2-23) and RealPlayer. You can download media players free from the web.

Internet Research

How do you subscribe to an iTunes podcast?

Search for: subscribe itunes podcast

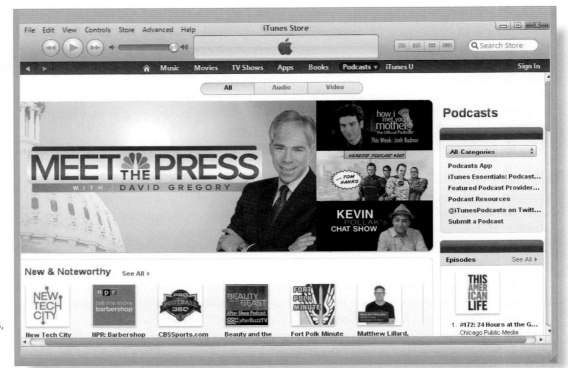

Figure 2-23 iTunes is a popular media player, through which you can access the iTunes Store to purchase and/or download music, movies, television shows, apps, books, and podcasts.

Source: Apple Inc.

Video

On the web, you can view video clips or watch live video. *Video* consists of images displayed in motion. Most video also has accompanying audio. You also can upload, share, or view video clips at a video sharing site. Educators, politicians, and businesses use video blogs and video podcasts to engage students, voters, and consumers.

Simple video applications on the web consist of individual video files, such as movie or television clips, that you must download completely before you can play them on a computer or mobile device. Video files often are compressed because they are quite large in size. Videos posted to the web often are short in length, usually less than 10 minutes, because they can take a long time to download. As with streaming audio files, streaming video files allows you to view longer or live videos by playing them as they download to your computer.

⚡ Internet Research

Internet Research

What is a Smart TV?

Search for: smart tv

Virtual Reality   **Virtual reality (VR)** is the use of computers to simulate a real or imagined environment that appears as a three-dimensional (3-D) space. VR involves the display of 3-D images that users explore and manipulate interactively. Using special VR software, a developer creates an entire 3-D environment that contains infinite space and depth, called a *VR world* (Figure 2-24). A VR world on the web, for example, might show a house for sale where potential buyers walk through rooms in the VR house by sliding their finger on a touch screen or moving an input device forward, backward, or to the side.

In addition to games and simulations, many practical applications of VR also exist. Science educators create VR models of molecules, organisms, and other structures for students to examine. Companies use VR to showcase products or create advertisements. Architects create VR models of buildings and rooms so that clients can see how a completed construction project will look before it is built.

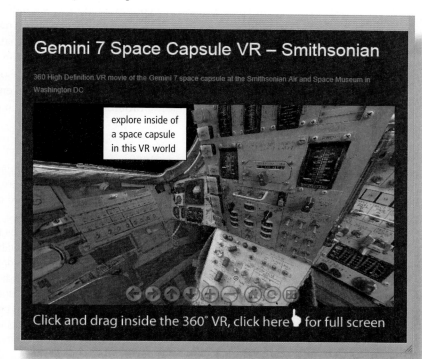

Figure 2-24   Users can explore a VR world using a touch screen or their input device. For example, users can explore the inside of the Gemini 7 space capsule, located at the Smithsonian Air and Space Museum in Washington, D.C., from their computer or mobile device.
Source: World VR

Plug-Ins

Most browsers have the capability of displaying basic multimedia elements on a webpage. Sometimes, however, a browser requires an additional program, called a plug-in, to display multimedia. A *plug-in*, or add-on, is a program that extends the capability of a browser. For example, your browser may require Adobe Reader to view and print PDF files, or Flash Player to view certain graphics or animations. You typically can download plug-ins at no cost from various websites. Some plug-ins run on all sizes of computers and mobile devices; others have special versions for mobile devices. Some mobile browsers do not support the use of plug-ins.

Other Internet Services

As previously mentioned, the web is only one of the many services on the Internet. Other Internet services include the following: email, email lists, instant messaging, chat rooms, discussion forums, VoIP (Voice over IP), and FTP (File Transfer Protocol).

Email

Email (short for electronic mail) is the transmission of messages and files via a computer network. Email was one of the original services on the Internet, enabling scientists and researchers working on government-sponsored projects to communicate with colleagues at other locations. Today, email is one of the primary communications methods for personal and business use.

You use an **email program** to create, send, receive, forward, store, print, and delete email messages. Email programs are available as desktop apps, web apps, and mobile apps. An email message can be simple text or can include an attachment such as a document, a graphic, an audio clip, or a video clip.

Just as you address a letter when using the postal system, you address an email message with the email address of your intended recipient. Likewise, when someone sends you a message, he or she must have your email address. Read How To 2-3 for the steps you can follow to send an email message.

An email address is a combination of a user name and a domain name that identifies a user so that he or she can receive Internet email. A **user name** is a unique combination of characters, such as letters of the alphabet and/or numbers, that identifies a specific user. Your user name must be different from the other user names in the same domain. For example, a user named Rick Claremont whose server has a domain name of esite.com might want to select rclaremont as his user name. If esite.com already has an rclaremont (for Rita Claremont) user name, then Rick will have to select a different user name, such as rick.claremont or r_claremont.

 HOW TO 2-3

Send Email Messages Using Various Email Programs and Web Apps

The process required to send an email message using a computer or mobile device from various email programs and web apps is very similar. The following steps describe how to send an email message using an email program or web app.

1. Run the email program or navigate to the email web app on your computer or mobile device.

2. Look for, and then tap or click the button to compose a new email message.

3. Type the recipient's email address in the To text box. If you are sending the email message to multiple recipients, separate each email address with a semicolon (;).

4. If you would like to send a copy of the email message to one or more people, type their email address(es) in the Cc text box (which stands for carbon copy).

5. To send a copy of the email message to someone while hiding their email address from the other recipients, enter his or her email address in the Bcc text box (which stands for blind carbon copy). The email recipients listed in the To or Cc text boxes will not be able to see the recipients you specified in the Bcc text box.

6. Enter a descriptive subject in the Subject text box. It is not good practice to leave the subject blank when you send email

messages because the recipient's email server may place messages without a subject in a spam or junk mail folder.

7. Type the body of the email message in the appropriate area.

8. If your email program supports it, check the spelling of your email message and correct any errors found.

9. Click the Send button, which sends the email message to everyone listed in the To, Cc, and Bcc text boxes.

✷ Under what circumstances might you want to send a blind carbon copy of an email message to one or more people?

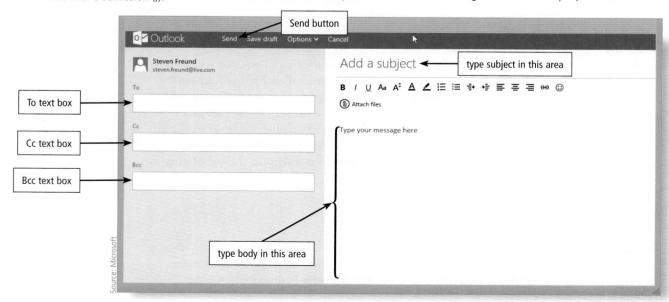

Send button

type subject in this area

To text box

Cc text box

Bcc text box

type body in this area

Source: Microsoft

Sometimes, organizations decide the format of user names for new users so that the user names are consistent across the company. In many cases, however, users select their own user names, often selecting a nickname or any other combination of characters for their user name. Many users select a combination of their first and last names so that others can remember it easily.

In an Internet email address, an @ (pronounced at) symbol separates the user name from the domain name. Your service provider supplies the domain name. A possible email address for Rick Claremont would be rclaremont@esite.com, which would be read as follows: R Claremont at e site dot com. Most email programs allow you to create a *contacts folder*, which contains a list of names, addresses, phone numbers, email addresses, and other details about people with whom you communicate.

Figure 2-25 illustrates how an email message may travel from a sender to a receiver. When you send an email message, an outgoing mail server determines how to route the message through the Internet and then sends the message. As you receive email messages, an incoming mail server holds the messages in your mailbox until you use your email program to retrieve them. Most email programs have a mail notification alert that informs you via a message and/or sound when you receive new mail.

 CONSIDER THIS

What are good practices to follow when using email?

1. Keep messages brief.
2. Respond to messages promptly.
3. Use proper grammar, spelling, and punctuation.
4. Never respond to unsolicited messages.
5. Use meaningful subject lines.
6. Read the message before you send it.
7. Use email when you want a permanent record of a communication.

How an Email Message May Travel from a Sender to a Receiver

Step 1 Using an email program, you create and send a message on a computer or mobile device.

Step 2 Your email program contacts software on the outgoing mail server.

Step 3 Software on the outgoing mail server determines the best route for the data and sends the message, which travels along Internet routers to the recipient's incoming mail server.

Step 4 When the recipient uses an email program to check for email messages, the message transfers from the incoming mail server to the recipient's computer or mobile device.

Figure 2-25 This figure shows how an email message may travel from a sender to a receiver.

Email Lists

An **email list**, or electronic mailing list, is a group of email addresses used for mass distribution of a message. When a message is sent to an email list, each person on the list receives a copy of the message in his or her mailbox. You *subscribe* to an email list by adding your email address to the mailing list, which is stored on a list server. To remove your name, you *unsubscribe* from the mailing list.

The original use of email lists, such as LISTSERV, allowed any subscriber to send a message, which created a discussion-type forum among all subscribers via email. Many mailing lists today, such as in Figure 2-26, however, are one-way communications and do not allow subscribers to send messages.

Figure 2-26 When you subscribe to a mailing list, you and all others in the list receive messages from the website. Shown here is a user who receives newsletters and alerts from FoxNews.com.
Source: FOX News Network, LLC

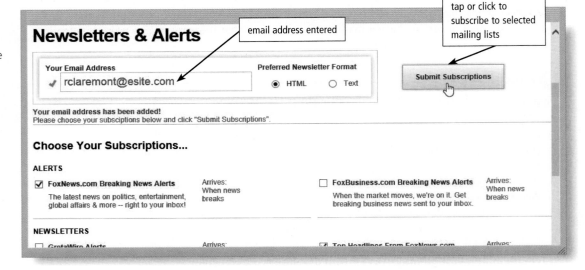

Instant Messaging

Instant messaging (**IM**) is a real-time Internet communications service that notifies you when one or more of your established contacts are online and then allows you to exchange messages or files or join a private chat room with them (Figure 2-27). *Real time* means that you and the people with whom you are conversing are online at the same time. Some IM services support voice and video conversations, allow you to send photos or other documents to a recipient, listen to streaming music, and play games with another online contact. Many can alert you to information such as calendar appointments, stock quotes, weather, or sports scores.

For IM to work, both parties must be online at the same time. Also, the receiver of a message must be willing to accept messages. To use IM, you may have to install instant messenger software on the computer or mobile device, such as a smartphone, you plan to use.

Many online social networks include an IM feature. To ensure successful communications, all individuals on the friend list need to use the same or a compatible instant messenger.

Figure 2-27 With IM, you and the person(s) with whom you are conversing are online at the same time. The conversation appears on all parties' screens at the same time.
© iStockphoto / Petar Chernaev; © Cengage Learning; © iStockphoto / Oleksiy Mark; © Cengage Learning

Chat Rooms

A **chat** is a real-time typed conversation that takes place on a computer or mobile device with many other online users. A **chat room** is a website or application that permits users to chat with others who are online at the same time. A server echoes the user's message to everyone in the chat room. Anyone in the chat room can participate in the conversation, which usually is specific to a particular topic. Businesses sometimes use chat rooms to communicate with customers.

As you type on your keyboard, others connected to the same chat room server also see what you have typed (Figure 2-28). Some chat rooms support voice chats and video chats, in which people hear or see each other as they chat. Most browsers today include the capability to connect to a chat server.

Figure 2-28 As you type, others in the same chat room see what you have typed.
© ARENA Creative / Shutterstock.com; © Cengage Learning; © topseller / Shutterstock.com; © Alex Staroseltsev / Shutterstock.com; © Oleksiy Mark / Shutterstock.com; © Oleksiy Mark / Shutterstock.com; © Tom Wang / Shutterstock.com; © vlad_star / Shutterstock.com; © artjazz / Shutterstock.com

Discussion Forums

A **discussion forum**, or *message board*, is an online area in which users have written discussions about a particular subject (Figure 2-29). To participate in a discussion, a user posts a message, called an article, to the newsgroup, and other users in the newsgroup read and reply to the message. A *thread*, or threaded discussion, consists of the original article and all subsequent related replies.

Some discussion forums require that you enter a user name and password to participate in the discussion. For example, a discussion forum for students taking a college course may require a user name and password to access the forum. This ensures that only students in the course participate in the discussion. Posts in a discussion forum usually are stored for a certain amount of time, such as a semester, in this example.

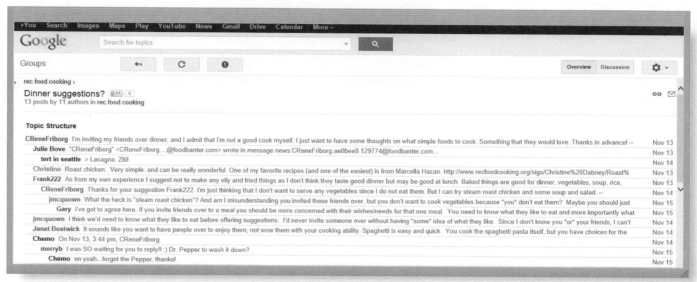

Figure 2-29 Users in a discussion forum read and reply to other users' messages.
© Google Inc.

VoIP

VoIP, short for Voice over IP (Internet Protocol), enables users to speak to other users via their Internet connection. That is, VoIP uses the Internet (instead of the public switched telephone network) to connect a calling party to one or more local or long-distance called parties.

To place an Internet telephone call, you need a broadband Internet connection, a microphone and speaker, both of which are included with a standard computer or mobile device, and VoIP software, such as Skype. Some VoIP services require that you purchase a separate telephone and VoIP router, and subscribe to their service. Others offer certain services free and require a subscription for additional services. Read How To 2-4 for instructions about how to set up a personal VoIP service and make a call.

BTW
VoIP Microphone
You also can use a headset connected to or that communicates with your computer or mobile device.

HOW TO 2-4

Set Up a Personal VoIP Service and Make a Call

VoIP services enable you to make free video or voice calls to others around the world. In many cases, the person you are calling also must use the same VoIP service. The following steps describe how to set up a VoIP service and make a call.

1. If you do not know the VoIP service you want to use, search for a program or app that enables you to place and receive VoIP calls.

2. If necessary, download the program or app for the VoIP service you will use.

3. Most VoIP services require you to have an account with their service before you can place or receive a call. When you start the VoIP program or app, search for the button or link to create a new account. Follow the steps in the program or app to finish creating the account.

4. Once the account has been created, if necessary, sign in to the VoIP service with your user name and password.

5. Make sure the person you are calling also has an account with the same VoIP service. You should know at least one person using this service to successfully

place a call. VoIP services typically allow you to locate and call someone by entering their user name or adding them to your list of contacts. If necessary, add the person you want to call to your list of contacts.

6. On the list of contacts, select the person you want to call and then tap or click the appropriate button to place the call.

7. When the other person answers, you can start your voice or video call.

8. When you are ready to end the call, tap or click the button to end the call.

9. When you are finished using the VoIP service, you should sign out of and exit the VoIP program or app.

☀ Survey your friends and family to see if they use a VoIP service. If so, which service is the most popular among them?

Source: Microsoft

FTP

FTP (File Transfer Protocol) is an Internet standard that permits file uploading and downloading to and from other computers on the Internet. *Uploading* is the process of transferring files from your computer or mobile device to a server on the Internet. Recall that downloading is the process of transferring files from a server on the Internet to your computer or mobile device. Webpage developers, for example, often use FTP to upload their webpages to a web server.

Many operating systems include FTP capabilities. If yours does not, you can download FTP programs from the web, usually for a small fee.

An *FTP server* is a computer that allows users to upload and/or download files using FTP. An FTP site is a collection of files that reside on an FTP server. Many FTP sites have *anonymous FTP*, whereby anyone can transfer some, if not all, available files. Some FTP sites restrict file transfers to those who have authorized accounts (user names and passwords) on the FTP server.

MINI FEATURE 2-3

Digital Communications

People, including home users, small/home office users, mobile users, power users, and enterprise users, use technology for many reasons, including communications, productivity, and information. This scenario, which assumes you are a student who balances school with a new internship, presents situations and questions regarding technology use during a single day.

7:30 a.m. Using your smartphone, you update your social networking status to say that today you start an internship. Within minutes, you receive many comments wishing you luck. Before leaving, you send a quick text message to your friends confirming they still want to meet for lunch today and then check the weather app on your smartphone. The local forecast calls for rain, so you take an umbrella.

✳ Should you include the company name for which you are interning in a social networking status? How might an app provider use your location information in ways you have not authorized?

8:15 a.m. At the subway station, you use your smartphone to pay the subway fare. On the subway, you receive a call from your new boss and debate whether you should answer it.

✳ How safe are mobile payment apps? Are you obligated to answer work calls on personal time? What courtesies should you extend to those around you while on a call in a public place?

8:45 a.m. In class, you use a tablet to take notes on the instructor's lecture. As she talks, you remember reading an article about the topic. You use the tablet to search for the article and share what you have learned. The sound is turned off, but you see notifications on your tablet about messages of congratulations based on your social networking post, as well as incoming email messages regarding a group presentation.

✳ Should your school or instructor be able to restrict Internet access during class? Is it acceptable to answer or look at email messages, text messages, or online social network posts when in class?

11:00 a.m. Before meeting friends for lunch, you use an app that uses search criteria, GPS, and user reviews to locate a Mexican restaurant between campus and your job. Once you find a restaurant that you like, you send the location to your friends via text message and

then check in to the restaurant via a status update through your online social network.

✳ How can you evaluate user reviews on websites for bias or accuracy? What should you consider when using apps or websites that enable you to check in to locations?

1:00 p.m. Taking a deep breath, you enter the advertising agency and introduce yourself to the receptionist. Your boss brings a laptop to the cubicle where you will be working. He shows you how to check company email and hands you a memo with the company's acceptable use policies.

✳ Can you use company resources, such as your email address, for personal use? Should you use your smartphone to send text messages or check your personal email during company time?

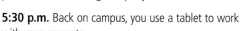

5:30 p.m. Back on campus, you use a tablet to work with your group to prepare a presentation, incorporating links to the source articles. You submit the presentation to your instructor using the school's educational portal.

✳ How important is it to credit sources when researching information on the web? When is it acceptable not to credit sources?

8:30 p.m. At home, you read assignments for tomorrow's classes using the e-book app on your tablet. You access the e-book's online content and take a quiz. You use the tablet to update your blog with a post about your first day, including a photo of your cubicle taken with your smartphone.

✳ How can technology be used to enhance education? What steps should you take to ensure your privacy on a blog?

11:30 p.m. You exchange several text messages with your brother to share information about your day, plug your phone and tablet into chargers, set the alarm on your smartphone, and then head to bed.

✳ How does technology enhance your daily life?

Netiquette

Netiquette, which is short for Internet etiquette, is the code of acceptable behaviors users should follow while on the Internet; that is, it is the conduct expected of individuals while online. Netiquette includes rules for all aspects of the Internet, including the web, social media, instant messaging, chat rooms, discussion forums, and FTP. Figure 2-30 outlines some of the rules of netiquette, with respect to online communications. Read Ethics & Issues 2-4 to consider issues related to an extreme misuse of online communications — online bullying.

 CONSIDER THIS

What are the various kinds of social media?

Social media consists of content that users create and share online, such as photos, videos, music, links, blog posts, Tweets, wiki entries, podcasts, and status updates. Social media websites facilitate the creation or publishing of social media online and include media sharing sites (for photo, video, and audio files), bookmarking sites, blogs and microblogs, wikis, podcasts, online social networks, and online gaming sites.

Netiquette Guidelines for Online Communications
Golden Rule: Treat others as you would like them to treat you.

Be polite. Avoid offensive language.

Avoid sending or posting *flames*, which are abusive or insulting messages. Do not participate in *flame wars*, which are exchanges of flames.

Be careful when using sarcasm and humor, as it might be misinterpreted.

Do not use all capital letters, which is the equivalent of SHOUTING!

Use **emoticons** to express emotion. Popular emoticons include:

| :) Smile | :\| Indifference | :o Surprised | :(Frown | :\ Undecided | ;) Wink |

Use abbreviations and acronyms for phrases:

| BTW | by the way | IMHO | in my humble opinion | FWIW | for what it's worth |
| FYI | for your information | TTFN | ta ta for now | TYVM | thank you very much |

Clearly identify a spoiler, which is a message that reveals an outcome to a game or ending to a movie or program.

Be forgiving of other's mistakes.

Read the *FAQ* (frequently asked questions), if one exists.

Figure 2-30 Some of the rules of netiquette, with respect to online communications.
© Cengage Learning

 ETHICS & ISSUES 2-4

Should Cyberbullying Be Illegal?

Sending or forwarding threatening text messages, posting embarrassing or altered pictures of someone without their permission, or setting up a fake social networking page where others make cruel comments and spread rumors about someone are all examples of cyberbullying. *Cyberbullying* is defined as harassment, often involving teens and preteens, using technology. Unlike verbal bullying, the perpetrators can hide behind the anonymity of the Internet and can reach a wide audience quickly. Because of people's reliance on smartphones, victims cannot just walk away or ignore bullying that comes in the form of text messages or other notifications sent to their smartphones.

Schools struggle to come up with policies because cyberbullying often takes place outside of school hours. Yet the ramifications affect the victim at school. Anti-bullying laws vary from state to state and often do not include specific statutes against cyberbullying. One argument against criminalizing cyberbullying is the protection of free speech. Awareness campaigns and parent monitoring of technology use are some ways to attempt to prevent cyberbullying, but they are not always effective. One group of teens recently worked together to create an app that enables anonymous reporting of bullying, including the time and location of the event(s).

Should cyberbullying be illegal? Why or why not? What are the positive and negative aspects of the freedom to remain anonymous on the Internet? What other measures can be taken to reduce cyberbullying? What role can parents play in reducing cyberbullying?

NOW YOU KNOW

Be sure you understand the material presented in the sections titled Media on the Web and Other Internet Services as it relates to the chapter objectives.
You now should know . . .

- Why you use media on the web (Objective 9)
- How you can benefit from using email, email lists, instant messaging, chat rooms, discussion forums, VoIP, and FTP (Objective 10)
- What rules you should follow in online communications (Objective 11)

Quiz Yourself Online: Check your knowledge of related content by navigating to this book's Quiz Yourself resource on Computer Concepts CourseMate and then tapping or clicking Objectives 9–11.

Chapter Summary

This chapter presented the evolution of the Internet, along with various ways to connect to the Internet, how data travels the Internet, and how the Internet works with domain names and IP addresses. It discussed the web at length, including topics such as browsing, navigating, web addresses, web apps and mobile apps, searching, and online social networks. It presented various types of websites, web publishing, and media on the web. It also introduced other services available on the Internet, such as email, email lists, instant messaging, chat rooms, discussion forums, VoIP, and FTP. Finally, the chapter listed rules of netiquette.

Test your knowledge of chapter material by accessing the Study Guide, Flash Cards, and Practice Test apps that run on your smartphone, tablet, laptop, or desktop.

 TECHNOLOGY @ WORK

Transportation

What is transportation like without computers and mobile devices? Delivery drivers use clipboards to hold their records. Human navigators use paper maps to track routes for pilots. Ship captains rely solely on experience to navigate through shallow waters. Today, the transportation industry relies heavily on computer and mobile device usage.

Many vehicles include onboard navigation systems to help you navigate from one location to another. These systems usually provide other services such as dispatching roadside assistance, unlocking the driver's side door if you lock the keys in your vehicle, and tracking the vehicle if it is stolen.

The shipping and travel industries identify items during transport using bar codes, which are identification codes that consist of lines and spaces of different lengths. When you ship a package, the shipping company, such as UPS or FedEx, places a bar code on the package to indicate its destination to a computer. Because a package might travel to its destination by way of several trucks, trains, and airplanes,

computers automatically route the package as efficiently as possible. You are able to visit a website to track a package's progress during shipment.

When you travel by airplane, baggage handling systems ensure that your luggage reaches its destination on time. When you check in your baggage at the airport, a bar code identifies the airplane on which the bags should be placed. If you change planes, automated baggage handling systems route your bags to connecting flights with very little, if any, human intervention. When the bags reach their destination, they are routed automatically to the baggage carousel in the airport's terminal building.

Pilots of high-technology commercial, military, and space aircraft today work in a glass cockpit, which features computerized instrumentation, navigation, communication, weather reports, and an autopilot. The electronic flight information shown on high-resolution displays is designed to reduce pilot workload, decrease fatigue, and enable pilots to concentrate on flying safely.

Boats and ships also are equipped with computers that include detailed electronic maps, which help the captain navigate, as well as calculate the water depth and provide a layout of the underwater surface so that the captain can avoid obstructions.

As you travel the roadways, airways, and waterways, bear in mind that computers often are responsible for helping you to reach your destination as quickly and safely as possible.

In what other ways do computers and technology play a role in the transportation industry?

© Digital Vision / Getty Images

Study Guide

The Study Guide exercise reinforces material you should know for the chapter exam. You will find answers to items with the **icon only in the e-book.**

 Access the Study Guide app that runs on your smartphone, tablet, laptop, or desktop by navigating to this book's Apps resource on Computer Concepts CourseMate.

Instructions: Answer the questions below using the format that helps you remember best or that is required by your instructor. Possible formats may include one or more of these options: write the answers; create a document that contains the answers; record answers as audio or video using a webcam, smartphone, or portable media player; post answers on a blog, wiki, or website; or highlight answers in the book/e-book.

1. Explain how ARPANET contributed to the growth of the Internet.

2. Describe the role of a host on a network.

3. Identify the role of the W3C.

4. Define the term, broadband. List popular wired and wireless broadband Internet services.

5. State the purpose of a hot spot and where you might find one.

6. ISP stands for _____.

7. Briefly describe how data and information travel the Internet.

8. Describe the purpose and composition of an IP address. What are IPv4 and IPv6?

9. Define the term, domain name.

10. Identify the purpose of several generic TLDs. Identify ICANN's role with TLDs.

11. Describe how and why cybersquatters register domain names.

12. State the purpose of a DNS server.

13. Differentiate between static and dynamic webpages.

14. Distinguish among the web, a webpage, a website, and a web server.

15. Explain the purpose of a browser. List ways you can browse safely.

16. Name examples of popular browsers for personal computers and mobile devices.

17. Describe the function of tabbed browsing.

18. Explain how a phishing filter can protect you.

19. Define the term, web address. Name a synonym.

20. Name and give examples of the components of a web address.

21. Describe the purpose of a web feed and the role of a feed reader.

22. Explain the relationship between web and mobile apps.

23. Describe the purpose of GPS receivers, and why they are embedded in smartphones.

24. Besides webpages, identify other items a search engine can find.

25. Name the products or services of Yahoo! and Google, with respect to browsing.

26. Describe how to use a search engine. What are some ways you can refine a search?

27. Differentiate between a search engine and a subject directory.

28. Explain how to use a social networking site for personal or business use.

29. List ways to use social networking sites securely.

30. Describe the purpose of these types of websites: informational; media sharing and bookmarking; news, weather, and sports; educational; business, governmental, and organizational; blogs; wikis; health and science; entertainment; financial; travel and mapping; shopping and auctions; career and employment; and portals.

31. List techniques to protect yourself from identity theft.

32. Describe ways you can shop online safely.

33. List some criteria you can use to narrow your search for a job online.

34. Define the term, e-commerce. Differentiate among B2C, C2C, and B2B e-commerce.

35. List the seven criteria for evaluating a website's content.

36. Identify and briefly describe the steps in web publishing.

37. _____ refers to any application that combines text with media.

38. Describe website accessibility guidelines.

39. Explain how webpages use graphics, animation, audio, video, virtual reality, and plug-ins.

40. Define the terms, thumbnail and infographic.

41. Name the types of graphics formats used on the web and how they use compression.

42. Describe the purpose of these Internet services and explain how each works: email, email lists, instant messaging, chat rooms, discussion forums, VoIP, and FTP.

43. Describe the components of an email address.

44. _____ refers to Internet communications in which both parties communicate at the same time.

45. Describe how the following use digital communications: home users, small/home office users, mobile users, power users, and enterprise users.

46. Define the term, netiquette.

47. Define the term, social media. List forms of social media.

48. Describe cyberbullying, and explain why it is difficult to catch the perpetrators.

You should be able to define the Primary Terms and be familiar with the Secondary Terms listed below.

Key Terms

 Access the Flash Cards app that runs on your smartphone, tablet, laptop, or desktop by navigating to this book's Apps resource on Computer Concepts CourseMate. **View definitions** for each term by navigating to this book's Key Terms resource on Computer Concepts CourseMate. **Listen to definitions** for each term on your portable media player by navigating to this book's Audio Study Tools resource on Computer Concepts CourseMate.

Primary Terms   (shown in **bold-black** characters in the chapter)

blog (72)	emoticons (90)	netiquette (90)	tabbed browsing (62)
blogger (72)	favorites (63)	online auction (76)	user name (84)
browser (62)	Firefox (64)	online social	virtual reality (VR) (83)
chat (87)	FTP (88)	network (68)	VoIP (88)
chat room (87)	graphic (80)	Opera (64)	web (61)
Chrome (64)	home page (62)	pop-up blocker (62)	web address (64)
cybercafé (57)	instant messaging	portal (78)	web publishing (78)
discussion forum (87)	(IM) (86)	Safari (64)	web server (61)
domain name (60)	Internet (54)	search engine (67)	webpage (61)
e-commerce (77)	Internet Explorer (64)	social media (90)	website (61)
email (84)	Internet service provider	social networking	wiki (73)
email list (86)	(ISP) (58)	site (68)	World Wide Web
email program (84)	IP address (59)	streaming (73)	(WWW) (61)

Secondary Terms   (shown in *italic* characters in the chapter)

animation (81)	*DSL (57)*	*message board (87)*	*timeline (69)*
anonymous FTP (88)	*dynamic webpage (61)*	*microblog (72)*	*top-level domain (TLD) (60)*
Anticybersquatting Consumer	*electronic storefront (75)*	*mobile app (65)*	*traffic (59)*
* Protection Act (60)*	*e-retail (75)*	*mobile broadband (57)*	*unsubscribe (86)*
ARPANET (54)	*extended contacts (69)*	*mobile browser (62)*	*uploading (88)*
Atom (65)	*FAQ (90)*	*mobile service provider (58)*	*URL (64)*
audio (81)	*Fiber to the Premises (FTTP) (57)*	*MP3 (82)*	*video (83)*
bandwidth (58)	*fixed wireless (57)*	*multimedia (79)*	*VR world (83)*
blogosphere (72)	*flames (90)*	*news feed (69)*	*W3C (56)*
bookmarks (63)	*flame wars (90)*	*PDF (81)*	*wall (69)*
bookmarking site (71)	*friends (69)*	*phishing (62)*	*Web 2.0 (62)*
broadband (56)	*FTP server (88)*	*phishing filter (62)*	*web app (65)*
business-to-business (B2B)	*gigabyte (GB) (58)*	*plug-in (83)*	*web feed (65)*
* e-commerce (77)*	*GPS (66)*	*PNG (81)*	*web hosting service (79)*
business-to-consumer (B2C)	*GPS receiver (66)*	*pop-up ad (62)*	*Wi-Fi (57)*
* e-commerce (77)*	*hashtag (72)*	*proxy server (62)*	*wireless modem (56)*
cable Internet service (57)	*bits (67)*	*pull (65)*	
cache (62)	*host (54)*	*real time (86)*	
ccTLD (60)	*hot spot (57)*	*RSS (65)*	
check in (69)	*http (64)*	*satellite Internet service (57)*	
cloud storage (65)	*ICANN (60)*	*search text (67)*	
consumer-to-consumer (C2C)	*infographic (80)*	*shopping cart (76)*	
* e-commerce (77)*	*Internet backbone (59)*	*static webpage (61)*	
contacts folder (85)	*JPEG (81)*	*status update (69)*	
content management system (79)	*keyloggers (74)*	*subject directory (68)*	
cyberbullying (90)	*like (69)*	*subscribe (86)*	
dial-up access (58)	*m-commerce (77)*	*tag (71)*	
DNS server (61)	*media player (82)*	*tethering (57)*	
domain name system (DNS) (61)	*media sharing site (70)*	*thread (87)*	
dongle (56)	*megabyte (MB) (58)*	*thumbnail (80)*	

infographic (80)

Checkpoint

The Checkpoint exercises test your knowledge of the chapter concepts. The page number containing the answer appears in parentheses after each exercise. The Consider This exercises challenge your understanding of chapter concepts.

Complete the Checkpoint exercises interactively by navigating to this book's Checkpoint resource on Computer Concepts CourseMate. **Access the Test Prep app** that runs on your smartphone, tablet, laptop, or desktop by navigating to this book's Apps resource on Computer Concepts CourseMate. After successfully completing the self-assessment through the Test Prep app, **take the Practice Test** by navigating to this book's Practice Test resource on Computer Concepts Coursemate.

True/False   Mark T for True and F for False.

_____ 1. No single person or government agency controls or owns the Internet. (56)

_____ 2. The W3C is responsible for maintaining all networks and content on the Internet. (56)

_____ 3. Users typically pay additional fees for mobile hot spot and tethering services. (58)

_____ 4. A gigabyte (GB) is the basic storage unit on a computer or mobile device and represents a single character. (58)

_____ 5. Visitors to a dynamic webpage can customize some or all of the viewed content, such as desired stock quotes, weather, or ticket availability for flights. (61)

_____ 6. Browsers usually are not included by default with mobile devices and smartphones. (63)

_____ 7. Mobile apps sometimes have fewer features than a web app. (66)

_____ 8. A subject directory is software that finds websites, webpages, images, videos, news, maps, and other information related to a specific topic. (67)

_____ 9. One technique you can use to improve search results is to use specific nouns. (68)

_____ 10. The term, blogosphere, refers to the worldwide collection of blogs. (72)

_____ 11. Unregistered wiki users can review the content, as well as edit it and add comments. (73)

_____ 12. Tethering is the process of transferring data in a continuous and even flow, which allows users to access and use a file while it is transmitting. (73)

Multiple Choice   Select the best answer.

1. A(n) _____ is any computer that provides services and connections to other computers on a network. (54)
   a. host
   b. client
   c. FTP site
   d. subject directory

2. _____ access takes place when a modem in a computer connects to the Internet via a standard telephone line that transmits data and information using an analog signal. (58)
   a. Wireless
   b. Broadband
   c. Dial-up
   d. Mobile

3. A(n) _____ is a sequence of numbers that uniquely identifies the location of each computer or device connected to the Internet. (59)
   a. Internet backbone
   b. domain name
   c. IP address
   d. ccTLD

4. You register a domain name through _____, which is an organization that sells and manages domain names. (60)
   a. a cybersquatter
   b. a registrar
   c. ICANN
   d. an ISP

5. One way to protect your identity while browsing is to use a(n) _____, which is another computer that screens all your incoming and outgoing messages. (62)
   a. password
   b. anonymous FTP
   c. phishing filter
   d. proxy server

6. _____ is a set of rules that defines how webpages transfer on the Internet. (64)
   a. Top-level domain
   b. Hypertext Transfer Protocol
   c. IPv4
   d. Web 2.0

7. A(n) _____ website contains factual information, such as libraries, encyclopedias, dictionaries, directories, guides, and other types of reference. (70)
   a. online social network
   b. media sharing
   c. business
   d. informational

8. A(n) _____, which consists of a number sign (#) followed by a keyword, describes and categorizes a Tweet. (72)
   a. hashtag
   b. microblog
   c. blog
   d. hit

Checkpoint

Matching   Match the terms with their definitions.

_____ 1. tethering (57)

_____ 2. Internet backbone (59)

_____ 3. domain name (60)

_____ 4. web server (61)

_____ 5. URL (64)

_____ 6. web feed (65)

_____ 7. plug-in (83)

_____ 8. chat (87)

_____ 9. cyberbullying (90)

_____ 10. social media (90)

a. text-based name that corresponds to the IP address of a server that hosts a website

b. program that extends the capability of a browser

c. harassment, often involving teens and preteens, using technology

d. websites and tools that foster communications and/or interactions among users, including online social networks, media sharing sites, blogs and microblogs, wikis, podcasts, and online gaming

e. technique that transforms a smartphone or Internet-capable tablet into a portable communications device that shares its Internet access with other computers and devices wirelessly

f. real-time typed conversation that takes place on a computer or mobile device with many other online users

g. computer that delivers requested webpages to your computer or mobile device

h. method of pulling content that has changed on a website

i. term used to refer to the major carriers of network traffic

j. a webpage's unique address

Short Answer   Write a brief answer to each of the following questions.

1. What is a cybersquatter? (60) What is the goal of the Anticybersquatting Consumer Protection Act (ACPA)? (60)

2. Define phishing. (62) What are some safe browsing techniques? (62)

3. Describe the different types of websites. (67) List some tips you can follow to protect yourself from privacy and security risks when using online social networks. (70)

4. List some tips to shop safely online. (76) Differentiate between e-commerce and m-commerce. (77–78)

5. What are some criteria you can use to evaluate a website or webpage before relying on its content? (78) List the steps in web publishing. (79)

✳ Consider This   Answer the following questions in the format specified by your instructor.

1. Answer the critical thinking questions posed at the end of these elements in this chapter: Ethics & Issues (60, 66, 80, 90), How To (77, 82, 84, 88), Mini Features (63, 69, 89), Secure IT (62, 70, 74, 76), and Technology @ Work (91).

2. What are the advantages of using a broadband Internet service? (56)

3. What is the relationship between domain names and IP addresses? (59)

4. Is cybersquatting ethical? Why or why not? (60)

5. How does Web 2.0 technology affect the way you interact with the Internet? (62)

6. What type of information is protected when you browse the web anonymously? (62)

7. What are the advantages and risks associated with allowing an app to track your location? (66)

8. Would you use a wiki as a resource when writing a research paper? Why or why not? (73)

9. Would you use a public computer to check email or do online banking? Why or why not? What are the risks? (74)

10. What information should you avoid using when answering a security question on a website? Why? (76)

11. 📖 Why is it important to have a LinkedIn account? (76)

12. What should you determine during the planning stage of a website? (79)

13. What is the purpose of website accessibility guidelines? (80)

14. What should you keep in mind when using email? (85)

15. 📖 How does a home user's use of digital communications differ from that of a power user? (89)

✹ How To: Your Turn

The How To: Your Turn exercises present general guidelines for fundamental skills when using a computer or mobile device and then require that you determine how to apply these general guidelines to a specific program or situation.

Instructions: You often can complete tasks using technology in multiple ways. Figure out how to perform the tasks described in these exercises by using one or more resources available to you (such as a computer or mobile device, articles on the web or in print, online or program help, user guides, blogs, podcasts, videos, other individuals, trial and error, etc.). Summarize your 'how to' steps, along with the resource(s) used, in the format requested by your instructor (brief report, presentation, discussion, blog post, video, or other means).

❶ Perform an Advanced Search

Performing an advanced search will help you locate desired search results more easily by filtering irrelevant content. The following steps guide you through the process of performing an advanced search using your browser.

a. Run your browser and then navigate to a search engine of your choice, such as google.com, bing.com, or yahoo.com.

b. Locate and then tap or click the link or button to perform an advanced search. You may have to perform a basic search before the link for an advanced search appears.

c. Enter as much information as possible on the advanced search form. Entering more information helps the search engine return more relevant results.

d. Tap or click the search (or similar) button to display the search results.

Source: Google Inc.

Exercises

1. Perform a basic search for a topic of your choice. Then, perform an advanced search for the same topic, but enter additional criteria on the advanced search form. How many results did the basic search return? How many results did the advanced search return? Are the advanced search results more relevant? Why or why not?

2. Which search engine did you use to perform your advanced search? Perform the same advanced search using a different search engine. After reviewing the search results, which search engine do you prefer? Why?

3. Will you use the advanced search feature more often? Why or why not?

❷ Create a Blog

Several websites are available that can assist you with setting up a blog for free or for a fee. The following steps guide you through the process of creating a blog.

a. Run your browser and then navigate to a search engine of your choice.

b. Perform a search for websites that allow you to create a free blog.

c. Review the search results and visit at least two websites that allow you to create a free blog.

d. After reviewing these websites, navigate to the website you want to use to create the blog.

e. Tap or click the button or link to sign up for a new account.

f. Follow the steps to sign up for a new account.

g. Once you have finished creating your account, configure the desired settings for your blog.

h. Tap or click the button or link to create a new post.

i. Specify a title for your post and then compose the post.

j. When you have finished creating your post, tap or click the button or link to save and publish the post.

k. Sign out of the blog website.

Source: Blog.com

Exercises

1. Summarize the process you used to sign up for an account on the blog website.

2. What topics will your blog discuss? What topics, if any, might not be appropriate for blogs?

3. Do you read other blogs on a regular basis? If so, which ones? If not, search the Internet for blogs that might interest you. Which ones did you find?

How To: Your Turn ✳

③ Determine Your IP (Internet Protocol) Address

Knowing a computer or mobile device's IP address can help you identify it on a network and can help you troubleshoot any problems you may experience connecting to the Internet or other computers and devices on your network. The following steps guide you through the process of determining your IP address.

a. Run your browser and then navigate to a search engine of your choice.

b. Search for a website that can determine your IP address and then navigate to one of these websites.

c. Your IP address should be displayed upon navigating to the website. If it does not, return to the search results and navigate to a different site.

or

a. Run your browser and then navigate to a search engine of your choice.

b. Search for a website that explains how to determine the IP address for your specific operating system and version (such as Windows 8, Mac OS X, iOS, or Android).

c. View the search results and then navigate to the website that provides you with the best guidance.

d. Follow the instructions on your computer or mobile device to determine the IP address.

Source: Microsoft Corporation

Exercises

1. Summarize the process you used to determine your IP address.
2. What is your IP address?
3. Is it possible for a computer to have more than one IP address at the same time? Why or why not?

④ Use an Online Auction

Online auctions allow consumers to bid on products that other people are selling. If you are the highest bidder at the end of the bidding period, you often can arrange payment through the online auction. The following steps guide you through the process of using an online auction.

WARNING: Do not purchase or bid on an item if you do not intend to purchase it. If you win the auction, you legally may be obligated to provide payment for the item.

a. Run your browser and then navigate to www.ebay.com.

b. Tap or click the link to register for a new account.

c. Enter the requested information to create the account.

d. Search for an item on which you would like to bid. If you want to browse items in a specific category instead, tap or click the link to browse for items by category.

e. When the search results appear, tap or click an item that interests you to see more details about the item.

f. Review the item details to determine whether you would like to bid on this item. If the item does not interest you, return to the search results and select another item.

g. The seller may have a "Buy It Now" option that allows you to purchase the item immediately at a predetermined price. Alternatively, you can bid on the item by making an offer. The highest bidder at the end of the auction will win the item. **Remember: if you bid on and win an item, you are obligated to provide payment.**

h. You will be notified if you are the winning bidder when the auction closes. At that time, follow the instructions to arrange to pay the seller.

i. When you are finished, sign out of eBay.

Exercises

1. What item(s) did you view? If the buyer had the "Buy It Now" option available, do you think the asking price was fair?
2. Would you purchase an item from an online auction? Why or why not?
3. What items might you post for sale on an online auction?

✹ Internet Research

The Internet Research exercises broaden your understanding of chapter concepts by requiring that you search for information on the web.

Instructions: Use a search engine or another search tool to locate the information requested or answers to questions presented in the exercises. Describe your findings, along with the search term(s) you used and your web source(s), in the format requested by your instructor (brief report, presentation, discussion, blog post, video, or other means).

① Making Use of the Web
Social Networks and Media Sharing

When Facebook recorded its one billionth user, the world took notice of this social networking site's milestone. Indeed, this service has experienced monumental growth since its inception in 2004. Other social networking sites, especially those featured in Mini Feature 2-2 on page 69, are some of the more popular among users of all ages. Likewise, media sharing sites, such as YouTube, which is shown in Figure 2-12 on page 70, are popular means of managing and sharing photos, videos, and music.

Visit two of the websites discussed in Mini Feature 2-2 or other social networking sites and create a profile if you do not currently have one. What personal information is required to join? Does either website ask for personal information that you are uncomfortable sharing? How does the content of these two websites differ? Which features are beneficial for casual users, and which are targeted toward business or professional users? Then, visit two social media sites. What personal information is required to join? Are these websites supported by advertisements? Locate the instructions for posting media. Are these instructions straightforward? Do these websites impose a limit on the number and/ or size of media files a user can post?

services. Unlike other commercial media, such as television, radio, and newspapers, advertisements generally are not used to fund the majority of operating costs, nor are users required to pay monthly or annual fees for basic services. One method that social media sites use to generate start-up and ongoing subsidies is through venture capitalists' funding. These investors scrutinize business plans and market trends in an effort to locate Internet start-up companies with the potential to generate substantial returns. Once the businesses are running, additional monies are needed to maintain and improve the websites. At this point, some websites display advertisements. The charge for companies to place an advertisement generally increases as the number of subscribers grows. Another method of generating income is to charge users for accessing premium content. Online dating services use this tactic successfully, for they allow people to browse online profiles free of charge but require them to pay to contact a potential dating match.

Locate venture capitalists who are seeking Internet start-up companies. Which criteria do they use to make investment decisions? Who are the successful venture capitalists, and which companies have they funded? Which types of ads are displayed on specific social media and social networking sites? How does the content of these ads pertain to the demographics and interests of users?

Source: Facebook

② Social Media

Most social media sites permit subscribers to create accounts and profiles at no cost. The companies have invested millions of dollars to develop and maintain the

③ Search Sleuth

(1) Who were the original developers of Skype, and how did they determine the name of their company? (2) Which partial word was the first message transmitted on ARPANET? (3) What is the cost of membership for a country to join the World Wide Consortium (W3C)? (4) In which city was the first public, commercial Internet café opened in the United States? In which year did this café open? What was the name of this cybercafé? (5) What was the first registered domain name? Which company registered this name? When was it registered? (6) What was the content of Twitter founder Jack Dorsey's first tweet? (7) Which browser first used the current web feed icon shown in Figure 2-9 on page 65 in this chapter?

Internet Research ☀

(8) Which U.S. president issued the first directive making GPS technology freely available for civilian use? Which branch of the U.S. military operates the GPS satellites orbiting the Earth? (9) Who is responsible for translating Twitter text into more than 20 languages so that it is available throughout the world? Which photo was retweeted the most in the history of Twitter? (10) What was eBay's original name, and what was the first item offered for auction?

4 Green Computing 📄

Employees' interest in working from home, or telecommuting, has steadily risen as apps, hardware, and increased broadband availability and speed have created more opportunities to take advantage of this perk. In one study, 83 percent of respondents claim to have worked at home, and 66 percent project their office will become completely virtual. They credit work-at-home tools such as Skype and other VoIP and collaboration software for helping them enjoy the benefits of telecommuting. They also would trade free meals, employer-paid mobile phone plans, paid vacation days, and a salary reduction in return for the benefit of working at home.

The environment also benefits in many ways when employers permit telecommuting. One major advantage is a reduction in the carbon footprint, or greenhouse gas emissions. Many websites offer tools to calculate individuals' carbon footprints, and a variety of apps measure CO_2 emissions and provide details about how to reduce this footprint.

Locate studies discussing employers' and employees' opinions of telecommuting. What are the advantages and challenges of working from home? Which companies are proponents of telecommuting? Which benefits would you relinquish in return for not commuting to the office at least part of a day? Visit some of the webpages or download at least two apps that allow you to calculate your ecological footprint. Which factors are used to determine your carbon footprint? What measures can you take to reduce greenhouse gas emissions?

5 Security

Secure IT 2-4 on page 76, which offers advice for shopping securely online, recommends creating a strong password and password questions. Despite suggestions and constant reminders from security experts to develop and then periodically change passwords, users continue to create weak passwords. These common passwords are broken easily and, therefore, never should be used. For many years, the most common password has been the word, password.

Locate at least two different company's lists of the 10 or 20 more common passwords in the past two years. Which passwords appear on both lists? Why do consumers continue to use these passwords despite repeated warnings to avoid them? Do you have accounts using one or more of these passwords? What advice is given for developing strong passwords, such as using the lyrics to the first line of a favorite song? How do the companies gather data to determine common passwords?

6 Ethics in Action

The conflict of Internet surveillance versus individuals' privacy rights has been raging for years. Major Internet and technology companies, including Microsoft, Google, eBay, Intel, and AT&T, are seeking to update the Electronic Communications Privacy Act (ECPA). The ECPA prohibits Internet service providers (ISPs) from releasing personal information, including names, addresses, phone numbers, and credit card account numbers, about their subscribers without a court order and protects the contents of files stored on individuals' personal computers.

With the advent of cloud storage and ubiquitous mobile phone usage since the ECPA was passed in 1986, prosecutors and the general public are at odds about whether police should be required to obtain a search warrant to retrieve an individual's email communications or to identify the location of a smartphone or mobile device. Some ISPs have monitored their users' bandwidth to monitor trafficking of copyrighted material. Some, however, have gone a step further by monitoring their users' website surfing activities without giving notice of this eavesdropping practice. Privacy experts claim these ISPs' practices violate the ECPA.

Should Congress enact laws requiring ISPs to formally track their customers' activities in an attempt to aid police investigating crimes, attorneys litigating divorce and insurance fraud cases, and the entertainment industry in locating illegally downloaded files? Should software companies such as Google, Yahoo!, and Facebook develop means for government surveillance of users? Do individuals have a privacy interest in their smartphones' locations? Should police be required to obtain a search warrant to read users' email?

Problem Solving

The Problem Solving exercises extend your knowledge of chapter concepts by seeking solutions to practical problems with technology that you may encounter at home, school, work, or with nonprofit organizations. The Collaboration exercise should be completed with a team.

Challenge yourself with additional Problem Solving exercises by navigating to this book's Problem Solving resource on Computer Concepts CourseMate.

Instructions: You often can solve problems with technology in multiple ways. Determine a solution to the problems in these exercises by using one or more resources available to you (such as a computer or mobile device, articles on the web or in print, blogs, podcasts, videos, television, user guides, other individuals, electronics or computer stores, etc.). Describe your solution, along with the resource(s) used, in the format requested by your instructor (brief report, presentation, discussion, blog post, video, or other means).

Personal

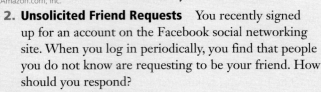

Source: Amazon.com, Inc.

1. **New Browser Windows**   While browsing the web, each time you tap or click a link, the link's destination opens in a new browser window. You prefer to have each link open in a new tab so that your taskbar does not become cluttered. How will you resolve this?

2. **Unsolicited Friend Requests**   You recently signed up for an account on the Facebook social networking site. When you log in periodically, you find that people you do not know are requesting to be your friend. How should you respond?

3. **Unexpected Search Engine**   A class project requires that you conduct research on the web. After typing the web address for Google's home page and pressing the ENTER key, your browser redirects you to a different search engine. What could be wrong?

4. **Images Do Not Appear**   When you navigate to a webpage, you notice that no images are appearing. You successfully have viewed webpages with images in the past and are not sure why images suddenly are not appearing. What steps will you take to show the images?

5. **Incorrect Home Page**   After running your browser, you notice that your home page has changed. You change your home page back to its previous setting, exit the browser, and then run the browser again. Surprisingly, your browser still navigates to a website other than the one you chose. What is your next step?

Professional

6. **Suspicious Website Visits**   The director of your company's information technology department sent you an email message stating that you have been spending an excessive amount of time viewing websites not related to your job. You periodically visit websites not related to work, but only on breaks, which the company allows. How does he know your web browsing habits? How will you respond to this claim?

7. **Automatic Response**   When you return from vacation, a colleague informs you that when she sent email messages to your email address, she would not always receive your automatic response stating that you were out of the office. Why might your email program not respond automatically to every email message received?

8. **Email Message Formatting**   A friend sent an email message containing a photo to your email account at work. Upon receiving the email message, the photo does not appear. You also notice that email messages never show any formatting, such as different fonts, font sizes, and font colors. What might be causing this?

9. **Sporadic Email Message Delivery**   The email program on your computer has been delivering new messages only every hour, on the hour. Historically, new email messages would arrive and be displayed immediately upon being sent by the sender. Furthermore, your coworkers claim that they sometimes do not receive your email messages until hours after they are sent. What might be the problem?

Collaboration

10. **Technology in Transportation**   Your project team has been accepted to present a business proposal to a group of potential investors. Because the presentation will take place in Kansas City, Missouri, you will need to transport people and ship some materials to that location. Form a team of three people and determine how to use technology to ship materials and how to make travel arrangements. One team member should research the steps required to use a website to make flight reservations, one team member should determine the steps necessary to print a package shipping label from his or her computer and track the package while it is en route, and another team member should find directions from Kansas City International Airport to a nearby hotel.

The Critical Thinking exercises challenge your assessment and decision-making skills by presenting real-world situations associated with chapter concepts. The Collaboration exercise should be completed with a team.

Critical Thinking ☀

 Challenge yourself with additional Critical Thinking exercises by navigating to this book's Critical Thinking resource on Computer Concepts CourseMate.

Instructions: Evaluate the situations below, using personal experiences and one or more resources available to you (such as articles on the web or in print, blogs, podcasts, videos, television, user guides, other individuals, electronics or computer stores, etc.). Perform the tasks requested in each exercise and share your deliverables in the format requested by your instructor (brief report, presentation, discussion, blog post, video, or other means).

1. Class Discussion

Source: Google Inc.

Mobile Browser Comparison   Although most mobile devices include a mobile browser, users have the option of downloading and installing other browsers. Evaluate and compare reviews of at least four mobile browsers, such as Opera, Android, Firefox, or Safari. Discuss the major differences among the browsers you researched, including number and types of features, for which devices they are available, how they display webpages, security features, and the speed at which they perform. Discuss any experiences you or your classmates have had with various browsers. Include in your discussion which mobile browser you would recommend and why.

2. Research and Share

Acceptable Use Policy   Most businesses provide Wi-Fi and Internet access to employees while they are at work. While the intention is for the Internet to be used for work-related purposes, employees often find it easy to become distracted with other activities on the Internet, such as social media, checking personal email, or visiting websites for entertainment. These activities can degrade Internet access for others or lead to poor performance, as well as expose the company to malware or other risks. Many businesses create an Acceptable Use Policy (AUP) that outlines how employees should use the Internet. It also may outline consequences for unauthorized Internet use. Locate two AUPs that are published online. Compare the two policies and then create a policy you believe would be fair to employees of a small business. Include guidelines for Internet use during breaks, use of smartphones, and restrictions for using social media. Compile your findings and then share them with the class.

3. Case Study

Farmers' Market   You are the new manager for a group of organic farmers who have a weekly market in season. The farmers' market needs a website. You prepare information about the website to present to the board of directors. First, you plan the website by determining its purpose and audience. Use a search engine to locate two farmers' market websites, and print their home pages. Identify what you like and do not like about each. Think about the design of the website for the farmers' market, and select the colors you would recommend. Describe the types of multimedia you would include on the webpage and give specific examples, such as a logo, photos or a slide show, or links to videos. Make a sketch of the home page layout, including navigation, multimedia, and text. Research content management systems. Evaluate whether you could use a preformatted template to meet your needs, and find what types of customization options are available. Determine whether you need a separate ISP for hosting the website, and calculate the costs. List ways you will maintain and update the site content. Compile your findings.

Collaboration

4. Website Evaluation

You and three teammates want to open a new chain of fast food sandwich shops. You envision a website that includes a menu, nutritional options, and allergy information, and that has regular promotions and special offers. With your teammates, evaluate existing fast food and sandwich websites by comparing the advantages and disadvantages of each. Assign each member the task of evaluating one chain. Team members should print the home page of the website to which they are assigned and evaluate their respective restaurants' websites, paying particular attention to the following areas: (1) design, (2) ease of use, (3) menu, (4) nutritional information, (5) allergy information, (6) special offers, (7) location information and directions, and (8) hours and contact information. Summarize your evaluations and rank the websites in terms of their effectiveness. Be sure to include brief explanations supporting your rankings.

✳ Beyond the Book

The Beyond the Book exercises expand your understanding of chapter concepts by requiring research.

🔲 **Access premium content** by visiting Computer Concepts CourseMate. If you have a Computer Concepts CourseMate access code, you can reinforce and extend your learning with MindTap Reader, practice tests, video, and other premium content for Discovering Computers. To sign in to Computer Concepts CourseMate at www.cengagebrain.com, you first must create a student account and then register this book, as described at www.cengage.com/ct/studentdownload.

Part 1 Instructions: Use the web or e-book to perform the task identified for each book element below. Describe your findings, along with the search term(s) you used and your web source(s), if appropriate, in the format requested by your instructor (brief report, presentation, discussion, blog post, video, or other means).

1. **Animations** 🔲   Review the animations associated with this chapter and then answer the questions they pose (77, 85). What search term would you use to learn more about a specific segment of each animation?

2. **Consider This**   Select a Consider This in this chapter (56, 58, 60, 64, 66, 68, 71, 72, 76, 78, 81, 85, 90) and find a recent article that elaborates on the topic. What information did you find that was not presented in this book or e-book?

3. **Drag-and-Drop Figures** 🔲   Complete the Drag-and-Drop Figure activities associated with this chapter (57, 59, 61, 65, 68, 81). What did you learn from each of these activities?

4. **Ethics & Issues**   Select an Ethics & Issues in this chapter (60, 66, 80, 90) and find a recent article that supports one view presented. Does the article change your opinion about the topic? Why or why not?

5. **Facebook & Twitter**   Review a recent Discovering Computers Facebook post or Twitter Tweet and read the referenced article(s). What did you learn from the article?

6. **High-Tech Talk** 🔲   Locate an article that discusses topics related to the IPv6 addressing scheme. Would you recommend the article you found? Why or why not?

7. **How To**   Select a How To in this chapter (77, 82, 84, 88) and find a recent article that elaborates on the topic. Who would benefit from the content of this article? Why?

8. **Innovative Computing** 🔲   Locate two additional facts about Internet2 or Pinterest and Delicious. Do your findings change your opinion about the future of this innovation? Why or why not?

9. **Internet Research**   Use the search term in an Internet Research (56, 57, 58, 62, 66, 67, 73, 82, 83) to answer the question posed in the element. What other search term could you use to answer the question?

10. **Mini Features**   Locate an article that discusses topics related to one of the mini features in this chapter (63, 69, 89). Do you feel that the article is appropriate for this course? Why or why not?

11. **Secure IT**   Select a Secure IT in this chapter (62, 70, 74, 76) and find a recent article about the topic that you find interesting. How can you relate the content of the article to your everyday life?

12. **Technology @ Work**   Locate three additional, unique usages of technology in the transportation industry (91). What makes the use of these technologies unique to the transportation industry?

13. **Technology Innovators** 🔲   Locate two additional facts about Tim Berners-Lee, Google, Yahoo!, and LinkedIn. Which Technology Innovator impresses you most? Why?

14. **Third-Party Links** 🔲   Visit one of the third-party links identified in this chapter (60, 61, 62, 66, 67, 70, 74, 76, 77, 91) and read the article or watch the video associated with the link. Would you share this link on your online social network account? Why or why not?

Part 2 Instructions: Find specific instructions for the exercises below in the e-book or on Computer Concepts CourseMate. Beside each exercise is a brief description of its online content.

1. 🔲 **You Review It**   Search for and review a video, podcast, or blog post about popular social media sites.

2. 🔲 **Windows and Mac**   Enhance your understanding and knowledge about using Windows and Mac computers by completing the Configure Your Browser and Find Your IP Address activities.

3. 🔲 **Android, iOS, and Windows Mobile**   Enhance your understanding of mobile devices by completing the Manage Airplane Mode, Configure Your Mobile Browser, and View Data Usage activities.

4. 🔲 **Exploring Computer Careers**   Read about a career as a web designer, search for related employment ads, and then answer related questions.

5. 🔲 **App Adventure**   Configure, read, send, and manage email using an app on your smartphone or tablet.

Computers and Mobile Devices

Evaluating the Possibilities

3

People use or interact with a variety of computers and mobile devices every day.

"I use desktops at work and my laptop at home and school. I send messages and access the Internet on my smartphone, take photos with my digital camera, and read books on my e-book reader. What more do I need to know about computers and mobile devices?"

True, you may be familiar with some of the material in this chapter, but do you know . . .

Whether you can be photographed in public without your knowledge?

How to protect devices from malware infections?

How a digital camera converts a photographed image to a digital signal?

How to connect your phone to a Wi-Fi network to save data charges?

How to identify a DVI or an HDMI port?

Which news, sports, and weather apps are best suited to your needs?

What to consider when purchasing a desktop, mobile computer, or mobile device?

How a touch screen recognizes taps and other gestures?

How you can minimize your risk of technology-related tendonitis or carpal tunnel syndrome?

How the meteorology field uses computers, mobile devices, and related technologies?

What NFC is, and when you might use it?

Which company's digital camera face recognition technology originally was developed for its toy robots?

How you can contribute to scientific research using your home or office computer?

What measures you can take to keep your computers and mobile devices from overheating?

For these answers and to discover much more information essential to this course, read this chapter and visit the associated Computer Concepts CourseMate at www.cengagebrain.com.

© Dragon Images / Shutterstock.com

✔ Objectives

After completing this chapter, you will be able to:

1 Describe the characteristics and uses of desktops, laptops, tablets, and handheld computers
2 Describe the characteristics and types of servers
3 Differentiate among POS terminals, ATMs, and self-service kiosks
4 Describe cloud computing and identify its uses
5 Describe the characteristics and uses of smartphones, digital cameras, portable media players, and e-book readers
6 Describe the characteristics of and ways to interact with game devices, including gamepads, joysticks and wheels, dance pads, and motion-sensing controllers
7 Identify uses of embedded computers
8 Differentiate a port from a connector, identify various ports and connectors, and differentiate among Bluetooth, Wi-Fi, and NFC wireless device connections
9 Identify safeguards against hardware theft and vandalism and hardware failure
10 Discuss ways to prevent health-related injuries and disorders caused from technology use, and describe ways to design a workplace ergonomically

Computers and Mobile Devices

 BTW
Peripheral Devices
A *peripheral device* is a device you connect to a computer or mobile device to expand its capabilities. Examples include a keyboard, mouse, microphone, monitor, printer, scanner, webcam, and speakers.

As Chapter 1 discussed, a **computer** is an electronic device, operating under the control of instructions stored in its own memory, that can accept data (input), process the data according to specified rules, produce information (output), and store the information for future use. A **mobile device** is a computing device small enough to hold in your hand. Types of computers and mobiles devices include desktop and mobile computers; servers and terminals; smartphones, digital cameras, e-book readers, and portable media players; game devices; and embedded computers. Figure 3-1 shows a variety of people using computers and mobile devices.

In addition to discussing features, functions, and purchasing guidelines of computers and mobile devices, this chapter also presents ways to connect peripheral devices, protect computers and mobile devices from theft and failure, and minimize your health risks while using computers and mobile devices.

Desktops and Mobile Computers

A **personal computer** (PC) is a computer that can perform all of its input, processing, output, and storage activities by itself and is intended to be used by one person at a time. Personal computers often are differentiated by the type of operating system they use, with Windows and Mac personal computers leading the market share. Companies such as Dell, Lenovo, and HP (Hewlett-Packard) sell personal computers that use the Windows operating system, and Apple sells personal computers that use the Mac operating system.

Types of personal computers include desktops, laptops, and tablets, and the latter two also are considered mobile computers. A *mobile computer* is a portable personal computer, designed so that a user easily can carry it from place to place.

Read Secure IT 3-1 on page 106 for suggestions about how to avoid malware infections on your computers and mobile devices.

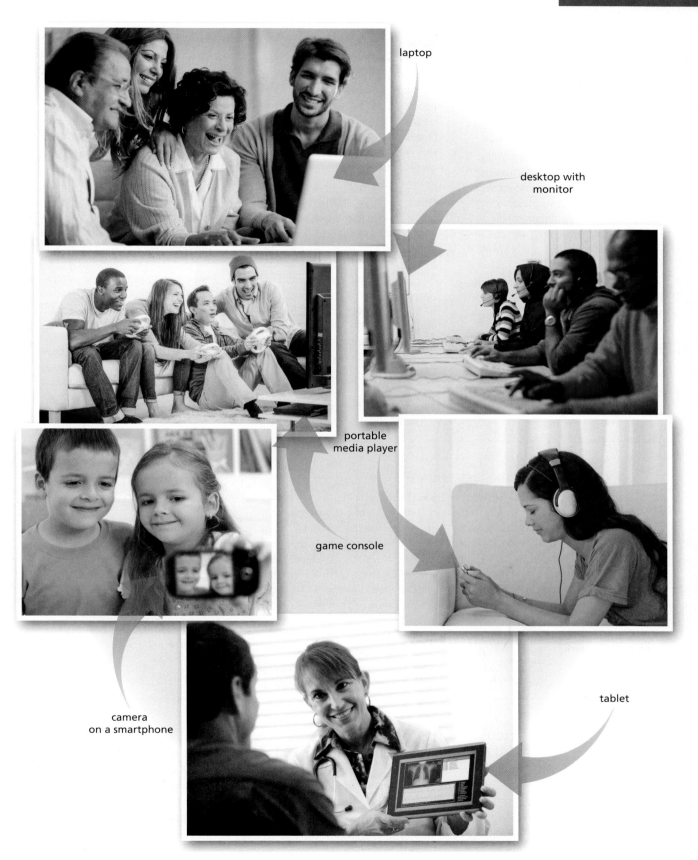

Figure 3-1 People use a variety of computers and mobile devices at home, at work, and at school.
© iStockphoto / kristian sekulic; © iStockphoto / ranplett; © Diego Cervo / Shutterstock.com; © Ilike / Shutterstock.com; © wavebreakmedia / Shutterstock.com; © iStockphoto / sjlocke

SECURE IT 3-1

Avoid Malware Infections

Some websites contain tempting offers to download free games and music, enter contests, and receive coupons on your computers or mobile devices. Danger, however, may lurk in those files, for they secretly could install malware with effects ranging from a mild annoyance to a severe problem such as identity theft. Recall that malware is malicious software that acts without your knowledge and deliberately alters operations of your computer or mobile device. As a general rule, do not install or download unfamiliar software. Follow these guidelines to minimize the chance of your computer or mobile device becoming infected with malware:

- **Websites:** Websites you visit or pop-up windows may present instructions to download new software or update current programs installed on a computer or mobile device. If you are uncertain of their legitimacy, exit and research the software by reading reviews online before you decide to install it.

- **Social media:** Malware authors often focus on social media, with the goal of stealing personal information, such as passwords, profiles, contact lists, and credit card account details. Their websites urge unsuspecting users to take surveys, click links to obtain free merchandise and games, and download antivirus programs. Ignore these deceitful tactics.

- **Email:** Spam (unsolicited email messages) can be loaded with malware, but even email messages from friends can be a culprit. If the message does not contain a subject line or contains links or an attachment, exercise caution. One option is to save the attachment to your computer so that antivirus software can scan the file for possible malware before you open it. Your best practice is to avoid opening suspicious messages at all costs.

- **Flash memory storage:** Colleagues and friends may hand you a USB flash drive or memory card with software, photos, and other files. Scan these media with security software before opening any files.

- **Pop-up windows:** At times, a window may open suddenly (called a pop-up window), with a warning that your computer is infected with a virus or that a security breach has occurred, and then make an urgent request to download free software to scan your computer and correct the alleged problem. Beware. Many of these offers actually are rogue security software that will infect a computer.

- **Software:** Occasionally, some seemingly safe software attempts to install malware. Read the dialog boxes that are displayed on your screen before tapping or clicking the OK or Agree buttons. If you are uncertain, cancel the installation. If possible, update software directly from manufacturers' websites.

⚹ What online activities might cause malware to be installed on your computer? What new techniques will you use to avoid malware?

 CONSIDER THIS

What is inside a personal computer?

The electronic components and circuitry of a personal computer usually are part of or are connected to a motherboard (Figure 3-2). A *motherboard*, sometimes called a system board, is the main circuit board of the personal computer. Many electronic components attach to the motherboard; others are built into it. Two main components on the motherboard are the processor and memory. Many motherboards also integrate sound, video, and networking capabilities.

 Internet Research

What is a computer chip?
Search for: computer chip

A *processor,* also called a *CPU* (central processing unit), is the electronic component that interprets and carries out the basic instructions that operate a computer. *Memory* consists of electronic components that store instructions waiting to be executed and data needed by those instructions.

motherboard

Figure 3-2 Shown here is the motherboard in a laptop.
© Raw Group / Shutterstock.com

Desktops

 BTW

Dell
Technology Innovator: You should be familiar with Dell and its founder, Michael Dell.

A **desktop**, or desktop computer, is a personal computer designed to be in a stationary location, where all of its components fit on or under a desk or table (Figure 3-3). Components include input devices such as a keyboard, mouse, and webcam; output devices such as a monitor, speakers, and printer; storage devices such as a hard disk drive and optical disc drive; system unit; and possibly a communications device(s) such as a modem, network card, or router.

Some people use the term, *system unit*, to refer to the case that contains and protects the motherboard, hard disk drive, memory, and other electronic components of the computer from damage. Many desktops have a system unit tower that is a separate device from a monitor. A *tower*, which is made of metal or plastic, is a frame that houses the system unit on a desktop.

Figure 3-3 The desktop with a tower shown in this figure is a Windows computer, and the all-in-one desktop is a Mac computer.
© George Dolgikh / Shutterstock.com;
© iStockphoto / Skip Odonnell;
© iStockphoto / Evgeny Kuklev;
© Cengage Learning

Towers are available in a variety of form factors, or shapes and sizes. Although they can range in height from 12 inches to 30 inches or more, the trend is toward smaller desktop tower form factors. Some desktops, called an *all-in-one desktop*, do not have a tower and instead house the screen and system unit in the same case. Many peripheral devices, such as keyboard, mouse, printer, speakers, and external hard disk, often occupy space outside a system unit.

BTW
Monitor Speakers
Many monitors have integrated speakers.

✵ CONSIDER THIS

Who uses desktops?
Home and business users who do not require the portability of a mobile computer may work with desktops for their everyday computing needs. Gaming enthusiasts often choose a *gaming desktop*, which offers high-quality audio, video, and graphics with optimal performance for sophisticated single-user and networked or Internet multiplayer games. Power users may work with a high-end desktop, sometimes called a *workstation*, that is designed to handle intense calculations and sophisticated graphics. For example, architects use powerful desktops to design buildings and homes, and graphic artists use them to create computer-animated special effects for full-length motion pictures and video games. Some users configure a desktop to function as a server on a network (servers are discussed later in this chapter).

Internet Research
Which movies use computer animation?
Search for: movies using computer animation

✵ MINI FEATURE 3-1

Desktop Computer Buyer's Guide

Desktops are a suitable option if you work mostly in one place and have plenty of space in a work area. Today, desktop manufacturers emphasize desktop style by offering bright colors, trendy displays, and theme-based towers so that the computer looks attractive if it is in an area of high visibility. If you have decided that a desktop is most suited to your technology needs, the next step is to determine specific software, hardware, peripheral devices, and services to purchase, as well as where to buy the computer. The following considerations will help you determine the appropriate desktop to purchase.

1. Determine the specific software to use on the desktop. Decide which software contains the features necessary for the tasks you want to perform. Your hardware requirements depend on the minimum requirements of the software you plan to use on the desktop.

2. Know the system requirements of the operating system. Determine the operating system you want to use because this also dictates hardware requirements. If, however, you purchase a new desktop, chances are it will have the latest version of your preferred operating system (Windows, Mac OS, or Linux).

3. Look for bundled software. Purchasing software at the same time you purchase a desktop may be less expensive than purchasing the software

continued on next page

continued from previous page

at a later date. At the very least, you probably will want word processing software and an antivirus program.

4. **Avoid purchasing the least powerful desktop available.** Computer technology changes rapidly, which means a desktop that seems powerful enough today may not serve your computing needs in the future. Purchasing a desktop with the most memory, largest hard disk, and fastest processor you can afford will help delay obsolescence.

5. **Consider upgrades to the keyboard, mouse, monitor, printer, microphone, and speakers.** You use these peripheral devices to interact with the desktop, so make sure they meet your standards.

6. **Consider a touch screen monitor.** A touch screen monitor will enable you to interact with the latest operating systems and apps using touch input.

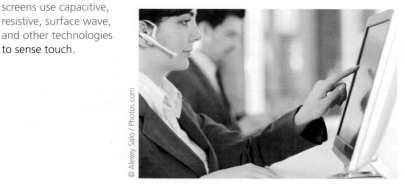

7. **Evaluate all-in-one desktops.** All-in-one desktops may be less expensive than purchasing a system unit and monitor separately. In addition, all-in-one desktops take up less space and often look more attractive than desktops with separate towers.

8. **If you are buying a new desktop, you have several purchasing options:** buy directly from a school bookstore, a local computer dealer, or a large retail store, or order from a vendor by mail, phone, or the web. Each purchasing option has its advantages. Explore each option to find the best combination of price and service.

9. **Be aware of hidden costs.** Along with the desktop itself, you also may need to make additional purchases. For example, you might purchase computer furniture, an uninterruptable power supply (UPS) or surge protector (discussed later in the chapter), an external hard disk, a printer, a router, a USB flash drive, or computer training classes.

10. **Consider purchasing an extended warranty or service plan.** If you use your computer for business or require fast resolution to major computer problems, consider purchasing an extended warranty or a service plan through a local dealer or third-party company. Most extended warranties cover the repair and replacement of computer components beyond the standard warranty.

⚘ Shop around for a desktop that meets your current needs. Which desktop would you purchase? Why?

BTW
Touch Screen Technology
High-Tech Talk: Touch screens use capacitive, resistive, surface wave, and other technologies to sense touch.

Laptops and Tablets

A **laptop**, also called a *notebook computer*, is a thin, lightweight mobile computer with a screen in its lid and a keyboard in its base (Figure 3-4). Designed to fit on your lap and for easy transport, laptops weigh up to 10 pounds (varying by manufacturer and specifications) and can be as powerful as the average desktop. Like desktops, laptops have input devices such as a keyboard, touchpad, and webcam; output devices such as a screen and speakers; a storage device(s) such as a hard disk and maybe an optical disc drive; and usually built-in wireless communications capability. Some laptops have touch screens. Most can operate on batteries or a power supply or both. Read Ethics & Issues 3-1 to consider issues related to laptops and other devices with cameras.

Figure 3-4 Traditional laptops weigh more than ultrathin laptops.
© Sergey Peterman / Shutterstock.com; © iStockphoto / Skip Odonnell

traditional laptop

ultrathin laptop

Netbooks and ultrathin laptops weigh less than traditional laptops, usually have a longer battery life, and do not include an optical disc drive. The difference is that a netbook focuses on affordability, while an ultrathin laptop focuses on power, speed, and durability. While netbooks are adequate for everyday computing tasks, you would want to use an ultrathin laptop to complete processor-intensive tasks, such as editing videos, working with complex software, or playing games.

Usually smaller than a laptop but larger than a smartphone, a **tablet** is a thin, lightweight mobile computer that has a touch screen. Two popular form factors of the tablet, or Tablet PC, are the slate and convertible (Figure 3-5). Resembling a letter-sized pad, a *slate tablet* is a type of tablet that does not contain a physical keyboard. A *convertible tablet* is a tablet that has a screen it its lid and a keyboard in its base, with the lid and base connected by a swivel-type hinge. You can use a convertible tablet like a traditional laptop, or you can rotate the display and fold it down over the keyboard so that it looks like a slate tablet. As with laptops, tablets run on batteries or a power supply or both; however, batteries in a tablet typically last longer than those in laptops.

Some tablets include a *stylus*, which looks like a small ink pen, that you can use instead of a fingertip to enter data, make selections, or draw on a touch screen. A stylus may include buttons you can press to simulate clicking a mouse. As an alternative to interacting with the touch screen, some users prefer to purchase a separate physical keyboard that attaches to or wirelessly communicates with the tablet.

Tablets are useful especially for taking notes in lectures, at meetings, at conferences, and in other forums where the standard laptop is not practical. Because slate tablets can have a more durable construction, they often are used in the medical field and other areas where exposure to heat, humidity, and dust is greater.

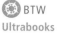
BTW
Ultrabooks
An ultrathin laptop that uses the Windows operating system often is called an *ultrabook*.

BTW
Pens
Some tablet manufacturers refer to a stylus as a pen.

slate tablet in stand

convertible tablet

Figure 3-5 Examples of slate and convertible tablets.
© iStockphoto / Pedro Castellano;
Courtesy of Lenovo

✳ ETHICS & ISSUES 3-1

What Punishment for Webcam Spying Is Appropriate?

While webcams and other cameras have many practical and harmless uses, they can also be used for spying. For example, a school district used software, which was supposed to track the school-distributed laptops in case of theft, to take 66,000 photos and screen captures of students. Wiretapping laws in general do not cover these types of acts. New Jersey was one of the first states to rule that secretly recording and broadcasting people without their permission is a crime. Previously, people could bring civil charges against the person who recorded them, but could not press criminal charges. Lawmakers continue to debate and expand current laws, as well as pass new ones.

While you assume that your at-home activities will remain private, this technology also allows people to take photos or videos in a public setting and broadcast them without your knowledge. A director at the American Civil Liberties Union stated that when you are in a public place, people have the right to photograph you. Privacy advocates criticize the Google Street View feature, however, which takes images captured using moving vehicles equipped with GPS and cameras, and then creates a panoramic view of an area, including people entering and exiting buildings or relaxing on a beach.

Should webcam spying be comparable to other types of spying? Why or why not? What kind of privacy should you expect when you are in a public place?

CONSIDER THIS

What is a phablet?
Some people use the term, *phablet*, to refer to a device that combines features of a smartphone with a tablet (Figure 3-6). These devices are larger than smartphones but smaller than full-sized tablets. The screen on a phablet usually measures five to seven inches diagonally. Some include a stylus.

Figure 3-6 A phablet combines features of a smartphone and a tablet.
© Iain Masterton / Alamy

 MINI FEATURE 3-2

Mobile Computer Buyer's Guide

If you need computing capability while traveling and during lectures or meetings, you may find a laptop or tablet to be an appropriate choice. With the abundance of mobile computer manufacturers, research each before making a purchase. The following are purchasing considerations unique to mobile computers.

1. Determine which mobile computer form factor fits your needs. Consider a tablet or netbook if you primarily will use the device to access the Internet and email. If you will use the computer to create and edit documents, work on spreadsheets, play graphic intensive games, or use other software that requires greater processing power, consider purchasing a traditional or ultrathin laptop.

2. Consider a mobile computer with a sufficiently large screen. Laptops and tablets are available with various screen sizes. For example, most traditional and ultrathin laptop screens range in size from 11 to 18 inches, while most tablet and netbook screens range in size from 7 to 10 inches.

3. Experiment with different keyboards and pointing devices. Mobile computers often vary in size, and for that reason have different keyboard layouts. Familiarize yourself with the keyboard layout of the computer you want to purchase, and make sure it is right for you. If you have large fingers, for example, you should not purchase a computer with a small, condensed keyboard. Laptops typically include a touchpad to control the pointer. Tablets have a touch screen and an on-screen keyboard.

4. Consider processor, memory, and storage upgrades at the time of purchase. As with a desktop, upgrading a mobile computer's memory and disk storage may be less expensive at the time of initial purchase.

Some disk storage is custom designed for mobile computer manufacturers, meaning an upgrade might not be available in the future.

5. The availability of built-in ports and slots is important. Determine which ports and slots (discussed later in this chapter) you require on the mobile computer. If you plan to transfer photos from a digital camera using a memory card, consider a mobile computer with a built-in card slot compatible with your digital camera's memory card. If you plan to connect devices such as a printer or USB flash drive to your mobile computer, consider purchasing one with one or more USB ports. In addition, evaluate mobile computers with ports enabling you to connect an external monitor.

© iStockphoto / Rüstem GÜRLER

ports and slots

6. If you plan to use your mobile computer for a long time without access to an electrical outlet, or if the battery life for the mobile computer you want to purchase is not sufficient, consider purchasing a second battery. Some mobile computers, such as most tablets, have built-in batteries that can be replaced only by a qualified technician. In that case, you might look into options for external battery packs or power sources.

7. Purchase a well-padded and well-designed carrying case. An amply padded carrying case will protect your mobile computer from the bumps it will receive while traveling. A well-designed carrying case will have room for accessories such as USB flash drives, pens, and paperwork. Although a mobile computer may be small enough to fit in a handbag, make sure that the bag has sufficient padding to protect the computer.

8. If you plan to connect your mobile computer to a video projector, make sure the mobile computer is compatible with the video projector. You should check, for example, to be sure that your mobile computer will allow you to display an image on the screen and projection device at the same time. Also, ensure that the mobile computer has the ports required or that you have the necessary dongle and cables to connect to the video projector.

⚛ Based on your current computing needs, should you purchase a traditional laptop, ultrathin laptop, netbook, or tablet? What are the specifications of the mobile computer you would purchase?

Handheld Computers

A **handheld computer** is a computer small enough to fit in one hand. Many handheld computers communicate wirelessly with other devices or computers. Some handheld computers have miniature or specialized keyboards. Others have a touch screen and also include a stylus for input.

Many handheld computers are industry-specific and serve the needs of mobile employees, such as parcel delivery people or warehouse employees (Figure 3-7), whose jobs require them to move from place to place. Handheld computers often send data wirelessly to central office computers.

Figure 3-7   This handheld computer is a lightweight computer that enables warehouse employees to take inventory and check supplies.
© iStockphoto / Ermin Gutenberger

Servers

A **server** is a computer dedicated to providing one or more services to other computers or devices on a network. Services provided by servers include storing content and controlling access to hardware, software, and other resources on a network. In many cases, a server accesses data, information, and programs on another server. In other cases, personal computers, devices, or terminals (discussed later in this chapter) access data, information, and programs on a server. Servers can support from two to several thousand connected computers or devices at the same time.

Some servers, called dedicated servers, perform a specific service and can be placed with other dedicated servers to perform multiple services (Table 3-1). Each type of dedicated server uses

Table 3-1   Dedicated Servers

Type	Main Service Provided
Application server	Stores and runs apps
Backup server	Backs up and restores files, folders, and media
Database server	Stores and provides access to a database
Domain name server	Stores domain names and their corresponding IP addresses
File server (or storage server)	Stores and manages files
FTP server	Stores files for user upload or download via FTP
Game server	Provides a central location for online game play
Home server	Provides storage, Internet connections, or other services to computers and devices in a household
List server	Stores and manages email lists
Mail server	Stores and delivers email messages
Network server	Manages network traffic
Print server	Manages printers and documents being printed
Web server	Stores and delivers requested webpages to a computer via a browser

© Cengage Learning

rack server blade server

rack tower server blade server chassis

 Figure 3-8 Shown here are a rack server, blade server, and tower server.
© iStockphoto / Godfried Edelman; © iStockphoto / luismmolina; © iStockphoto / evirgen; © iStockphoto / Alexander Shirokov; © iStockphoto / luismmolina

software designed specifically to manage its service. Dedicated servers typically require a faster processor, more memory, and additional storage.

Servers include a processor, memory, storage, and network connections. Depending on its function, a server may not require a monitor or input device. Some are controlled remotely. Form factors for servers include rack server, blade server, and tower server (Figure 3-8):

- A *rack server*, sometimes called a rack-mounted server, is a server that is housed in a slot (bay) on a metal frame (rack). A rack can contain multiple servers, each in a different bay. The rack is fastened in place to a flat surface.
- A *blade server* is a server in the form of a single circuit board, or blade. The individual blades insert in a blade server chassis that can hold many blades. Like a rack server, the chassis is fastened in place to a flat surface.
- A *tower server* is a server built into an upright cabinet (tower) that stands alone. The tower can be similar in size and shape to a desktop tower or larger.

✹ **CONSIDER THIS**

Which server should you use?
Home or small business users and organizations with ample floor space often choose tower servers. (Some home users even use a desktop tower or powerful laptop to act as a home server.) Data centers and other organizations looking to conserve floor space often choose rack servers or blade servers. Organizations that require a large quantity of servers usually opt for blade servers.

Figure 3-9 Server farms and mainframes can handle thousands of connected computers and process millions of instructions per second.
© Sashkin / Shutterstock.com

Some organizations use virtualization to improve utilization of technology. *Virtualization* is the practice of sharing or pooling computing resources, such as servers and storage devices. *Server virtualization* uses software to divide a physical server logically into many virtual servers. That is, virtual servers use software to configure and emulate physical servers. From the end user's point of view, a virtual server behaves just like a physical server. The advantages are that a virtual server can be created and configured quickly, does not require a new physical server, and is easier to manage. Cloud computing, discussed later in this chapter, uses server virtualization.

Major corporations use server farms, mainframes, or other types of servers for business activities to process everyday transactions (Figure 3-9). A *server farm* is a network of several servers together in a single location. Server farms make it possible to combine the power of multiple servers. A *mainframe* is a large, expensive, powerful server that can handle hundreds or thousands of connected users simultaneously. Enterprises use server farms, mainframes, or other large servers to bill millions of customers, prepare payroll for thousands of employees, and manage millions of items in inventory.

Supercomputers

A *supercomputer* is the fastest, most powerful computer — and the most expensive (Figure 3-10). Supercomputers are capable of processing many trillions of instructions in a single second. With weights that exceed 100 tons, these computers can store more than 20,000 times the data and information of an average desktop.

Applications requiring complex, sophisticated mathematical calculations use supercomputers. For example, large-scale simulations and applications in medicine, aerospace, automotive design, online banking, weather forecasting, nuclear energy research, and petroleum exploration use a supercomputer.

Figure 3-10   Supercomputers can process more than one quadrillion instructions in a single second.
Los Alamos National Laboratory

Terminals

A *terminal* is a computer, usually with limited processing power, that enables users to send data to and/or receive information from a server, or host computer. The host computer processes the data and then, if necessary, sends information (output) back to the terminal. Terminals may include a monitor and/or touch screen, keyboard, and memory.

A *thin client* is a terminal that looks like a desktop but has limited capabilities and components. Because thin clients typically do not contain a hard disk, they run programs and access data on a network or the Internet. Public locations, such as libraries and schools, and enterprises sometimes use thin clients because they cost less, are easier to maintain, last longer, use less power, and are less susceptible to malware attacks than desktops.

Special-purpose terminals perform specific tasks and contain features uniquely designed for use in a particular industry. Three widely used special-purpose terminals are point-of-sale terminals, ATMs, and self-service kiosks.

Point-of-Sale Terminals

The location in a retail or grocery store where a consumer pays for goods or services is the point of sale (POS). Most retail stores use a *POS terminal* to record purchases, process credit or debit cards, and update inventory.

In a grocery store, the POS terminal is a combination of an electronic cash register, bar code reader, and printer (Figure 3-11). A *bar code reader* is an input device that uses laser beams to read bar codes on products. When the checkout clerk or customer scans the bar code on the grocery item, the computer uses the manufacturer name and item numbers to look up the price of the item and the complete product name. Then, the price of the item shows on the display device, the name of the item and its price print on a receipt, and the item being sold is recorded so that the inventory can be updated. Thus, the output from a POS terminal serves as input to other computers to maintain sales records, update inventory, verify credit, and perform other activities associated with the sales transactions that are critical to running the business. Some POS terminals are Internet capable, which allows updates to inventory at geographically separate locations.

touch screen

204

bar code reader scans bar code on item being purchased

Figure 3-11   Many grocery stores offer self-service checkouts, where consumers use POS terminals to scan purchases, scan their store or saver card and coupons, and then pay for the goods.
© Dennis Macdonald / Getty Images

card reader

Figure 3-12 An ATM is a self-service banking terminal that allows customers to access their bank accounts.
© AlikeYou / Shutterstock.com

Many POS terminals handle credit card or debit card payments. After swiping your card through the reader, the POS terminal connects to a system that authenticates the purchase. Once the transaction is approved, the terminal prints a receipt for the customer.

ATMs

An *ATM* (automated teller machine) is a self-service banking terminal that connects to a host computer through a network (Figure 3-12). Banks place ATMs in public locations, including grocery stores, convenience stores, retail outlets, shopping malls, sports and concert venues, and gas stations, so that customers can access their bank accounts conveniently.

Using an ATM, people withdraw cash, deposit money, transfer funds, or inquire about an account balance. Some ATMs have a touch screen; others have special buttons or keypads for entering data. To access a bank account, you insert a plastic bank card in the ATM's card reader. The ATM asks you to enter a numeric password, called a *PIN* (personal identification number), which verifies that you are the holder of the bank card. When your transaction is complete, the ATM prints a receipt for your records. Read Secure IT 3-2 for ATM safety tips.

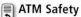 **SECURE IT 3-2**

ATM Safety

Visiting an ATM to withdraw or deposit money is convenient, but it also is riddled with potential for criminal activity. Avoid being a victim by exercising common sense and following these guidelines.

- **Location:** Choose an ATM in a well-lit public area away from bushes and dividers and near the center of a building. If using a drive-up ATM, keep the engine running and doors locked, roll windows up while waiting for the ATM to process your request, and leave adequate room to maneuver between your vehicle and the one in the lane in front of you. Observe your surroundings and be suspicious of people sitting in vehicles or loitering nearby.

- **ATM card and PIN:** Handle the ATM card like cash by keeping it in a safe location and storing it in a protective sleeve. Do not write the PIN on the back of the card; instead, memorize the numbers. Report a lost or stolen card immediately.

- **Transaction:** Minimize time by having the ATM card ready as you approach the machine. Do not allow people to watch your activity. Cover the keypad or screen with

one hand as you enter the PIN, and use your body to block as much of the area as possible. If the ATM screen appears different, behaves unusually, or offers options with which you are unfamiliar or uncomfortable, cancel the transaction and leave the area.

- **Be suspicious of skimmers:** Thieves can capture a credit card number and PIN by placing a *skimmer* on an ATM (shown in the figure to the right). A sophisticated skimmer is an entire panel placed directly on top of the ATM face and virtually is undetectable, but less-technical devices are false card readers secured to the card slot with double-sided tape and a hidden camera or an overlay on the keypad.

- **Valuables:** Expensive clothes and jewelry can be incentives to potential assailants. Dress modestly and leave jewels at home.

- **Exiting:** Do not count cash in public; immediately put it in your pocket or fold it in your hand. If you receive a receipt, take it with you and do not discard it in a trash can near the area. As you leave, be certain you are not being followed. If you suspect

skimmer

© Jochen Tack / Alamy

someone is tracking you, immediately walk to a crowded location or business, or drive to a police or fire station.

- **Statements:** Review your balances and bank statements frequently. Be certain all deposits and withdrawals are listed, and look for unusual or unfamiliar activity.

✳ Which of these tips do you follow, and how will you change your behavior the next time you visit an ATM? Which ATMs in your neighborhood appear to be in safe locations?

Self-Service Kiosks

A self-service *kiosk* is a freestanding terminal that usually has a touch screen for user interaction. Table 3-2 identifies several widely used self-service kiosks. Because users interact with self-service kiosks independently, without a salesperson nearby, it is important the kiosk is simple and easy to use.

Table 3-2	Self-Service Kiosks
Type	**Typical Services Provided**
Financial kiosk	Pay bills, add minutes to phone plans, add money to prepaid cards, and perform other financial activities.
Photo kiosk	Print photos from digital images. Some allow editing of digital photos. Users may print directly at the kiosk or may send an order to a photo lab to be printed.
Ticket kiosk	Print tickets. Located in airports, amusement parks, movie theaters, rental companies, and train stations.
Vending kiosk	Dispense item after payment is received. Examples include DVD rentals and license plate renewals.
Visitor kiosk	Manage and track visitors upon check-in. Located in businesses, schools, hospitals, and other areas where access is controlled or registration is required.

© Cengage Learning

A *DVD kiosk*, for example, is a self-service DVD rental machine that connects to a host computer through a network (Figure 3-13). DVD kiosks are associated with a particular vendor. To rent a movie online, for example, a customer establishes an account or connects to an existing account on the vendor's website, selects the desired movie, and then chooses a nearby DVD kiosk where the movie will be picked up. Customers also usually can select movies directly at the DVD kiosk via a touch screen or some other input device on the kiosk. After presenting identifying information and swiping a credit card through the reader, the DVD kiosk dispenses the rented movie to the customer. The customer returns it to any of the vendor's nationwide DVD kiosks, at which time the customer's account is charged a fee based on the time elapsed.

touch screen

insert returned DVDs in this slot

Figure 3-13 A DVD kiosk is a self-service DVD rental terminal.
© Getty Images

✔ NOW YOU KNOW

Be sure you understand the material presented in the sections titled Computers and Mobile Devices, Desktops and Mobile Computers, Servers, Supercomputers, and Terminals, as it relates to the chapter objectives.
You now should know . . .

- What you should consider when purchasing a desktop or mobile computer (Objective 1)
- When you would use specific types of servers (Objective 2)
- How you use a POS terminal, ATM, and self-service kiosk (Objective 3)

Quiz Yourself Online: Check your knowledge of related content by navigating to this book's Quiz Yourself resource on Computer Concepts CourseMate and then tapping or clicking Objectives 1–3.

Cloud Computing

Cloud computing refers to an environment of servers that house and provide access to resources users access through the Internet (Figure 3-14). Resources include email messages, schedules, music, photos, videos, games, websites, programs, web apps, servers, storage, and more. That is, instead of accessing these resources locally, you access them on the cloud. For example, you use cloud computing capabilities when you store or access documents, photos, videos, and other media online; use programs and apps online (i.e., email, productivity, games, etc.); and share ideas, opinions, and content with others online (i.e., social networking sites).

Businesses use cloud computing to more efficiently use resources, such as servers and programs, by shifting usage and consumption of these resources from a local environment to the Internet. For example, an employee working during the day in California could use computing resources located in an office in Paris that is closed for the evening. When the company uses the computing resources, it pays a fee that is based on the amount of computing time and other resources it consumes, much in the way that consumers pay utility companies for the amount of electricity used.

Cloud computing allows a company to diversify its network and server infrastructure. Some cloud computing services automatically add more network and server capacity to a company's website as demand for services of the website increases. The network and server capacity may be duplicated around the world so that, for example, an outage of a single server does not affect the company's operations.

 CONSIDER THIS ─────────────────────────────

Are all cloud services available to everyone?
Some cloud services are public and others are private. A public cloud is made available free or for a fee to the general public or a large group, usually by a cloud service provider. A private cloud is dedicated to a single organization. Some cloud services are hybrid, combining two or more cloud types.

 Internet Research

How secure is the cloud?
Search for: cloud privacy issues

 BTW

The Cloud
The cloud-shaped symbol, which today universally represents cloud computing, stems from early diagrams that visually portrayed the Internet as a cloud, intangible and widespread.

Figure 3-14 Users access resources on the cloud through their Internet connections.
© iStockphoto / Petar Chernaev; © iStockphoto / cotesebastien; © Cengage Learning; © iStockphoto / Jill Fromer; © Cengage Learning; © iStockphoto / 123 render; © Cengage Learning; © Pablo Eder / Shutterstock.com; © Peter Gudella / Shutterstock.com; © Mr.Reborn55 / Shutterstock.com; Courtesy of LG Electronics USA Inc.; © Cengage Learning

Mobile Devices

A mobile device is a computing device small enough to hold in your hand. Because of their reduced size, the screens on mobile devices are small — often between 3 and 5 inches. Popular types of mobile devices are smartphones, digital cameras, portable media players, and e-book readers. Read Ethics & Issues 3-2 to consider issues related to recycling computers and mobile devices.

 ETHICS & ISSUES 3-2

Should Recycling of Electronics Be Made Easier?

As technology advances and prices fall, many people think of computers and mobile devices as disposable. Americans discard millions of electronic items annually, resulting in tons of e-waste. E-waste releases lead, mercury, barium, and other elements into soil and water. A large amount of e-waste ends up polluting developing countries, who accept the materials for profit.

Only about 20 percent of e-waste is recycled. Electronics recycling can take several forms: reusing parts from computers, mobile devices, and other electronics; creating new products from old products; or melting down or reducing parts to basic elements or materials. In the past, recycling programs that focused on outdated electronic equipment have not been as accessible as recycling programs for paper, glass, and plastic. Today, however, electronic recycling programs have become successful business ventures, with many companies focusing exclusively on e-waste recycling.

Lawmakers at the federal and state levels are working to address e-waste problems. A proposed bill makes it illegal for companies to export e-waste to developing countries. Currently, several states have laws that mandate e-waste recycling.

How can companies make it easier to recycle electronics? Should the government, manufacturers, or users be responsible for recycling of obsolete equipment? Why? What impact does exporting toxic waste have on developing nations? Should the state or federal government mandate a recycling program for electronics? Why or why not?

Smartphones

A **smartphone** is an Internet-capable phone that usually also includes a calendar, an appointment book, an address book, a calculator, a notepad, games, browser, and numerous other apps. In addition to basic phone capabilities, many smartphones include these features:

- Send and receive email messages and access the web — via Wi-Fi or a mobile data plan
- Communicate wirelessly with other devices or computers
- Function as a portable media player
- Include a built-in digital camera
- Talk directly into the smartphone's microphone or into a Bluetooth headset that wirelessly communicates with the phone
- Conduct live video calls, where the parties can see each other as they speak
- Receive GPS signals to provide users with maps and directions from their current location
- Synchronize data and information with a computer or another mobile device
- Support voice control so that you can speak instructions to the phone and it speaks responses back to you
- Serve as a wireless access point

Many smartphones have touch screens. Instead of or in addition to a touch screen, some have a built-in mini keyboard on the front of the phone or a keyboard that slides in and out from behind the phone. Others have keypads that contain both numbers and letters. Some also include a stylus.

 BTW

Samsung
Technology Innovator:
You should be familiar
with Samsung.

 CONSIDER THIS

How do you type text messages on a phone that has only a numeric keypad and no touch screen?
Each key on the keypad represents multiple characters, which are identified on the key. For example, the 2 key on the phone's keypad displays the letters a, b, and c on the key's face. On many phones, you cycle through the number, letters, and other symbols associated with a particular key by pressing a key on the keypad multiple times. To type the word, hi, for instance, you would press the 4 key (labeled with the letters g, h, and i) twice to display the letter h, pause momentarily to advance the cursor, and then press the 4 key three times to display the letter i.

A variety of options are available for typing on a smartphone (Figure 3-15). Many can display an *on-screen keyboard*, where you press keys on the screen using your fingertip or a stylus. Some phones support a swipe keyboard app, on which users enter words by tracing a path on an on-screen keyboard with their fingertip or stylus from one letter to the next in a continuous motion. With other phones, you press letters on the phone's keyboard or keypad. Some phones use *predictive text input*, where you press one key on the keyboard or keypad for each letter in a word, and software on the phone predicts the word you want. Swipe keyboard apps and predictive text input save users time when entering text on the phone.

Instead of typing on a phone's keyboard or keypad, users can enter text via a *portable keyboard*, which is a full-sized keyboard that communicates with a smartphone via a dock, cables, or wirelessly. Some portable keyboards physically attach to and remove from the device; others are wireless. Another option is a *virtual keyboard* that projects an image of a keyboard on a flat surface.

Figure 3-15 A variety of options for typing on a smartphone.
© iStockphoto / TommL; Courtesy of Nuance; © FreezeFrameStudio / Photos.com; © iStockphoto / webphotographeer; Bloomberg via Getty Images; Courtesy of Jorno; © Italianestro / dreamstime.com

on-screen keyboard

swipe keyboard app

mini keyboard

keypad

slide out keyboard

portable keyboard

virtual keyboard

Wireless messaging services enable users to send and receive text messages and picture/video messages to and from smartphones, mobile phones, handheld game devices, and other mobile devices and computers. The type of messages you send depends primarily on the services offered by the mobile service provider that works with the phone or other mobile device you select. Many users have unlimited wireless messaging plans, while others pay a fee per message sent or received.

Text Message Services   With text message service, or *SMS (short message service)*, users can send and receive short text messages, typically fewer than 300 characters, on a phone or other mobile device or computer. Text message services typically provide users with several options for sending and receiving messages:

- Mobile to Mobile: Send a message from your mobile device to another mobile device.
- Mobile to Email: Send a message from your mobile device to an email address anywhere in the world.
- Web to Mobile: Send a message from a text messaging website to a mobile device, or request that a website alert a mobile device with messages of breaking news and other updates, such as sports scores, stock prices, and weather forecasts.
- Mobile to Provider: Send a message by entering a *common short code (CSC)*, which is a four- or five-digit number assigned to a specific content or mobile service provider, sometimes followed by the message, for example, to a vote for a television program contestant or donate to a charity.

Picture/Video Message Services   With picture message services, users can send photos and audio files, as well as short text messages, to a phone or other mobile device or computer. With video messages services, users can send short video clips, usually about 30 seconds in length, in addition to all picture message services. Smartphones and other mobile devices with picture/video message services, also called *MMS* (*multimedia message service*), typically have a digital camera built into the device. Users who expect to receive numerous picture/video messages should verify the phone has sufficient memory.

Picture/video message services typically provide users these options for sending and receiving messages:

• Mobile to Mobile: Send the picture/video from your mobile device to another mobile device.
• Mobile to Email: Send the picture/video from your mobile device to any email address.

If you send a picture message to a phone that does not have picture/video message capability, the phone usually displays a text message directing the user to a webpage that contains the picture/video message. Some online social networks allow you to send a picture/video message directly to your online profile.

Voice mail, which functions much like an answering machine, allows someone to leave a voice message for one or more people. Unlike answering machines, however, a computer in the voice mail system converts an analog voice message into digital form. Once digitized, the message is stored in a voice mailbox. A voice mailbox is a storage location on a hard disk in the voice mail system. To help users manage voice mail messages, some systems offer visual voice mail. With *visual voice mail*, users can view message details such as the length of calls and, in some cases, read message contents instead of listening to them. Some voice mail systems can convert a voice mail message to a text message for display on a computer or mobile device such as a smartphone, which you then can manage like any other text message.

Wireless messaging services and voice mail systems also may be able to send messages to groups of phone numbers or email addresses. Read Secure IT 3-3 for tips about safely using smartphones and other mobile devices in public.

 BTW

Analog vs. Digital
Human speech is analog because it uses continuous (wave form) signals that vary in strength and quality. Most computers and electronic devices are digital, which use only two discrete states: on and off.

 SECURE IT 3-3

 Safe Mobile Device Use in Public Areas

Sending a text message, updating a Facebook status, posting a Tweet, selecting a new playlist, and checking email messages are tasks you may perform using a mobile device many times each day. They all require some concentration as you focus on the device, usually while looking downward, and they distract you from events occurring around you. Using technology responsibly and safely can prevent theft and injuries.

One common method of thwarting a smartphone thief is to not use the phone to check the time. Potential thieves randomly ask people for the correct time. If a person stops and takes a phone out of a pocket or purse, the thief glances at the make and model and decides if it is worth snatching.

Bus stops and train stations are common places for mobile device theft. People in

these locations tend to use their smartphones to check schedules, send text messages, and make phone calls. Headphones and earbuds are giveaways that you are using a mobile device and may not be focused on your surroundings. Apple's white earbuds or EarPods are a clear indication that the person is using an Apple product; one out of every seven crimes in New York City is an Apple theft. Thieves are likely to snatch the devices while the doors are closing just before the train or bus departs from a station so that the victim is unable to pursue the thief. To decrease the chance of theft or pickpocketing, keep your mobile device(s) in a front pocket or in a zippered backpack. Keep your head up and look around at the surroundings. If possible, when in public, avoid using accessories that indicate the type of device to which they are connected.

Cognitive psychologists have studied the effects of *inattentional blindness*, which occurs when a person's attention is diverted while performing a natural activity, such as walking. The researchers have determined that diverted attention is particularly pronounced when people are talking on a mobile phone and, to a lesser extent, using a portable media player. Emergency room reports indicate that distracted walking accidents are on the rise, especially when people trip over cracks in sidewalks or run into fixed objects, such as parked cars and telephone poles.

Do you know anyone who has had a mobile device stolen? If so, how did the theft occur? Have you ever experienced inattentional blindness or distracted walking?

Digital Cameras

A **digital camera** is a mobile device that allows users to take photos and store the photographed images digitally. While many digital cameras look like a traditional camera, mobile devices such as smartphones and portable media players often have a built-in digital camera.

In addition to cameras built into phones and other devices, types of digital cameras include point-and-shoot cameras and SLR cameras (Figure 3-16). A *point-and-shoot camera* is an affordable and lightweight digital camera with lenses built into it and a screen that displays an approximation of the image to be photographed. Point-and-shoot cameras, which range in size and features, provide acceptable quality photographic images for the home or small business user. An *SLR camera* (single-lens reflex camera), by contrast, is a high-end digital camera that has interchangeable lenses and uses a mirror to display on its screen an exact replica of the image to be photographed. SLR cameras are much heavier and larger than point-and-shoot cameras. They also can be quite expensive, with a variety of available lens sizes and other attachments.

Most point-and-shoot cameras include zoom and autofocus capability, use a built-in flash, store images on memory cards, and enable you to view and sometimes edit images directly on the camera. Many can take video in addition to still photos. Some have a GPS; others are waterproof. Figure 3-17 illustrates how a point-and-shoot digital camera might work.

Digital cameras store captured images on storage in the camera or on some type of memory card. Although many cameras enable you to edit, print, and share photos directly from the camera, some users prefer to download photos from a digital camera or the memory card to a computer's hard disk to perform these tasks. Read How To 3-1 for instructions about how to transfer photos to a computer.

BTW

Sony
Technology Innovator:
You should be familiar
with Sony.

Internet Research

What is an SD card?
Search for: sd card
information

point-and-
shoot camera

SLR camera

camera in
smartphone

Figure 3-16 SLR digital cameras have lenses and other attachments, whereas the lenses on point-and-shoot cameras are built into the device. Many smartphones also have built-in digital cameras.
© iStockphoto / andrew-thief; © Pawel Gaul / Photos.com; © iStockphoto / Stephen Krow

How a Digital Camera Might Work

Step 1
Point to the image to photograph and take the photo. Light passes into the lens of the camera.

Step 2
The image is focused on a chip called a *charge-coupled device* (CCD).

Step 3
The CCD generates an analog signal that represents the image.

Step 4
The analog signal is converted to a digital signal by an analog-to-digital converter (ADC).

Step 5
A processor in the camera adjusts the quality of the image and usually stores the digital photo on media inserted in the camera.

Figure 3-17   This figure shows how a point-and-shoot digital camera might work.
© iStockphoto / David Birkbeck; © iStockphoto / David Birkbeck; © Johan Larson / Shutterstock.com; Courtesy of Kingston Technology Company, Inc

---

 HOW TO 3-1

Transfer Photos from a Mobile Device to a Computer

Many individuals take hundreds of photos each year using mobile devices such as digital cameras, smartphones, and tablets. After taking the photos, transferring them to a computer allows you easily to create backup copies, edit the photos using photo editing software, and create digital photo albums. The following steps describe multiple ways to transfer photos from a mobile device to a computer.

To transfer photos from a mobile device to a computer using a memory card:

1. Safely remove the memory card from the mobile device.
2. Properly insert the memory card into the appropriate memory card slot on the computer.
3. When the computer detects the memory card, navigate to the location of the photos to transfer.
4. Select the files to transfer and then drag them to the destination folder on the computer.
5. Safely remove the memory card from the computer and insert it back in the mobile device.

To transfer photos from a mobile device to a computer using a USB cable:

1. Connect the cable to the mobile device and to the computer.
2. When the computer detects the mobile device, navigate to the location on the mobile device containing the photos to transfer.
3. Select the files to transfer and then drag them to the destination folder on the computer.
4. Disconnect the USB cable from the computer and from the mobile device.

Some mobile devices also allow you to transfer photos using wireless technologies such as Bluetooth and Wi-Fi. The steps required to transfer photos wirelessly vary greatly for each device. Thus, read your mobile device's documentation to see if and how you can transfer photos to your computer wirelessly. Be aware that transferring photos wirelessly could increase your data charges.

☀ Of the above techniques, which way do you find is easiest to transfer files from your mobile device to a computer? Why? What other techniques might you use to accomplish this task?

CONSIDER THIS ————————————————————————————————

Do you need a digital camera if you have a camera built into your mobile phone?
If you use a camera only for posts on social media sites, then your mobile phone's built-in camera probably is adequate. If you want more flexibility and options when photographing images, you should purchase a digital camera. Features typically not found in cameras built into mobile phones include optical zoom, additional lenses, scene modes, autofocus, image stabilization, and burst mode (capturing a series of images in rapid succession).

pixel

Figure 3-18   A pixel is a single point in an electronic image.
© Lingong / Dreamstime.com

Photo Quality   Resolution affects the quality of digital camera photos. **Resolution** is the number of horizontal and vertical pixels in a display device. A *pixel* (short for picture element) is the smallest element in an electronic image (Figure 3-18). Digital camera resolution typically is stated in megapixels, or millions of pixels. For example, a 16 MP resolution means 16 million pixels. The greater the number of pixels the camera uses to capture a picture, the better the quality of the picture but the larger the file size and the more expensive the camera. Most digital cameras provide a means to adjust the resolution. At a lower resolution, you can capture and store more images in the camera.

The actual photographed resolution is known as the *optical resolution*. Some manufacturers state enhanced resolution, instead of, or in addition to, optical resolution. The *enhanced resolution* usually is higher because it uses a special formula to add pixels between those generated by the optical resolution. Be aware that some manufacturers compute a digital camera's megapixels from the enhanced resolution, instead of optical resolution.

Portable Media Players

A **portable media player**, sometimes called a *personal media player*, is a mobile device on which you can store, organize, and play or view digital media (Figure 3-19). Smartphones and other mobile devices often can function as a portable media player. Portable media players enable you to listen to music; view photos; watch videos, movies, and television shows; and even record audio and video. Some include a digital camera and also offer a calendar, address book, games, and other apps. Others communicate wirelessly with other devices or computers and enable you to synchronize your digital media with a computer, another mobile device, or cloud storage.

Figure 3-19   Some portable media players have touch screens; others have touch-sensitive pads or buttons that enable you to access your media library.
© iStockphoto / Stephen Krow;
© iStockphoto / rzelich;
© iStockphoto / AleksVF

earbuds

portable media player with button controls

portable media player with touch screen

portable media player with touch-sensitive pad

Portable media players usually include a set of *earbuds*, which are small speakers that rest inside each ear canal. Available in a variety of sizes and colors, some portable media player models have a touch screen. Others have a *touch-sensitive pad*, which is an input device that contains buttons and/or wheels you operate with a thumb or finger. Using the touch-sensitive pad, you can scroll through and play music; view pictures; watch videos or movies; navigate through song, picture, or movie lists; display a menu; adjust volume; customize settings; and perform other actions. Some portable media players have only button controls.

Your collection of stored digital media is called a *media library*. Portable media players house your media library on a storage device in the player and/or on some type of memory card. With most, you transfer the digital media from a computer or the Internet, if the device is Internet capable, to the portable media player's media library. Read How To 2-2 on page 82 for instructions about how to transfer digital media from online services to a mobile device, such as a portable media player.

 BTW
EarPods
Apple uses the term, *EarPods*, to refer to earbuds they designed to match the shape of the human ear.

 MINI FEATURE 3-3

Mobile Device Buyer's Guide

Mobile devices such as smartphones, digital cameras, and portable medial players are quite popular among people who are frequently on the go. Research the manufacturers and then consider the following guidelines before purchasing a mobile device.

Smartphone Purchase Guidelines

1. Choose a wireless carrier and plan that satisfies your needs and budget.

2. Decide on the size, style, and weight of the smartphone that will work best for you.

3. Determine whether you prefer an on-screen keyboard, keypad, or mini keyboard.

4. Select a smartphone that is compatible with the program you want to use for synchronizing your email messages, contacts, calendar, and other data.

5. Choose a smartphone with sufficient battery life that meets your lifestyle.

6. Make sure your smartphone has enough memory and storage for contacts, email messages, photos, videos, and apps.

7. Consider purchasing accessories such as extra batteries, earbuds, screen protectors, and carrying cases.

© iStockphoto / luxxtek; Courtesy of Nokia; Courtesy of Nokia

Digital Camera Purchase Guidelines

1. Determine the type of digital camera that meets your needs, such as a point-and-shoot camera or SLR camera.

2. Choose a camera with an appropriate resolution.

3. Evaluate memory cards because different cameras require different memory cards.

© iStockphoto / tomprout

4. Consider a camera with built-in photo editing features.

5. Make sure that you can see the screen easily.

6. If the photos you plan to take will require you to zoom, choose a camera with an appropriate optical zoom.

7. Purchase accessories such as extra batteries and battery chargers, extra memory cards, lenses, and carrying cases.

© iStockphoto / Vasiliki Varvaki

Portable Media Player Purchase Guidelines

1. Choose a portable media player with sufficient storage capacity for your media library.

2. Consider a portable media player that can play video.

continued on next page

continued from previous page

3. Read reviews about sound quality. Consider higher-quality earbuds, headphones, or external speakers.

4. Select an appropriate size and style.

5. Consider additional memory cards to increase the storage capacity of your portable media player.

6. Consider rechargeable batteries instead of disposable batteries.

✷ Although most smartphones also can function as portable media players and digital cameras, would you have a separate portable media player and digital camera? Why?

E-Book Readers

An **e-book reader** (short for electronic book reader), or *e-reader*, is a mobile device that is used primarily for reading e-books and other digital publications (Figure 3-20). An *e-book*, or digital book, is an electronic version of a printed book, readable on computers and other mobile devices. Digital publications include books, newspapers, and magazines. Mobile computers and devices that display text also can function as e-book readers.

E-book readers usually are smaller than tablets but larger than smartphones. Most e-book reader models can store thousands of books, have a touch screen, and are Internet capable with built-in wireless technology. You use an on-screen keyboard to navigate, search, make selections, take notes, and highlight. Some have a text-to-speech feature, where the device speaks the contents of the printed page. E-book readers are available with an electronic paper black-and-white screen or with a color screen. Most have settings to adjust text size and for various lighting conditions, such as bright sunlight or dim lighting. Batteries usually have a long life, providing more than 75 hours of use before needing to be recharged.

Similar to how a portable media player stores digital media, e-book readers store digital publications in a library on a storage device in the e-book reader and/or on memory cards. You typically transfer the digital publication from a computer or the Internet, if the device is Internet capable, to the e-book reader. Read How To 2-2 on page 82 for instructions about how to transfer digital media from online services to a mobile device such as an e-book reader. Read Ethics & Issues 3-3 to consider library circulation of e-books.

Figure 3-20
E-book readers enable you to read e-books and other digital publications such as newspapers and magazines.
© iStockphoto / pressureUA

⊕ BTW

Electronic Paper Screen
Some users of e-books prefer the electronic paper black-and-white screen over the models with color screens because the electronic paper resembles a paper page from a book.

✷ ETHICS & ISSUES 3-3

Should Limits Be Placed on Libraries' Lending of E-Books?
Each time you check out a printed book from the library, the mere act of thumbing through the pages as you read causes subtle damage to the book. E-books have no wear and tear, which means that libraries can circulate them an unlimited number of times. Libraries add e-books to their circulation by partnering with companies that offer an inventory system and enable libraries and library networks to license content from publishers.

These companies allow the publishers to set certain limits, such as number of consecutive checkouts, length of checkout, and so forth.

One publisher states that, on average, libraries replace a print book after 26 checkouts. That publisher used the statistic to set its policy so that libraries have to repurchase e-book content after 26 checkouts. The publisher cited loss of revenue and author royalties if libraries do not repurchase e-books as they do print books. Some publishers do not offer e-books to

libraries at all because of the same concern. Criticism from some librarians is that when a print book is purchased, the library can circulate it as many times as it wants, or until the book falls apart; therefore, no limits should be placed on e-books.

Should publishers be able to put a limit on how many times a library can circulate an e-book? Why or why not? How do the limits affect library patrons, libraries, authors, and publishers?

Do you need a separate e-book reader if you have a tablet or other device that can function as an e-book reader?
If you want the flexibility of reading on one device while using a tablet or other device for separate tasks, you will want to purchase a separate e-book reader. Also, e-book readers have a design suited for optimal readability of on-screen text and a longer battery life.

Game Devices

A **game console** is a mobile computing device designed for single-player or multiplayer video games. Gamers often connect the game console to a television or a monitor so that they can view gameplay on the screen. Some models also allow you to listen to music and watch movies or view photos. Typically weighing between 3 and 11 pounds, many game console models include internal disk drives or memory to store games and other media. Optical disc drives in the game consoles provide access to games and movies on optical disc. Some use memory cards and accept USB flash drives. Game consoles that are Internet capable enable gamers to download games, stream games or movies, and play with others online. Some gamers connect keyboards or webcams so that they more easily can send text messages or conduct video chats with other gamers.

A **handheld game device** is a small mobile device that contains a screen, speakers, controls, and game console all in one unit. Some include a stylus. Some handheld game device models have touch screens and built-in digital cameras. Some are Internet capable for downloading games and apps. Most handheld game devices can communicate wirelessly with other similar devices for multiplayer gaming.

With a game console or computer video game, players direct movements and actions of on-screen objects via a controller, voice, or air gestures. Game controllers include gamepads, joysticks and wheels, dance pads, and a variety of motion-sensing controllers (Figure 3-21). The list on the next page describes each of these types of game controllers. Most communicate via wired or wireless technology.

BTW
Nintendo
Technology Innovator: You should be familiar with Nintendo.

gamepad   joystick   pedals and wheel   dance pad

motion-sensing game controller   guitar   balance board

Figure 3-21   Game players have a variety of ways to direct movements and actions of on-screen objects.
© iStockphoto / peng wu; © aquariagirl1970 / Shutterstock.com; © George Dolgikh / Shutterstock.com; Courtesy of DDR Game; © iStockphoto / Florea Marius Catalin; Handout / MCT / Newscom; © Stuartkey / Dreamstime.com

126 **Chapter 3** Computers and Mobile Devices

 Internet Research

Which video games are the most widely used?

Search for: popular video games

- A *gamepad*, which is held with both hands, controls the movement and actions of players or objects in video games or computer games. On the gamepad, users press buttons with their thumbs or move sticks in various directions to trigger events. Several gamepads can communicate with the game console simultaneously for multiplayer gaming.

- Users running flight and driving simulation software often use a joystick or wheel. A *joystick* is a handheld vertical lever, mounted on a base, that you move in different directions to control the actions of the simulated vehicle or player. The lever usually includes buttons, called triggers, that you press to initiate certain events. A *wheel* is a steering-wheel-type input device that users turn to simulate driving a car, truck, or other vehicle. Most wheels also include foot pedals for acceleration and braking actions.

- A *dance pad* is a flat, electronic device divided into panels that users press with their feet in response to instructions from a music video game. These games test the user's ability to step on the correct panel at the correct time, following a pattern that is synchronized with the rhythm or beat of a song.

- *Motion-sensing game controllers* allow the user to guide on-screen elements with air gestures, that is, by moving their body or a handheld input device through the air. Some motion-sensing game controllers are sold with a particular type of game; others are general purpose. Sports games, for example, use motion-sensing game controllers, such as baseball bats and golf clubs. With general-purpose motion-sensing game controllers, you simulate batting, golfing, and other actions with a universal handheld device or no device at all.

- Controllers that resemble musical instruments, such as guitars, drums, keyboards, and microphones work with music video games that enable game players to create sounds and music by playing the instrument.

- Fitness games often communicate with a *balance board*, which is shaped like a weight scale and contains sensors that measure a game player's balance and weight. Read Ethics & Issues 3-4 to consider whether games and apps are qualified to provide medical advice.

✹ ETHICS & ISSUES 3-4

Are Fitness Video Games and Apps Qualified to Provide Medical Advice?

Most video games and smartphone apps provide a workout only for your fingers. A host of games and apps, however, attempt to track calories, suggest workout routines, and more. Because you can take your smartphone anywhere, one advantage is that apps can provide tips for eating healthfully at a restaurant, act as a pedometer to track your steps, and send reminders to exercise. Another advantage is you can receive instant feedback and support from fitness apps and games that allow you to post workouts,

calorie counts, and even weight loss to social media sites.

Some critics find fault with these systems, claiming that neither the game or app developers, nor the games and apps themselves, have been evaluated by medical personnel. Because they do not take into account the amount of lean muscle mass and body fat, health and weight loss goals can be miscalculated. Experts say that games that simulate sports, such as tennis, burn half the calories you would burn if you participated in the actual sport. Some medical experts note also that apps do not consider a participant's

medical history when recommending activities. Proponents of fitness-related games and apps say that the games encourage people to be more active, especially the elderly and children who might otherwise not get much physical activity.

Should game and app developers be permitted to provide medical advice? Why or why not? Can fitness-related games provide a quality workout? Can an app give accurate calorie recommendations? Why or why not? As long as the games make people more active, should the games' shortcomings be ignored? Why or why not?

Embedded Computers

An **embedded computer** is a special-purpose computer that functions as a component in a larger product. Embedded computers are everywhere — at home, in your car, and at work. The following list identifies a variety of everyday products that contain embedded computers.

- **Consumer electronics:** Mobile phones, digital phones, digital televisions, cameras, video recorders, DVD players and recorders, answering machines
- **Home automation devices:** Thermostats, sprinkling systems, security systems, vacuum systems, appliances, lights
- **Automobiles:** Antilock brakes, engine control modules, electronic stability control, airbag controller, cruise control, navigation systems and GPS receivers

- **Process controllers and robotics:** Remote monitoring systems, power monitors, machine controllers, medical devices
- **Computer devices and office machines:** Keyboards, printers, fax and copy machines

Because embedded computers are components in larger products, they usually are small and have limited hardware. These computers perform various functions, depending on the requirements of the product in which they reside. Embedded computers in printers, for example, monitor the amount of paper in the tray, check the ink or toner level, signal if a paper jam has occurred, and so on. Figure 3-22 shows some of the many embedded computers in vehicles. Read Ethics & Issues 3-5 to consider whether in-vehicle technology fosters a false sense of security.

Cars equipped with wireless communications capabilities, called *telematics*, include features such as navigation systems, remote diagnosis and alerts, and Internet access.

Adaptive cruise control systems detect if vehicles in front of you are too close and, if necessary, adjust the vehicle's throttle, may apply brakes, and/or sound an alarm.

Tire pressure monitoring systems send warning signals if tire pressure is insufficient.

Advanced airbag systems have crash-severity sensors that determine the appropriate level to inflate the airbag, reducing the chance of airbag injury in low-speed accidents.

Electronic stability control automatically applies brakes, and may reduce engine power, when you lose control of steering or traction.

Drive-by-wire systems sense pressure on the gas pedal and communicate electronically to the engine how much and how fast to accelerate.

Figure 3-22   Some of the embedded computers designed to improve your safety, security, and performance in today's vehicles.
© Nir Levy / Shutterstock.com; © Santiago Cornejo / Shutterstock.com; © Patti McConville / Getty Images; © iStockphoto / narvikk; © iStockphoto / kenneth-cheung; © iStockphoto / Marcin Laska

✳ ETHICS & ISSUES 3-5

Does In-Vehicle Technology Foster a False Sense of Security?
Embedded computers in vehicles can guide you when backing out of a driveway or alert you to unsafe road conditions. You can use GPS technology to help reach a destination. Hands-free and voice-activated technology allows you to use a phone and play music or send text messages while driving. Apps can track gas mileage or tell you when an oil change is due. Recently, all new cars were required to include electronic stability control, which can assist with steering the car in case of skidding. All of this technology is supposed to make driving safer.

Critics of in-vehicle technology claim that it can provide drivers with a false sense of security. If you rely on a sensor for assistance while backing up, for example, you may fail to look for obstructions behind the vehicle. Using GPS and hands-free technology to find a location or talk on the phone ultimately can be distracting. The electronic stability control may cause you to drive faster than conditions allow.

Teen drivers statistically are more susceptible to being distracted while driving. If they learn to drive using vehicles equipped with features such as video rearview mirrors, they may be unable to drive older, less-equipped vehicles

safely. Without GPS step-by-step guidance, teen drivers may have difficulty navigating using a paper map. Many apps and devices help parents protect their teens while driving. Mobile devices can be programmed to block incoming calls or text messages while the vehicle is moving. GPS can be used to track a vehicle's location and speed, as well as seatbelt usage and number of passengers in the vehicle.

Does in-vehicle technology make driving safer? Why or why not? What basic skills should all drivers have, regardless of their vehicle's technology?

CONSIDER THIS ────────────────────────────────────

Can embedded computers use the Internet to communicate with other computers and devices?
Many already do, on a small scale. For example, a *Smart TV* enables you to browse the web, stream video from online media services, listen to Internet radio, communicate with others on social media sites, play online games, and more — all while watching a television show.

A trend, called the *Internet of Things*, describes an environment where processors are embedded in every product imaginable (things), and those 'things' communicate with each other via the Internet (i.e., alarm clocks, coffeemakers, apps, vehicles, refrigerators, phones, washing machines, doorbells, streetlights, thermostats, navigation systems, etc.). For example, when your refrigerator detects the milk is low, it sends your phone a text message that you need milk and adds a 'buy milk' task to your scheduling app. On the drive home, your phone determines the closest grocery store that has the lowest milk price and sends the address of that grocery store to your vehicle's navigation system, which in turn gives you directions to the store. In the store, your phone directs you to the dairy aisle, where it receives an electronic coupon from the store for the milk. Because this type of environment provides an efficient means to track or monitor status, inventory, behavior, and more — without human intervention — it sometimes is referred to as machine-to-machine (M2M) communications.

BTW
Volunteer Computing
Innovative Computing: You should be familiar with innovations of volunteer computing, where you can donate your computer's resources to promote scientific research projects.

Putting It All Together

Industry experts typically classify computers and mobile devices in six categories: personal computers (desktop), mobile computers and mobile devices, game consoles, servers, supercomputers, and embedded computers. A computer's size, speed, processing power, and price determine the category it best fits. Due to rapidly changing technology, however, the distinction among categories is not always clear-cut. Table 3-3 summarizes the categories of computers discussed on the previous pages.

Table 3-3   Categories of Computers and Mobile Devices

Category	Physical Size	Number of Simultaneously Connected Users	General Price Range
Personal computers (desktop)	Fits on a desk	Usually one (can be more if networked)	Several hundred to several thousand dollars
Mobile computers and mobile devices	Fits on your lap or in your hand	Usually one	Less than a hundred dollars to several thousand dollars
Game consoles	Small box or handheld device	One to several	Several hundred dollars or less
Servers	Small cabinet to room full of equipment	Two to thousands	Several hundred to several million dollars
Supercomputers	Full room of equipment	Hundreds to thousands	Half a million to several billion dollars
Embedded computers	Miniature	Usually one	Embedded in the price of the product

NOW YOU KNOW —————————————————————————

Be sure you understand the material presented in the sections titled Cloud Computing, Mobile Devices, Game Devices, Embedded Computers, and Putting It All Together as it relates to the chapter objectives.
You now should know…

- When you are using cloud computing (Objective 4)
- What you should consider when purchasing a mobile device (Objective 5)
- What types of controllers you might use with game consoles (Objective 6)
- When you are using an embedded computer (Objective 7)

 Quiz Yourself Online: Check your knowledge of related content by navigating to this book's Quiz Yourself resource on Computer Concepts CourseMate and then tapping or clicking Objectives 4–7.

Ports and Connections

Computers and mobile devices connect to peripheral devices through ports or by using wireless technologies. A **port** is the point at which a peripheral device (i.e., keyboard, printer, monitor, etc.) attaches to or communicates with a computer or mobile device so that the peripheral device can send data to or receive information from the computer or mobile device. Most computers and mobile devices have ports (Figure 3-23). Some ports have a micro or mini version for mobile devices because of the smaller sizes of these devices.

BTW
Jacks
Instead of the term, port, the term, *jack*, sometimes is used to identify audio and video ports (i.e., audio jack or video jack).

Figure 3-23 Most computers and mobile devices have ports so that you can connect the computer or device to peripherals.

A **connector** joins a cable to a port. A connector at one end of a cable attaches to a port on the computer or mobile device, and a connector at the other end of the cable attaches to a port on the peripheral device. Table 3-4 shows a variety of ports you may find on a computer or mobile device. Notice that many are color-coded to help you match the connector to the correct port. USB and Thunderbolt are more general-purpose ports that allow connections to a wide variety of devices; other ports are more specific and connect a single type of device. Read How To 3-2 on page 131 for instructions about how to connect peripheral devices and accessories to a computer or mobile device.

Table 3-4 Popular Ports and Connectors

Port Type	Connector Photo	Port Photo	Port Type	Connector Photo	Port Photo
DisplayPort (audio/video)			Mini HDMI (audio/video)		
DVI (digital video interface)			Network (Ethernet)		
FireWire			Speaker		
HDMI (audio/video)			Thunderbolt		
Headphones			USB (Type A)		
Lightning			USB (Type B)		
Microphone			VGA		
Mini USB					

✸ HOW TO 3-2

Connect Peripheral Devices and Accessories to a Computer or Mobile Device

You connect peripheral devices and accessories to computers or mobile devices either to enhance the capabilities of the computer or mobile device or to transfer data or information from a peripheral device or an accessory to a computer or mobile device. The following steps describe how to connect peripheral devices and accessories to a computer or mobile device.

1. If the peripheral device or accessory packaging included an installation disc, insert the disc in the computer. Install any necessary software and drivers required for the computer to recognize the device or accessory.

2. Connect the peripheral device or accessory to the computer or mobile device using the cable that came with the device or accessory. If a cable was not included or you are unable to locate the cable, you may be able to purchase one either from the device's or accessory's manufacturer or from a company that sells various cables. Cables also are available with multiple connectors that fit many common devices.

3. If the computer recognizes the device or accessory, you should be able to begin using it.

4. If the computer does not recognize the device or accessory, refer to its documentation to determine whether any additional steps are required to use the device or accessory.

✸ Why is it sometimes necessary to install a program on a computer before the computer is able to recognize the device or accessory you are connecting?

© Dmitry DG / Fotolia

USB Ports

A **USB port**, short for universal serial bus port, can connect up to 127 different peripheral devices together with a single connector. Devices that connect to a USB port include the following: card reader, digital camera, external hard disk, game console, joystick, modem, mouse, optical disc drive, portable media player, printer, scanner, smartphone, speakers, USB flash drive, and webcam. In addition to computers and mobile devices, you find USB ports in vehicles, airplane seats, and other public locations.

Several USB versions have been released, with newer versions (i.e., USB 3.0) transferring data and information faster than earlier ones (i.e., USB 2.0). Newer versions are *backward compatible*, which means they support older USB devices as well as newer ones. Keep in mind, though, that older USB devices do not run any faster in a newer USB port. In addition to transferring data, cables plugged into USB ports also may be able to transfer power to recharge many smartphones and tablets. Newer versions of USB can charge connected mobile devices even when the computer is not in use.

To attach multiple peripheral devices using a single USB port, you can use a USB hub. A *USB hub* is a device that plugs in a USB port on the computer or mobile device and contains multiple USB ports, into which you plug cables from USB devices. Some USB hubs are wireless. That is, a receiver plugs into a USB port on the computer and the USB hub communicates wirelessly with the receiver.

Port Replicators and Docking Stations

Instead of connecting peripheral devices directly to ports on a mobile computer, some mobile users prefer the flexibility of port replicators and docking stations. A *port replicator* is an external device that provides connections to peripheral devices through ports built into the device. The mobile user accesses peripheral devices by connecting the port replicator to a USB port or a special port on the mobile computer. Port replicators sometimes disable ports on the mobile computer to prevent conflicts among the devices on the computer and port replicator.

tablet in docking station

close-up of docking station

USB ports

docking station

stylus

wireless keyboard

Figure 3-24 Docking stations often are used with tablets and other mobile computers, providing connections to peripheral devices.
Courtesy of Fujitsu Technology Solutions; © Cengage Learning

A docking station is similar to a port replicator, but it has more functionality. A *docking station*, which is an external device that attaches to a mobile computer or device, contains a power connection and provides connections to peripheral devices (Figure 3-24). Docking stations also may include slots for memory cards, optical disc drives, and other devices. With the mobile computer or device in the docking station, users can work with a full-sized keyboard, a mouse, and other desktop peripheral devices from their traditional laptop, ultrathin laptop, or tablet.

Wireless Device Connections

Instead of connecting computers and mobile devices to peripheral devices with a cable, some peripheral devices use wireless communications technologies, such as Bluetooth, Wi-Fi, and NFC.

Bluetooth   **Bluetooth** technology uses short-range radio signals to transmit data between two Bluetooth-enabled computers or devices. In addition to computers, mobile devices and many peripheral devices, such as a mouse, keyboard, printer, or headset, and many vehicles and consumer electronics are Bluetooth enabled. Bluetooth devices have to be within about 33 feet of each other, but the range can be extended with additional equipment. If you have a computer that is not Bluetooth enabled, you can purchase a *Bluetooth wireless port adapter* that will convert an existing USB port into a Bluetooth port. Read How To 3-3 for instructions about setting up two Bluetooth devices to communicate with each other.

✸ HOW TO 3-3

Pair Bluetooth Devices

Before two Bluetooth devices will communicate with each other, they might need to be paired. **Pairing** is the process of initiating contact between two Bluetooth devices and allowing them to communicate with each other. It is important to have the documentation for the Bluetooth devices you are pairing readily available. The following steps will help you pair two Bluetooth devices.

1. Make sure the devices you intend to pair are charged completely or plugged into an external power source.

2. Turn on the devices to pair, ensuring they are within your immediate reach.

3. If necessary, enable Bluetooth on the devices you are pairing.

4. Place one device in *discoverable mode,* which means it is waiting for another Bluetooth device to locate its signal. If you

are connecting a smartphone to a Bluetooth headset, for example, the smartphone would need to be in discoverable mode.

5. Refer to the other device's documentation and follow the necessary steps to locate the discoverable device from the other device you are pairing.

6. After no more than about 30 seconds, the devices should initiate communications.

7. You may be required to enter a passkey (similar to a PIN) on one device for the other device with which you are pairing. For example, if you are pairing a smartphone with a Bluetooth headset, you may be required to enter the Bluetooth headset's passkey on the smartphone. In this case, you would refer to the Bluetooth headset's documentation to obtain the passkey. Common passkeys are 0000 and 1234.

8. After entering the correct passkey, the two devices should be paired successfully.

✸ Why is a passkey required when pairing two Bluetooth devices? Do you need to pair Bluetooth devices before each use?

© iStockphoto / Moncherie; © Norman Chan / Shutterstock.com

Wi-Fi   Short for wireless fidelity, **Wi-Fi** uses radio signals that conform to 802.11 standards, which were developed by the Institute of Electrical and Electronics Engineers (IEEE). Computers and devices that have the appropriate Wi-Fi capability can communicate via radio waves with other Wi-Fi computers or devices. Most mobile computers and devices are Wi-Fi enabled, along with routers and other communications devices. For successful Wi-Fi communications in open or outdoor areas free from interference, the Wi-Fi computers or devices should be within 300 feet of each other. In closed areas, the wireless range is about 100 feet. To obtain communications at the maximum distances, you may need to install extra hardware. Read How To 3-4 for instructions about connecting a phone to a Wi-Fi network.

✷ HOW TO 3-4

Connect Your Phone to a Wi-Fi Network to Save Data Charges

Many of today's data plans limit the amount of data you can transfer each month on your mobile service provider's network. Connecting a smartphone to a Wi-Fi network enables you to transfer data without using your phone's data plan and risking costly overages. The following steps describe how to connect your phone to a Wi-Fi network.

1. Make sure you are in a location where a Wi-Fi network is available. Obtain any necessary information you need to connect to the Wi-Fi network.
2. Navigate to the settings on your phone.
3. Locate and enable Wi-Fi in your phone's settings.
4. When your phone displays a list of available wireless networks, choose the network to which you want to connect.

5. If necessary, enter any additional information, such as a password, required to connect to the network.
6. Your phone should indicate when it successfully is connected to the network.
7. When you are finished using the Wi-Fi connection or are not within range of the Wi-Fi network, disable Wi-Fi on your phone to help conserve battery life.

✷ If you have a data plan allowing unlimited data and you are within range of a Wi-Fi network, is it better to use your mobile service provider's network or the Wi-Fi network? Why?

icon indicates phone connected to Wi-Fi network

Source: Google Inc.

NFC   **NFC** (*near field communications*) uses close-range radio signals to transmit data between two NFC-enabled devices. Examples of NFC-enabled devices include smartphones, digital cameras, computers, televisions, and terminals. Other objects, such as credit cards and tickets, also use NFC technology. For successful communications, the devices either touch or are within an inch or two of each other.

✷ CONSIDER THIS

What are some uses of NFC devices?

- Pay for goods and services (i.e., smartphone to terminal)
- Share contacts, photos, and other files (i.e., smartphone to smartphone or digital camera to television)
- Download apps (i.e., computer to smartphone)
- Gain access or admittance (i.e., smartphone to terminal)

Protecting Hardware

Users rely on computers and mobile devices to create, store, and manage important information. Thus, you should take measures to protect computers and devices from theft, vandalism, and failure.

Hardware Theft and Vandalism

Companies, schools, and other organizations that house many computers are at risk of hardware theft and vandalism, especially those with smaller computers that easily can fit in a backpack or briefcase. Mobile users are susceptible to hardware theft because the size and weight of their computers and devices make them easy to steal. Thieves may target laptops of company executives so that they can use the stolen computer to access confidential company information illegally.

To help reduce the chances of theft, companies and schools use a variety of security measures. Physical access controls, such as locked doors and windows, usually are adequate to protect the equipment. Many businesses, schools, and some homeowners install alarm systems for additional security. School computer labs and other facilities with a large number of semifrequent users often attach additional physical security devices such as cables that lock the equipment to a desk (Figure 3-25), cabinet, or floor. Mobile users sometimes lock their mobile computers temporarily to a stationary object, for example, a table in a hotel room. Small locking devices also exist that require a key to access a hard disk or optical disc drive.

Figure 3-25 Using cables to lock computers can help prevent theft of equipment.
Courtesy of Kensington

Some users install a security or device-tracking app on their mobile computers and devices. Some security apps shut down the computer and sound an alarm if the computer moves beyond a specified distance. Others can be configured to photograph the thieves when they use the computer. Device-tracking apps use GPS, Wi-Fi, IP addresses, and other means to determine the location of a lost or stolen computer or device.

Users can configure computers and mobile devices to require identification before allowing access. For example, you can require entry of a user name and password to use the computer or device. Some computers have built-in or attached fingerprint readers (Figure 3-26), which can be used to verify a user's identity before allowing access. A *fingerprint reader* captures curves and indentations of a fingerprint. This type of security does not prevent theft, but it renders the computer or device useless if it is stolen.

Hardware Failure

Hardware can fail for a variety of reasons: aging hardware; random events such as electrical power problems; and even errors in programs or apps. Not only could hardware failure require you to replace or repair a computer or mobile device, but it also can cause loss of software, data, and information.

Figure 3-26 Some mobile computers include fingerprint readers, which can be used to verify a user's identity.
© Jochen Tack / Alamy

One of the more common causes of system failure is an electrical power variation, which can cause loss of data and loss of equipment. If computers and mobile devices are connected to a network, a single power disturbance can damage multiple devices at once. Electrical disturbances that can cause damage include undervoltages and overvoltages.

- An **undervoltage** occurs when the electrical supply or voltage drops, often defined as more than five percent, below the normal volts. A *brownout* is a prolonged (more than a minute) undervoltage. A *blackout* is a complete power failure. Undervoltages can cause data loss but generally do not cause equipment damage.
- An **overvoltage**, or **power surge**, occurs when the incoming electrical supply or voltage increases, often defined as more than five percent, above the normal volts. A momentary overvoltage, called a *spike*, occurs when the increase in power lasts for less than one millisecond (thousandth of a second). Uncontrollable disturbances such as lightning bolts can cause spikes. Overvoltages can cause immediate and permanent damage to hardware.

To protect against electrical power variations, use a surge protector. A **surge protector**, also called a *surge suppressor*, uses electrical components to provide a stable current flow and minimize the chances of an overvoltage reaching the computer and other electronic equipment (Figure 3-27). Sometimes resembling a power strip, the computer and other devices plug in the surge protector, which plugs in the power source.

Figure 3-27 Circuits inside a surge protector safeguard against electrical power variations.
Courtesy of Tripp Lite

The surge protector absorbs small overvoltages — generally without damage to the computer and equipment. To protect the computer and other equipment from large overvoltages, such as those caused by a lightning strike, some surge protectors stop working completely when an overvoltage reaches a certain level. Surge protectors also usually protect the computer from undervoltages. No surge protectors are 100 percent effective. Large power surges can bypass the protector. Repeated small overvoltages can weaken a surge protector permanently. Some experts recommend replacing a surge protector every two to three years.

For additional electrical protection, some users connect an uninterruptible power supply to the computer. An **uninterruptible power supply** (**UPS**) is a device that contains surge protection circuits and one or more batteries that can provide power during a temporary or permanent loss of power (Figure 3-28). A UPS connects your computer and a power source. Read Secure IT 3-4 on the next page for purchasing suggestions regarding surge protectors and UPSs.

Figure 3-28 If power fails, a UPS uses batteries to provide electricity for a limited amount of time.
Courtesy of Tripp Lite

 CONSIDER THIS

What other measures can organizations implement if their computers must remain operational at all times?
Some companies use duplicate components or duplicate computers to protect against hardware failure. A *fault-tolerant computer* has duplicate components so that it can continue to operate when one of its main components fail. Airline reservation systems, communications networks, ATMs, and other systems that must be operational at all times use duplicate components, duplicate computers, or fault-tolerant computers.

SECURE IT 3-4

Avoid System Failure with Surge Protectors and UPSs

Electrical power surges are a part of everyday life, and they are especially prevalent during thunderstorms and peak energy consumption periods. These unavoidable occurrences can damage or ruin sensitive electronic equipment. The processor in a computer is particularly sensitive to the current fluctuations. Two devices can help protect electronic components: a surge protector and an uninterruptible power supply (UPS).

Purchase the best surge protector you can afford. Typically, the amount of protection offered by a surge protector is proportional to its cost. That is, the more expensive the surge protector, the more protection it offers. At a minimum, it should cost more than $15 and meet or exceed these specifications:

- Sufficient outlets to accommodate each device needing protection
- Individual on/off switch for each device
- Built-in fuse
- UL 1449 rating (ensures quality control and testing)

- Joule rating of at least 600 (a Joule is the unit of energy the device can absorb before it can be damaged; the higher the Joule rating, the better the protection)
- Indicator light (shows it is functioning properly)
- Warranty for damages to any connected equipment (best units offer replacement guarantee)
- Low clamping voltage (the level when electricity is diverted)
- High energy-absorption rating (allows electricity to flow before failing)
- Low response time (time between the spike and the protector's response), preferably less than ten nanoseconds (billionths of a second)
- Protection for a modem, communications lines, and cables, if your computer connects to a network or the Internet

If the home has many audio and video technologies in different rooms, a whole-house surge protector may be convenient and cost effective. Another advantage is that it might prevent a house fire caused when faulty wiring overheats and then ignites. A whole-house surge protector, which costs at least $300, connects to the electric meter or to the breaker box. This device should be installed by a licensed electrician.

If your electric service fails frequently, a UPS may offer peace of mind. Two types of UPS devices are standby and online. A *standby UPS*, sometimes called an *offline UPS*, switches to battery power when a problem occurs in the power line. The amount of time a standby UPS allows a user to continue working depends on the electrical requirements of the computer and the size of the batteries in the UPS. A UPS for a home user should provide enough time to save current work and shut down the computer properly. An *online UPS* always runs off the battery, which provides continuous protection. An online UPS is much more expensive than a standby UPS.

☀ How do you protect your computer and other electrical devices from power surges? Would a UPS be a good investment given the reliability of your electric service?

Health Concerns of Using Technology

The widespread use of technology has led to some important user health concerns. You should be proactive and minimize your chance of risk.

Repetitive Strain Injuries

A *repetitive strain injury* (*RSI*) is an injury or disorder of the muscles, nerves, tendons, ligaments, and joints. Technology-related RSIs include tendonitis and carpal tunnel syndrome.

- Tendonitis is inflammation of a tendon due to repeated motion or stress on that tendon.
- Carpal tunnel syndrome (CTS) is inflammation of the nerve that connects the forearm to the palm of the wrist.

Repeated or forceful bending of the wrist can cause tendonitis or CTS of the wrist. Symptoms of tendonitis of the wrist include extreme pain that extends from the forearm to the hand, along with tingling in the fingers. Symptoms of CTS include burning pain when the nerve is compressed, along with numbness and tingling in the thumb and first two fingers.

Long-term computer work can lead to tendonitis or CTS. Factors that cause these disorders include prolonged typing, prolonged mouse usage, or continual shifting between the mouse and the keyboard. If untreated, these disorders can lead to permanent physical damage.

What can you do to prevent technology-related tendonitis or CTS?

Follow these precautions:

- Take frequent breaks to exercise your hands and arms (Figure 3-29).
- Do not rest your wrists on the edge of a desk. Instead, place a wrist rest between the keyboard and the edge of your desk.
- Place the mouse at least six inches from the edge of the desk. In this position, your wrist is flat on the desk.
- Minimize the number of times you switch between the mouse and the keyboard.
- Keep your forearms and wrists level so that your wrists do not bend.
- Avoid using the heel of your hand as a pivot point while typing or using the mouse.
- Keep your shoulders, arms, hands, and wrists relaxed while you work.
- Maintain good posture.
- Stop working if you experience pain or fatigue.

Hand Exercises

- Spread fingers apart for several seconds while keeping wrists straight.
- Gently push back fingers and then thumb.
- Dangle arms loosely at sides and then shake arms and hands.

Figure 3-29 To reduce the chance of developing tendonitis or carpal tunnel syndrome, take frequent breaks during computer sessions to exercise your hands and arms.
© iStockphoto / Denis Kartavenko; © Oleksiy Mark / Shutterstock.com; © Cengage Learning

Other Physical Risks

Computer vision syndrome (*CVS*) is a technology-related health condition that affects eyesight. You may have CVS if you have sore, tired, burning, itching, or dry eyes; blurred or double vision; distance blurred vision after prolonged staring at a display device; headache or sore neck; difficulty shifting focus between a display device and documents; difficulty focusing on the screen image; color fringes or after-images when you look away from the display device; and increased sensitivity to light. Eyestrain associated with CVS is not thought to have serious or long-term consequences. Figure 3-30 outlines some techniques you can follow to ease eyestrain.

People who spend their workday using the computer sometimes complain of lower back pain, muscle fatigue, and emotional fatigue. Lower back pain sometimes is caused from poor posture. Always sit properly in the chair while you work. To alleviate back pain, muscle fatigue, and emotional fatigue, take a 15- to 30-minute break every 2 hours — stand up, walk around, stretch, and relax.

Techniques to Ease Eyestrain

- Every 10 to 15 minutes, take an eye break.
  - Look into the distance and focus on an object for 20 to 30 seconds.
  - Roll your eyes in a complete circle.
  - Close your eyes and rest them for at least one minute.
- Blink your eyes every five seconds.
- Place your display device about an arm's length away from your eyes with the top of the screen at or below eye level.
- Use large fonts.
- If you wear glasses, ask your doctor about computer glasses.
- Adjust the lighting.

Figure 3-30 Following these tips may help reduce eyestrain while using technology.
© grublee / Shutterstock.com

Internet Research

What is a treadmill desk?

Search for: treadmill desk

Another way to help prevent these injuries is to be sure your workplace is designed ergonomically. **Ergonomics** is an applied science devoted to incorporating comfort, efficiency, and safety into the design of items in the workplace. Ergonomic studies have shown that using the correct type and configuration of chair, keyboard, display device, and work surface helps users work comfortably and efficiently and helps protect their health (Figure 3-31). You can hire an ergonomic consultant to evaluate your workplace and recommend changes.

viewing angle: 20° to center of screen **viewing distance:** 18 to 28 inches

arms: elbows at about 90° and arms and hands approximately parallel to flooor

keyboard height: 23 to 28 inches depending on height of user

adjustable height chair with 4 or 5 legs for stability

feet flat on floor

Figure 3-31 A well designed work area should be flexible to allow adjustments to the height and build of different individuals. Good lighting and air quality also are important considerations.

© C Squared Studios / Getty Images

Behavioral Health Risks

Some technology users become obsessed with computers, mobile devices, and the Internet. **Technology addiction** occurs when the technology consumes someone's entire social life. Technology addiction is a growing health problem but can be treated through therapy and support groups.

People suffering from *technology overload* feel distressed when deprived of technology, even for a short length of time, or feel overwhelmed with the amount of technology they are required to manage. To cope with the feelings of distraction and to control the impact that technology can have on work and relationships, set aside technology-free time.

 CONSIDER THIS

How can you tell if you are addicted to technology?
Symptoms of a user with technology addiction include the following:

- Craves computer time
- Overjoyed when using a computer or mobile device
- Unable to stop using technology
- Irritable when not using technology
- Neglects family and friends
- Problems at work or school

NOW YOU KNOW ———————————————————————————————————————

Be sure you understand the material presented in the sections titled Ports and Connections, Protecting Hardware, and Health Concerns of Using Technology as it relates to the chapter objectives.
You now should know…

• How you can connect a peripheral device to a computer or mobile device (Objective 8)

• How you can protect your hardware from theft, vandalism, and failure (Objective 9)

• How you can minimize your risk of health-related injuries and disorders that can result from using technology (Objective 10)

> Quiz Yourself Online: Check your knowledge of related content by navigating to this book's Quiz Yourself resource on Computer Concepts CourseMate and then tapping or clicking Objectives 8–10.

Chapter Summary

This chapter presented characteristics of and purchasing guidelines for desktops, laptops, tablets, smartphones, digital cameras, and portable media players. It also discussed handheld computers, servers, supercomputers, point-of-sale terminals, ATMs, self-service kiosks, e-book readers, game devices, embedded computers, and cloud computing. It presented a variety of ports and connections, ways to protect hardware, and health concerns of using technology use along with preventive measures.

Test your knowledge of chapter material by accessing the Study Guide, Flash Cards, and Practice Test apps that run on your smartphone, tablet, laptop, or desktop.

TECHNOLOGY @ WORK ——

Meteorology

With the television tuned to the local weather station, you anxiously are awaiting to see the projected path of a hurricane in the tropics. Having experienced hurricanes in the past, you rely heavily on the accuracy of weather forecasts so that you can prepare adequately if a storm travels through the area. Computers allow meteorologists to better estimate the severity and path of storms, enabling people to make potentially life-saving preparations.

The National Hurricane Center uses powerful computers to generate multiple computer models to determine a storm's path. These models consider factors such as the storm's current strength, the effects of nearby weather systems, the storm's central pressure, and whether the storm may travel over land. These models also may consider previous storms that traveled a similar path. While these models are not 100 percent accurate, they do ensure that everyone who may be affected by the storm has enough time to prepare.

Violent, rotating thunderstorms potentially can spawn tornadoes, which sometimes cause catastrophic damage. For this reason, it is important for everyone to watch or listen closely to the weather during the storm. Meteorologists can monitor weather systems on multiple radars and send additional severe weather warnings automatically to weather radios and apps. Computer technology enables these messages to be broadcast automatically to weather radios and apps only in areas that may be affected.

In addition to computers helping us stay safe during severe storms, they also assist with day-to-day weather forecasting. Several years ago, meteorologists could predict the weather for only a few days into the future. Beyond that point, the forecast was very uncertain. Meteorologists presently are able to predict the weather, including temperature and chance of precipitation, one week or more into the future with much greater accuracy because computers create models using historical weather data and behavior to predict the future path of various weather systems.

News and weather stations have weather apps and also post their weather forecasts

National Oceanographic and Atmospheric Administration

online. In fact, several websites have interactive radars that allow visitors to zoom in and view how weather is affecting their immediate neighborhood.

The meteorology field has made significant advancements because of computer technologies. Weather forecasts are more accurate, which not only helps us prepare on land, but also helps to protect those traveling by air or by sea.

☀ In what other ways do computers and technology play a role in the meteorology field?

Study Guide

The Study Guide exercise reinforces material you should know for the chapter exam. You will find answers to items with the icon only in the e-book.

Access the Study Guide app that runs on your smartphone, tablet, laptop, or desktop by navigating to this book's Apps resource on Computer Concepts CourseMate.

Instructions: Answer the questions below using the format that helps you remember best or that is required by your instructor. Possible formats may include one or more of these options: write the answers; create a document that contains the answers; record answers as audio or video using a webcam, smartphone, or portable media player; post answers on a blog, wiki, or website; or highlight answers in the book/e-book.

1. List types of computers and mobile devices.

2. Explain how to avoid malware infections.

3. Describe how personal computers often are differentiated.

4. Name the contributions of Dell and Michael Dell, with respect to personal computers and peripherals.

5. Define the term, motherboard.

6. Describe the roles of the processor and memory.

7. Identify types of desktop users and explain how each user's computer needs may differ.

8. List considerations when purchasing a desktop. A(n) _____ desktop may be less expensive and take up less space.

9. Differentiate among traditional and ultrathin laptops, netbooks, tablets, phablets, and handheld computers.

10. To interact with a tablet, you may use a touch screen or a(n) _____.

11. List considerations when purchasing a mobile computer. Explain the importance of built-in ports and slots.

12. Describe the purpose and functions of a server. Differentiate among rack, blade, and tower servers.

13. Define virtualization as it relates to servers. Define the terms, server farm and mainframe.

14. A(n) _____ is used to solve complex, sophisticated mathematical calculations such as petroleum exploration.

15. Define the terms, terminal and thin client. List the advantages of a thin client.

16. Identify situations where POS terminals, ATMs, and self-service kiosks might be used. List ATM safety guidelines.

17. List cloud computing resources. Describe how businesses use cloud computing to manage resources.

18. List types of mobile devices. Describe features of a smartphone.

19. Explain the issues surrounding the recycling of e-waste.

20. Differentiate among types of smartphone keyboards.

21. Name the products and/or services of Samsung, with respect to technology.

22. List options provided by text and picture/video message services.

23. _____ occurs when a person's attention is diverted, such as by talking on a mobile phone.

24. Describe the types of digital cameras, how they store captured images, and how to transfer photos to a computer.

25. Explain how resolution affects digital picture quality.

26. Identify the features of a portable media player.

27. List considerations when purchasing mobile devices. List accessory options for various device types.

28. List features of e-book readers. Explain the issues surrounding library circulation of e-books.

29. Identify types of game controllers.

30. Explain whether fitness video games are an effective form of exercise.

31. List products that contain embedded computers. List the disadvantages of in-vehicle technology.

32. With _____ computing, you can donate your computer's resources for scientific research.

33. Explain how a computer uses ports and connectors.

34. List devices that connect to a USB port. Explain the role of a USB hub.

35. Define the term, backward compatible.

36. Distinguish between a port replicator and a docking station.

37. Describe the following technologies: Bluetooth, Wi-Fi, and NFC.

38. _____ is the process of initiating contact between two Bluetooth devices.

39. List steps to connect your phone to a Wi-Fi network.

40. List methods for securing against hardware theft and vandalism.

41. Define the terms, undervoltage and overvoltage, and explain how each can damage a computer or data.

42. Describe the purposes of surge protectors and UPS devices. Explain the purpose a fault-tolerant computer.

43. Identify causes and types of repetitive strain injuries.

44. List symptoms of CVS.

45. Describe the role of ergonomics in a workplace.

46. List symptoms of technology addiction. Define the term, technology overload.

You should be able to define the Primary Terms and be familiar with the Secondary Terms listed below.

Key Terms

Access the Flash Cards app that runs on your smartphone, tablet, laptop, or desktop by navigating to this book's Apps resource on Computer Concepts CourseMate. View definitions for each term by navigating to this book's Key Terms resource on Computer Concepts CourseMate. Listen to definitions for each term on your portable media player by navigating to this book's Audio Study Tools resource on Computer Concepts CourseMate.

Primary Terms (shown in **bold-black** characters in the chapter)

Bluetooth (132)	embedded computer (126)	pairing (132)	tablet (109)
cloud computing (116)	ergonomics (138)	personal computer (104)	technology addiction (138)
computer (104)	game console (125)	port (129)	undervoltage (135)
computer vision	handheld computer (111)	portable media player (122)	uninterruptible power
syndrome (137)	handheld game device (125)	power surge (135)	supply (UPS) (135)
connector (129)	laptop (108)	resolution (122)	USB port (131)
desktop (106)	mobile device (104)	server (111)	Wi-Fi (133)
digital camera (120)	NFC (133)	smartphone (117)	
e-book reader (124)	overvoltage (135)	surge protector (135)	

Secondary Terms (shown in *italic* characters in the chapter)

all-in-one desktop (107)	*enhanced resolution (122)*	*network server (111)*	*Smart TV (128)*
application server (111)	*e-reader (124)*	*notebook computer (108)*	*SMS (short message service)*
ATM (114)	*fault-tolerant computer (135)*	*offline UPS (136)*	*(118)*
backup server (111)	*file server (111)*	*online UPS (136)*	*spike (135)*
backward compatible (131)	*fingerprint reader (134)*	*on-screen keyboard (117)*	*standby UPS (136)*
balance board (126)	*FTP server (111)*	*optical resolution (122)*	*storage server (111)*
bar code reader (113)	*game server (111)*	*peripheral device (104)*	*stylus (109)*
blackout (135)	*gamepad (126)*	*personal media player (122)*	*supercomputer (113)*
blade server (112)	*gaming desktop (107)*	*phablet (110)*	*surge suppressor (135)*
Bluetooth wireless port adapter	*home server (111)*	*PIN (114)*	*system unit (106)*
(132)	*inattentional blindness (119)*	*pixel (122)*	*technology overload (138)*
brownout (135)	*Internet of Things (128)*	*point-and-shoot camera (120)*	*telematics (127)*
charge-coupled device (CCD) (121)	*jack (129)*	*port replicator (131)*	*terminal (113)*
common short code (CSC) (118)	*joystick (126)*	*portable keyboard (118)*	*thin client (113)*
convertible tablet (109)	*kiosk (115)*	*POS terminal (113)*	*touch-sensitive pad (123)*
CPU (106)	*list server (111)*	*predictive text input (117)*	*tower (106)*
CVS (137)	*mail server (111)*	*print server (111)*	*tower server (112)*
dance pad (126)	*mainframe (112)*	*processor (106)*	*ultrabook (109)*
database server (111)	*media library (123)*	*rack server (112)*	*USB hub (131)*
discoverable mode (132)	*memory (106)*	*repetitive strain injury (RSI)*	*virtual keyboard (118)*
docking station (132)	*MMS (multimedia message service)*	*(136)*	*virtualization (112)*
domain name server (111)	*(119)*	*server farm (112)*	*visual voice mail (119)*
DVD kiosk (115)	*mobile computer (104)*	*server virtualization (112)*	*voice mail (119)*
earbuds (123)	*motherboard (106)*	*skimmer (114)*	*web server (111)*
EarPods (123)	*motion-sensing game controller (126)*	*slate tablet (109)*	*wheel (126)*
e-book (124)	*near field communications (133)*	*SLR camera (120)*	*workstation (107)*

slate tablet (109)
© iStockphoto / Pedro Castellano

Checkpoint

The Checkpoint exercises test your knowledge of the chapter concepts. The page number containing the answer appears in parentheses after each exercise. The Consider This exercises challenge your understanding of chapter concepts.

Complete the Checkpoint exercises interactively by navigating to this book's Checkpoint resource on Computer Concepts CourseMate. **Access the Test Prep app** that runs on your smartphone, tablet, laptop, or desktop by navigating to this book's Apps resource on Computer Concepts CourseMate. After successfully completing the self-assessment through the Test Prep app, **take the Practice Test** by navigating to this book's Practice Test resource on Computer Concepts Coursemate.

True/False   Mark T for True and F for False.

_____ 1. Malware authors focus on social media, with the goal of stealing personal information. (106)

_____ 2. Although they can save space, all-in-one desktops usually are more expensive than a system unit and monitor purchased separately. (108)

_____ 3. Most traditional and ultrathin laptop and ultrabook screens range in size from 7 to 10 inches, and most tablet and netbook screens range in size from 11 to 18 inches. (110)

_____ 4. Dedicated servers typically require a faster processor, more memory, and additional storage. (112)

_____ 5. Most computers and electronic devices are analog, which use only two discrete states: on and off. (119)

_____ 6. Some mobile devices allow you to transfer photos using wireless technologies such as Bluetooth and Wi-Fi. (121)

_____ 7. Most smartphones also can function as portable media players and digital cameras. (122)

_____ 8. Because embedded computers are components in larger products, they usually are small and have limited hardware. (127)

_____ 9. Instead of the term, port, the term, connector, sometimes is used to identify audio and video ports. (129)

_____ 10. Newer versions of USB are backward compatible, which means they support only new USB devices, not older ones. (131)

_____ 11. Because the processor in a computer is particularly sensitive to current fluctuations, you always should use a surge protector. (136)

_____ 12. An offline UPS always runs off the battery. (136)

Multiple Choice   Select the best answer.

1. Examples of a(n) _____ device include keyboard, mouse, microphone, monitor, printer, USB flash drive, scanner, webcam, and speakers. (104)
   a. output
   b. input
   c. mobile
   d. peripheral

2. Some people use the term _____ to refer to the case that contains and protects the motherboard, hard disk drive, memory, and other electronic components of the computer from damage. (106)
   a. system unit
   b. phablet
   c. thin client
   d. USB hub

3. Some desktops, called a(n) _____, do not have a tower and instead house the screen and system unit in the same case. (107)
   a. peripheral unit
   b. system unit
   c. all-in-one desktop
   d. gaming computer

4. Power users may work with a high-end desktop, sometimes called a(n) _____, that is designed to handle intense calculations and powerful graphics. (107)
   a. laptop
   b. gaming desktop
   c. server farm
   d. workstation

5. Services provided by _____ include storing content and controlling access to hardware, software, and other resources on a network. (111)
   a. jacks
   b. servers
   c. fault-tolerant computers
   d. mainframes

6. A dedicated server that backs up and restores files, folders, and media is referred to as a(n) _____. (111)
   a. web server
   b. file server
   c. storage server
   d. backup server

7. A four- or five-digit number assigned to a specific content or mobile service provider is referred to as a(n) _____. (118)
   a. CSC
   b. MMS
   c. SMS
   d. SLR

8. A(n) _____ can connect up to 127 different peripheral devices together with a single connector. (131)
   a. SLR device
   b. USB port
   c. port replicator
   d. docking station

Checkpoint

Matching   Match the terms with their definitions.

_____ 1. peripheral device (104)

_____ 2. motherboard (106)

_____ 3. CPU (106)

_____ 4. tower (106)

_____ 5. phablet (110)

_____ 6. virtualization (112)

_____ 7. thin client (113)

_____ 8. resolution (122)

_____ 9. pairing (132)

_____ 10. standby UPS (136)

a. term used to refer to a device that combines the features of a smartphone with a tablet

b. power supply that switches to battery power when a problem occurs in the power line

c. metal or plastic frame that houses the system unit on a desktop

d. component you connect to a computer or mobile device to expand its capabilities

e. terminal that looks like a desktop but has limited capabilities and components

f. the practice of sharing or pooling computing resources, such as servers and storage devices

g. electronic component that interprets and carries out the basic instructions that operate a computer

h. the number of horizontal and vertical pixels in a display device

i. process of initiating contact between two Bluetooth devices and allowing them to communicate with each other

j. the main circuit board of a personal computer

Short Answer   Write a brief answer to each of the following questions.

1. Describe the different types of desktops. (107) What should you consider when purchasing a desktop? (107–108)

2. How do netbooks and ultrathin laptops differ from traditional laptops? (109) What privacy issues have arisen with webcams in mobile devices? (109)

3. Describe the different types of tablets. (109) What is a stylus? (109)

4. List the three form factors for servers. (112) What are the advantages of virtual servers? (112)

5. What typing options are available on smartphones? (117–118) Differentiate between predictive text input and a swipe keyboard app. (117)

✹ Consider This   Answer the following questions in the format specified by your instructor.

1. Answer the critical thinking questions posed at the end of these elements in this chapter: Ethics & Issues (109, 117, 124, 126, 127), How To (121, 131, 132, 133), Mini Features (107, 110, 123), Secure IT (106, 114, 119, 136), and Technology @ Work (139).

2. How do malware authors use social media to spread infection? (106)

3. What are the two main components of the motherboard? What is in the system unit? (106)

4. What are the features of a gaming desktop? What is a workstation? (107)

5. How do netbooks and ultrathin laptops differ? When might you use each? (109)

6. What additional requirements are associated with a dedicated server? (111)

7. How does a POS terminal serve as input? Why would a grocery store use a POS terminal? (113)

8. What information might you receive from a web to mobile text message? For what purpose is a common short code (CSC) used? (118)

9. What is the difference between enhanced and optical resolution? (122)

10. 📱 When purchasing a smartphone, what should you consider when choosing a wireless plan? (123)

11. What is the purpose of a docking station? (132)

12. Why might you want to connect your phone to a Wi-Fi network? (133)

13. How can you configure your computer or mobile device to help track it in case of theft? (134)

14. How does a surge protector work? What is the purpose of an uninterruptible power supply? (135)

15. How can you prevent technology-related tendonitis and CTS? (136)

✲ How To: Your Turn

The How To: Your Turn exercises present general guidelines for fundamental skills when using a computer or mobile device and then require that you determine how to apply these general guidelines to a specific program or situation.

Instructions: You often can complete tasks using technology in multiple ways. Figure out how to perform the tasks described in these exercises by using one or more resources available to you (such as a computer or mobile device, articles on the web or in print, online or program help, user guides, blogs, podcasts, videos, other individuals, trial and error, etc.). Summarize your 'how to' steps, along with the resource(s) used, in the format requested by your instructor (brief report, presentation, discussion, blog post, video, or other means).

❶ Synchronize a Device

© Iain Masterton / Alamy

Synchronizing a mobile device with the cloud or a computer provides a backup location for your data should your device fail, or become lost or stolen. While companies such as Google and Apple typically will allow you to download your purchased apps again free of charge, you also should synchronize your data so that it is available in the event a problem with your device arises. The following steps guide you through the process of synchronizing a device.

Synchronize with the Cloud

a. Search for an app compatible with your device that allows you to synchronize the data on your device with the cloud. Some device manufacturers, such as Apple, provide a service to synchronize your device with the cloud.
b. If necessary, download and install the app.
c. The first time you run the app, you may need to enter some personal information so that you are able to sign in and access your data in the future.
d. Configure the app to synchronize at your desired interval. If you are synchronizing a smartphone, keep in mind that synchronizing with the cloud will require a data plan. Be sure your data plan supports the amount of data that will be synchronized.
e. Once you have configured the synchronization settings successfully, select the option to manually synchronize your device at this time.

Synchronize with a Computer

a. Install and run the app designed to synchronize your device with your computer. For instance, iTunes is used to synchronize Apple devices with a computer.
b. Connect the device to the computer using the synchronization cable provided.
c. When the synchronization is complete, a message will inform you that it is safe to disconnect the device. Do not disconnect the device before the synchronization is complete, as that may damage the data on the device.

Retrieve Synchronized Data

If you lose your device or the data on your device, you can retrieve the data previously synchronized. To retrieve data synchronized previously, follow the instructions in the program or app used to synchronize your data.

Exercises

1. What type of device are you attempting to synchronize? What programs and apps are available to synchronize your device with the cloud? What programs and apps are available to synchronize your device with a computer?
2. Which program or app did you use to synchronize your device? Why did you choose that program or app instead of the others?
3. How long did it take to synchronize your device? What data on your device did the program or app synchronize?

❷ Evaluate Earbuds and Headphones

Earbuds and headphones are used to listen to music and other audio files on computers and mobile devices. Selecting the proper product not only depends on the style you prefer, but also the type of audio you will be playing. Prices for earbuds and headphones can range from only a few dollars to several hundred dollars, so it is important to know what you are purchasing. The following guidelines describe what to look for when evaluating earbuds and headphones.

- Determine which style you prefer. Earbuds rest inside your ear, while headphones rest over your ear. Experiment with both types and determine which is more comfortable for you.
- Determine the quality you desire. If you listen to music casually and typically do not notice variations in sound quality, a higher-end product might not be necessary. Alternatively, if sound quality is important, you may consider a more expensive set. Note that a higher price does not always indicate better quality; read online product reviews for information about the sound quality of various products.

- Decide whether you would like a noise cancelling feature. Noise cancelling headphones help block external noise while you are listening to the audio on your device. Noise cancelling headphones sometimes require batteries, and you are able to turn the noise cancelling feature on and off. If you will be listening to audio in locations where you also need to hear what is going on around you, consider purchasing a product without this feature.

Exercises

1. Do you prefer earbuds or headphones? Why?
2. Is sound quality important to you? Why or why not?
3. Based on your preferences and needs, which type of product (earbuds or headphones) is best for you? Locate a product online that meets your specifications. What brand is it? How much does it cost? Where is this product available?

❸ Ergonomically Arrange Your Computer Work Area

Maintaining an ergonomic work area will help keep you comfortable while working with your computer. In addition to providing comfort, an ergonomic work area also will help minimize health risks associated with using a computer frequently. The following guidelines will help you set up an ergonomic work area:

- Set up a work area of at least two feet by four feet.
- The viewing angle between your eyes and the center of the screen should be 20 degrees, and your eyes should be 18 to 28 inches away from the screen.
- Your elbows should be at about 90 degrees and your arms and hands should be approximately parallel to the floor.
- The height of the keyboard from the floor should be 23 to 28 inches, depending on the height of the user.
- Use a chair with four or five legs that allows you to adjust the height.
- Your feet should rest flat on the floor.

Exercises

1. Evaluate your current work area. Is it ergonomic? Why or why not?
2. What types of health risks might a nonergonomic work area pose?
3. What are some additional guidelines you can follow to help minimize health risks while using your computer?

How To: Your Turn ✳

❹ Find, Download, and Read an E-Book on an E-Book Reader

© iStockphoto / pressureUA

Most e-book readers enable you to find and download new e-books without having to connect to a computer first. To search for and download an e-book, you need to establish an Internet connection through either Wi-Fi or a mobile data plan. The following steps guide you through the process of finding, downloading, and reading an e-book on an e-book reader.

a. Turn on your e-book reader and establish an Internet connection.
b. Navigate to the store on your e-book reader where you can search for and download e-books.
c. Locate the option to search available e-books and then enter the desired search text. You usually can search by the book's title, author, or genre.
d. Perform the search and then browse the search results for the book you want to download and install.
e. Select the option to download the book. Please note that many books cost money to download. If your payment information was entered previously, you may be charged for downloading this e-book. If you do not want to be charged, locate and download an e-book that is free.
f. When the download is complete, return to your list of installed e-books.
g. Select the e-book you have just downloaded to read the e-book.

Exercises

1. What type of e-book reader do you have? Are you happy with the selection of e-books on your e-book reader?
2. In addition to e-book readers, what other types of devices allow you to read e-books?
3. Do e-books cost more or less than traditional print books? What are the advantages and disadvantages of using e-books?

✳ Internet Research

The Internet Research exercises broaden your understanding of chapter concepts by requiring that you search for information on the web.

Instructions: Use a search engine or another search tool to locate the information requested or answers to questions presented in the exercises. Describe your findings, along with the search term(s) you used and your web source(s), in the format requested by your instructor (brief report, presentation, discussion, blog post, video, or other means).

❶ Making Use of the Web
Shopping and Auctions

E-retailers are changing the ways consumers shop for goods. One market research firm reports that nearly three-fourths of shoppers complete one-half of all their transactions online. As shoppers grow increasingly loyal to e-commerce, shopping sites have become more sophisticated, and brick-and-mortar stores have adapted to the online presence. Nearly 50 percent of smartphone and mobile device owners use apps to compare prices and purchase items every month.

Online auctions offer another convenient method of shopping for and selling practically anything imaginable. Most auction sites organize products in categories and provide photos and descriptions. eBay is one of thousands of Internet auction websites and is the world's largest personal online trading community. In addition, craigslist is a free online equivalent of classified advertisements.

(a) Visit two shopping websites and search for the latest iPhone or Android phone. Which features do these websites offer compared with the same offerings in brick-and-mortar stores? What are the advantages and disadvantages of shopping online? What policies do these websites offer for returning items? Which items have you purchased online?

(b) Visit an auction website and search for two objects pertaining to your hometown or a favorite vacation destination. For example, if you are from

Boston, search for a Red Sox or Bruins jersey. Describe these two items. How many people have bid on these items? Who are the sellers? What are the opening and current bids?

❷ Social Media

Businesses are discovering that using social media is an efficient and effective method of building brand loyalty and promoting the exchange of ideas. According to a recent study, 80 percent of American Internet users visit social networking sites and blogs, and 60 percent discover particular brands and companies by reading material posted on these websites when conducting research using a variety of online sources. The informal communication between consumers and company representatives can help maintain credibility and promote trust. Twitter, Facebook, and other social media often are used to befriend customers, give a positive feeling about services and goods, engage readers, and market new ideas. Subscribers share their opinions, thoughts, and experiences, either positive or negative, through product and service reviews.

Visit at least three Twitter, Facebook, or other social media sites and review the content. How many Twitter followers or Facebook 'likes' does the website have? Which posts are engaging and promote positive attitudes about the companies and the products or services offered? How many user-generated reviews and product ratings are shown? How do the websites encourage sharing opinions? In which ways do the companies respond to and interact with customers? If negative posts are written, does the company respond professionally and positively?

❸ Search Sleuth

(1) What are four 10-letter words composed of letters on a keyboard's top row? (2) Which company is

Source: ebay

Internet Research ✳

credited with developing the first phablet? (3) Who wrote the official five-note Intel signature jingle? How many weeks did he need to write this jingle? (4) What trait do Belle, Deep Blue, Hydra, Gravity Pipe, MDGRAPE-3, and Deep Crack share? (5) For which purpose was the Barcode Battler developed? (6) In which shopping center was the first ATM installed in the United States? When was it installed? (7) Which company has self-service kiosks located in the Empire State Building in New York City and the Willis Tower in Chicago? (8) What is the name of the predictive text input method that Martin King and Cliff Kushler developed? (9) JPL's Frederic C. Billingsley used the word, pixel, to describe which images in 1965? (10) Who created the first video game joystick in 1967?

4 Green Computing

When your computer is turned on, many of the components generate heat. The processor and video card become so hot that, in theory, they could be used as a hot plate to cook food. If heat builds up inside the case, the components could become seriously damaged.

Most computers have a cooling system that consists of an intake fan on the front and sometimes the sides of the case and an exhaust fan on the back inside the power supply. These two fans work together to move cool air over the components and force hot air out the opposite side.

It is important to keep the computer as cool as possible, and the most effective method of meeting this requirement is to not restrict the airflow. Remove all obstructions on all sides of the case, especially the rear. Most likely the fans will become caked with dust and pet hair, so occasionally unplug the computer, open the case, and blow canned air over the fins. Place a cooling mat with an integrated fan under a laptop to keep temperatures in the normal range. If you are interested in checking the computer's internal heat, install temperature monitoring software.

Locate the intake and exhaust fans in your computer. How much space is allocated on all sides of the computer so that these fans can work efficiently? Can you remove any obstructions or position the case in a location that increases the airflow? Visit some websites that advertise cooling mats and temperature monitoring software. What are their costs, and which features do they have?

5 Security

Surge protectors and uninterruptible power supplies offer electrical protection, and Secure IT 3-4 on page 136 gives suggestions about features to consider when purchasing these devices. Visit an electronics store or view websites with a variety of surge protectors from several manufacturers. Read the packaging to determine many of the specifications listed in Secure IT 3-4. Compare at least three surge protectors by creating a table using these headings: manufacturer, model, price, Joule rating, warranty, clamping voltage, energy-absorption rating, response time, and other features. Which surge protector do you recommend?

Courtesy of Tripp Lite

6 Ethics in Action

Instant background checks on United States citizens are available through several websites. Computers search several decades of public record databases with billions of records containing warrants, state and local arrests, convictions, felonies, probation violations, revoked licenses, driving infractions, average income, bankruptcies, marriage and divorce history, reverse phone and email lookups, estimated income, property sales transactions, births, deaths, and census figures.

The companies that provide this information in an uncensored format offer a variety of methods of looking into an individual's criminal history. For example, some websites offer a free trial or have a free directory that allows a preliminary search for a person's name. If the name is found, then a full criminal background check can be ordered.

Do you believe people who run a background check are using the report only for personal reasons, or is the information being used to make employment or leasing decisions? When might a background check be useful, in addition to the desire to locate lost family members and friends or to verify that a babysitter does not have a criminal history? Would you consider running a background check on yourself? Visit at least two background check sites. What is the cost to run a search? Which databases are used? Do the websites offer an opportunity to individuals to remove information, or opt out, from the page?

✳ Problem Solving

The Problem Solving exercises extend your knowledge of chapter concepts by seeking solutions to practical problems with technology that you may encounter at home, school, work, or with nonprofit organizations. The Collaboration exercise should be completed with a team.

💻 **Challenge yourself** with additional Problem Solving exercises by navigating to this book's Problem Solving resource on Computer Concepts CourseMate.

Instructions: You often can solve problems with technology in multiple ways. Determine a solution to the problems in these exercises by using one or more resources available to you (such as a computer or mobile device, articles on the web or in print, blogs, podcasts, videos, television, user guides, other individuals, electronics or computer stores, etc.). Describe your solution, along with the resource(s) used, in the format requested by your instructor (brief report, presentation, discussion, blog post, video, or other means).

Personal

1. **Slow Computer Performance** Your computer is running exceptionally slow. Not only does it take the operating system a long time to start, but programs also are not performing as well as they used to perform. How might you resolve this?

2. **Faulty ATM** When using an ATM to deposit a check, the ATM incorrectly reads the amount of the check and credits your account the incorrect amount. What can you do to resolve this?

3. **Insufficient Memory** When trying to download a photo to your smartphone, an error message is displayed stating that no more storage space is available. What types of items might you remove from your phone to obtain additional storage space?

© iStockphoto / Oleksiy Mark;
© Cengage Learning

4. **Touch Input Does Not Work** While working with your tablet, it suddenly stops responding to your touch gestures. What might be wrong, and how can you try to fix this problem?

5. **Potential Virus Infection** While using your laptop, a message is displayed stating that your computer is infected with a virus and you should click a link to download a program designed to remove the virus. How will you respond?

Professional

6. **New Computer** Your boss has given you the authority to purchase a new computer, but you are unsure of which one to buy. Each computer you review has a different type of processor, and you are having difficulty determining which one will suit your needs. How will you obtain this information?

7. **Server Not Connecting** While traveling on a business trip, your phone suddenly stops synchronizing your email messages, calendar information, and contacts. Upon further investigation you notice an error message stating that your phone is unable to connect to the server. What are your next steps?

8. **Mobile Device Synchronization** When you plug your smartphone into your computer to synchronize the data, the computer does not recognize that the smartphone is connected. What might be the problem?

9. **Cloud Service Provider** Your company uses a cloud service provider to back up the data on each employee's computer. Your computer recently crashed, and you need to obtain the backup data to restore to your computer; however, you are unable to connect to the cloud service provider's website. What are your next steps?

10. **Connecting to a Projector** Your boss asked you to give a presentation to your company's board of directors. When you enter the boardroom and attempt to connect your laptop to the projector, you realize that the cable to connect your laptop to the projector does not fit in any of the ports on your laptop. What are your next steps?

Collaboration

11. **Technology in Meteorology** Your environmental sciences instructor is teaching a lesson about how technology has advanced the meteorology field. Form a team of three people to prepare a brief report about how technology and meteorology are connected. One team member should research how meteorologists predicted weather patterns before computer use became mainstream. Another team member should create a timeline illustrating when and how technology was introduced to the meteorology field, and the third team member should research the technology required for a typical news station to forecast and present the weather.

The Critical Thinking exercises challenge your assessment and decision-making skills by presenting real-world situations associated with chapter concepts. The Collaboration exercise should be completed with a team.

Critical Thinking ✳

 Challenge yourself with additional Critical Thinking exercises by navigating to this book's Critical Thinking resource on Computer Concepts CourseMate.

Instructions: Evaluate the situations below, using personal experiences and one or more resources available to you (such as articles on the web or in print, blogs, podcasts, videos, television, user guides, other individuals, electronics or computer stores, etc.). Perform the tasks requested in each exercise and share your deliverables in the format requested by your instructor (brief report, presentation, discussion, blog post, video, or other means).

1. Class Discussion

Technology Purchases   You are the director of information technology at a company that specializes in designing and selling customizable sportswear for local high school and college sports teams. Most of the computer equipment is out of date and must be replaced. You need to evaluate the technology requirements of individual employees so that you can order replacements. Determine the type of computer or mobile device that might be most appropriate for the following employees: a graphic designer who exclusively works in the office, a cashier who is responsible for assisting customers with purchases, and a sales representative who travels to various locations and needs wireless communications capabilities. Consider the varying requirements of each, including mobility, security, and processing capabilities. Discuss various options that might work for each user, and considerations when purchasing each type of device.

2. Research and Share

Game Devices   You manage a youth recreation center and have been given a grant to purchase a game console and accessories, along with fitness games, for use at the center. Use the web to research three popular recent game consoles. Choose five characteristics to compare the game consoles, such as Internet capabilities, multiplayer game support, storage capacity, television connection, and game controllers. Research fitness games for each console and what accessories are needed to run the games. Determine the goals of each game, such as skill-building, weight loss, or entertainment. Read user reviews of each game as well as professional reviews by gaming industry experts. If possible, survey your friends and classmates to learn about their experiences with each game, such as heart rate while playing the games, any fitness goals reached, and their enjoyment of the game. Compile your findings and then share with the class.

3. Case Study

Farmers' Market   You are the new manager for a group of organic farmers who have a weekly market in season. The farmers' market would like to purchase a digital camera to upload pictures of its vendors and events to its Facebook page and its website. You prepare information about digital camera options to present to the board of directors. First, you research the cost and quality differences between point-and-shoot cameras and SLR cameras. Use the web to find a recent model of both camera types and compare the reviews, as well as the costs, for each. Make a list of additional features, such as video capabilities, editing capabilities, lens, megapixels, GPS, flash, and zoom. Determine how each camera stores the images, the amount of storage available, and how to transfer images to a computer. Explore whether software is included with the camera that can be used to edit, store, or organize the images after they are transferred to a computer. Compare your findings with the camera capabilities of a recent model smartphone. Determine what type of camera would be best for the market's needs and the capabilities that are most important. Compile your findings.

© Skylines / Shutterstock.com

Collaboration

4. **Technology in the Military**   Technology is an integral part of military operations. Many military research projects use simulators that resemble civilian computer games. Your company has been contacted by the Department of Defense for a research project. Form a four-member team, and then form two two-member groups. Assign each group one of the following topics to research: (1) How have mobile computers and cloud computing affected issues of national security? (2) How can the utilization of microchips worn by soldiers, or wearable computers, be integrated into civilian use? Meet with your team and discuss your findings. Compile and organize your findings to include both topics and share with your class. Include any advantages or disadvantages, as well as any legal ramifications that may arise.

Beyond the Book

The Beyond the Book exercises expand your understanding of chapter concepts by requiring research.

Access premium content by visiting Computer Concepts CourseMate. If you have a Computer Concepts CourseMate access code, you can reinforce and extend your learning with MindTap Reader, practice tests, video, and other premium content for Discovering Computers. To sign in to Computer Concepts CourseMate at www.cengagebrain.com, you first must create a student account and then register this book, as described at www.cengage.com/ct/studentdownload.

Part 1 Instructions: Use the web or e-book to perform the task identified for each book element below. Describe your findings, along with the search term(s) you used and your web source(s), if appropriate, in the format requested by your instructor (brief report, presentation, discussion, blog post, video, or other means).

1. **Animation** Review the animation associated with this chapter and then answer the question(s) it poses (121). What search term would you use to learn more about a specific segment of the animation?

2. **Consider This** Select a Consider This in this chapter (106, 107, 110, 112, 116, 118, 122, 125, 128, 133, 135, 137, 138) and find a recent article that elaborates on the topic. What information did you find that was not presented in this book or e-book?

3. **Drag-and-Drop Figures** Complete the Drag-and-Drop Figure activities associated with this chapter (111, 112, 115, 118, 120, 121, 128, 140). What did you learn from each of these activities?

4. **Ethics & Issues** Select an Ethics & Issues in this chapter (109, 117, 124, 126, 127) and find a recent article that supports one view presented. Does the article change your opinion about the topic? Why or why not?

5. **Facebook & Twitter** Review a recent Discovering Computers Facebook post or Twitter Tweet and read the referenced article(s). What did you learn from the article?

6. **High-Tech Talk** Locate an article that discusses topics related to touch screens. Would you recommend the article you found? Why or why not?

7. **How To** Select a How To in this chapter (121, 131, 132, 133) and find a recent article that elaborates on the topic. Who would benefit from the content of this article? Why?

8. **Innovative Computing** Locate two additional facts about IBM's Watson or volunteer computing. Do your findings change your opinion about the future of this innovation? Why or why not?

9. **Internet Research** Use the search term in an Internet Research (106, 107, 113, 116, 120, 125, 134, 138) to answer the question posed in the element. What other search term could you use to answer the question?

10. **Mini Features** Locate an article that discusses topics related to one of the mini features in this chapter (107, 110, 123). Do you feel that the article is appropriate for this course? Why or why not?

11. **Secure IT** Select a Secure IT in this chapter (106, 114, 119, 136) and find a recent article about the topic that you find interesting. How can you relate the content of the article to your everyday life?

12. **Technology @ Work** Locate three additional, unique usages of technology in the meteorology industry (139). What makes the use of these technologies unique to the meteorology industry?

13. **Technology Innovators** Locate two additional facts about Dell and Michael Dell, Samsung, Sony, and Nintendo. Which Technology Innovator impresses you most? Why?

14. **Third-Party Links** Visit one of the third-party links identified in this chapter (104, 106, 107, 109, 110, 114, 117, 119, 120, 121, 123, 124, 125, 126, 133, 136, 139) and read the article or watch the video associated with the link. Would you share this link on your online social network account? Why or why not?

Part 2 Instructions: Find specific instructions for the exercises below in the e-book or on Computer Concepts CourseMate. Beside each exercise is a brief description of its online content.

1. **You Review It** Search for and review a video, podcast, or blog post about current models and features of desktops, traditional laptops, or ultrathin laptops.

2. **Windows and Mac** Enhance your understanding and knowledge about using Windows and Mac computers by completing the Power Management and Using Removable Flash Memory activities.

3. **Android, iOS, and Windows Mobile** Enhance your understanding of mobile devices by completing the Power Management and Transfer Photos from a Digital Camera or Mobile Device to a Computer activities.

4. **Exploring Computer Careers** Read about a career as a help desk specialist, search for related employment ads, and then answer related questions.

5. **App Adventure** Check the news, sports, and weather using apps on your smartphone or tablet.

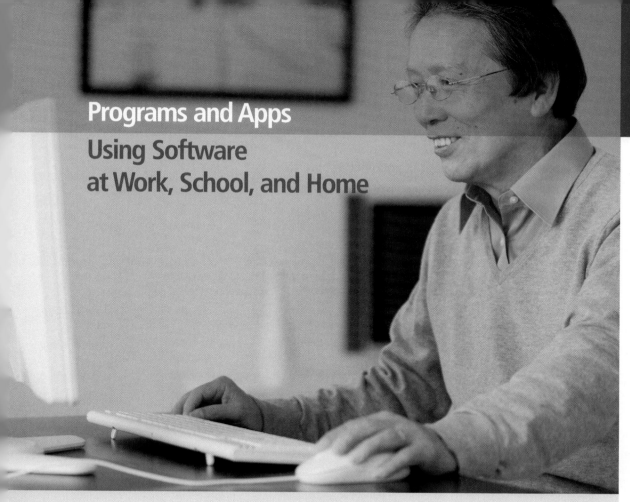

Programs and Apps
Using Software at Work, School, and Home

4

People use a variety of programs and apps on their computers and mobile devices.

"I use my computer and mobile devices to complete homework assignments, pay bills, edit digital photos, post social media updates, and play games. I also use an antivirus program. What other programs and apps could I need?"

True, you may be familiar with some of the material in this chapter, but do you know . . .

How to recognize a virus hoax?

If you should copy information from the web into a research paper?

Whether health and fitness apps can help you reach your goals?

How to back up your computer?

Why you should use a personal firewall?

Who uses iTunes U?

How to avoid risks when using payment apps?

Why you would use a QR code?

How antivirus programs detect viruses?

How the entertainment industry uses programs and apps?

Which office web and mobile apps are best suited to your needs?

Which software company is named after a creek?

How to recognize a phishing message?

How to defragment a hard disk?

For these answers and to discover much more information essential to this course, read this chapter and visit the associated Computer Concepts CourseMate at www.cengagebrain.com.

© AID / a.collectionRF / Getty Images

✓ Objectives

After completing this chapter, you will be able to:

1 Identify the general categories of programs and apps

2 Describe how an operating system interacts with applications and hardware

3 Differentiate among the ways you can acquire programs and apps: retail, custom, web app, mobile app, open source, shareware, freeware, and public-domain

4 Identify the key features of productivity applications: word processing, presentation, spreadsheet, database, note taking, calendar and contact management, project management, accounting, personal finance, legal, tax preparation, document management, support services, and enterprise computing

5 Identify the key features of graphics and media applications: computer-aided design, desktop publishing, paint/image editing, photo editing and photo management, clip art/image gallery, video and audio editing, multimedia and website authoring, media player, and disc burning

6 Identify the uses of personal interest applications: lifestyle, medical, entertainment, convenience, and education

7 Identify the purpose of software used in communications

8 Identify the key features of security tools: personal firewall, antivirus programs, malware removers, and Internet filters

9 Identify the key features of file and disk management tools: file manager, search, image viewer, uninstaller, disk cleanup, disk defragmenter, screen saver, file compression, PC maintenance, and backup and restore

Programs and Apps

Using programs and apps, you can accomplish a variety of tasks on computers and mobile devices. Recall from Chapter 1 that a **program**, or **software**, consists of a series of related instructions, organized for a common purpose, that tells the computer what tasks to perform and how to perform them. An **application**, or **app**, sometimes called *application software*, consists of programs designed to make users more productive and/or assist them with personal tasks.

An *operating system* is a set of programs that coordinates all the activities among computer or mobile device hardware. Other programs, often called *tools* or *utilities*, enable you to perform maintenance-type tasks usually related to managing devices, media, and programs used by computers and mobile devices. The operating system and other tools are collectively known as *system software* because they consist of the programs that control or maintain the operations of the computer and its devices.

With programs and apps, you can create letters, memos, reports, and other documents; develop presentations; prepare and file taxes; draw and alter images; record and enhance audio and video clips; obtain directions or maps; play games individually or with others; compose email messages and instant messages; protect your computers and mobile devices from malware; organize media; locate files; and much more. Table 4-1 categorizes popular categories of programs and apps by their general use.

Table 4-1   Programs and Apps by Category

Category	Types of Programs and Apps	
Productivity (Business and Personal)	• Word Processing • Presentation • Spreadsheet • Database • Note Taking • Calendar and Contact Management • Project Management	• Accounting • Personal Finance • Legal • Tax Preparation • Document Management • Support Services • Enterprise Computing
Graphics and Media	• Computer-Aided Design (CAD) • Desktop Publishing • Paint/Image Editing • Photo Editing and Photo Management • Clip Art/Image Gallery	• Video and Audio Editing • Multimedia and Website Authoring • Media Player • Disc Burning
Personal Interest	• Lifestyle • Medical • Entertainment • Convenience • Education	
Communications	• Blogging • Browser • Chat Room • Discussion Forum • Email • FTP	• Instant Messaging • VoIP • Videoconference • Web Feeds • Wireless Messaging
Security	• Personal Firewall • Antivirus • Malware Removers • Internet Filters	
File and Disk Management	• File Manager • Search • Image Viewer • Uninstaller • Disk Cleanup	• Disk Defragmenter • Screen Saver • File Compression • PC Maintenance • Backup and Restore

✸ CONSIDER THIS

Are the categories of programs and apps shown in Table 4-1 mutually exclusive?

Programs and apps listed in one category may be used in other categories. For example, photo editing applications, which appear in the graphics and media category, often also are used for business or personal productivity. Additionally, the programs and apps in the last three categories (communications, security, and file and disk management) often are used in conjunction with or to support programs and apps in the first three categories (productivity, graphics and media, and personal interest). For example, users may use file transfer software (FTP) to publish webpages created with website authoring programs.

Internet Research

Which mobile operating system is the most widely used?

Search for: mobile operating system market share

The Role of the Operating System

The operating system serves as the interface between the user, the applications, and the computer or mobile device's hardware (Figure 4-1). To use applications, such as a browser or email program on a personal computer, your computer must be running an operating system. Similarly, a mobile device must be running an operating system to run a mobile app, such as a navigation or payment app. Desktop operating systems include Mac OS, Windows, and Linux. Mobile operating systems include Android, iOS, and Windows Phone.

Each time you start a computer or mobile device, the operating system is loaded (copied) from the computer's hard disk or mobile device's storage media into memory. Once the operating system is loaded, it coordinates all the activities of the computer or mobile device.

An Example of How an Operating System Interacts with a User, an Application, and Hardware

Step 2
The user instructs the operating system to run an application, such as a word processing application, which appears on the user's screen. The user then instructs the application to print a document.

document to be printed

Step 1
An operating system user interface is displayed on the screen when a user turns on a computer.

Print button

Step 3
The application sends the print instruction to the computer's operating system (software), which is running on the computer.

Step 4
The operating system sends the print instruction to the printer (hardware), which prints the document.

Figure 4-1 This figure shows how the operating system is the interface between the user, the application, and the hardware.

This includes running applications and transferring data among input and output devices and memory. While the computer or mobile device is running, the operating system remains in memory.

Software Availability

Software is available in a variety of forms: retail, custom, web app, mobile app, mobile web app, open source, shareware, freeware, and public domain.

- *Retail software* is mass-produced, copyrighted software that meets the needs of a wide variety of users, not just a single user or company. Some retail software, such as an operating system, typically is preinstalled on new computers. You also can purchase retail software from local stores and on the web. With online purchases, you may be able to download purchased programs immediately instead of waiting for the software to arrive by mail. Some retail programs have a *trial version*, which is an application you can use at no charge for a limited time, to see if it meets your needs. Some trial versions have limited functionality.

- *Custom software* performs functions specific to a business or industry. Sometimes a company cannot locate retail software that meets its unique requirements. In this case, the company may use software developers to create tailor-made custom software. Custom software usually costs more than retail software.

- A *web app* is an application stored on a web server that you access through a browser. Users typically interact with web apps directly at a website. Many websites provide free access to their apps. Some charge a one-time fee, while others charge recurring monthly or annual subscription fees. You may be able to use part of a web app free and pay for access to a more comprehensive program or pay a fee when a certain action occurs.

- A *mobile app* is an application you download from a mobile device's app store, sometimes called a marketplace, or other location on the Internet to a smartphone or other mobile device. Some mobile apps are preinstalled on a new mobile computer or device. Many mobile apps are free; others have a minimal cost — often less than a few dollars.

- A *mobile web app* is a web app that is optimized for display in a browser on a mobile device. Many app developers opt for web delivery because they do not have to create a different version for each mobile device's app store. Many web apps use a responsive design, which means the app displays properly on any computer or device.

- *Open source software* is software provided for use, modification, and redistribution. This software has no restrictions from the copyright holder regarding modification of the software's internal instructions and its redistribution. Open source software usually can be downloaded from a web server on the Internet, often at no cost. Promoters of open source software state two main advantages: users who modify the software share their improvements with others, and customers can personalize the software to meet their needs.

- *Shareware* is copyrighted software that is distributed at no cost for a trial period. To use a shareware program beyond that period, you send payment to the software developer. Some developers trust users to send payment if software use extends beyond the stated trial period. Others render the software useless if no payment is received after the trial period expires. In some cases, a scaled-down version of the software is distributed free, and payment entitles the user to the fully functional product.

- *Freeware* is copyrighted software provided at no cost by an individual or a company that retains all rights to the software. Thus, software developers typically cannot incorporate freeware in applications they intend to sell. The word, free, in freeware indicates the software has no charge.

- *Public-domain software* has been donated for public use and has no copyright restrictions. Anyone can copy or distribute public-domain software to others at no cost.

BTW
Copyright
A copyright gives authors, artists, and other creators of original work exclusive rights to duplicate, publish, and sell their materials.

Thousands of shareware, freeware, and public-domain programs are available on the Internet for users to download. Examples include communications, graphics, and game programs. Read Secure IT 4-1 for tips about safely downloading shareware, freeware, or public-domain software.

Recall from Chapter 1 that you typically need to install desktop apps on a computer. Installing is the process of setting up the software to work with a computer, printer, and other hardware. Mobile apps typically install automatically after you download the app from the device's app store. You usually do not need to install web apps before you can use them.

During installation of software or before the first use, a program or app may ask you to register and/or activate the software. *Software registration* typically is optional and usually involves submitting your name and other personal information to the software manufacturer or developer. Registering the software often entitles you to product support. *Product activation* is a technique that some software manufacturers use to ensure that you do not install the software on more computers than legally licensed. Usually, the software can be run a preset number of times, has limited functionality, or does not function until you activate it via the Internet or by phone. Thus, activation is a required process for programs that request it. Some software allows multiple activations; for example, you can install it and run it on a desktop and a laptop. Registering and/or activating software also usually entitles you to free program updates for a specified time period, such as a year.

Many desktop and mobile apps use an *automatic update* feature, where the updates can be configured to download and install automatically. With web apps, by contrast, you always access the latest version of the software.

 CONSIDER THIS

What is a license agreement?

A *license agreement* is the right to use a program or app. The license agreement provides specific conditions for use of the software, which a user typically must accept before using the software (Figure 4-2). Unless otherwise specified by a license agreement, you do not have the right to copy, loan, borrow, rent, or in any way distribute programs or apps. Doing so is a violation of copyright law; it also is a federal crime.

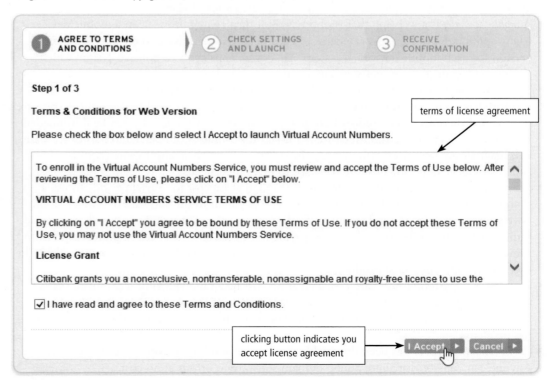

Figure 4-2   A user must accept the terms in a license agreement before using the software.
Source: Citigroup Inc

SECURE IT 4-1

Safe Downloading Websites

The temptation to download shareware, freeware, and public-domain software is high, especially when the cost of such useful or fun programs is free or extremely reasonable. Danger lurks, however, when websites tempt potential customers with catchy offers promising to speed up the computer or to acquire the latest versions of games and music. Many of these websites are filled with virus-infected software just waiting to be installed on an unsuspecting user's computer or mobile device.

Before downloading any software, consider these factors when locating and evaluating shareware, freeware, or public-domain websites:

- Search for popular shareware, freeware, and public-domain download websites.

The software generally is organized into evaluation categories, such as outstanding and recommended, or grouped into purpose, such as tools and gaming.

- Look for websites with programs for your particular type of computer or mobile device. Some websites exclusively offer Windows- or Apple-based products.

- Determine whether the latest versions of shareware, freeware, or public-domain software are available. Many developers update their programs frequently in an effort to thwart viruses and include new features. The newest versions, therefore, often are safer and easier to use than previous versions.

- Find websites with search engines to help you locate a variety of programs in a specific category. For example, if you need

antivirus software, you can search to find which shareware, freeware, and public-domain software is available.

- Seek websites with ratings for and reviews of products. Often, comments from users provide guidance in selecting the most desirable software for your needs.

If you follow these tips, you may find shareware, freeware, and public-domain software to be one of the best software bargains in the marketplace.

Have you ever used or downloaded programs or apps from a shareware, freeware, or public-domain software website? If so, what software did you acquire? If not, would you consider locating shareware, freeware, or public-domain software for your particular needs? Why or why not?

Productivity Applications

Productivity applications can assist you in becoming more effective and efficient while performing daily activities at work, school, and home. Productivity applications include word processing, presentation, spreadsheet, database, note taking, calendar and contact management, project management, accounting, personal finance, legal, tax preparation, document management, support services, and enterprise computing.

A variety of manufacturers offer productivity apps in each of these areas, ranging from desktop to mobile to web apps. Many have a desktop version and a corresponding mobile version adapted for smaller screen sizes and/or touch screens.

BTW

Apple and Microsoft

Technology Innovators: You should be familiar with Microsoft and Apple.

Project Development

With productivity applications, users often create, edit, format, save, and distribute projects. Projects include documents, presentations, calendars, and more. During the process of developing a project, you likely will switch back and forth among these activities.

1. When you *create* a project, you enter text or numbers, insert images, and perform other tasks using a variety of input methods, such as a keyboard, a mouse, touch, or voice.
2. To *edit* a project means to make changes to its existing content. Common editing tasks include inserting, deleting, cutting, copying, and pasting.
   a. Inserting involves adding text, images, or other content.
   b. Deleting means that you are removing text, images, or other content.
   c. Cutting is the process of removing content and storing it in a temporary storage location, called a *clipboard*.
   d. Copying is the process of placing content on a clipboard, with the content remaining in the document. Read Ethics & Issues 4-1 on the next page for a discussion about unethical copying.
   e. Pasting is the process of transferring content from a clipboard to a specific location in a project.
3. When users *format* a project, they change its appearance. Formatting is important because the overall look of a document significantly can affect its capability to communicate

BTW
Points
The text you are reading in this book is about 10 points, which makes each character about 10/72, or approximately one-sixth, of an inch in height.

clearly. Examples of formatting tasks are changing the font, font size, and font style (Figure 4-3).

a. A *font* is a name assigned to a specific design of characters. Cambria and Calibri are examples of fonts.

b. *Font size* indicates the size of the characters in a particular font. Font size is gauged by a measurement system called points. A single point is about 1/72 of an inch in height.

c. A *font style* adds emphasis to a font. Bold, italic, underline, and color are examples of font styles.

4. During the process of creating, editing, and formatting a project, the computer or mobile device holds it in memory. To keep the project for future use requires that you save it. When you *save* a document, the computer transfers the project from memory to a local storage medium, such as a USB flash drive or hard disk, or cloud storage. Once saved, a project is stored permanently as a file.

5. You can distribute a project as a hard copy or electronically. A *hard copy* is information that exists on a physical medium, such as paper. To generate a hard copy, you *print* a project. Sending electronic files via email or posting them for others to view, on websites for example, saves paper and printer supplies. Many users opt for electronic distribution because it contributes to green computing.

 CONSIDER THIS

How often should you save a project?
Saving at regular intervals, such as every 5 or 10 minutes, ensures that the majority of your work will not be lost in the event of a power loss or system failure. Many programs have an AutoSave feature that automatically saves open projects at specified time intervals, such as every 10 minutes. Some web apps save your work instantly as you type.

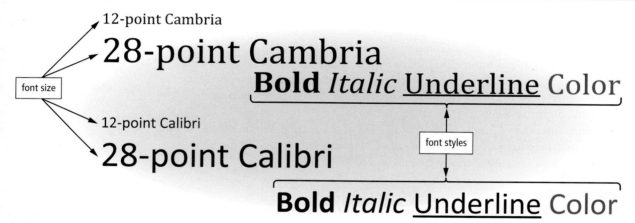

Figure 4-3 The Cambria and Calibri fonts are shown in two font sizes and a variety of font styles.
© Cengage Learning

 ETHICS & ISSUES 4-1

How Should Schools Deal with Internet Plagiarism?

If you ask a student whether plagiarism and cheating are ethical, would you be surprised to receive a response other than a resounding "No"? According to a survey, 55 percent of college presidents believe that plagiarism has increased during the last 10 years. Further, 89 percent of college presidents blame the Internet and computers for the increase. The Internet offers many ways to cheat purposefully, including websites that allow you to purchase or download a research paper. What students may not realize is

that copying information without properly citing it also is plagiarism.

Students who intentionally plagiarize blame peer pressure and competition as some reasons to cheat. Teachers have several tools to catch plagiarists, including a variety of Internet-based services that compare suspect papers to those found on the Internet and produce a report highlighting text that may have been copied. Some instructors, however, are reluctant to confront students with the evidence of plagiarism.

Some educators argue that the best way to prevent cheating is to educate students. First, teach them values and discuss the

consequences of cheating. Next, teach students how to cite sources properly and summarize information in their own words. Armed with this information, the student fully knows right from wrong and hopefully will make the responsible decision not to cheat.

How should educators deal with plagiarism? How should schools educate students about using the Internet for research? Should schools use a paper-comparison service in an attempt to stop cheating? Why or why not? Would you notify an instructor if you knew a classmate had plagiarized material for a research paper? Why or why not?

Word Processing

Word processing software, sometimes called a word processor, is an application that allows users to create and manipulate documents containing mostly text and sometimes graphics (Figure 4-4). Millions of people use word processing software on their computers and mobile devices every day to develop documents such as letters, memos, reports, mailing labels, newsletters, and webpages.

A major advantage of using word processing software is that it enables users to change their written words easily. Word processing software also has many features to make documents look professional and visually appealing. For example, you can change the shape, size, and color of characters; apply special effects, such as three-dimensional shadows; use built-in styles to format documents; and organize text in newspaper-style columns.

Most word processing software allows users to incorporate graphics, such as digital photos and clip art, in documents. **Clip art** is a collection of drawings, photos, and other images. In Figure 4-4, a user inserted an graphic of a tractor in the document. With word processing software, you easily can modify the appearance of an image after inserting it in the document.

You can use word processing software to define the size of the paper on which to print and to specify the margins. A feature, called wordwrap, allows users to type words in a paragraph continually without pressing the ENTER key at the end of each line. As you type more lines of text than can be displayed on the screen, the top portion of the document moves upward, or scrolls, off the screen.

Word processing software typically includes a spelling checker, which reviews the spelling of individual words, sections of a document, or the entire document.

Internet Research
What are the guidelines for writing business letters?
Search for: business letter writing

document is displayed in window

image

printed document

Figure 4-4 Word processing software enables users to create professional and visually appealing documents.
Source: Microsoft; © Cengage Learning

Figure 4-5 This presentation created with presentation software consists of five slides.

The spelling checker compares the words in the document with an electronic dictionary that is part of the word processing software. Some word processing programs also check for contextual spelling errors, such as a misuse of homophones (words pronounced the same but have different spellings or meanings, such as one and won).

Presentation

Presentation software is an application that allows users to create visual aids for presentations to communicate ideas, messages, and other information to a group. The presentations can be viewed as slides, sometimes called a *slide show*, that are displayed on a large monitor or on a projection screen from a computer or mobile device (Figure 4-5).

Presentation software typically provides a variety of predefined presentation formats that define complementary colors for backgrounds, text, and graphical accents on the slides. This software also provides a variety of layouts for each individual slide such as a title slide, a two-column slide, and a slide with clip art, a chart, a table, or a diagram. In addition, you can enhance any text, charts, and graphics on a slide with 3-D effects, animation, and other special effects, such as shading, shadows, and textures.

When building a presentation, users can set the slide timing so that the presentation automatically displays the next slide after a preset delay. Presentation software allows you to apply special effects to the transition between slides. One slide, for example, might fade away as the next slide appears.

Presentation software typically includes a clip gallery that provides images, photos, video clips, and audio clips to enhance presentations. Some audio and video editing applications work with presentation software, providing users with an easy means to record and insert video, music, and audio commentary in a presentation.

You can view or print a finished presentation in a variety of formats, including a hard copy outline of text from each slide and audience handouts that show completed slides. Presentation software also incorporates features such as checking spelling, formatting, researching, and creating webpages from existing slide shows.

Spreadsheet

Spreadsheet software is an application that allows users to organize data in rows and columns and perform calculations on the data. These rows and columns collectively are called a **worksheet**. Most spreadsheet software has basic features to help users create, edit, and format worksheets. A spreadsheet file is similar to a spiral notebook that can contain thousands of related individual worksheets. Data is organized vertically in columns and horizontally in rows on each worksheet (Figure 4-6).

Each worksheet usually can have thousands of columns and rows. One or more letters identify each column, and a number identifies each row. Only a small fraction of these columns and rows are visible on the screen at one time. Scrolling through the worksheet displays different parts of it on the screen.

A cell is the intersection of a column and row. The spreadsheet software identifies cells by the column and row in which they are located. For example, the intersection of column B and row 4 is referred to as cell B4. As shown in Figure 4-6, cell B4 contains the number, $1,000.29, which represents the wages for January.

Many of the worksheet cells shown in Figure 4-6 contain a number, called a value, that can be used in a calculation. Other cells, however, contain formulas that generate values. A formula performs calculations on the data in the worksheet and displays the resulting value in a cell, usually the cell containing the formula. When creating a worksheet, you can enter your own formulas. In Figure 4-6, for example, cell B17 could contain the formula =B9+B10+B11+B12+B13+B14+B15+B16, which would add (sum) the contents of cells B9, B10, B11, B12, B13, B14, B15, and B16. That is, this formula calculates the total expenses for January.

A *function* is a predefined formula that performs common calculations such as adding the values in a group of cells or generating a value such as the time or date. For example, the function =SUM(B9:B16) instructs the spreadsheet application to add all of the numbers in the range of cells B9 through B16. Spreadsheet applications contain many built-in functions.

One of the more powerful features of spreadsheet software is its capability of recalculating the rest of the worksheet when data in a worksheet changes. Spreadsheet software's capability of recalculating data also makes it a valuable budgeting, forecasting, and decision-making tool. Another standard feature of spreadsheet software is charting, which depicts the data in graphical form, such as bar charts or pie charts. A visual representation of data through charts often makes it easier for users to see at a glance the relationship among the numbers.

BTW

Dan Bricklin

Technology Innovator: You should be familiar with Dan Bricklin (cocreator of the first spreadsheet program).

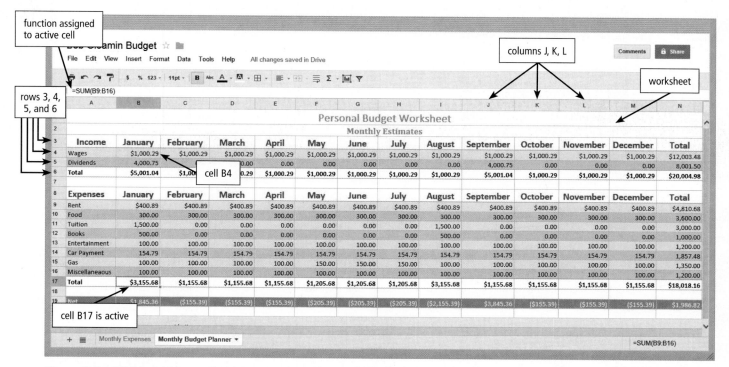

Figure 4-6 With spreadsheet software, you create worksheets that contain data arranged in rows and columns, and you can perform calculations on the data in the worksheets.
Source: Google Inc.

Database

A **database** is a collection of data organized in a manner that allows access, retrieval, and use of that data. In a manual database, you might record data on paper and store it in a filing cabinet. With a computerized database, such as the one shown in Figure 4-7, the computer stores the data in an electronic format on a local storage medium, such as a hard disk or optical disc, or on cloud storage.

Database software is an application that allows users to create, access, and manage a database. Using database software, you can add, change, and delete data in a database; sort and retrieve data from the database; and create forms and reports using the data in the database.

With most personal computer database programs, a database consists of a collection of tables, organized in rows and columns. Each row, called a record, contains data about a given item in the database, which is often a person, product, object, or event. Each column, called a field, contains a specific category of data within a record. The Publisher database shown in Figure 4-7 consists of two tables: a Customer table and a Book Rep table. The Customer table contains 15 records (rows), each storing data about one customer. The customer data is grouped into 10 fields (columns): CU # (customer number), Customer Name, Street, City, State, Postal Code, Amount Paid, Current Due, Returns, and BR # (book rep number). The Current Due field, for instance, contains the amount of money the customer owes the publisher. The Customer and Book Rep tables relate to one another through a common field, BR # (book rep number).

Users run queries to retrieve data. A query is a request for specific data from the database. For example, a query might request a list of customers whose balance is greater than $20,000. After obtaining the results of a query, database applications can present them on the screen, send them to the printer, or save them in a file.

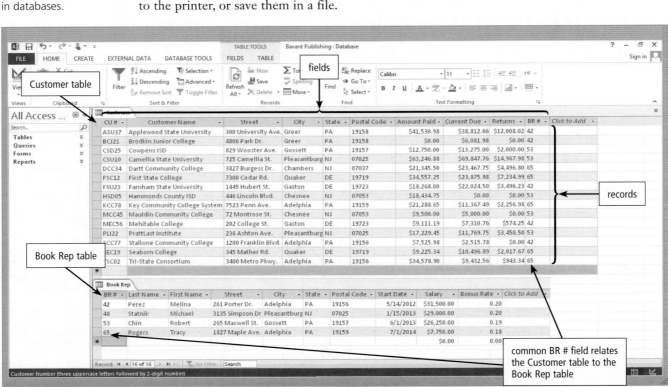

Figure 4-7 This database contains two tables: one for customers and one for book reps. The Customer table has 15 records and 10 fields; the Book Rep table has 4 records and 10 fields.
Source: Microsoft

Note Taking

Note taking software is an application that enables users to enter typed text, handwritten comments, drawings, sketches, photos, and links anywhere on a page and then save the page as part of a notebook (Figure 4-8). Users also can include audio recordings as part of their notes. Many note taking applications also include a calendar feature.

Users find note taking software convenient during meetings, class lectures and conferences, and in libraries and other settings that previously required a pencil and tablet of paper for recording thoughts and discussions.

Calendar and Contact Management

Calendar and contact management software is an application that helps you organize your calendar, keep track of contacts, and share this information with other devices or users (Figure 4-9). This software provides a way for individuals and workgroups to organize,

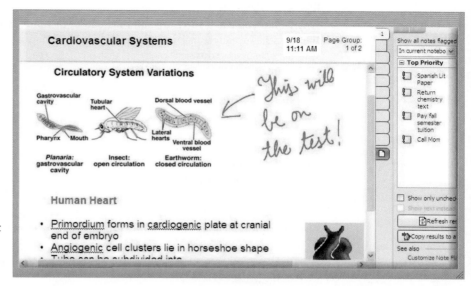

Figure 4-8 With note taking software, mobile users can handwrite notes, draw sketches, insert photos and links, and type text.
Source: Microsoft

find, view, and share appointment and contact information easily. Although sometimes available separately, calendar and contact management software typically exists as a unit in a single program. Many email applications include calendar and contact management features.

Calendar and contact management applications enable you to synchronize information. This means that all of your computers and mobile devices, along with your organization's server or cloud storage, have the latest version of any updated information.

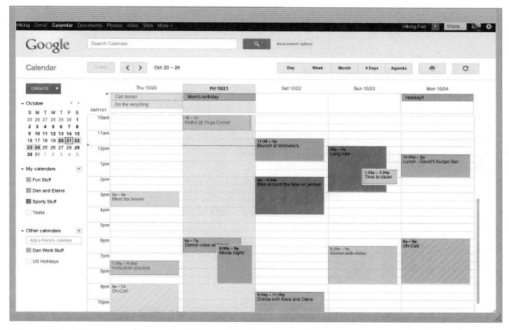

Figure 4-9 Users can share schedules with other computers, mobile devices, and users via calendar and contact management applications.
Source: Google Inc.

Software Suite

A **software suite** is a collection of individual applications available together as a unit. Productivity software suites typically include, at a minimum, word processing, presentation, spreadsheet, and email applications.

✳ **CONSIDER THIS**

Why would you use a software suite instead of a stand-alone application?
Software suites offer three major advantages: lower cost, ease of use, and integration. When you purchase a software suite, the suite usually costs significantly less than purchasing each application individually, or as stand-alone applications. Software suites provide ease of use because the applications in the suite normally use a consistent interface and share features such as clip art and spelling checker. Lastly, applications in a software suite often are integrated, which makes it easy to share information among them. For example, your email program can access your contact list to find recipients' email addresses.

Project Management

Project management software is an application that allows a user to plan, schedule, track, and analyze the events, resources, and costs of a project. Project management software helps users manage project variables, allowing them to complete a project on time and within budget. A marketing manager, for example, might use project management software to schedule the processes required in an advertising campaign (Figure 4-10).

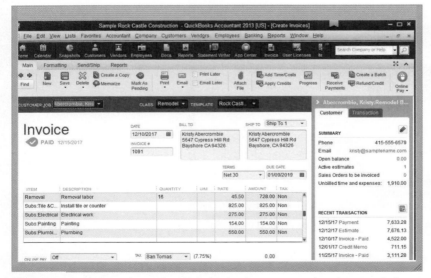

Figure 4-10   With project management software, you can plan and schedule a project.
Courtesy of CS Odessa

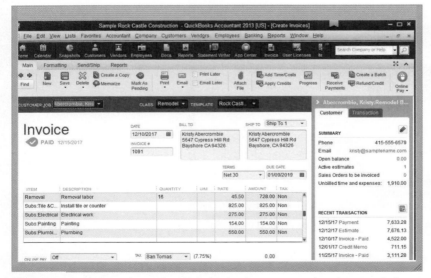

Figure 4-11   Accounting software helps businesses record and report their financial transactions.
Courtesy of Intuit

Accounting

Accounting software is an application that helps businesses of all sizes record and report their financial transactions. With accounting software, business users perform accounting activities related to the general ledger, accounts receivable, accounts payable, purchasing, invoicing (Figure 4-11), and payroll functions. Accounting software also enables business users to write and print checks, track checking account activity, and update and reconcile balances on demand.

Most accounting software supports online credit checks, bill payment, direct deposit, and payroll services. Some offer more complex features, such as job costing and estimating, time tracking, multiple company reporting, foreign currency reporting, and forecasting the amount of raw materials needed for products. The cost of accounting software for small businesses ranges from less than one hundred to several thousand dollars. Accounting software for large businesses can cost several hundred thousand dollars.

Personal Finance

Personal finance software is a simplified accounting application that helps home users and small/home office users balance their checkbooks, pay bills, track personal income and expenses, verify account balances, transfer funds, track investments, and evaluate financial plans (Figure 4-12). Personal finance software helps determine where, and for what purpose, you are spending money so that you can manage your finances.

Most personal finance software includes financial planning features, such as analyzing home and personal loans, preparing income taxes, and managing retirement savings. Other features include managing home inventory and setting up budgets. Most of these applications also offer a variety of online services, such as online banking and online investing. Read Secure IT 4-2 for safety tips when using personal finance apps on your smartphone or other mobile device.

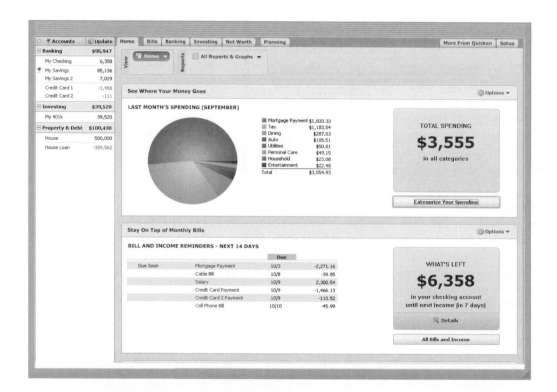

Figure 4-12   Personal finance software assists home users with tracking personal accounts.
Courtesy of Intuit

SECURE IT 4-2

Using Personal Finance Apps Safely

Using personal finance apps on a smartphone to pay bills, deposit checks, verify payments, and transfer funds is convenient and easy. It also is a magnet for cybercriminals to snatch personal information and money from unsuspecting users. In recent years, Google and other companies with app marketplaces have removed more than 50 finance apps filled with malicious instructions to invade users' smartphones and gain access to information stored on their devices. By using caution and common sense, however, you can take steps to safeguard your funds and your identity by following these practices:

- **Evaluate the apps.** Fraudulent apps may resemble legitimate apps from financial institutions. They often, however, are riddled with misspellings and awkward

sentences. In addition, legitimate companies rarely promote downloading an app from a pop-up advertisement. If you desire an app from a bank or other financial institution, visit that company's website for instructions about downloading and installing its authentic apps.

- **Use strong passwords to access the apps.** Many of the more secure personal finance apps have dual passwords that involve typing a string of characters and also validating a picture.

- **Guard your smartphone.** One security firm estimates that the collective value of smartphones lost each year exceeds $30 billion. With that figure in mind, store as little personal information as possible on your phone so that if the mobile device is lost, the chances of losing your identity

and having your accounts compromised is lessened. Be certain to password protect your mobile device. Also install software to locate your lost or stolen device and to wipe (erase) its content remotely.

- **Verify the transactions.** Always verify your transactions by scrutinizing monthly statements. In addition, periodically check balances and alert your financial institution if any activity seems abnormal.

Have you used finance apps? If so, which ones? When making transactions, do you follow some of the tips described above? If not, would you consider downloading an app to complete some common banking transactions? Why or why not?

Legal

Legal software is an application that assists in the preparation of legal documents and provides legal information to individuals, families, and small businesses (Figure 4-13). Legal software provides standard contracts and documents associated with buying, selling, and renting property; estate planning; marriage and divorce; and preparing a will or living trust. By answering a series of questions or completing a form, the legal software tailors the legal document to specific needs. Read Ethics & Issues 4-2 on the facing page to consider whether an attorney should review documents created with legal software.

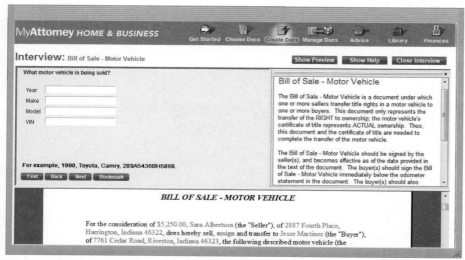

Figure 4-13 Legal software assists individuals, families, and small businesses in the preparation of legal documents.
Source: Avanquest Software

Tax Preparation

Tax preparation software is an application that can guide individuals, families, or small businesses through the process of filing federal taxes (Figure 4-14). These programs forecast tax liability and offer money-saving tax tips, designed to lower your tax bill. After you answer a series of questions and complete basic forms, the software creates and analyzes your tax forms to search for missed potential errors and deduction opportunities.

Once the forms are complete, you can print any necessary paperwork; then, they are ready for filing. Some tax preparation programs also allow you to file your tax forms electronically, a process called *e-filing*.

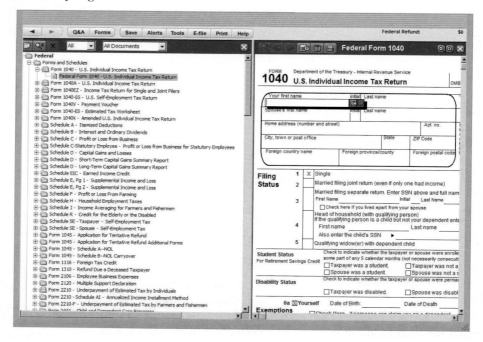

Figure 4-14 Tax preparation software guides individuals, families, or small businesses through the process of filing federal taxes.
Source: 2ⁿᵈ Story Software

BTW

Adobe

Technology Innovator:
You should be familiar
with Adobe Systems.

Document Management

Document management software is an application that provides a means for sharing, distributing, and searching through documents by converting them into a format that can be viewed by any user. The converted document, which mirrors the original document's

✳ **ETHICS & ISSUES 4-2**

Should an Attorney Review Documents Created with Legal Software?

Hiring an attorney to create a will or prepare a contract can cost you thousands of dollars. Legal software or website services, on the other hand, typically cost less than $100 and sometimes are free. While it is tempting to opt for the route that will save money, you should evaluate the program to make sure it is up to date, addresses the latest laws and provisions that are specific to your state, and includes a legal dictionary. If you use a program that is out of date or creates an incomplete or invalid legal document, the cost for an attorney to correct the

document could exceed the amount you originally spent on the program.

In nearly all states in the U.S., it is legal to create your own will. Each state, however, has complex laws that govern the types of information a will should contain, how any taxes associated with the estate are paid, and more. Legal software, therefore, should account for all laws, allow you to create and change your will easily, and cost less than using an attorney. Regardless of whether you use an attorney or legal software, in most states a will must be printed, signed, witnessed, and notarized in order to be valid.

Attorneys caution against using legal software unless you intend to have an attorney review the document. Not only can they validate the accuracy of the document, attorneys claim they can provide for gaps in the software, such as successors to businesses, complexities that arise from second marriages, and provisions for children with special needs.

Would you use legal software to create a will or contract? Why or why not? Do you think it is wise to prepare a will using legal software? Why or why not? How do mistakes made as a result of using legal software differ from mistakes that result from human error?

appearance, can be viewed and printed without the software that created the original document. Some document management software allows users to edit content and add comments to the converted document (Figure 4-15).

Many businesses use document management software to share and distribute company brochures, literature, and other documents electronically. Home users distribute flyers, announcements, and graphics electronically. A popular electronic image file format that document management software uses to save converted documents is **PDF** (Portable Document Format), developed by Adobe Systems. To view and print a PDF file, you need Acrobat Reader software, which can be downloaded free from Adobe's website.

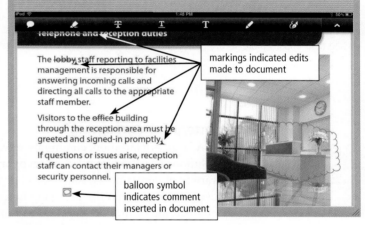

Figure 4-15   Users can edit content and add comments to a converted document.
Source: Adobe Systems Incorporated

✳ **CONSIDER THIS**

Can you create a PDF file only in document management applications?

No. Many productivity applications, such as word processing and spreadsheet programs, provide a method of saving a project as a PDF. This enables other users to view your document without requiring the application that created the project.

 Internet Research

Are there alternatives to Adobe Reader?

Search for: adobe reader alternatives

Support Services

A variety of desktop, mobile, and web apps provide a service intended to make business or personal tasks easier to accomplish. Some applications focus on a single service, while others provide several services in a single application. Examples include reference, travel, and retail applications.

- Reference applications: Look up definitions, synonyms, addresses, directions, and more; or translate text from one language to another.
- Travel applications: Compare rates and prices of flights, hotels, and rental cars; order airline tickets; print boarding passes; make hotel or vehicle reservations; check traffic conditions; or send a package.
- Retail applications: Check product availability, compare prices locally or online, locate stores, pay for purchases (read Secure IT 4-3 on the next page for safety tips when using payment apps), manage rewards, use coupons, or track a shipment.

SECURE IT 4-3

Avoiding Risks Using Payment Apps

Paying for coffee at Starbucks or purchasing clothing at Macy's has become streamlined with the advent of mobile payment apps. More than 12 percent of smartphone users have paid for items at the cash register using an app, such as Google Wallet, on their phone instead of using cash or credit cards; this number is expected to increase as more merchants accept this form of payment and the apps become more secure. The users enjoy the convenience of maintaining control when they scan the phone at the checkout counter instead of handing a credit card to a clerk. This security factor becomes even more pronounced at restaurants, where unscrupulous employees take credit cards away from the table and then have full access to the personal information the cards contain.

Mobile payment providers state that using their apps is more secure than using plastic credit cards. The apps use a payment system on phones with a GPS system, which allows the provider to verify that the sales transition is legitimate. A smartphone user never enters an account number at the cash register because all the financial information is stored on the mobile payment system. If, however, an unauthorized charge is made, the Electronic Fund Transfer Act protects users as long as the claim is made promptly, generally within two days.

If you use your smartphone to make purchases, follow this advice from the security experts:

- Use a password on your phone.
- Select a payment app that requires you to enter a password to start the transaction.
- Choose a payment app that issues a receipt so that you can verify every purchase.

- Be vigilant about checking mobile transactions against monthly statements from the credit card company.

✳ Should additional merchants allow payments using mobile apps? Should merchants be required to pay when customers use payment apps (like they do when customers use credit cards)? Why or why not? Where would you like to pay for transactions using your smartphone?

Source: Google Inc.

Enterprise Computing

A large organization, commonly referred to as an enterprise, requires special computing solutions because of its size and geographic distribution. A typical enterprise consists of a wide variety of departments, centers, and divisions — collectively known as functional units. Nearly every enterprise has the following functional units: human resources, accounting and finance, engineering or product development, manufacturing, marketing, sales, distribution, customer service, and information technology.

Software used in functional units is not mutually exclusive; however, each functional unit in an enterprise uses specific software, as outlined below.

- Human resources software manages employee information such as pay rate, benefits, personal information, performance evaluations, training, and vacation time.
- Accounting software manages everyday transactions, such as sales and payments to suppliers. Finance software helps managers budget, forecast, and analyze.
- Engineering or product development software allows engineers to develop plans for new products and test their product designs.
- Manufacturing software assists in the assembly process, as well as in scheduling and managing the inventory of parts and products.
- Marketing software allows marketing personnel to create marketing campaigns, target demographics, and track their effectiveness.
- Sales software enables the salesforce to manage contacts, schedule meetings, log customer interactions, manage product information, and take customer orders.
- Distribution software analyzes and tracks inventory and manages product shipping status.
- Customer service software manages the day-to-day interactions with customers, such as phone calls, email messages, web interactions, and instant messaging sessions.
- Information technology staff use a variety of programs and apps to maintain and secure the hardware and software in an enterprise.

MINI FEATURE 4-1

Web and Mobile Apps for Personal and Business Productivity

Whether you are checking appointments, sending or reading email messages, scanning business cards or bar codes, banking or looking up information online, making a purchase, arranging travel, or checking in with friends on social networking sites, web and mobile apps can assist your personal and business productivity.

Office Productivity

Maintaining an appointment calendar, accessing and editing documents, and checking email messages are common tasks of office productivity web and mobile apps. Calendar apps keep track of your appointments and synchronize information entered on a mobile device with your online or desktop calendar software. Email mobile apps assist you by displaying names from your phone's contact list that match a recipient's name as you enter it. Advanced features often found in office productivity web apps, such as sending email messages with attachments and formatting documents with fonts and colors, usually are omitted from their mobile counterparts to simplify the interaction.

Scanning

QR code readers, bar code scanners, and business card scanning apps all require use of the camera on a mobile device to scan a code or card. A QR code (quick response code) is a square-shaped coded graphic that corresponds to a web address or other information. A QR code reader app scans the QR code, as shown on the phone in the figure, and then displays the corresponding webpage in a browser. A bar code scanner reads the code and then looks up the product's ratings and reviews online. A business card scanner takes a photo of a business card and

© iStockphoto / franckreporter

deciphers the name, address, and other information on the card to add it immediately to your device's contacts list.

Financial

You can access bank accounts or investments using a financial app. Financial mobile apps help you track expenses as you spend money and notify you when a bill is due. To help secure information, financial mobile apps can disable access if your device is stolen or lost. Some banking mobile apps allow you to take a photo of a check with the device's camera and upload it to a server to process the deposit.

Reference

Dictionaries, encyclopedias, books, and directories are available online as reference apps. Many have associated mobile apps that format information for or take advantage of features on mobile devices. For example, rather than typing a search term in a dictionary web app to look up its definition, the corresponding mobile app also might offer voice input. On the mobile version of an encyclopedia app, you might shake the device to display random topics or redisplay the app's home screen. Some reference mobile apps also can download information directly to your phone for offline access.

Retail

Online marketplaces and payment services support buying and selling items and transferring funds from one party to another. Marketplace apps enable customers to read about products, enter or examine product reviews, and make purchases. A retail store mobile app might use a device's GPS to determine sellers or special deals closest to the customer's location. You also might use a device's camera to scan a product's bar code and then place the item in a shopping cart. Payment services allow customers to send money or pay for items using mobile devices.

Travel

Researching or purchasing flights, hotels, rental cars, or travel services is a common online task for personal and business travelers. Travel apps allow you to display and filter the results. Many allow you to share travel plans with others in your online social networks or display your itinerary and destination information on a map.

Source: KAYAK.com

Social Networking

Many users connect with their family, friends, and coworkers on social networking sites using mobile apps. Social networking web apps integrate instant messaging, video chat, and other interactive communications. Social networking mobile web apps use GPS technology to locate others nearby and generally do not have the real-time audio and video capabilities as their web-based counterparts.

✺ Compare the web and mobile versions of the same app for personal and business productivity. What features are common to both? Are there any features in the mobile version that are not found in the web version? Are there any features in the web version that are not found in the mobile version? Why do you think the developers made these decisions? What features would you like to see that are missing from either version of the app?

Graphics and Media Applications

In addition to productivity applications, many people work with software designed specifically for their field of work. Power users such as engineers, architects, desktop publishers, and graphic artists often use sophisticated software that allows them to work with graphics and media. Many of these applications incorporate user-friendly interfaces or scaled-down versions, making it possible for the home and small business users also to create documents using these types of programs.

Graphics and media applications include computer-aided design, desktop publishing, paint/image editing, photo editing and photo management, clip art/image gallery, video and audio editing, multimedia and website authoring, media players, and disc burning.

Computer-Aided Design

Computer-aided design (CAD) software is a type of application that assists professionals and designers in creating engineering, architectural, and scientific designs and models. For example, engineers create design plans for vehicles and security systems. Architects design building structures and floor plans (Figure 4-16). Scientists design drawings of molecular structures.

Three-dimensional CAD programs allow designers to rotate designs of 3-D objects to view them from any angle. Some CAD software even can generate material lists for building designs.

Home and small business users work with less sophisticated design and modeling software. These applications usually contain thousands of predrawn plans that users can customize to meet their needs. For example, *home design/landscaping*

Figure 4-16 Architects use CAD software to design building structures.
© Cyberstock / Alamy

software is an application that assists users with the design, remodeling, or improvement of a home, deck, or landscape.

Desktop Publishing

Desktop publishing software (DTP software) is an application that enables designers to create sophisticated publications that contain text, graphics, and many colors. Professional DTP software is ideal for the production of high-quality color documents such as textbooks, corporate newsletters, marketing literature, product catalogs, and annual reports. Designers and graphic artists can print finished publications on a color printer, take them to a professional printer, or post them on the web in a format that can be viewed by those without DTP software.

Home and small business users create newsletters, brochures, flyers, advertisements, postcards, greeting cards, letterhead, business cards, banners, calendars, logos, and webpages using personal DTP software (Figure 4-17). Although many word processing programs include DTP features, home and small business users often prefer to create DTP documents using DTP software because of its enhanced features. These programs typically guide you through the development of a project by asking a series of questions. Then, you can print a finished publication on a color printer or post it on the web.

Many personal DTP programs also include paint/image editing software and photo editing and photo management software (discussed next), enabling users to embellish their publications with images.

Figure 4-17   With personal DTP software, home users can create greeting cards.
Courtesy of Broderbund / Encore Software

Paint/Image Editing

Graphic artists, multimedia professionals, technical illustrators, and desktop publishers use paint software and image editing software to create and modify graphics such as those used in DTP documents and webpages. **Paint software**, also called *illustration software*, is an application that allows users to draw pictures, shapes, and other graphics with various on-screen tools such as a pen, brush, eyedropper, and paint bucket. **Image editing software** is an application that provides the capabilities of paint software and also includes the capability to enhance and modify existing photos and images. Modifications can include adjusting or enhancing image colors, adding special effects such as shadows and glows, creating animations, and image stitching (combining multiple images into a larger image).

Paint/image editing software for the home or small business user provides an easy-to-use interface; includes various simplified tools that allow you to draw pictures, shapes, and other images (Figure 4-18); and provides the capability of modifying existing graphics and photos. These products also include many templates to assist you in adding images to documents such as greeting cards, banners, calendars, signs, labels, business cards, and letterhead.

Photo Editing and Photo Management

Photo editing software is a type of image editing software that allows users to edit and customize digital photos. With photo editing software, users can retouch photos, crop images, remove red-eye, erase blemishes, restore aged photos, add special effects, enhance image quality, change image shapes, color-correct images, straighten images, remove or rearrange

Figure 4-18   Home users can purchase affordable paint/image editing programs that enable them to draw images.
DrawPlus X5 © Serif (Europe) Ltd, | www.serif.com

objects in a photo, and more (Figure 4–19). Many applications also provide a means for creating digital photo albums.

When you purchase a digital camera, it usually includes photo editing software. Some digital cameras even have basic photo editing software built in so that you can edit the image directly on the camera. Read How To 4-1 for instructions about editing photos.

Figure 4-19 With photo editing software, users can edit digital photos, such as by adjusting the appearance of images as shown here.

PhotoPlus X6 © Serif (Europe) Ltd | www.serif.com

HOW TO 4-1

Edit Photos

When you take a photo using a digital camera or smartphone, you sometimes may want to edit the photo to remove unwanted areas, correct imperfections, or change its file size. Many apps allow you to edit photos easily. Several are easy to use and do not require advanced photo editing experience. Before editing a photo, you first should make a backup of the original photo. The table below describes common ways to edit photos using a photo editing app.

After you have edited a photo to your satisfaction, you may want to share the photo with others. Many mobile devices such as smartphones and tablets, as well as most photo editing apps, have built-in options that allow you to share photos. To share a photo on a mobile device or from within a photo editing app, follow these steps:

1. Open the photo to share.
2. Select the sharing option in the photo editing app or on the mobile device.

3. Choose the method by which to share the photo. Common ways to share photos include sending the photo as an email attachment, posting the photo to a social media site, and sending the photo as a picture message to another mobile device.

☀ Examine your digital camera or other mobile device with a camera feature. Which of the photo editing features discussed here does it have? Did you notice any photo editing features in addition to those listed here?

ACTION	PURPOSE	STEPS
Crop	Removes unwanted areas of a photo	1. Select cropping tool. 2. Adjust photo border to define area(s) of the photo to keep and discard.
Remove *red-eye*	Removes the appearance of red eyes caused by the camera flash	1. Select red-eye removal tool. 2. Tap or click areas of the photo with the red-eye effect *or* drag a border around the affected areas.
Resize	Changes the physical dimensions of the photo	1. Select resizing tool. 2. Drag sizing handles to increase or decrease the photo's dimensions *or* type the desired height and width in the appropriate text boxes.
Compress	Decreases the photo's file size	1. Select option to compress photo. 2. Choose desired level of compression.
Adjust *sharpness*	Increases or decreases crispness of objects in the photo	1. Select option to adjust sharpness. 2. Drag sharpness slider to desired value *or* type the desired sharpness level into appropriate text box.
Adjust *brightness*	Adjusts lightness or darkness in the photo	1. Select option to adjust brightness. 2. Drag brightness slider to desired value *or* type the desired brightness level into appropriate text box.
Adjust *contrast*	Adjusts the difference in appearance between light and dark areas of the photo	1. Select option to adjust contrast. 2. Drag contrast slider to desired value *or* type the desired contrast level into appropriate text box.

With **photo management software**, you can view, organize, sort, catalog, print, and share digital photos. Some photo editing software includes photo management functionality. Read Ethics & Issues 4-3 to consider issues related to altering digital photos.

 ETHICS & ISSUES 4-3

Is It Ethical to Alter Digital Photos?
Many commercial artists, photojournalists, and creators of cartoons, book covers, and billboards use photo editing software to alter photos. Artists can use graphic software to alter digital photos by changing colors, resizing, adding or removing objects, and more.

In several high-profile cases, major news sources published intentionally altered photos. The alterations were more than just touching up a blemish. Instead, they were attempts to alter the facts, such as the instance where an unknown person combined separate photos of an anti-war activist and

a presidential candidate so that it looked like the candidate was protesting. Also making news are celebrity or model photos that artists retouch to change their physical appearance. Real estate agents on occasion have altered photos of homes for online listings or print brochures.

The National Press Photographers Association expresses reservations about digital altering and subscribes to the following belief: "As [photo]journalists we believe the guiding principle of our profession is accuracy; therefore, we believe it is wrong to alter the content of a photo in any way

... that deceives the public." Yet, some insist that the extent to which a photo "deceives the public" is in the eye of the beholder.

Is it ethical to alter digital photos? Why or why not? Does the answer depend on the reason for the alteration, the extent of the alteration, or some other factor? If some alteration is accepted, can photographic integrity still be guaranteed? Why or why not? Should magazines stop altering pictures of people to change their appearance? Why or why not?

Clip Art/Image Gallery

Applications often include a **clip art/image gallery**, which is a collection of clip art and photos. Some applications contain links to additional clips available on the web or are available as web apps. You also can purchase clip art/image gallery software that contains thousands of images (Figure 4-20).

In addition to clip art, many clip art/image galleries provide fonts, animations, sounds, video clips, and audio clips. You can use the images, fonts, and other items from the clip art/image gallery in all types of projects, including documents, brochures, worksheets, and slide shows.

Video and Audio Editing

Video editing software is an application that allows professionals to modify a segment of a video, called a clip. For example, users can reduce the length of a video clip, reorder a series of clips, or add special effects such as words that move across the screen. Video editing software typically includes audio editing capabilities. **Audio editing software** is an application that enables users to modify audio clips, produce studio-quality soundtracks, and add audio to video clips (Figure 4-21). Most television shows and movies are created or enhanced using video and audio editing software.

Figure 4-20 Clip art/image gallery software contains thousands of images.
Courtesy of IMSI / Design, LLC

 BTW
Instagram
Innovative Computing: You should be familiar with the photo sharing app, Instagram.

Figure 4-21 With audio editing software, users modify audio clips.
Source: Adobe Systems Incorporated

Many home users work with easy-to-use video and audio editing software, which is much simpler to use than its professional counterpart, for small-scale movie making projects. With these programs, home users can edit home movies, add music or other sounds to the video, and share their movies on the web. Some operating systems include video editing and audio editing applications.

Multimedia and Website Authoring

Multimedia authoring software allows users to combine text, graphics, audio, video, and animation in an interactive application (Figure 4-22). With this software, users control the placement of text and images and the duration of sounds, video, and animation. Once created, multimedia presentations often take the form of interactive computer-based presentations or web-based presentations designed to facilitate learning, demonstrate product functionality, and elicit direct-user participation. Training centers, educational institutions, and online magazine publishers use multimedia authoring software to develop interactive applications. These applications may be distributed on an optical disc, over a local area network, or via the Internet as web apps.

Website authoring software helps users of all skill levels create webpages that include graphics, video, audio, animation, and special effects with interactive content. In addition, many website authoring programs allow users to organize, manage, and maintain websites. Website authoring software often has capabilities of multimedia authoring software.

Productivity apps, such as word processing and spreadsheets, often include the capability of saving projects as webpages. This allows home and small business users to create basic webpages using an application they already own. For more sophisticated websites, however, users work with website authoring software.

 CONSIDER THIS

What is computer-based or web-based training?
Computer-based training (*CBT*) is a type of education in which students learn by using and completing exercises with instructional software. *Web-based training* (*WBT*) is a type of CBT that uses Internet technology to deliver the training. CBT and WBT typically consist of self-directed, self-paced instruction about a topic so that the user becomes actively involved in the learning process instead of being a passive recipient of information. Beginning athletes use CBT programs to learn the intricacies of participating in a sport. The military and airlines use CBT simulations to train pilots to fly in various conditions and environments. WBT is popular in business, industry, and schools for teaching new skills or enhancing existing skills of employees, teachers, and students.

Figure 4-22
Multimedia authoring software allows you to create dynamic presentations that include text, graphics, audio, video, and animation.
Courtesy of Matchware Inc.

Media Player

A **media player** is a program that allows you to view images and animations, listen to audio, and watch video files on your computer or mobile device (Figure 4-23). Media players also may enable you to organize media files by genre, artist, or other category; create playlists; convert files to different formats; connect to and purchase media from an online media store or marketplace; tune into radio stations; download podcasts; burn audio CDs; and transfer media to portable media players. Read Ethics & Issues 4-4 to consider whether media downloads should be taxed.

Figure 4-23
A media player.
Source: Rhapsody

 ETHICS & ISSUES 4-4

Should the Government Tax Media Downloads?

When you walk into a store and purchase a DVD of your favorite movie, chances are you also pay a state and/or local sales tax. If you purchase and download or stream the same movie online digitally, however, you are less likely to pay a sales tax. Some government taxing bodies seek to change that discrepancy. The main reason for the pressure to tax is lost revenue. State and local governments lose sales tax revenue when consumers purchase and legally download digital content instead of purchasing taxable, physical media. Another reason for pressure to tax stems

from the media industry looking to recoup lost sales due to illegally downloaded digital content. Some state laws attempt to distinguish between tangible goods (that include packaging and/or printed documentation) and intangible goods (that have no physical components to them), such as streaming video. Other laws express that if you can sense the goods (i.e., you can view or hear them), they are taxable.

Critics of the taxes claim that government should not tax the greenest form of media purchases. When you download and stream digital media, you eliminate packaging, optical discs, and use of delivery vehicles.

Critics also argue that governments single out media content due to pressure from the media industry. For example, some governments tax the purchase of newspapers, magazines, and books, but often the same content is sold online and is not taxed.

Should the government tax media downloads, such as music, video, e-books, newspaper articles, and magazine articles? Why or why not? Should digital content delivery be considered a service rather than a good by taxing bodies? Why?

Disc Burning

Disc burning software writes text, graphics, audio, and video files on a recordable or rewritable disc. This software enables home users easily to back up contents of their hard disk on an optical disc (CD/DVD) and make duplicates of uncopyrighted music or movies. Disc burning software usually also includes photo editing, audio editing, and video editing capabilities. When you buy a recordable or rewritable disc, it typically includes disc burning software.

Personal Interest Applications

Countless desktop, mobile, and web apps are designed specifically for lifestyle, medical, entertainment, convenience, or education activities. Most of the programs in this category are relatively inexpensive; many are free. Some applications focus on a single service, while others provide several services in a single application.

- Lifestyle applications: Access the latest news or sports scores, check the weather forecast, compose music, research genealogy, find recipes, or locate nearby restaurants, gas stations, or points of interest.
- Medical applications: Research symptoms, establish a fitness or health program, track exercise activity, refill prescriptions, count calories, or monitor sleep patterns.
- Entertainment applications: Listen to music or the radio, view photos, watch videos or shows, read a book or other publication, organize and track fantasy sports teams, and play games individually or with others.
- Convenience applications: Obtain driving directions or your current location, remotely start your vehicle or unlock/lock the doors, set an alarm or timer, check the time, calculate a tip, or use a flashlight.
- Education applications: Access how-to guides, learn or fine-tune a particular skill, follow a tutorial, run a simulation, assist children with reading and other elementary skills, or support academics (read How To 4-2 for instructions about using help with programs and apps).

 Internet Research

What is geocaching?
Search for: geocaching basics

 BTW

iTunes U
Innovative Computing:
You should be familiar with the education app, iTunes U.

 HOW TO 4-2

Obtain Help about Programs and Apps

Multiple ways are provided to obtain help while using the programs and apps on a computer or mobile device. The program or app developer usually includes a Help feature in the program and/or online. In addition, third parties often post resources online that can provide further assistance. The following sections describe the various ways to obtain help about a program or app.

Help System

You typically can access help in a program or app using one of the following methods:

- Tap or click the Help or Information icon in the program or app. The appearance of Help or Information icons may vary, but they typically are identified by a question mark or the letter 'i' formatted in italic.

- Navigate the program or app's menu to locate the Help command.

- If you are using a program or app on a Windows desktop or laptop, press the F1 key on the keyboard to display Help content.

Online Help

Online help usually is available from the program or app developer. The following steps describe how to obtain online help.

1. Navigate to the program or app developer's website.
2. Search for, and then tap or click a Help or Support link.
3. Select the program or app for which you wish to obtain help to display the help information.

Searching for Help

In addition to obtaining help from within a program or app or on the developer's website, you also can search the web for help as described in the following steps.

1. Navigate to a search engine such as google.com or yahoo.com.
2. Type the program or app name, as well as the type of help for which you are searching, as the search text, and then press the ENTER key or tap or click the search button.
3. Scroll the search results and then tap or click the search result to display more information. Be aware that not all help originates from reputable or accurate sources.

⚙ Under what circumstances would you use each of these methods to obtain help with a program or app you are using? Justify your answer.

MINI FEATURE 4-2

Web and Mobile Apps for Graphics, Media, and Personal Interests

Whether sharing, viewing, and purchasing media, such as photos; streaming audio and video; or playing games by yourself or with others, countless web and mobile apps are available to meet your needs. You also can use web and mobile apps to look up news, sports, and weather; obtain maps and directions; help you reach your health and fitness goals; and assist you with academic objectives.

Media Sharing

With media sharing mobile apps, you use the digital camera on your mobile device to take quality photos and/or videos and then instantly can share the photos or videos on social media sites. Using the corresponding media sharing web app, you can categorize, tag, organize, and rank the media posted by you, your friends, and your contacts.

Streaming Audio and Video

Podcasts, video blogs, clips or episodes from a television show, or even an entire movie are available through a variety of streaming media web and mobile apps, often with a membership or monthly fee. Streaming media enables you to view and listen to content without downloading it to your computer or device, saving valuable disc or media storage space.

Game

Game web and mobile apps often offer a social component, enabling you to chat within the game environment, find friends who play the same game apps, and post your scores on social media. Word, puzzle, and board games are just some examples of apps you can play by yourself or with friends or others using the same apps.

Source: Zynga, Inc.

News, Sports, and Weather

Many apps provide access to the latest news, stories, current events, sports scores, sporting events, and weather forecasts. Some of these mobile apps use GPS technology to provide current or customized information based on the location of your mobile device. You also can configure these apps to send text messages and other types of alerts when certain events occur, such as when a football team scores a touchdown or when severe weather is near.

Mapping

Using GPS technology in your mobile device, you can use mapping mobile apps to obtain directions, maps, and recommendations for restaurants or other points of interest based on your current location. Some mapping apps even help you to locate friends based on their GPS signals (if they enable you to do so). Others allow you to share your current location on social media using a check-in feature. Web apps help you decide on a route, print directions or a map, and even find amenities along your route, such as public rest stops or restaurants.

Health and Fitness

Losing weight, training for a race, or following a low-calorie diet are some uses of health and fitness apps. Using a mobile device as a pedometer or GPS receiver can help you count your steps or create a map of a route you run and then update your profile with the data it tracked. You can use corresponding web apps to chart and analyze your progress, schedule your next workout, or determine the next steps to reach your goals. These apps also can help plan your meals and track the nutritional value of food you consume.

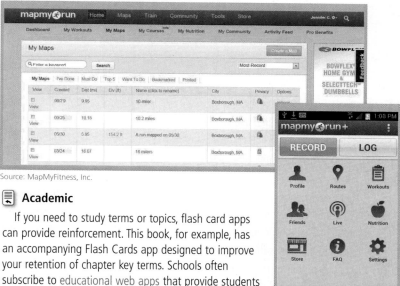
Source: MapMyFitness, Inc.

Academic

If you need to study terms or topics, flash card apps can provide reinforcement. This book, for example, has an accompanying Flash Cards app designed to improve your retention of chapter key terms. Schools often subscribe to educational web apps that provide students with games, quizzes, and lessons about course topics. Using these apps, teachers can keep track of students' progress and pinpoint where they may need extra help. You even can access complete college or high school courses and take advantage of free or fee-based digital content provided by publishers and teachers.

✹ Which web and mobile apps have you used for media sharing; streaming audio and video; gaming; news, sports, and weather; mapping; health and fitness; and education? Will you try others after reading this mini feature? Why or why not?

Communications Applications

One of the main reasons people use computers is to communicate and share information with others. Earlier chapters presented a variety of communications applications, which are summarized in Table 4-2.

Table 4-2 Communications Applications

Blogging
- Time-stamped articles, or posts, in diary or journal format, usually listed in reverse chronological order
- Blogger (author) needs *blog software*, or blogware, to create/maintain blog
  - Some websites do not require installation of blog software

Instant Messaging
- Real-time exchange of messages, files, audio, and/or video with another online user
- Requires instant messenger software
  - Integrated in some operating systems
  - Available for download on the web, usually for free
  - Included with some paid ISPs

Browsing
- Allows users to access and view webpages on the Internet
- Requires browser
  - Integrated in some operating systems
  - Available for download on the web, usually for free

Videoconference
- Meeting between geographically separated people who use a network to transmit video/audio
- Requires videoconferencing software, a microphone, a speaker, and a webcam

Chat Room
- Real-time, online typed conversation with many users
- Requires chat client software
  - Integrated in some operating systems and browsers
  - Available for download on the web, usually for free
  - Included with some paid ISPs
  - Built into some websites

VoIP
- Allows users to speak to other users via an Internet connection
- Requires a microphone, a speaker, a high-speed Internet connection, and VoIP software
  - Some subscription services also require a separate phone and VoIP router
  - With a webcam, some services also support video chat or videoconferences

Discussion Forum
- Online areas where users have written discussions
- May require a reader program
  - Integrated in some operating systems, email programs, and browsers

Web Feeds
- Keeps track of changes made to websites by checking feeds
- Requires a feed reader
  - Integrated in some email programs and browsers
  - Available for download on the web, usually for free

Email
- Messages and files sent via a network such as the Internet
- Requires an email program
  - Integrated in many software suites and operating systems
  - Available free at portals on the web
  - Included with a paid ISP
  - Can be purchased separately

Wireless Messaging
- Short text, picture, or video messages sent and received, mainly on mobile devices
- May require messaging plan from mobile service provider
- Requires messaging software
  - Integrated in most mobile devices
  - Available for download on the web, usually for free

FTP
- Method of uploading and downloading files with other computers on the Internet
- May require an FTP program
  - Integrated in some operating systems
  - Available for download on the web, usually for a small fee

NOW YOU KNOW

Be sure you understand the material presented in the sections titled Graphics and Media Applications, Personal Interest Applications, and Communications Applications, as it relates to the chapter objectives.
You now should know . . .

- When you might use a graphics or media application (Objective 5)

- Which personal interest applications you would find useful (Objective 6)

- When you are interacting with communications applications (Objective 7)

Quiz Yourself Online: Check your knowledge of related content by navigating to this book's Quiz Yourself resource on Computer Concepts CourseMate and then tapping or clicking Objectives 5–7.

Security Tools

To protect your computers and mobile devices, you can use one or more security tools. Security tools include personal firewalls, antivirus programs, malware removers, and Internet filters. Although some of these tools are included with the operating system, you also can purchase stand-alone programs that offer improvements or added functionality.

BTW
Security Suites
A *security suite* is a collection of individual security tools available together as a unit. These programs often are called Internet security programs.

Personal Firewall

A **personal firewall** is a security tool that detects and protects a personal computer and its data from unauthorized intrusions (Figure 4-24). Personal firewalls constantly monitor all transmissions to and from a computer and may inform a user of attempted intrusions. When connected to the Internet, your computer is vulnerable to attacks from nefarious individuals who try to access a computer or network illegally. These attacks may destroy your data, steal information, damage your computer, or carry out some other malicious action.

BTW
Hacker
The term, *hacker,* refers to someone who accesses a computer or network illegally.

 CONSIDER THIS

What is a hardware firewall?
A hardware firewall is a device intended to stop network intrusions before they attempt to affect your computer or network maliciously. Many routers also can function as a hardware firewall.

Figure 4-24
This personal firewall detected a threat to the computer and provided a means to remove the threat.
Courtesy of Checkpoint Software Technologies Ltd.

MINI FEATURE 4-3

Viruses and Malware

A computer **virus** is a potentially damaging computer program that affects, or infects, a computer negatively by altering the way the computer works without the user's knowledge or permission. Once the virus is in a computer, it can spread throughout and may damage your files and operating system.

Computer viruses do not generate by chance. The programmer of a virus, known as a virus author, intentionally writes a virus program. Writing a virus program usually requires significant programming skills. The virus author ensures the virus can replicate itself, conceal itself, monitor for certain events, and then deliver its *payload* — the destructive event or prank the virus was created to deliver. Viruses can infect all types of computers and mobile devices, including smartphones and tablets. Despite the many variations of viruses, most have two phases involved in their execution: infection and delivery.

To start the infection phase, the virus must be activated. Today, the most common way viruses spread is by users running infected programs or apps. During the infection phase, viruses typically perform one or more of the following actions:

1. First, a virus replicates by attaching itself to program files. A macro virus hides in a macro, which is a standard feature of many productivity applications such as word processing and spreadsheet apps. A boot sector virus targets the computer's start-up files. A file virus attaches itself to program files. The next time an infected program or app is run, the virus executes and infects the computer.

2. Viruses also conceal themselves to avoid detection. A stealth virus disguises itself by hiding in fake code sections, which it inserts within working code in a file. A polymorphic virus actually changes its code as it infects computers.

3. Finally, viruses watch for a certain condition or event and activate when that condition or event occurs. The event might be starting the computer or reaching a date on the system clock. A logic bomb activates when it detects a specific condition (say, a name deleted from the employee list). A time bomb

is a logic bomb that activates on a particular date or time. If the triggering condition does not exist, the virus simply replicates.

During the delivery phase, the virus unleashes its payload, which might be a harmless prank that displays a meaningless message — or it might be destructive, corrupting or deleting data and files. The most dangerous viruses do not have an obvious payload; instead they quietly modify files. One way antivirus software detects computer viruses is by monitoring files for unknown changes.

In addition to viruses, other malware includes worms, trojan horse programs, and rootkits.

- A *worm* resides in active memory and replicates itself over a network to infect computers and devices, using up the system resources and possibly shutting down the system.

- A *trojan horse* is a destructive program disguised as a real program, such as a screen saver. When a user runs a seemingly innocent program, a trojan horse hiding inside can capture information, such as user names and passwords, from your computer or enable someone remotely to control your computer. Unlike viruses, trojan horses do not replicate themselves.

- A *rootkit* is a program that easily can hide and allow someone to take full control of your computer from a remote location, often for nefarious purposes. For example, a rootkit can hide in a folder on your computer, and the folder will appear empty. This is because the rootkit has instructed your computer not to display the contents of the folder. Rootkits can be very dangerous and often require special software to detect and remove.

Studies show that an unprotected computer can be infected by malware within minutes after being connected to the Internet. Due to the increasing threat of viruses attacking your computer, it is more important than ever to protect your computer from viruses and other malware. Secure IT 1-2 on page 23 in Chapter 1 lists steps you can follow to protect your computer from a virus infection.

✹ If your computer or mobile device becomes infected with a virus or malware, where can you obtain information about removing the virus or malware?

Signs of Virus Infection

- An unusual message or image is displayed on the computer screen.
- An unusual sound or music plays randomly.
- The available memory is less than what should be available.
- A program or file suddenly is missing.
- An unknown program or file mysteriously appears.
- The size of a file changes without explanation.
- A file becomes corrupted.
- A program or file does not work properly.
- System properties change.
- The computer operates much slower than usual.

Antivirus Programs

To protect a computer from virus attacks, users should install an antivirus program and keep it updated by purchasing revisions or upgrades to the software. An **antivirus program** protects a computer against viruses by identifying and removing any computer viruses found in memory, on storage media, or on incoming files (Figure 4-25). Antivirus programs scan for programs that attempt to modify a computer's start-up files, the operating system, and other programs that normally are read from but not modified. In addition, many antivirus programs automatically scan files downloaded from the web, email attachments, opened files, and all types of removable media inserted in the computer or mobile device.

If an antivirus program identifies an infected file, it attempts to remove the malware. If the antivirus program cannot remove the infection, it often quarantines the infected file. A *quarantine* is a separate area of a hard disk that holds the infected file until the infection can be removed. This step ensures other files will not become infected. Quarantined files remain on your computer or mobile device until you delete them or restore them.

Most antivirus programs also include protection against other malware such as worms, trojan horses, and spyware. When you purchase a new computer, it may include a trial version of antivirus software. Many email servers also have antivirus programs installed to check incoming and outgoing email messages for viruses and other malware. Read Secure IT 4-4 for tips about recognizing virus hoaxes.

Figure 4-25   An antivirus program scans memory, media, and incoming email messages and attachments for viruses and attempts to remove any viruses it finds.
Source: AVG Technologies

 SECURE IT 4-4

Recognizing Virus Hoaxes

Many years ago, people mailed chain letters to friends and relatives promising riches, good health, and other unverifiable claims. Today's equivalent of the chain letter is a computer hoax, which spreads across the Internet in record time and often is the source of urban legends. The hoaxes take several forms and often disappear for months or years at a time, only to resurface some time later.

Most alarming to some users are the computer virus hoaxes, which warn that the computer is infected and needs immediate

attention. Occasionally, the claims state the problem is so severe that the computer will explode or that the entire hard disk will be erased in a matter of seconds. The warning cites prominent companies, such as Microsoft and McAfee. These messages claim to offer a solution to the problem, generally requesting a fee for a program to download. Snopes.com compiles these hoaxes and describes their sources and histories.

In reality, these fake messages are generated by unscrupulous scammers preying upon gullible people who panic and follow

the directions in the message. These users divulge credit card information and then often download files riddled with viruses.

If you receive one of these virus hoaxes, never respond to the message. Instead, delete it. Most importantly, never forward it to an unsuspecting friend or coworker. If you receive the virus hoax from someone you know, send him or her a separate email message with information about the hoax.

☀ Have you ever received a virus hoax? If so, what action did you take?

CONSIDER THIS

How do antivirus programs detect viruses?

Many antivirus programs identify viruses by looking for virus signatures. A *virus signature*, also called a virus definition, is a known specific pattern of virus code. Computer users should update their antivirus program's signature files regularly. This extremely important activity allows the antivirus program to protect against viruses written since the antivirus program was released and/or its last update. Most antivirus programs contain an automatic update feature that regularly prompts users to download the updated virus signatures, usually at least once a week. The vendor usually provides this service to registered users at no cost for a specified time.

Spyware, Adware, and Other Malware Removers

Spyware is a program placed on a computer or mobile device without the user's knowledge that secretly collects information about the user and then communicates the information it collects to some outside source while the user is online. Some vendors or employers use spyware to collect information about program usage or employees. Internet advertising firms often collect information about users' web browsing habits. Spyware can enter your computer when you install a new program, through a graphic on a webpage or in an email message, or through malware.

Adware is a program that displays an online advertisement in a banner or pop-up window on webpages, email messages, or other Internet services. Sometimes, Internet advertising firms hide spyware in adware.

A **spyware remover** is a program that detects and deletes spyware and similar programs. An **adware remover** is a program that detects and deletes adware. Malware removers detect and delete spyware, adware, and other malware. Read Secure IT 4-5 for measures you can take to protect your mobile device from malware.

 CONSIDER THIS

Are cookies spyware?

A *cookie* is a small text file that a web server stores on your computer. Cookie files typically contain data about you, such as your user name, viewing preferences, or shopping cart contents. Cookies are not considered spyware because website programmers do not attempt to conceal the cookies.

 SECURE IT 4-5

Malware Risks to Mobile Devices

Hackers aggressively are taking advantage of the surge in mobile device purchases and are spreading malware to unsuspecting users. Threats to Android devices are growing in record numbers due to the rising popularity of tablets and smartphones and the variety of marketplace sources for downloading apps. The Federal Bureau of Investigation issues consumer alerts warning users of the serious risks for theft of personal and sensitive information. Often the malware steals phone numbers; it also can allow hackers to control the mobile device from remote locations. Once the hacker takes over the device, all the information on it is available, including passwords and account numbers. One of the fastest growing threats within mobile apps is *toll fraud malware*, which is a malicious mobile app that uses a variety of fraudulent schemes to charge unsuspecting users for premium messaging services.

Smartphone users can take several precautions to guard against malware threats. They include:

- Read reviews of apps and the company that creates them before downloading the apps to your mobile device.
- Use mobile malware and antivirus protection.
- Turn off location-based apps that track your movements.

- Do not connect to unknown wireless networks.
- Keep the operating system up to date.
- Enable the screen lock feature, and use a strong password to unlock the device.
- Reset the mobile device before selling or trading it in.
- Practice the same safe computing measures you take on your home computer.

 Which of these guidelines do you follow now when using your mobile device? How will you modify your usage after reading these tips?

Internet Filters

Filters are programs that remove or block certain items from being displayed. Four widely used Internet filters are anti-spam programs, web filters, phishing filters, and pop-up blockers.

Anti-Spam Programs **Spam** is an unsolicited email message or posting sent to many recipients or forums at once. Spam is considered Internet junk mail. The content of spam ranges from selling a product or service, to promoting a business opportunity, to advertising offensive material. Spam also may contain links or attachments that contain malware.

An **anti-spam program** is a filtering program that attempts to remove spam before it reaches your Inbox or forum. If your email program does not filter spam, many anti-spam programs are available at no cost on the web. ISPs often filter spam as a service for their subscribers.

Web Filters **Web filtering software** is a program that restricts access to certain material on the web. Some restrict access to specific websites; others filter websites that use certain words or phrases. Many businesses use web filtering software to limit employee's web access. Some schools, libraries, and parents use this software to restrict access to websites that are not educational.

Phishing Filters **Phishing** is a scam in which a perpetrator sends an official look-ing email message that attempts to obtain your personal and/or financial information (Figure 4-26). Some phishing messages ask you to reply with your information; others direct you to a phony website or a pop-up window that looks like a legitimate website, which then collects your information.

A **phishing filter** is a program that warns or blocks you from potentially fraudulent or suspicious websites. Some browsers include phishing filters.

Pop-Up Blockers A *pop-up ad* is an Internet advertisement that suddenly appears in a new window on top of a webpage. A **pop-up blocker** is a filtering program that stops pop-up ads from displaying on webpages. Many browsers include a pop-up blocker. You also can download pop-up blockers from the web at no cost.

Figure 4-26 An example of a phishing email message.
Source: Andrew Levine

File and Disk Management Tools

To perform maintenance-type tasks related to managing a computer, its devices, or its programs, you can use one or more file and disk management tools. Functions provided by these tools include the following: managing files, searching, viewing images, uninstalling software, cleaning up disks, defragmenting disks, setting up screen savers, compressing files, maintaining a personal computer, and backing up files and disks. Although some of these tools are included with the operating system, you also can purchase stand-alone programs that offer improvements or added functionality.

File Manager

A **file manager** is a tool that performs functions related to file management. Some of the file management functions that a file manager performs are displaying a list of files on a storage medium (Figure 4-27); organizing files in folders; and copying, renaming, deleting, moving, and sorting files. A **folder** is a specific named location on a storage medium that contains related documents. Operating systems typically include a file manager.

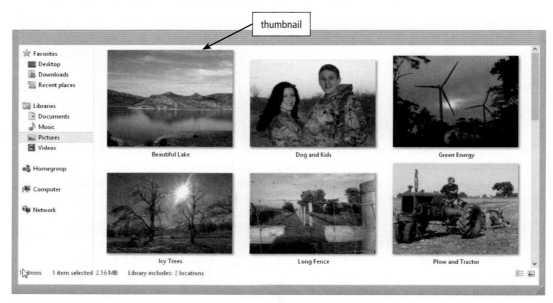

Figure 4-27 With a file manager, you can view files containing documents, photos, and music. In this case, thumbnails of photos are displayed.
Source: Microsoft

Search

A **search tool** is a program, usually included with an operating system, that attempts to locate a file on your computer or mobile device based on criteria you specify (Figure 4-28). The criteria could be a word or words contained in a file, date the file was created or modified, size of the file, location of the file, file name, author/artist, and other similar properties. Search tools can look through documents, photos, music, and other files on your computer or mobile device and/or on the Internet, combining search results in a single location.

Search tools typically use an index to assist with locating files quickly. An *index* stores a variety of information about a file, including its name, date created, date modified, author name, and so on. When you enter search criteria, instead of looking through every file and folder on the storage medium, the search tool looks through the index first to find a match. Each entry in the index contains a link to the actual file on the storage media for easy retrieval.

Figure 4-28 This search displays all files on the mobile device that match the search critieria, Map. Notice the search results show map apps, email with a map, and a calendar event.
Source: Apple Inc

Image Viewer

An **image viewer** is a tool that allows users to display, copy, and print the contents of a graphics file, such as a photo (Figure 4-29). With an image viewer, users can see images without having to open them in a paint or image editing program. Many image viewers include some photo editing capabilities. Most operating systems include an image viewer.

Uninstaller

An **uninstaller** is a tool that removes a program, as well as any associated entries in the system files. When you install a program, the operating system records the information it uses to run the software in the system files. The uninstaller deletes files and folders from the hard disk, as well as removes program entries from the system files. Read How To 4-3 for instructions about uninstalling programs and apps from your computers and mobile devices.

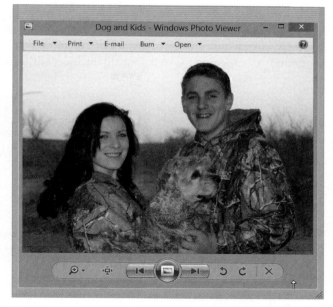

Figure 4-29   An image viewer allows users to see the contents of a photo file.
Source: Microsoft

 CONSIDER THIS

Can you use a file manager to delete a program?
If an uninstaller exists and you remove software from a computer by deleting the files and folders associated with the program without running the uninstaller, the system file entries might not be updated. This may cause the operating system to display error messages when you start the computer.

 HOW TO 4-3

Uninstall a Program or Remove an App

You may choose to uninstall a program or remove an app from your computer or mobile device for a variety of reasons. For example, you may uninstall a program if you need more space on your hard disk, or if you no longer have a use for that program. Uninstalling unwanted programs and apps will keep your hard disk free from clutter and maximize your computer or mobile device's performance. The following steps describe how to uninstall a program or remove an app.

Windows
1. Open the Control Panel.
2. Tap or click the option to uninstall a program.

3. Tap or click to select the program to uninstall.
4. Tap or click the Uninstall button and then follow the prompts on the screen.

Mac
1. Open the Finder.
2. Tap or click Applications in the left pane.
3. Scroll to display the app you wish to uninstall.
4. Drag the app's icon to the Trash.

iPhone, iPad, or iPod Touch
1. Press and hold the icon for the app you wish to delete until the app icons begin to animate.

2. Tap the X on the icon for the app you wish to delete to remove the app from your device.

Android
1. Display the Settings menu.
2. Tap Applications.
3. Tap the application to uninstall.
4. Tap the Uninstall button.
5. Tap the OK button.

✸ In addition to the reasons stated here, what other reasons might you choose to uninstall an app from your computer or mobile device?

Disk Cleanup

A **disk cleanup** tool searches for and removes unnecessary files (Figure 4-30). Unnecessary files may include downloaded program files, temporary Internet files, deleted files, and unused program files. Operating systems usually include a disk cleanup tool.

searching for unnecessary files

Figure 4-30 A disk cleanup tool searches for and removes unnecessary files.
Source: Microsoft

Disk Defragmenter

A **disk defragmenter** is a tool that reorganizes the files and unused space on a computer's hard disk so that the operating system accesses data more quickly and programs run faster. When an operating system stores data on a disk, it places the data in the first available sector (a storage location on a disk in the shape of an arc). The operating system attempts to place data in sectors that are contiguous (next to each other), but this is not always possible. When the contents of a file are scattered across two or more noncontiguous sectors, the file is fragmented.

Fragmentation slows down file access and thus the performance of the entire computer. **Defragmenting** the disk, or reorganizing it so that the files are stored in contiguous sectors, solves this problem (Figure 4-31). Operating systems usually include a disk defragmenter. Read How To 4-4 for instructions about defragmenting a hard disk.

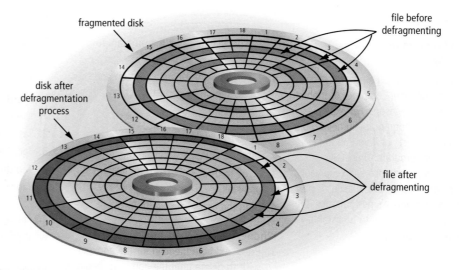

Figure 4-31 A fragmented disk has many files stored in noncontiguous sectors. Defragmenting reorganizes the files so that they are located in contiguous sectors, which speeds access time.
© Cengage Learning

HOW TO 4-4

 Defragment a Hard Disk

Defragmenting a hard disk can improve your computer's performance by storing all related files for a particular program together. This can reduce the amount of time it takes the hard disk to locate and access the files necessary for programs to run. Windows has a built-in tool to defragment a computer's hard disk. If you are using a Mac, you should obtain a program to defragment your hard disk. The following steps describe how to defragment a hard disk using the Windows 8 operating system.

1. Tap or click the Desktop tile to run the Desktop app.
2. Swipe from the right or point to the upper-right corner of the screen to display the Charms bar.
3. Tap or click the Settings charm.
4. Tap or click the Control Panel link on the Settings menu to display the Control Panel.
5. Tap or click the 'System and Security' link.
6. If necessary, scroll to display the 'Defragment and optimize your drives' link.

7. Tap or click the 'Defragment and optimize your drives' link.
8. Tap or click the hard disk you wish to defragment.
9. Tap or click the Optimize button to begin defragmenting the selected hard disk. This

process may take from several minutes to more than one hour.

What other tools can help optimize the performance of your computer?

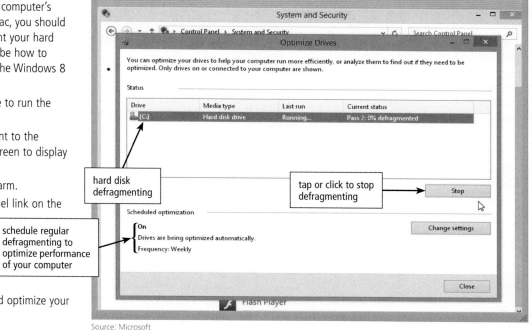

Source: Microsoft

Screen Saver

A **screen saver** is a tool that causes a display device's screen to show a moving image or blank screen if no keyboard or mouse activity occurs for a specified time. When you press a key on the keyboard or move the mouse, the screen saver disappears and the screen returns to the previous state.

CONSIDER THIS

What is the purpose of a screen saver?
Screen savers originally were developed to prevent a problem called ghosting, in which images could be etched permanently on a monitor's screen. Although ghosting is not as severe of a problem with today's displays, manufacturers continue to recommend that users install screen savers for this reason. Screen savers also are popular for security, business, and entertainment purposes. To secure a computer, users configure their screen saver to require a password to deactivate.

File Compression

A **file compression tool** shrinks the size of a file(s). A compressed file takes up less storage space than the original file. Compressing files frees up room on the storage media. You may need to compress a file so that it will fit on a smaller storage medium, such as a USB flash drive. Attaching a compressed file to an email message, for example, reduces the time needed for file transmission. Uploading and downloading compressed files to and from the Internet reduces the file transmission time.

 Internet Research
How are files compressed?
Search for: how file compression works

Compressed files sometimes are called **zipped files**. When you receive or download a compressed file, you must uncompress it. To **uncompress** (or unzip or expand) a file, you restore it to its original form. Some operating systems include file compression and uncompression capabilities. Read How To 4-5 for instructions about using file compression tools.

HOW TO 4-5

Compress and Uncompress Files and Folders

While the operating system may be able to compress some files by 50 percent or more, other files' sizes may not decrease significantly when they are compressed. Compressed files typically are stored by default in a file with a .zip file extension. The following steps describe how to compress a file or folder and then uncompress (expand or extract) the compressed file.

1. Press and hold or right-click the file(s) or folders you wish to compress to display a shortcut menu.

2. Tap or click the option to compress the file(s) or folder(s). (You may need to select a Send to or other command to display the compression options.)

3. If necessary, type the desired file name for the compressed file.

Uncompressing (or expanding) compressed files or folders returns them to their original form. The following steps uncompress a compressed file.

1. Double-tap or double-click the compressed file.

2. If necessary, tap or click the option to uncompress (expand or extract) the file.

or

1. Press and hold or right-click the compressed file to display a shortcut menu.

2. Tap or click the option to uncompress (expand or extract) the file.

✹ In addition to the operating system's built-in functionality to compress files and folders, what other programs and apps exist that can compress files and folders?

PC Maintenance

A **PC maintenance tool** is a program that identifies and fixes operating system problems, detects and repairs disk problems, and includes the capability of improving a computer's performance. Additionally, some personal computer maintenance utilities continuously monitor a computer while you use it to identify and repair problems before they occur.

Backup and Restore

A **backup tool** allows users to copy, or back up, selected files or the contents of an entire storage medium to another storage location, such as another hard disk, optical disc, USB flash drive, or cloud storage (Figure 4-32). During the backup process, the backup tool monitors progress and alerts you if it needs additional media, such as another disc. Many backup programs compress files during the backup process. By compressing the files, the backup program requires less storage space for the backup files than for the original files.

Because they are compressed, you usually cannot use backup files in their backed up form. In the event you need to use a backup file, a **restore tool** reverses the process and returns backed up files to their original form. Backup tools work with a restore tool. You should back up files and disks regularly in the event your originals are lost, damaged, or destroyed.

Figure 4-32 A backup tool allows users to copy files, folders, or the entire contents from one storage medium to another location.
Source: Acronis

✔ NOW YOU KNOW

Be sure you understand the material presented in the sections titled Security Tools and File and Disk Management Tools as it relates to the chapter objectives.
You now should know . . .

- Why you should use personal firewalls, antivirus programs, malware removers, and Internet filters (Objective 8)
- Which file and disk management tools you would find useful (Objective 9)

Quiz Yourself Online: Check your knowledge of related content by navigating to this book's Quiz Yourself resource on Computer Concepts CourseMate and then tapping or clicking Objectives 8–9.

✔ Chapter Summary

This chapter presented a variety of programs and apps available for computers and mobile devices. You learned about the role of the operating system and the various ways software is distributed. The chapter presented the features of a variety of productivity applications, graphics and media applications, and personal interest applications. It reviewed several communications applications and then presented features of a variety of security tools and file and disk management tools.

Test your knowledge of chapter material by accessing the Study Guide, Flash Cards, and Practice Test apps that run on your smartphone, tablet, laptop, or desktop.

⚡ TECHNOLOGY @ WORK

Entertainment

Do you wonder how music on the radio sounds so perfectly in tune, how animated motion pictures are created, or how one controls lighting during a concert? Not only does the entertainment industry rely on computers to advertise and sell their services, computers also assist in other aspects, including audio and video composition, lighting control, computerized animation, and computer gaming.

Entertainment websites provide music and movies you can purchase and download to your computer or mobile device; live news broadcasts, performances, and sporting events; games you can play with other online users; and much more.

As early as 1951, computers were used to record and play music. Today, computers play a much larger role in the music industry. For example, if you are listening to a song on the radio and notice that not one note is out of tune, it is possible that a program or app was used to change individual notes without altering the rest of the song.

Many years ago, creating cartoons or animated motion pictures was an

extremely time-consuming task because artists were responsible for sketching thousands of drawings by hand. Currently, artists use computers to create these drawings in a fraction of the time, which significantly reduces the time and cost of development.

Computers also are used in the game industry. While some game developers create games from scratch, others might use game engines that simplify the development process. For example, LucasArts created the GrimE game engine, which is designed to create adventure games.

During a concert, lighting technicians use computer programs to control lights by turning them off and on, changing their color, or changing their placement at specified intervals. In fact, once a performance begins, the technicians often merely are standing by, monitoring the computer as it performs most of the work. A significant amount of time and effort, however, is required to program the computer to execute its required tasks during a live show.

The next time you listen to a song, watch a movie, play a game, or attend a concert, think

about the role computers play in contributing to your entertainment.

✳ How else might computers and technology be used in the entertainment industry?

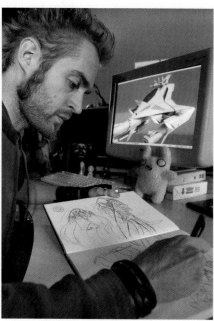

© Horizons WWP / Alamy

Study Guide

The Study Guide exercise reinforces material you should know for the chapter exam. You will find answers to items with the icon only in the e-book.

Access the Study Guide app that runs on your smartphone, tablet, laptop, or desktop by navigating to this book's Apps resource on Computer Concepts CourseMate.

Instructions: Answer the questions below using the format that helps you remember best or that is required by your instructor. Possible formats may include one or more of these options: write the answers; create a document that contains the answers; record answers as audio or video using a webcam, smartphone, or portable media player; post answers on a blog, wiki, or website; or highlight answers in the book/e-book.

1. List categories of programs and apps.

2. Define the terms: operating system, tools, and system software.

3. List examples of desktop and mobile operating systems.

4. Describe how an operating system interacts with the computer.

5. _____ software is tailor-made for a specific business or industry.

6. Differentiate among web apps, mobile apps, and mobile web apps.

7. List any restrictions for open source, shareware, freeware, and public-domain software.

8. Describe steps to register and activate software.

9. Explain the purpose of a license agreement.

10. List types of productivity applications.

11. Name the contributions of Microsoft and Apple, with respect to productivity applications.

12. Describe the activities that occur during project development.

13. Differentiate among font, font size, and font style.

14. Explain how the Internet has expanded plagiarism.

15. Identify functions of the following software: word processing, presentation, spreadsheet, database, note taking, calendar and contact management, project management, accounting, personal finance, legal, tax preparation, and document management.

16. List advantages of using a software suite.

17. Define the following terms: worksheet and function.

18. Name the contributions of Dan Bricklin, with respect to spreadsheet programs, and of Adobe Systems, with respect to document management software.

19. Name the products and/or services of Evernote.

20. List safety considerations when using personal finance apps.

21. Describe issues that might arise when using legal software.

22. Describe the functions of reference, travel, and retail applications.

23. Identify risks when using payment apps.

24. Name the types of software used by various functional units in an enterprise.

25. Identify functions of the following apps: office productivity, scanning, financial, reference, retail, travel, and social networking.

26. Identify functions of the following software: computer-aided design, desktop publishing, paint/image editing, photo editing and photo management, clip art/image gallery, video and audio editing, multimedia and website authoring, media player, and disc burning.

27. List ways to edit digital photos.

28. Identify issues surrounding altered digital photos.

29. Name the products and/or services of Instagram, with respect to photo sharing.

30. Define the terms, CBT and WBT.

31. List types of personal interest applications.

32. Describe ways to obtain help about a program or app.

33. Identify functions of the following apps: media sharing; streaming audio and video; game; news, sports, and weather; mapping; health and fitness; and academic.

34. Name the products and/or services of iTunes U.

35. Identify types of communications applications.

36. A(n) _____ includes time-stamped articles in a journal format.

37. Identify functions of the following tools: personal firewalls, antivirus programs, malware removers, and Internet filters.

38. Describe ways a virus infects programs or apps.

39. List types of malware. Identify signs of a virus infection.

40. Explain the risks of and how to avoid computer virus hoaxes.

41. Identify ways to avoid malware when using a mobile device.

42. Identify functions of the following tools: file manager, search, image viewer, uninstaller, disk cleanup, disk defragmenter, screen saver, file compression, PC maintenance, and backup and restore.

43. Define the terms, folder and index.

44. List steps to uninstall a program or remove an app.

45. Describe the disk defragmentation process.

46. Compressed files are sometimes called _____ files. List steps to uncompress a file.

47. List storage media for backups.

48. Describe uses of technology in the entertainment industry.

You should be able to define the Primary Terms and be familiar with the Secondary Terms listed below.

Key Terms

Access the Flash Cards app that runs on your smartphone, tablet, laptop, or desktop by navigating to this book's Apps resource on Computer Concepts CourseMate. View definitions for each term by navigating to this book's Key Terms resource on Computer Concepts CourseMate. Listen to definitions for each term on your portable media player by navigating to this book's Audio Study Tools resource on Computer Concepts CourseMate.

Primary Terms   (shown in **bold-black** characters in the chapter)

accounting software (164)
adware remover (182)
anti-spam program (183)
antivirus program (181)
app (152)
application (152)
audio editing software (173)
backup tool (188)
calendar and contact management software (163)
clip art (159)
clip art/image gallery (173)
computer-aided design (170)
database (162)
database software (162)
defragmenting (186)

desktop publishing software (170)
disc burning software (176)
disk cleanup (186)
disk defragmenter (186)
document management software (166)
file compression tool (187)
file manager (183)
folder (184)
image editing software (171)
image viewer (185)
legal software (166)
media player (175)
multimedia authoring software (174)
note taking software (162)
paint software (171)

PC maintenance tool (188)
PDF (167)
personal finance software (164)
personal firewall (179)
phishing (183)
phishing filter (183)
photo editing software (171)
photo management software (173)
pop-up blocker (183)
presentation software (160)
program (152)
project management software (164)
restore tool (188)
screen saver (187)
search tool (184)

software (152)
software suite (163)
spam (183)
spreadsheet software (160)
spyware remover (182)
tax preparation software (166)
uncompress (188)
uninstaller (185)
video editing software (173)
virus (180)
web filtering software (183)
website authoring software (174)
word processing software (159)
worksheet (160)
zipped files (188)

Secondary Terms   (shown in *italic* characters in the chapter)

adware (182)
application software (152)
automatic update (156)
blog software (178)
brightness (172)
clipboard (157)
compress (172)
computer-based training (CBT) (174)
contrast (172)
cookie (182)
create (157)
crop (172)
custom software (155)
edit (157)
e-filing (166)
font (158)

font size (158)
font style (158)
format (157)
freeware (155)
function (161)
hacker (179)
hard copy (158)
home design/landscaping software (170)
illustration software (171)
index (184)
license agreement (156)
mobile app (155)
mobile web app (155)
open source software (155)
operating system (152)

payload (180)
pop-up ad (183)
print (158)
product activation (156)
productivity applications (157)
public-domain software (155)
QR code (169)
QR code reader (169)
quarantine (181)
red-eye (172)
resize (172)
retail software (155)
rootkit (180)
save (158)
security suite (179)
shareware (155)

sharpness (172)
slide show (160)
software registration (156)
spyware (182)
system software (152)
toll fraud malware (182)
tools (152)
trial version (155)
trojan horse (180)
utilities (152)
virus signature (182)
web app (155)
web-based training (WBT) (174)
worm (180)

note taking software (162)

Source: Microsoft

Checkpoint

The Checkpoint exercises test your knowledge of the chapter concepts. The page number containing the answer appears in parentheses after each exercise. The Consider This exercises challenge your understanding of chapter concepts.

 Complete the Checkpoint exercises interactively by navigating to this book's Checkpoint resource on Computer Concepts CourseMate. **Access the Test Prep app** that runs on your smartphone, tablet, laptop, or desktop by navigating to this book's Apps resource on Computer Concepts CourseMate. After successfully completing the self-assessment through the Test Prep app, **take the Practice Test** by navigating to this book's Practice Test resource on Computer Concepts Coursemate.

True/False   Mark T for True and F for False.

_____ 1. Application software serves as the interface between the user, the apps, and the computer's or mobile device's hardware. (154)

_____ 2. Each time you start a computer or mobile device, the system software is loaded from storage into memory. (154)

_____ 3. Open source software is mass-produced, copyrighted software that meets the needs of a wide variety of users. (155)

_____ 4. When downloading shareware, freeware, or public-domain software, it is good practice to seek websites with ratings for and reviews of products. (157)

_____ 5. While a computer or mobile device is running, the operating system remains in memory. (155)

_____ 6. With database software, users run functions to retrieve data. (162)

_____ 7. Software suites offer three major advantages: lower cost, ease of use, and integration. (164)

_____ 8. A PDF file can be viewed and printed without the software that created the original document. (167)

_____ 9. The military and airlines might use CBT simulations to train pilots to fly in various conditions and environments. (174)

_____ 10. An antivirus program automatically deletes quarantined files. (181)

_____ 11. One of the fastest growing threats in mobile apps is toll fraud malware. (182)

_____ 12. Cookies typically are considered a type of spyware. (182)

Multiple Choice   Select the best answer.

1. Programs called _____ enable you to perform maintenance-type tasks usually related to managing devices, media, and programs used by computers and mobile devices. (152)
   a. productivity tools
   b. tools or utilities
   c. operating systems
   d. multimedia software

2. _____ software performs functions specific to a business or industry. (155)
   a. Retail   c. Shareware
   b. Open source   d. Custom

3. A(n) _____ is the right to use a program or app. (156)
   a. license agreement   c. software registration
   b. product activation   d. automatic update

4. _____ software is an application that allows users to organize data in rows and columns and perform calculations on the data. (160)
   a. Spreadsheet   c. Presentation
   b. Database   d. Document management

5. _____ is a type of application that assists professionals and designers in creating engineering, architectural, and scientific designs and models. (170)
   a. Enterprise software
   b. CAD software
   c. Public-domain software
   d. A software suite

6. The term _____ refers to decreasing a photo's file size. (172)
   a. crop   c. compress
   b. resize   d. shrink

7. A _____ is a destructive program disguised as a real program. (180)
   a. worm   c. pop-up ad
   b. trojan horse d. rootkit

8. A(n) _____ is a known, specific pattern of virus code. (182)
   a. index
   b. quarantine
   c. cookie
   d. virus signature

Checkpoint

Matching   Match the terms with their definitions.

_____ 1. tools (152)

_____ 2. open source software (155)

_____ 3. shareware (155)

_____ 4. QR code (169)

_____ 5. payload (180)

_____ 6. rootkit (180)

_____ 7. worm (180)

_____ 8. quarantine (181)

_____ 9. phishing (183)

_____ 10. defragmenting (186)

a. destructive event or prank a virus was created to deliver

b. copyrighted software that is distributed at no cost for a trial period

c. malware that resides in active memory and replicates itself over a network to infect computers and devices, using up the system resources and possibly shutting down the system

d. program that enables you to perform maintenance-type tasks usually related to managing devices, media, and programs used by computers and mobile devices

e. software provided for use, modification, and redistribution that has no restrictions from the copyright holder regarding modification of the software

f. process of reorganizing a hard disk's files so that the files are stored in contiguous sectors

g. malware that can hide and allow someone to take full control of a computer from a remote location

h. scam in which a perpetrator sends an official looking email message that attempts to obtain personal and/or financial information

i. square-shaped coded graphic that corresponds to a web address or other information

j. separate area of a hard disk that holds an infected file until the infection can be removed

Short Answer   Write a brief answer to each of the following questions.

1. What is the difference between software registration and product activation? (156) What activities does a license agreement restrict? (156)

2. What is the clipboard? (157) List some uses of the clipboard. (157)

3. List some security tools you can use to protect your computers and mobile devices. (179) What is a personal firewall? (179)

4. Differentiate among a virus, worm, trojan horse, and rootkit. (180) In reference to malware, what is a quarantine? (181)

5. List the different types of file and disk management tools. (183) What functions do they provide? (183)

✳ Consider This   Answer the following questions in the format specified by your instructor.

1. Answer the critical thinking questions posed at the end of these elements in this chapter: Ethics & Issues (158, 166, 173, 175), How To (172, 176, 185, 187, 188), Mini Features (169, 177, 180), Secure IT (156, 165, 168, 181, 182), and Technology @ Work (189).

2. What is the role of the operating system? (152, 154)

3. What are the advantages of open source software? What are some examples of open source software? (155)

4. What does it mean to edit a project? How does editing differ from formatting? (157)

5. How does a spreadsheet organize data? How are cells identified in a spreadsheet? (160)

6. What kind of information can you find using a reference application? (167)

7. How can you ensure your safety when using mobile payment apps? (168)

8. What are some examples of office productivity apps? What can you accomplish using these apps? (157, 169)

9. Should journalists edit or enhance digital photos? Why or why not? (173)

10. What tasks can you accomplish using mapping apps? (177)

11. How does a personal firewall protect your computer? (179)

12. What happens during the delivery phase of a virus? (180)

13. Why is spam potentially dangerous? What is a phishing scam? (183)

14. How does a search tool locate a file on your computer or mobile device? (184)

15. What is a fragmented disk? How does fragmentation affect a computer's performance? (186)

❋ How To: Your Turn

The How To: Your Turn exercises present general guidelines for fundamental skills when using a computer or mobile device and then require that you determine how to apply these general guidelines to a specific program or situation.

Instructions: You often can complete tasks using technology in multiple ways. Figure out how to perform the tasks described in these exercises by using one or more resources available to you (such as a computer or mobile device, articles on the web or in print, online or program help, user guides, blogs, podcasts, videos, other individuals, trial and error, etc.). Summarize your 'how to' steps, along with the resource(s) used, in the format requested by your instructor (brief report, presentation, discussion, blog post, video, or other means).

1 Obtain Directions with Mapping Applications and Websites

If you need directions to walk, drive, bike, or even take public transportation to your destination, you can use mapping applications or websites to obtain directions. These applications and websites often provide very accurate directions, but it is important to verify the directions before venturing into unfamiliar areas. If the directions you obtain require using public transportation, you should verify with the transportation provider's website that the routes and time schedules provided by your mapping application still are accurate. The following steps describe how to obtain directions using a mapping application.

a. Search for and install a mapping application or navigate to a mapping website of your choice on your computer or mobile device. Many computers and mobile devices include a mapping application. You also can access websites that provide directions and updated maps. If you are using a mapping application that is installed on your computer or mobile device, make sure the application is updated with the latest maps. Using an application with outdated maps can result in it providing directions that are not accurate.

b. Tap or click the option to obtain directions. Then, if necessary, specify whether you want to obtain driving, biking, walking, or public transportation directions.

c. If you require directions from your current location, mapping applications and websites may be able to use the GPS feature on your mobile device to detect your location automatically. To use this feature, make sure the GPS feature on your mobile device is enabled and then, if necessary, tap or click the button to detect your current location automatically.

d. Enter the address to which you want directions. Make sure you enter the full street address, city, state, and postal code, and then tap or click the button to retrieve the directions.

e. Review the directions and make sure you understand them before beginning your trip.

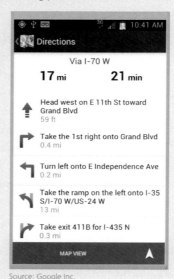

Source: Google Inc.

f. Print the directions and carry them with you during the journey to your destination. If the directions are on a mobile device that you can take with you as you travel to your destination, consider activating the audio feature so that directions can be read aloud as you navigate the route.

g. Upon arriving at your destination, exit the mapping application.

Exercises

1. Research three different mapping applications. Which one would you use, and why?

2. Research three web apps that can provide directions. In your opinion, is it better to use a web app to obtain directions than an application installed on your computer or mobile device? Why or why not?

3. Use a mapping application or web app to obtain directions from your home to your preferred shopping mall. Did the web app or application display directions similar to the route you travel? If not, will you consider traveling the route that the mapping web app or application provided?

2 View Current Virus Threats

One important way to protect your computer or mobile device from viruses is to be aware of current threats. Several websites exist that not only provide a list of current virus threats but also describe how best to protect your computer or mobile device from these threats. As new virus threats are introduced, it is important to make sure your antivirus program is updated and running properly. The following steps describe how to view a list of current virus threats.

a. Run a browser and then navigate to a search engine of your choice.

How To: Your Turn

b. Perform a search for websites that display current virus threats.

c. Review the search results and visit at least two websites that display current virus threats.

d. View the list of virus threats on each of these websites.

or

a. Run a browser and then navigate to a search engine of your choice.

b. Perform a search for websites created by companies that make antivirus software. Some companies that make antivirus software include Symantec, McAfee, and Microsoft.

c. Navigate to one of these company's websites and search for a link to a webpage displaying current virus threats.

d. Tap or click the link to display current virus threats.

Source: McAfee.com

Exercises

1. Which websites did you access? Compare these websites and determine which you think provided the most helpful information. Why, in your opinion, does the website you chose provide the best information?

2. Has your computer or mobile device ever been infected with a virus? If so, what steps have you taken to remove the virus?

3. Is your computer or mobile device adequately protected from viruses? What steps do you take to keep your computer safe?

❸ Back Up Your Computer

Backing up your computer is an important way to protect your programs, apps, and data from loss. The frequency at which people back up their computers can vary. For instance, if you create and modify a lot of files on your computer, you may choose to back up your computer frequently. If you rarely use

your computer or primarily use your computer for answering email messages and browsing the web, you might not back up your computer as often. The following steps guide you through the process of backing up a computer.

a. Decide which backup program you wish to use. Some operating systems have built-in tools you can use to back up a computer, or you can install a third-party program.

b. Run the program you will use to back up the computer.

c. If necessary, connect the storage device, such as an external hard disk, you will use to store the backup. If you plan to store the backup on an optical disc or another hard disk that already is installed, you will not need to connect an additional storage device.

d. Make sure the storage medium has enough available space for the backed up files. If you are storing the backup on optical discs, make sure you have enough optical discs for the backup.

e. Select the type of backup (full, incremental, differential, or selective) you wish to perform.

f. If you are performing a selective backup, choose the files, programs, and apps you wish to include in the backup.

g. Run the backup. The backup process may take up to several hours, depending on the number of files you are including in the backup.

h. If you are storing the backup on optical discs, the backup program may prompt you to insert new, blank optical discs throughout the backup process.

i. When the backup is complete, store the backup in a safe location. In the event you lose data or information on the computer, you will need to retrieve the backup.

Source: Acronis

Exercises

1. How often do you feel you should back up your computer? Justify your answer.

2. What storage medium do you feel is most appropriate for your backup? Justify your answer.

3. Research at least three programs that you can use to back up your computer. Which programs did you research? Which program or app do you feel is the best? Why?

✳ Internet Research

The Internet Research exercises broaden your understanding of chapter concepts by requiring that you search for information on the web.

Instructions: Use a search engine or another search tool to locate the information requested or answers to questions presented in the exercises. Describe your findings, along with the search term(s) you used and your web source(s), in the format requested by your instructor (brief report, presentation, discussion, blog post, video, or other means).

❶ Making Use of the Web
Travel and Mapping

Pack your bags and grab some great deals on airfare, hotels, rental cars, and resorts just by visiting websites geared toward your travel needs. Some websites compare multiple airlines' fares to cities worldwide and allow you to search for the lowest fares on a particular date or a range of dates, for destinations within a specific price range, or for locations with preferred activities, such as skiing or hiking. Others send alerts when lodging rates or fares drop below a specified price point or give predictions of whether the rates will increase or decrease during the upcoming weeks. The websites also offer reviewers' ratings of hotels, restaurants, and activities.

Getting to a vacation destination can be an adventure in itself, and websites can offer assistance in pointing travelers in the right direction. Some provide interactive maps, display satellite and aerial imagery of the Earth, and recommended restaurants and tourist attractions en route to specific cities.

(a) Visit two travel websites and search for airfares to your favorite vacation destination on your next birthday. Which airlines offer the lowest fares to this location? What hotels or resorts are reviewed favorably? Which aspects of this lodging do the travelers like and dislike? What are the similarities and differences between the two travel websites? Which website is easier to search and locate desired information? Have you used websites to obtain travel information or to make reservations?

(b) Visit a mapping website and obtain the distance from your campus to the Indianapolis Motor Speedway (Speedway, IN), Kennedy Space Center (Merritt Island,

FL), or Navy Pier (Chicago, IL). What is the estimated travel time? Locate an aerial or a satellite image of this destination. What features are visible in the picture?

❷ Social Media 📑

Gaming via social media has seen explosive growth in recent years, with an estimated 235 million people participating in online games each month. Exponential gaming growth has spawned companion businesses that facilitate and manage the gaming experience. Some mobile and desktop apps provide gamers a portal for tracking all their online gaming results in a central location that can be shared with friends and others with similar game interests. These apps integrate with the major instant messaging services, have personalized news feeds, and incorporate a "suggestion" engine for new game discoveries. Many gaming blogs offer game tricks, work-arounds, and hidden features. Beginning gamers can engage their minds during downtime and expand their circle of online friends.

Visit at least two social networks for gamers. How many games are shown? Which topics are featured in community discussions and live chats? Are rewards available? If so, what are they? Which online leagues and tournaments are offered? What are some of the latest news articles about specific games and the gaming industry? Have you participated in gaming social networks? If so, which ones?

❸ Search Sleuth

(1) Who was sitting under an apple tree in Apple's original corporate logo? (2) In what year was the first phone using the Android operating system sold in the United States? (3) Which software developer appeared in the movies *Triumph of the Nerds* and *Aardvark'd: 12 Weeks with Geeks*? (4) Which United States president's speech did Peter Norvig turn into a lighthearted PowerPoint presentation? (5) What is the difference between a serif and sans serif font? Which sans serif font did the German Bauhaus movement develop in 1928? (6) In which year did the United States Department of Revenue first provide tax forms and booklets in Adobe PDF format on its website?

Source: Google Inc.

Internet Research ✺

(7) What company did Bruce Artwick form in 1977, and what game did it license to Microsoft in 1982? (8) Which company coined the term, word processing, in the late 1960s? (9) Microsoft included the Disk Volume Organization Optimizer in its early operating system to defragment which storage medium? (10) Bernd Fix, Atari ST, G Data, and UVK 2000 are names of which category of security tools?

fragmented disk

disk after defragmentation process

file before defragmenting

file after defragmenting

© Cengage Learning

④ Green Computing

When it comes to software recycling, going green may just leave you in the black. Software from that desktop you once cherished, now gathering dust in the corner of your basement, may have some value in its dormant bytes. A niche industry of software brokers now exists that purchases used software and resells it to customers that may not need the latest versions. These customers may have older computers or operating systems that do not support new software revisions. In such cases, vintage software may be a necessity to avoid upgrading to new hardware. Some software recycling companies buy popular used software, such as Microsoft Office, which often is bundled and preinstalled on new computers. These recycling brokers work with organizations that are replacing old hardware with software installed. The brokers first verify that the used software exists and the licensing terms are not violated. They then buy the software and offer it for resale. Recycled software may not be green for the environment, but it can provide some green for your bottom line.

Locate at least two software recycling company websites. Which software titles are available in the inventory? What is the cost of the more popular titles, such as Microsoft Office or Adobe Creative Suite? How much will the companies pay to obtain software? Do they have restrictions on how new the software must be? Are incomplete software packages accepted? How do the companies verify authenticity? Software manufacturers may not update older versions of their products, so recycled software may leave a computer vulnerable to Internet and network security attacks.

Would this security risk dissuade you from purchasing recycled software?

⑤ Security

Virus hoaxes are widespread and sometimes cause panic among Internet users. Secure IT 4-4 on page 181 gives advice on recognizing and avoiding virus hoaxes. Snopes.com provides further insight on the sources and variations of a wide variety of rumors, deceptions, and folklore.

Visit snopes.com and review the list of the more recent real (indicated by a green dot) and false (indicated by a red dot) rumors circulating on the Internet. Which are the three newest actual warnings, and which are the three latest virus hoaxes? What harm is predicted to occur if a user downloads each of these real or false viruses or views a website laden with malware? What is the origin of the website's name, Snopes?

⑥ Ethics in Action

As you read in this chapter, a hacker is someone who tries to access a computer or network illegally. Although hacking activity sometimes is a harmless prank, at times it causes extensive damage. Some hackers claim their activities are a form of civil disobedience that forces companies to make their products more secure. Others say their activities allow them to test their skills. Many of these hackers are able to participate in activities and share their knowledge each year at DEF CON, one of the world's largest and continuous-running conferences for hackers. The International Council of E-Commerce Consultants administers professional accreditation to become a Certified Ethical Hacker. Also, community-based hacking projects test researchers' programs and apps under development.

View online websites that provide information about when hackers provide some benefit to the Internet society. In which circumstances are hackers valuable contributors to the computer field? What are the requirements to become a Certified Ethical Hacker? The DefCon Kids event teaches children ages 8 to 16 how to hack hardware, open master locks, break codes, and prevent spying over wireless networks. Should children be taught hacking activities? Will learning these techniques at an early age encourage them to fight cybercrime or entice them to participate in it?

✸ Problem Solving

The Problem Solving exercises extend your knowledge of chapter concepts by seeking solutions to practical problems with technology that you may encounter at home, school, work, or with nonprofit organizations. The Collaboration exercise should be completed with a team.

 Challenge yourself with additional Problem Solving exercises by navigating to this book's Problem Solving resource on Computer Concepts CourseMate.

Instructions: You often can solve problems with technology in multiple ways. Determine a solution to the problems in these exercises by using one or more resources available to you (such as a computer or mobile device, articles on the web or in print, blogs, podcasts, videos, television, user guides, other individuals, electronics or computer stores, etc.). Describe your solution, along with the resource(s) used, in the format requested by your instructor (brief report, presentation, discussion, blog post, video, or other means).

Personal

1. Antivirus Program Not Updating You are attempting to update your antivirus program with the latest virus definitions, but you receive an error message. What steps will you take to resolve this issue?

Source: AVG Technologies

2. Operating System Does Not Load Each time you turn on your computer, the operating system attempts to load for approximately 30 seconds and then the computer restarts. You have tried multiple times to turn your computer off and on, but it keeps restarting when the operating system is trying to load. What are your next steps?

3. Tablet App Malfunctioning When you attempt to run an app on your tablet, the tablet displays an error message stating that the app is unable to run and then returns to the home screen. You have run this app successfully in the past and are unsure of why this problem suddenly is occurring. What are your next steps?

4. News Not Updating Each morning you run an app on your smartphone to view the news for the current day. For the past week, however, you notice that the news displayed in the app is out of date. In fact, the app now is displaying news that is nearly one week old. Why might the app not be updating? What are your next steps?

5. Incompatible App You are using your Android tablet to browse for apps in the Google Play store. You found an app you want to download, but you are unable to download it because a message states it is incompatible with your device. Why might the app be incompatible with your device?

Professional

6. Email Program Freezing Each time you run the email program on your computer and it attempts to download your new email messages, the program freezes and you have to restart the computer. You are able to retrieve your email messages on your mobile device without any issues and do not know why you are having problems with the email program on your computer. What are your next steps?

7. License Agreement You are planning to work from home for several days, but you are unsure of whether you are allowed to install a program you use at work on your home computer. What steps will you take to determine whether you are allowed to install the software on your home computer?

8. Presentation Problems While rehearsing for a presentation you plan to give to some colleagues, you notice that the presentation software automatically is advancing the slides. Instead, you would like the slides to advance when you tap the screen or click your mouse. What steps will you take to fix this problem?

9. Unacceptable File Size Your boss has asked you to design a new company logo using a graphics application installed on your computer. When you save the logo and send it to your boss, she responds that the file size is too large and tells you to find a way to decrease the file size. What might you do to make the image file size smaller?

10. Disc Burning Not Working While attempting to back up some files on your computer on an optical disc, the disc burning software on your computer reports a problem and ejects the disc. When you check the contents of the disc, the files you are trying to back up are not there. What might be wrong?

Collaboration

11. Technology in Entertainment The film department at a local high school is considering developing a movie and has asked for your help. The film teacher would like to incorporate technology wherever possible, in hopes that it would decrease the cost of the movie's production. Form a team of three people to determine what technology can be used to assist in the movie's production. One team member should research the type of technology that can be used during the filming process. Another team member should research the types of hardware and software available for editing footage, and the third team member should research the hardware and software requirements for producing and distributing the media.

The Critical Thinking exercises challenge your assessment and decision-making skills by presenting real-world situations associated with chapter concepts. The Collaboration exercise should be completed with a team.

Critical Thinking ☀

 Challenge yourself with additional Critical Thinking exercises by navigating to this book's Critical Thinking resource on Computer Concepts CourseMate.

Instructions: Evaluate the situations below, using personal experiences and one or more resources available to you (such as articles on the web or in print, blogs, podcasts, videos, television, user guides, other individuals, electronics or computer stores, etc.). Perform the tasks requested in each exercise and share your deliverables in the format requested by your instructor (brief report, presentation, discussion, blog post, video, or other means).

1. Class Discussion

File and Disk Management Tools   You are the director of information technology at a company that hires student interns frequently. The interns tend to have limited experience with using file and disk management tools. As part of your job, you lead workshops that teach the interns the many tasks and functions they can perform using these tools. Choose three categories of tools, such as disk cleanup, PC maintenance, and file compression. Determine whether your computer's operating system includes these tools. Use the web to research popular tools for each category; whether they can be purchased separately or if they are available only as part of an operating system; and the costs for each tool. Choose one program from each category, and read user reviews and articles by industry experts. Describe situations where you would use each type of tool. Share any experiences you have with using the tools.

2. Research and Share

Web and Mobile App Comparison   You recently purchased a new smartphone and want to research mobile apps that also have accompanying web apps. Choose three categories of apps, and find an example for each that has both a free web and mobile version. Read user reviews of each app, and search for articles by industry experts. Research any known safety risks for the apps. If you determine the app is safe and have the appropriate device, and would like to test the mobile app, you can download it to your smartphone or other mobile device. Try accessing the web app on a computer. Using your experience or research, note the differences in functionality between the web and mobile app. Is one or the other easier to use? Why or why not? Compile your findings and then share with the class.

3. Case Study

Farmers' Market   You are the new manager for a group of organic farmers who have a weekly market in season. The farmers' market needs productivity software in order to keep track of vendor and budget information and prepare flyers. You prepare information about productivity software options to present to the board of directors. Use the web to research popular word processing, spreadsheet, and accounting software. Choose three programs from each category. List common features of each, find pricing information, and note any feedback or ratings by users. Which programs would you recommend? Why? Describe the steps involved in developing a project, creating a flyer for the farmers' market as an example. Identify possible uses the farmers' market may have for the spreadsheet and accounting software. Compile your findings.

Source: Google Inc.

Collaboration

4. **Educational Program and App Effectiveness**   The principal of the local elementary school has recommended that educational applications should play a major role in the learning process. She stated that educational applications enable students to learn at their own pace. Some enable teachers to track an individual student's progress and understanding. Form a three-member team and research the use of educational applications. Each member of your team should choose a different type of application, such as flash cards, testing, or CBT. List the advantages and disadvantages of using that type of application. If possible, download or access a free version of an educational application from each category and spend some time using it. Read user reviews of popular applications, and search for articles by industry experts. Would you recommend using an application for educational purposes? Why or why not? Meet with your team, discuss and compile your findings, and then share with the class.

STUDENT ASSIGNMENTS

✳ Beyond the Book

The Beyond the Book exercises expand your understanding of chapter concepts by requiring research.

💻 **Access premium content** by visiting Computer Concepts CourseMate. If you have a Computer Concepts CourseMate access code, you can reinforce and extend your learning with MindTap Reader, practice tests, video, and other premium content for Discovering Computers. To sign in to Computer Concepts CourseMate at www.cengagebrain.com, you first must create a student account and then register this book, as described at www.cengage.com/ct/studentdownload.

Part 1 Instructions: Use the web or e-book to perform the task identified for each book element below. Describe your findings, along with the search term(s) you used and your web source(s), if appropriate, in the format requested by your instructor (brief report, presentation, discussion, blog post, video, or other means).

1. **Animation** 📱 Review the animation associated with this chapter and then answer the question(s) it poses (154). What search term would you use to learn more about a specific segment of the animation?

2. **Consider This** Select a Consider This in this chapter (153, 156, 158, 164, 167, 174, 179, 182, 185, 187) and find a recent article that elaborates on the topic. What information did you find that was not presented in this book or e-book?

3. **Drag-and-Drop Figures** 📱 Complete the Drag-and-Drop Figure activities associated with this chapter (153, 154, 172, 178, 186). What did you learn from each of these activities?

4. **Ethics & Issues** Select an Ethics & Issues in this chapter (158, 166, 173, 175) and find a recent article that supports one view presented. Does the article change your opinion about the topic? Why or why not?

5. **Facebook & Twitter** Review a recent Discovering Computers Facebook post or Twitter Tweet and read the referenced article(s). What did you learn from the article?

6. **High-Tech Talk** 📱 Locate an article that discusses topics related to 3-D graphics. Would you recommend the article you found? Why or why not?

7. **How To** Select a How To in this chapter (172, 176, 185, 187, 188) and find a recent article that elaborates on the topic. Who would benefit from the content of this article? Why?

8. **Innovative Computing** 📱 Locate two additional facts about Instagram, iTunes U, or Evernote. Do your findings change your opinion about the future of this innovation? Why or why not?

9. **Internet Research** Use the search term in an Internet Research (154, 159, 167, 176, 183, 187) to answer the question posed in the element. What other search term could you use to answer the question?

10. **Mini Features** Locate an article that discusses topics related to one of the mini features in this chapter (169,

177, 180). Do you feel that the article is appropriate for this course? Why or why not?

11. **Secure IT** Select a Secure IT in this chapter (156, 165, 168, 181, 182) and find a recent article about the topic that you find interesting. How can you relate the content of the article to your everyday life?

12. **Technology @ Work** Locate three additional, unique usages of technology in the entertainment industry (189). What makes the use of these technologies unique to the entertainment industry?

13. **Technology Innovators** 📱 Locate two additional facts about Microsoft, Apple, Dan Bricklin, and Adobe Systems. Which Technology Innovator impresses you most? Why?

14. **Third-Party Links** 📱 Visit one of the third-party links identified in this chapter (157, 158, 161, 165, 166, 168, 173, 175, 177, 181, 182, 187, 189) and read the article or watch the video associated with the link. Would you share this link on your online social network account? Why or why not?

Part 2 Instructions: Find specific instructions for the exercises below in the e-book or on Computer Concepts CourseMate. Beside each exercise is a brief description of its online content.

1. 📱 **You Review It** Search for and review a video, podcast, or blog post about the most popular mobile apps that users of mobile devices downloaded this week.

2. 📱 **Windows and Mac** Enhance your understanding and knowledge about using Windows and Mac computers by completing the Creating Documents Using a Text Editor and Creating, Accessing, and Storing Notes Online activities.

3. 📱 **Android, iOS, and Windows Mobile** Enhance your understanding of mobile devices by completing the Organize Your Apps, Widgets, or Tiles and Creating, Accessing, and Storing Notes Online activities.

4. 📱 **Exploring Computer Careers** Read about a career as a game designer, search for related employment ads, and then answer related questions.

5. 📱 **App Adventure** Stay organized by keeping a to-do list of your tasks using apps on your smartphone or tablet.

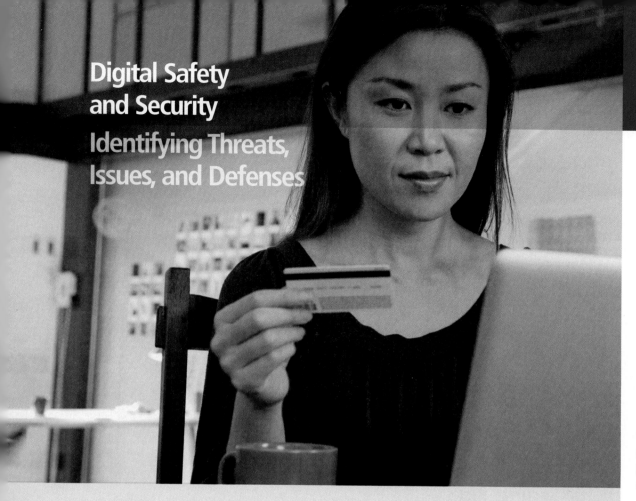

Digital Safety and Security
Identifying Threats, Issues, and Defenses

5

Users should take precautions to protect their digital content.

"I am careful when browsing the web, use antivirus software, and never open email messages from unknown senders. I use a cloud storage provider to back up my computer and mobile devices. What more do I need to know about digital safety and security?"

True, you may be familiar with some of the material in this chapter, but do you know . . .

How to secure a wireless network?

When an organization can be punished for weak security?

How to tell if your computer or device is functioning as a zombie?

How to use anonymous browsing?

How a digital forensics examiner collects and analyzes cybercrime evidence?

When you might see a CAPTCHA?

How to avoid risks when playing online games?

Which security company's code of conduct expects its employees to raise ethical issues?

How to protect yourself from social engineering scams?

How the federal and local governments use technology?

Why computer vision helps to increase security?

How public key encryption works?

Which retail apps are best suited to your needs?

How to secure a mobile device?

For these answers and to discover much more information essential to this course, read this chapter and visit the associated Computer Concepts CourseMate at www.cengagebrain.com.

✔ Objectives

After completing this chapter, you will be able to:

1   Define the term, digital security risks, and briefly describe the types of cybercriminals

2   Describe various types of Internet and network attacks (malware, botnets, denial of service attacks, back doors, and spoofing) and explain ways to safeguard against these attacks, including firewalls

3   Discuss techniques to prevent unauthorized computer access and use, including access controls, user names, passwords, possessed objects, and biometric devices

4   Explain ways that software manufacturers protect against software piracy

5   Discuss how encryption, digital signatures, and digital certificates work

6   Identify safeguards against hardware theft, vandalism, and failure

7   Explain options available for backing up

8   Identify risks and safeguards associated with wireless communications

9   Recognize issues related to information accuracy, intellectual property rights, codes of conduct, and green computing

10 Discuss issues surrounding information privacy, including electronic profiles, cookies, phishing, spyware and adware, social engineering, privacy laws, employee monitoring, and content filtering

Digital Security Risks

Today, people rely on technology to create, store, and manage their critical information. Thus, it is important that computers and mobile devices, along with the data and programs they store, are accessible and available when needed. It also is crucial that users take measures to protect or safeguard their computers, mobile devices, data, and programs from loss, damage, and misuse. For example, organizations must ensure that sensitive data and information such as credit records, employee and customer data, and purchase information is secure. Home users must ensure that their credit card numbers are secure when they make online purchases.

A **digital security risk** is any event or action that could cause a loss of or damage to computer or mobile device hardware, software, data, information, or processing capability. The more common digital security risks include Internet and network attacks, unauthorized access and use, hardware theft, software theft, information theft, and system failure (Figure 5-1).

While some breaches to digital security are accidental, many are intentional. Some intruders do no damage; they merely access data, information, or programs on the computer or mobile device before signing out. Other intruders indicate some evidence of their presence either by leaving a message or by deliberately altering or damaging data.

Cybercrime

An intentional breach to digital security often involves a deliberate act that is against the law. Any illegal act involving the use of a computer or related devices generally is referred to as a **computer crime**. The term **cybercrime** refers to online or Internet-based illegal acts such as distributing malicious software or committing identity theft. Software used by cybercriminals sometimes is called *crimeware*. Today, combating cybercrime is one of the FBI's top priorities.

unauthorized access
and use

intercepting
wireless
communications

**Internet and
network attacks**

virus attack

hardware theft

stolen computer

**Security
Risks**

system failure

lightning strike

software theft

illegal copying

information theft

stolen identity

Figure 5-1 Computers and mobile devices, along with the data and programs they store, are exposed to several types of security risks.

Perpetrators of cybercrime typically fall into one of these basic categories: hacker, cracker, script kiddie, corporate spy, unethical employee, cyberextortionist, and cyberterrorist.

🌀 **Internet Research**

What is a white hat hacker?

Search for: white hat hacker

- The term **hacker**, although originally a complimentary word for a computer enthusiast, now has a derogatory meaning and refers to someone who accesses a computer or network illegally. Some hackers claim the intent of their security breaches is to improve security.
- A **cracker** also is someone who accesses a computer or network illegally but has the intent of destroying data, stealing information, or other malicious action. Both hackers and crackers have advanced computer and network skills.
- A **script kiddie** has the same intent as a cracker but does not have the technical skills and knowledge. Script kiddies often use prewritten hacking and cracking programs to break into computers and networks.
- Some corporate spies have excellent computer and networking skills and are hired to break into a specific computer and steal its proprietary data and information, or to help identify security risks in their own organization. Unscrupulous companies hire corporate spies, a practice known as corporate espionage, to gain a competitive advantage.
- Unethical employees may break into their employers' computers for a variety of reasons. Some simply want to exploit a security weakness. Others seek financial gains from selling confidential information. Disgruntled employees may want revenge.
- A **cyberextortionist** is someone who demands payment to stop an attack on an organization's technology infrastructure. These perpetrators threaten to expose confidential information, exploit a security flaw, or launch an attack that will compromise the organization's network — if they are not paid a sum of money.
- A **cyberterrorist** is someone who uses the Internet or network to destroy or damage computers for political reasons. The cyberterrorist might target the nation's air traffic control system, electricity-generating companies, or a telecommunications infrastructure. The term, *cyberwarfare*, describes an attack whose goal ranges from disabling a government's computer network to crippling a country. Cyberterrorism and cyberwarfare usually require a team of highly skilled individuals, millions of dollars, and several years of planning.

Read Ethics & Issues 5-1 to consider how cybercriminals should be punished. Some organizations hire individuals previously convicted of computer crimes to help identify security risks and implement safeguards because these individuals know how criminals attempt to breach security.

✳️ **ETHICS & ISSUES 5-1**

📓 **How Should Cybercriminals Be Punished?**
A hacker was sentenced to 20 years in jail for stealing credit card information from several large corporations and then selling the information, costing one company approximately $200 million. Legislators have made efforts to deter cybercrime. For example, one country proposed legislation that attempts to specify punishments for cybercrime, such as those involving identity theft, unauthorized access and use, obscene material, and libel. Critics of this type of law claim that including libel as a cybercrime is a threat to free speech, privacy, and democracy.

The proposed legislation received international attention and scrutiny, and the country's supreme court issued a temporary restraining order against the legislation.

Cybercrime laws vary between states and countries, making it difficult to reach a consensus as to what is illegal, and whether a crime is a civil or criminal case. Determining who has jurisdiction over a case can create more legal hassles. For example, which area has jurisdiction: where the victim(s) resides or where the perpetrator lives? The anonymity of the Internet makes it difficult even to find out who has committed the crime.

Some legal experts claim that weak security on the part of corporations using the Internet to conduct business is to blame. The Federal Trade Commission (FTC) has punished companies whose security flaws enabled hackers to breach their systems.

Should the government create new laws specifically aimed at punishing cybercriminals? Why or why not? Should corporations be liable for damages caused by hackers? Why or why not? Who should decide the extent of the true damages caused by a cybercrime? Why?

Internet and Network Attacks

Information transmitted over networks has a higher degree of security risk than information kept on an organization's premises. In an organization, network administrators usually take measures to protect a network from security risks. On the Internet, where no central administrator is present, the security risk is greater. Internet and network attacks that jeopardize security include malware, botnets, denial of service attacks, back doors, and spoofing.

Malware

Recall that **malware**, short for *malicious software*, consists of programs that act without a user's knowledge and deliberately alter the operations of computers and mobile devices. Table 5-1 summarizes common types of malware, all of which have been discussed in previous chapters. Some malware contains characteristics in two or more classes. For example, a single threat could contain elements of a virus, worm, and trojan horse. Some websites maintain lists of known malware.

Malware can deliver its *payload*, or destructive event or prank, on a computer or mobile device in a variety of ways, such as when a user opens an infected file, runs an infected program, connects an unprotected computer or mobile device to a network, or when a certain condition or event occurs, such as the computer's clock changing to a specific date. A common way that computers and mobile devices become infected with viruses and other malware is through users opening infected email attachments (Figure 5-2). Read Secure IT 5-1 on the next page to learn about how malware can affect online gaming.

Table 5-1	Common Types of Malware
Type	**Description**
Virus	A potentially damaging program that affects, or infects, a computer or mobile device negatively by altering the way the computer or device works without the user's knowledge or permission.
Worm	A program that copies itself repeatedly, for example in memory or on a network, using up resources and possibly shutting down the computer, device, or network.
Trojan horse	A program that hides within or looks like a legitimate program. Unlike a virus or worm, a trojan horse does not replicate itself to other computers or devices.
Rootkit	A program that hides in a computer or mobile device and allows someone from a remote location to take full control of the computer or device.
Spyware	A program placed on a computer or mobile device without the user's knowledge that secretly collects information about the user and then communicates the information it collects to some outside source while the user is online.
Adware	A program that displays an online advertisement in a banner or pop-up window on webpages, email messages, or other Internet services.

How a Virus Can Spread via an Email Message

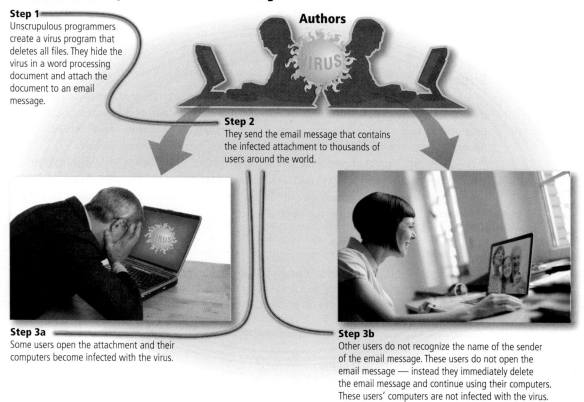

Step 1
Unscrupulous programmers create a virus program that deletes all files. They hide the virus in a word processing document and attach the document to an email message.

Authors

Step 2
They send the email message that contains the infected attachment to thousands of users around the world.

Step 3a
Some users open the attachment and their computers become infected with the virus.

Step 3b
Other users do not recognize the name of the sender of the email message. These users do not open the email message — instead they immediately delete the email message and continue using their computers. These users' computers are not infected with the virus.

Figure 5-2   This figure shows how a virus can spread via an email message.

CONSIDER THIS

What if you cannot remove malware?

In extreme cases, in order to remove malware from a computer or mobile device, you may need to erase, or reformat, an infected computer's hard disk, or reset a mobile device to its factory settings. For this reason, it is critical you have uninfected (clean) backups of all files. Seek advice from a technology specialist before performing a format or reformat instruction on your media.

Internet Research

What are the latest malware threats?

Search for: malware news

SECURE IT 5-1

Play It Safe to Avoid Online Gaming Risks

Anyone experiencing the joys of playing games online or playing games with others through online services needs to realize the perils of finding real-life predators lurking behind the scenes. Thieves and hackers take advantage of security holes and vulnerabilities that can turn a gaming session into a nightmare. While gamers often understand general security issues regarding online behavior, they may not be aware of a different set of technology and social risks they may encounter as they interact in the online world.

Viruses, worms, and malware can be hidden in email message attachments, downloaded game files, and instant messaging software. In addition, messages on social networks may encourage gamers to visit fraudulent websites filled with malware. If the game requires a connection to the Internet, then any

computer connected to the game's server is subject to security cyberthreats. Thieves can take control of a remote computer that does not have a high level of security protection and use it to control other computers, or they break into the computer and install malware to discover personal information. The Computer Emergency Response Team Coordination Center (CERT/CC) describes many vulnerabilities found in online games and online gaming services used with game consoles and devices.

Malicious users know that the gaming community uses social media intensely, so they also create accounts and attempt to mislead uninformed users into revealing personal information. The thieves may claim to have software updates and free games, when they really are luring users to bogus websites that ask users to set up profiles and accounts.

Gamers should follow these practices to increase their security:

- Before downloading any software, including patches to games, or disclosing any private details, be certain the website or the person making the request is legitimate.

- Exercise extreme caution if the game requires ActiveX or JavaScript to be enabled or if it must be played in administrator mode.

- Use a firewall and make exceptions to allow only trusted individuals to access your computer or mobile device when playing multiplayer online games.

- Do not share personal information with other gamers whom you meet online.

Have you played online games and followed the advice listed here? How will you change your gaming behavior now that you are aware of specific security threats?

Botnets

A **botnet**, or *zombie army*, is a group of compromised computers or mobile devices connected to a network such as the Internet that are used to attack other networks, usually for nefarious purposes. A compromised computer or device, known as a **zombie**, is one whose owner is unaware the computer or device is being controlled remotely by an outsider.

A *bot* is a program that performs a repetitive task on a network. Cybercriminals install malicious bots on unprotected computers and devices to create a botnet. The perpetrator then uses the botnet to send spam via email, spread viruses and other malware, or commit a distributed denial of service attack (discussed in the next section).

CONSIDER THIS

How can you tell if your computer or mobile device is functioning as a zombie?

Your computer or mobile device may be a zombie if you notice an unusually high disk activity, a slower than normal Internet connection, or connected devices becoming increasingly unresponsive. The chances of your computer or devices becoming part of a botnet greatly increase if they are not running an effective firewall.

Denial of Service Attacks

A **denial of service attack** (**DoS attack**) is an assault whose purpose is to disrupt computer access to an Internet service such as the web or email. Perpetrators carry out a DoS attack in a variety of ways. For example, they may use an unsuspecting computer to send an influx of confusing data messages or useless traffic to a computer network. The victim computer network slows down considerably and eventually becomes unresponsive or unavailable, blocking legitimate visitors from accessing the network.

A more devastating type of DoS attack is the *distributed DoS attack (DDoS attack)* in which a zombie army is used to attack computers or computer networks. DDoS attacks have been able to stop operations temporarily at numerous websites, including powerhouses such as Yahoo!, eBay, Amazon.com, and CNN.com.

The damage caused by a DoS or DDoS attack usually is extensive. During the outage, retailers lose sales from customers, news websites and search engines lose revenue from advertisers, and time-sensitive information may be delayed. Repeated attacks could tarnish reputations, causing even greater losses.

Internet Research

Are DoS attacks still prevalent?

Search for: news of dos attacks

 CONSIDER THIS ——————————————————————————

Why would someone execute a Dos or DDoS attack?
Perpetrators have a variety of motives for executing a DoS or DDoS attack. Those who disagree with the beliefs or actions of a particular organization claim political anger motivates their attacks. Some perpetrators use the attack as a vehicle for extortion. Others simply want the recognition, even though it is negative.

Back Doors

A **back door** is a program or set of instructions in a program that allows users to bypass security controls when accessing a program, computer, or network. Once perpetrators gain access to unsecure computers, they often install a back door or modify an existing program to include a back door, which allows them to continue to access the computer remotely without the user's knowledge. A rootkit can be a back door. Some worms leave back doors, which have been used to spread other worms or to distribute spam from the unsuspecting victim computers.

Programmers often build back doors into programs during system development. These back doors save development time because the programmer can bypass security controls while writing and testing programs. Similarly, a computer repair technician may install a back door while troubleshooting problems on a computer. If a programmer or computer repair technician fails to remove a back door, a perpetrator could use the back door to gain entry to a computer or network.

Spoofing

Spoofing is a technique intruders use to make their network or Internet transmission appear legitimate to a victim computer or network. Two common types of spoofing schemes are email and IP spoofing.

- *Email spoofing* occurs when the sender's address or other components of an email header are altered so that it appears that the email message originated from a different sender. Email spoofing commonly is used in virus hoaxes, spam, and phishing scams (Figure 5-3).
- *IP spoofing* occurs when an intruder computer fools a network into believing its IP address is associated with a trusted source. Perpetrators of IP spoofing trick their victims into interacting with the phony website. For example, the victim may provide confidential information or download files containing viruses, worms, or other malware.

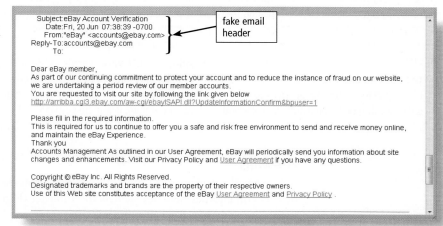

Figure 5-3 With email spoofing, the components of an email header are altered so that it appears the email message originated from a different sender.
© Cengage Learning

BTW

Antivirus Programs
In addition to protecting against viruses and other malware, many antivirus programs also include protection from DoS and DDoS attacks.

Safeguards against Internet and Network Attacks

Methods that protect computers, mobile devices, and networks from attacks include the following:

- Use antivirus software.
- Be suspicious of unsolicited email attachments.
- Scan removable media for malware before using it.
- Implement firewall solutions.
- Back up regularly.

Secure IT 1-2 on page 23 in Chapter 1 provided some measures you can take to protect your computers and mobile devices from malware. Read Secure IT 5-2 for additional tips to protect home users against Internet and network attacks. The next section discusses firewalls in more depth.

 CONSIDER THIS

How can you determine if your computer or mobile device is vulnerable to an Internet or network attack?

You could use an **online security service**, which is a web app that evaluates your computer or mobile device to check for Internet and email vulnerabilities. The online security service then provides recommendations of how to address the vulnerabilities.

Organizations requiring assistance or information about Internet security breaches can contact or visit the website for the *Computer Emergency Response Team Coordination Center*, or *CERT/CC*, which is a federally funded Internet security research and development center.

 SECURE IT 5-2

Safeguarding Home Computers and Devices

Sophisticated cybercriminals take advantage of the fact that most home users employ poor security measures. In fact, one study found that home users are victims of 86 percent of all attacks. Instead of resorting to large-scale attacks affecting thousands of users simultaneously, these criminals develop fraud, data theft, and other wealth-generating schemes affecting individual users. In these cases, the users are forced to be reactive in repairing the damage done. The following measures, however, can help home users become proactive by preventing Internet and network attacks.

- **Use routers and firewalls.** These devices can help detect suspicious activities by continuously monitoring activity and blocking unauthorized entry into the computer. Antivirus software can help thwart attacks that slip by the firewall.

- **Disable macro security settings.** *Macros* are useful to record, save, and then execute a set of keystrokes and instructions repeatedly, and they commonly are found in word processing and spreadsheet files. Macros, however, can be disastrous when hidden in a file and then run without permission. In many office productivity applications, you can change the macro security settings so that macros are executed only with your permission.

- **Address software warnings.** Be wary of tapping or clicking buttons or security bars that seek permission to download or run a program. If you are suspicious of the authenticity, exit the program or leave the website.

- **Keep software updated.** Major software companies release software patches to repair known vulnerabilities. Many times, home users could have prevented their attacks if they had updated their software with the available patches.

- **Stay informed.** News media and technology websites report current security breaches and threats. Seek out these articles and take preventive measures.

 Which of these techniques do you use on your home computer or mobile devices? What new techniques will you use to help prevent security attacks?

Firewalls

A **firewall** is hardware and/or software that protects a network's resources from intrusion by users on another network such as the Internet (Figure 5-4). All networked and online users should implement a firewall solution.

Organizations use firewalls to protect network resources from outsiders and to restrict employees' access to sensitive data, such as payroll or personnel records. They can implement a firewall solution themselves or outsource their needs to a company specializing in providing firewall protection.

hardware firewall

Internet

firewall

network

software firewall installed on server

Figure 5-4 A firewall is hardware and/or software that protects a network's resources from intrusion by users on another network, such as the Internet.

Large organizations often route all their communications through a proxy server, which typically is a component of the firewall. A *proxy server* is a server outside the organization's network that controls which communications pass in and out of the organization's network. That is, a proxy server carefully screens all incoming and outgoing messages. Proxy servers use a variety of screening techniques. Some check the domain name or IP address of the message for legitimacy. Others require that the messages have digital signatures (discussed later in this chapter).

Home and small/home office users often protect their computers with a personal firewall. As discussed in Chapter 4, a **personal firewall** is a software firewall that detects and protects a personal computer and its data from unauthorized intrusions. Personal firewalls constantly monitor all transmissions to and from the computer and may inform a user of any attempted intrusions. Both Windows and Mac operating systems include firewall capabilities, including monitoring Internet traffic to and from installed applications. Read How To 5-1 on the next page for instructions about setting up a personal firewall.

Some small/home office users purchase a hardware firewall, such as a router or other device that has a built-in firewall, in addition to or instead of a personal firewall. Hardware firewalls stop intrusions before they attempt to affect your computer or network maliciously.

BTW

AVG, McAfee, and Symantec

Technology Innovators: You should be familiar with AVG, McAfee, and Symantec (security product developers).

HOW TO 5-1

Set Up a Personal Firewall

A personal firewall is a program that helps protect your computer from unauthorized access by blocking certain types of communications. For example, if somebody knows the IP address of your computer and attempts to access it using a browser or other program, the personal firewall can be configured to deny the incoming connection. The following steps describe how to set up a personal firewall.

1. Locate and purchase a personal firewall. You can purchase personal firewalls online and in stores that sell software. Many operating systems include a personal firewall. Computers typically can have only one active personal firewall running at a time. If you purchase a personal firewall, you may need to disable the one that is included with the operating system.

2. If you purchase a personal firewall, follow the instructions to install the program on your computer.

3. Run the personal firewall.

4. If necessary, ensure the personal firewall is enabled.

5. Review the settings for the incoming and outgoing rules. Incoming rules display programs and services that are allowed to access your computer. Outgoing rules display programs and services on your computer that are allowed to communicate with other computers and mobile devices on your network or the Internet.

6. Back up or export your current list of incoming and outgoing rules. If your computer does not function properly after you adjust the rules (in Steps 7 and 8), you will be able to restore the current rules.

7. Adjust your incoming rules to disallow devices, programs, and services you do not want accessing your computer. Be careful adjusting these settings,

as adding or removing rules may hinder a legitimate program's capability to work properly.

8. Adjust your outgoing rules to allow only appropriate programs on your computer to communicate with other computers and mobile devices on your network or the Internet. Examples include a browser, email program, or other communications programs.

9. Save your settings.

10. Test programs on your computer that require Internet access. If any do not function properly, restore the list of rules you backed up or exported in Step 6.

11. Exit the personal firewall.

✳ Which programs on your computer should have access to the Internet? Which programs should not?

Unauthorized Access and Use

Unauthorized access is the use of a computer or network without permission. *Unauthorized use* is the use of a computer or its data for unapproved or possibly illegal activities.

Home and business users can be a target of unauthorized access and use. Unauthorized use includes a variety of activities: an employee using an organization's computer to send personal email messages, an employee using the organization's word processing software to track his or her child's soccer league scores, or a perpetrator gaining access to a bank computer and performing an unauthorized transfer.

Safeguards against Unauthorized Access and Use

Organizations take several measures to help prevent unauthorized access and use. At a minimum, they should have a written *acceptable use policy (AUP)* that outlines the activities for which the computer and network may and may not be used. An organization's AUP should specify the acceptable use of technology by employees for personal reasons. Some organizations prohibit such use entirely. Others allow personal use on the employee's own time, such as a lunch hour. Whatever the policy, an organization should document and explain it to employees. The AUP also should specify the personal activities, if any, that are allowed on company time. For example, can employees check personal email messages or respond to personal text messages during work hours?

To protect your personal computer from unauthorized intrusions, you should disable file and printer sharing in your operating system (Figure 5-5). This security measure attempts to ensure that others cannot access your files or your printer. You also should be sure to use a firewall. The following sections address other techniques for protecting against unauthorized access and use. The technique(s) used should correspond to the degree of risk that is associated with the unauthorized access.

Figure 5-5 To protect files on your local hard disk from hackers and other intruders, turn off file and printer sharing on your Internet connection.
Source: Microsoft

Libraries and devices

When you share content, other homegroup members can see it, but only you can change it.

Documents
Not shared

Music
Not shared

Pictures
Not shared

Videos
Not shared

Printers and devices
Not shared

Media devices

Allow all devices on the network such as TVs and game consoles to play my shared content

Off

Access Controls

Many organizations use access controls to minimize the chance that a perpetrator intentionally may access or an employee accidentally may access confidential information on a computer, mobile device, or network. An *access control* is a security measure that defines who can access a computer, device, or network; when they can access it; and what actions they can take while accessing it. In addition, the computer, device, or network should maintain an *audit trail* that records in a file both successful and unsuccessful access attempts. An unsuccessful access attempt could result from a user mistyping his or her password, or it could result from a perpetrator trying thousands of passwords.

Organizations should investigate unsuccessful access attempts immediately to ensure they are not intentional breaches of security. They also should review successful access for irregularities, such as use of the computer after normal working hours or from remote computers. The security program can be configured to alert a security administrator whenever suspicious or irregular activities are suspected. In addition, an organization regularly should review users' access privilege levels to determine whether they still are appropriate.

User Names and Passwords

A **user name**, or *user ID* (identification), is a unique combination of characters, such as letters of the alphabet or numbers, that identifies one specific user. A **password** is a private combination of characters associated with the user name that allows access to certain computer resources.

Most operating systems that enable multiple users to share computers and devices or that access a home or business network require users to correctly enter a user name and a password before they can access the data, information, and programs stored on a computer, mobile device, or network. Many systems that maintain financial, personal, and other confidential information also require a user name and password as part of their sign-in procedure (Figure 5-6).

Some systems assign a user name and/or password to each user. For example, a school may use a student ID as a user name. Some websites use your email address as the user name. Information technology (IT) departments may assign passwords so that they have a record in case the employee leaves or forgets the password.

With other systems, users select their own user names and/or passwords. Many users select a combination of their first and last names for their user names. Read Secure IT 1-3 on page 24 in Chapter 1 for tips about creating strong passwords. Once you select a password, change it frequently. Do not disclose it to anyone or write it on a slip of paper kept near the computer, especially taped to the monitor or under the keyboard. Email and telemarketing scams often ask unsuspecting users to disclose their credit card numbers, so be wary if you did not initiate the inquiry or phone call.

Figure 5-6 Many websites that maintain personal and confidential data, such as Citibank's credit card system, require a user to enter a user name (user ID) and password.
Source: Citigroup Inc

BTW
Microsoft Account
Some computers can be configured so that you can sign in using your Microsoft account. Signing in with your Microsoft account makes additional Windows features available and also enables you to synchronize settings if you sign in to multiple computers.

✳ CONSIDER THIS

Why do some websites allow me to use my email address as a user name?
No two users can have the same email address; that is, your email address is unique to you. This means you can use your email address and password from one website to validate your identity on another website. Facebook, Google, and Twitter, for example, are three popular websites that provide authentication services to other applications. By using your email address from one of these websites to access other websites, you do not have to create or remember separate user names and passwords for the various websites you visit.

BTW

Default Passwords
If a program or device has a default or preset password, such as admin, be sure to change it to prevent unauthorized access.

In addition to a user name and password, some systems ask users to enter one of several pieces of personal information. Such items can include a grandparent's first name, your mother's maiden name, or the name of the elementary school you attended. These items should be facts that you easily remember but are not easy for others to discover about you when using a search engine or examining your profiles on social networking sites. As with a password, if the user's response does not match information on file, the system denies access. Read Secure IT 5-3 to learn about two-step verification, an authentication technique you might encounter with user names and passwords.

Instead of passwords, some organizations use passphrases to authenticate users. A *passphrase* is a private combination of words, often containing mixed capitalization and punctuation, associated with a user name that allows access to certain computer resources. Passphrases, which often can be up to 100 characters in length, are more secure than passwords, yet can be easy to remember because they contain words.

✸ **CONSIDER THIS**

Why do some websites display distorted characters you must reenter along with your password?
These websites use a CAPTCHA, which stands for Completely Automated Public Turing test to tell Computers and Humans Apart. A *CAPTCHA* is a program developed at Carnegie Mellon University that displays an image containing a series of distorted characters for a user to identify and enter in order to verify that user input is from humans and not computer programs (Figure 5-7). A CAPTCHA is effective in blocking computer-generated attempts to access a website, because it is difficult to write programs for computers to detect distorted characters, while humans generally can recognize them. For visually impaired users or if words are too difficult to read, the CAPTCHA text can be read aloud; you also have the option of generating a new CAPTCHA.

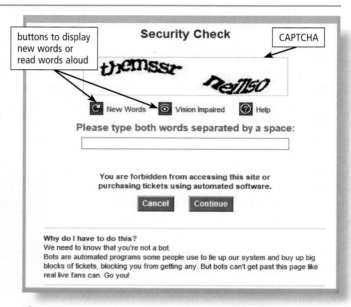

Figure 5-7   To continue with the ticket order process at the Ticketmaster website, the user must enter the characters in the CAPTCHA, which consists of the letters, themssr neillso, in this case.
Source: Carnegie Mellon University

✸ **SECURE IT 5-3**

Using the Two-Step Verification Process

If you use the same password to access several accounts, you are not alone. More than 10 percent of people think their password is sufficient protection for all their vital online accounts. Cyberthieves are aware of this flawed thinking and take advantage of this practice.

In an attempt to thwart the thieves' actions, financial institutions, universities, and businesses are using a two-step verification process, also known as two-factor authentication. This method requires a mobile phone and a computer. When users sign in to a computer account, they enter a user name and a password. Next, they are prompted to enter another authentication code, which is sent as a text or voice message or via an app on a smartphone. This second code generally is valid for a set time, sometimes only for a few hours. If users do not sign in during this time limit, then they must repeat the process and request another verification code.

One method of circumventing this two-step verification process is to specify one computer as a trusted device. The computer must accept cookies for this designation to be assigned. (Cookies are discussed later in the chapter.) Only limited-use computers in safe areas should be identified as being secure.

A flaw in using the two-step process arises when users lose their mobile phones.

If individuals who own these phones use the two-step process, they would be unable to access their online accounts. Some software developers have created work-arounds; in one instance, a series of images is sent to the computer and one photo from the series is sent to another mobile device. The user must match the photos to authenticate and gain access to the account.

✸ Is the two-step verification process a sufficient practice of adding an extra layer of protection to accounts? Or, is this measure overkill? Is it a better process than requiring users to type a long, complex password? Why or why not?

Possessed Objects

A possessed object is any item that you must carry with you in order to gain access to a computer or computer facility. Examples of possessed objects are badges, cards, smart cards, and keys. The card you use in an ATM (automated teller machine), for example, is a possessed object that allows access to your bank account.

Possessed objects often are used in combination with PINs. A **PIN** (*personal identification number*) is a numeric password, either assigned by a company or selected by a user. PINs provide an additional level of security. An ATM card typically requires a four-digit PIN. Most debit cards and some credit cards use PINs. If someone steals these cards, the thief must enter the user's PIN to access the account. PINs are passwords. Select them carefully and protect them as you do any other password. For example, do not use the same four digits, sequential digits, or dates others could easily determine, such as birth dates.

Biometric Devices

A **biometric device** authenticates a person's identity by translating a personal characteristic, such as a fingerprint, into a digital code that is compared with a digital code stored in a computer verifying a physical or behavioral characteristic. If the digital code in the computer does not match the personal characteristic code, the computer denies access to the individual.

Biometric devices grant access to programs, computers, or rooms using computer analysis of some biometric identifier. Examples of biometric devices and systems include fingerprint readers, face recognition systems, hand geometry systems, voice verification systems, signature verification systems, iris recognition systems, and retinal scanners.

Figure 5-8   A fingerprint reader.
© Flynavyjp / Dreamstime.com

Fingerprint Reader   A **fingerprint reader**, or scanner, captures curves and indentations of a fingerprint (Figure 5-8). Organizations use fingerprint readers to secure doors, computers, and software. With the cost of fingerprint readers often less than $100, some home and small business users install fingerprint readers to authenticate users before they can access a personal computer. The reader also can be set up to perform different functions for different fingers; for example, one finger starts a program and another finger shuts down the computer. External fingerprint readers usually plug into a USB port. Some newer laptops have a fingerprint reader built into their keyboards, which allows users to sign in to programs and websites via their fingerprint instead of entering a user name and password.

Face Recognition System   A *face recognition system* captures a live face image and compares it with a stored image to determine if the person is a legitimate user. Some buildings use face recognition systems to secure access to rooms. Law enforcement, surveillance systems, and airports use face recognition to protect the public. Some mobile devices use face recognition systems to unlock the device. Face recognition programs are becoming more sophisticated and can recognize people with or without glasses, makeup, or jewelry, and with new hairstyles.

BTW
Face Recognition
Innovative Computing: You should be familiar with the FBI's face recognition technology project.

Hand Geometry System   A *hand geometry system* measures the shape and size of a person's hand (Figure 5-9). Because hand geometry systems can be expensive, they often are used in larger companies to track workers' time and attendance or as security devices. Colleges use hand geometry systems to verify students' identities. Daycare centers and hospital nurseries use them to identify parents who pick up their children.

Voice Verification System   A *voice verification system* compares a person's live speech with their stored voice pattern. Larger organizations sometimes use voice verification systems as time and attendance devices. Many companies also use this technology for access to sensitive files and networks. Some financial services use voice verification systems to secure phone banking transactions.

Figure 5-9   A hand geometry system verifies identity based on the shape and size of a person's hand.
Courtesy of Ingersoll Rand Security Technologies

Signature Verification System   A *signature verification system* recognizes the shape of your handwritten signature, as well as measures the pressure exerted and the motion used to write the signature. Signature verification systems use a specialized pen and tablet. Signature verification systems often are used to reduce fraud in financial institutions.

 CONSIDER THIS

Do retailers use a signature verification system for credit card purchases?
No. With a credit card purchase, users sign their name on a signature capture pad using a stylus attached to the device. Software then transmits the signature to a central computer, where it is stored. Thus, the retailers use these systems simply to record your signature.

Iris Recognition System   High security areas use iris recognition systems. The camera in an *iris recognition system* uses iris recognition technology to read patterns in the iris of the eye (Figure 5-10). These patterns are as unique as a fingerprint. Iris recognition systems are quite expensive and are used by government security organizations, the military, and financial institutions that deal with highly sensitive data. Some organizations use retinal scanners, which work similarly but instead scan patterns of blood vessels in the back of the retina.

Figure 5-10   An iris recognition system.
© Robert F. Balazik / Shutterstock.com; AP Photo / Canadian Press, Adrian Wyld;
© Cengage Learning

 CONSIDER THIS

How popular are biometric devices?
Biometric devices are gaining popularity as a security precaution because they are a virtually foolproof method of identification and authentication. For example, some grocery stores, retail stores, and gas stations use *biometric payment*, where the customer's fingerprint is read by a fingerprint reader that is linked to a payment method such as a checking account or credit card. Users can forget their user names and passwords. Possessed objects can be lost, copied, duplicated, or stolen. Personal characteristics, by contrast, are unique and cannot be forgotten or misplaced.

Biometric devices do have disadvantages. If you cut your finger, a fingerprint reader might reject you as a legitimate user. Hand geometry readers can transmit germs. If you are nervous, a signature might not match the one on file. If you have a sore throat, a voice recognition system might reject you. Many people are uncomfortable with the thought of using an iris scanner.

Digital Forensics

Digital forensics, also called *cyberforensics*, is the discovery, collection, and analysis of evidence found on computers and networks. Digital forensics involves the examination of media, programs, data and log files on computers, mobile devices, servers, and networks. Many areas use digital forensics, including law enforcement, criminal prosecutors, military intelligence, insurance agencies, and information security departments in the private sector.

A digital forensics examiner must have knowledge of the law, technical experience with many types of hardware and software products, superior communication skills, familiarity with corporate structures and policies, a willingness to learn and update skills, and a knack for problem solving. For more information about digital forensics, read Mini Feature 5-1 (available in the e-book).

NOW YOU KNOW ────────────────────────────────

Be sure you understand the material presented in the sections titled Digital Security Risks, Internet and Network Attacks, and Unauthorized Access and Use, as it relates to the chapter objectives.
You now should know . . .

- How cybercriminals' backgrounds and intent vary (Objective 1)
- How you can protect your computers and devices from malware, botnets, DoS attacks, back doors, and spoofing (Objective 2)
- Why you should use a firewall (Objective 2)
- How you can prevent unauthorized users from accessing your home or office computers and devices (Objective 3)

Quiz Yourself Online: Check your knowledge of related content by navigating to this book's Quiz Yourself resource on Computer Concepts CourseMate and then tapping or clicking Objectives 1–3.

Software Theft

Software theft occurs when someone steals software media, intentionally erases programs, illegally registers and/or activates a program, or illegally copies a program.
- Physically stealing software: A perpetrator physically steals the media that contains the software, or steals the hardware that contains the media that contains the software. For example, an unscrupulous library patron might steal a game CD/DVD.
- Intentionally erasing software: A perpetrator erases the media that contains the software. For example, a programmer who is terminated from a company may retaliate by removing or disabling the programs he or she has written from company computers.
- Illegal registration/activation: A perpetrator illegally obtains registration numbers and/or activation codes. A program called a *keygen*, short for key generator, creates software registration numbers and sometimes activation codes. Some unscrupulous individuals create and post keygens so that users can install software without legally purchasing it.
- Illegal copying: A perpetrator copies software from manufacturers. **Software piracy**, often referred to simply as **piracy**, is the unauthorized and illegal duplication of copyrighted software. Piracy is the most common form of software theft.

 BTW
BSA
To promote understanding of software piracy, a number of major worldwide software companies formed the *Business Software Alliance* (*BSA*). The BSA operates a website and antipiracy hotlines around the world.

Safeguards against Software Theft

To protect software media from being stolen, owners should keep original software boxes and media or the online confirmation of purchased software in a secure location, out of sight of prying eyes. All computer users should back up their files and disks regularly, in the event of theft. When some companies terminate a programmer or if the programmer quits, they escort the employee off the premises immediately. These companies believe that allowing terminated employees to remain on the premises gives them time to sabotage files and other network procedures.

Many manufacturers incorporate an activation process into their programs to ensure the software is not installed on more computers than legally licensed. During the **product activation**, which is conducted either online or by phone, users provide the software product's identification number to associate the software with the computer or mobile device on which the software is installed. Usually, the software can be run a preset number of times, has limited functionality, or does not function until you activate it.

To further protect themselves from software piracy, software manufacturers issue users license agreements. As discussed in Chapter 4, a **license agreement** is the right to use software. That is, you do not own the software. The most common type of license included with software purchased by individual users is a *single-user license agreement*, also called an *end-user license agreement* (*EULA*). The license agreement provides specific conditions for use of the software, which a user must accept before using the software. These terms usually are displayed when you install the software. Use of the software constitutes acceptance of the terms on the user's part. Figure 5-11 on the next page identifies the conditions of a typical single-user license agreement.

 Internet Research
What are the penalties for piracy?
Search for: piracy penalties

Typical Conditions of a Single-User License Agreement

You can…

- Install the software on only one computer. (Some license agreements allow users to install the software on one desktop and one laptop.)
- Make one copy of the software as a backup.
- Give or sell the software to another individual, but only if the software is removed from the user's computer first.

You cannot…

- Install the software on a network, such as a school computer lab.
- Give copies to friends and colleagues, while continuing to use the software.
- Export the software.
- Rent or lease the software.

Figure 5-11   A user must accept the terms of a license agreement before using the software.
© Cengage Learning

To support multiple users' access of software, most manufacturers sell network versions or site licenses of their software, which usually costs less than buying individual stand-alone copies of the software for each computer. A *network license* is a legal agreement that allows multiple users to access the software on the server simultaneously. The network license fee usually is based on the number of users or the number of computers attached to the network. A *site license* is a legal agreement that permits users to install the software on multiple computers — usually at a volume discount.

✳ **CONSIDER THIS**

Can you install software on work computers or work-issued smartphones?
Many organizations and businesses have strict written policies governing the installation and use of software and enforce their rules by checking networked or online computers or mobile devices periodically to ensure that all software is licensed properly. If you are not completely familiar with your school's or employer's policies governing installation of software, check with the information technology department or your school's technology coordinator.

Information Theft

Information theft occurs when someone steals personal or confidential information. Both business and home users can fall victim to information theft. An unethical company executive may steal or buy stolen information to learn about a competitor. A corrupt individual may steal credit card numbers to make fraudulent purchases. Information theft often is linked to other types of cybercrime. For example, an individual first might gain unauthorized access to a computer and then steal credit card numbers stored in a firm's accounting department.

Safeguards against Information Theft

Most organizations will attempt to prevent information theft by implementing the user identification and authentication controls discussed earlier in this chapter. These controls are best suited for protecting information on computers located on an organization's premises. To further protect information on the Internet and networks, organizations and individuals use a variety of encryption techniques.

Encryption

Encryption is the process of converting data that is readable by humans into encoded characters to prevent unauthorized access. You treat encrypted data just like any other data. That is, you can store it or send it in an email message. To read the data, the recipient must **decrypt**, or decode it. For example, users may specify that an email application encrypt a message before sending it securely. The recipient's email application would need to decrypt the message in order for the recipient to be able to read it.

In the encryption process, the unencrypted, readable data is called *plaintext*. The encrypted (scrambled) data is called *ciphertext*. An *encryption algorithm*, or *cypher*, is a set of steps that can convert readable plaintext into unreadable ciphertext. Table 5-2 shows examples of some simple encryption algorithms. Encryption programs typically use more than one encryption algorithm, along with an encryption key. An *encryption key* is a set of characters that the originator of the data uses to encrypt the plaintext and the recipient of the data uses to decrypt the ciphertext.

 BTW

Encryption Algorithms
High-Tech Talk: Most secure encryption uses complex encryption algorithms.

Table 5-2 Simple Encryption Algorithms

Name	Algorithm	Plaintext	Ciphertext	Explanation
Transposition	Switch the order of characters	SOFTWARE	OSTFAWER	Adjacent characters swapped
Substitution	Replace characters with other characters	INFORMATION	WLDIMXQUWIL	Each letter replaced with another
Expansion	Insert characters between existing characters	USER	UYSYEYRY	Letter Y inserted after each character
Compaction	Remove characters and store elsewhere	ACTIVATION	ACIVTIN	Every third letter removed (T, A, O)

❋ CONSIDER THIS

What is the Caesar cipher?

The *Caesar cipher* is a substitution encryption algorithm that replaces each character in the plaintext with a different letter by shifting the alphabet a certain number of positions. For example, the plaintext word, computer, would become dpnqvufs when the alphabet shifts one position. The Caesar cipher is named after Julius Caesar because it is believed he used it in his private correspondence.

Two basic types of encryption are private key and public key. With *private key encryption*, also called *symmetric key encryption*, both the originator and the recipient use the same secret key to encrypt and decrypt the data. *Public key encryption*, also called *asymmetric key encryption*, uses two encryption keys: a public key and a private key (Figure 5-12). Public key encryption software generates both the private key and the public key. A message encrypted with a public key can be decrypted only with the corresponding private key, and vice versa. The public key is made known to message originators and recipients. For example, public keys may be posted on a secure webpage or a public-key server, or they may be emailed. The private key, by contrast, should be kept confidential.

An Example of Public Key Encryption

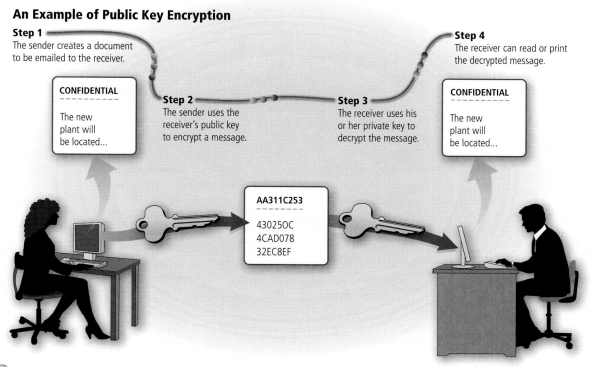

Step 1
The sender creates a document to be emailed to the receiver.

Step 2
The sender uses the receiver's public key to encrypt a message.

Step 3
The receiver uses his or her private key to decrypt the message.

Step 4
The receiver can read or print the decrypted message.

CONFIDENTIAL
The new plant will be located...

AA311C253
430250C
4CAD078
32EC8EF

CONFIDENTIAL
The new plant will be located...

Figure 5-12 This figure shows an example of public key encryption.
© Cengage Learning

Some operating systems and email programs allow you to encrypt the contents of files and messages that are stored on your computer. You also can purchase an encryption program to encrypt files. Many browsers use encryption when sending private information, such as credit card numbers, over the Internet.

Mobile users today often access their company networks through a virtual private network. When a mobile user connects to a main office using a standard Internet connection, a *virtual private network* (*VPN*) provides the mobile user with a secure connection to the company network server, as if the user has a private line. VPNs help ensure that data is safe from being intercepted by unauthorized people by encrypting data as it transmits from a laptop, smartphone, or other mobile device.

indicates secure webpage

Choose your shipping options

Shipping Details: DBROTH (Learn more)

Choose a shipping speed:
- ⦿ Standard (3-5 business days)
- ◯ Two-Day Shipping (2 business days)

Figure 5-13   Web addresses of secure sites, such as the Amazon.com checkout, often begin with https instead of http. Browsers also often display a lock symbol in the window.
Source: Amazon.com; Microsoft

Digital Signatures and Certificates

A **digital signature** is an encrypted code that a person, website, or organization attaches to an electronic message to verify the identity of the message sender. Digital signatures often are used to ensure that an impostor is not participating in an Internet transaction. That is, digital signatures can help to prevent email forgery. A digital signature also can verify that the content of a message has not changed.

A **digital certificate** is a notice that guarantees a user or a website is legitimate. E-commerce applications commonly use digital certificates. Browsers often display a warning message if a website does not have a valid digital certificate. Read Secure IT 5-4 to learn about ways digital certificates and signatures verify authenticity.

A website that uses encryption techniques to secure its data is known as a **secure site** (Figure 5-13). Web addresses of secure sites often begin with https instead of http. Secure sites typically use digital certificates along with security protocols.

 SECURE IT 5-4

Verifying Authenticity with Digital Certificates and Signatures

When you are in the security line at the airport, a security administration agent may compare a government-issued photo ID to your boarding pass to verify your identity. When you receive a document as an email attachment or download a file posted online, however, it is difficult for you to verify who actually created that file. At this point, a digital certificate or digital signature could identify and verify the sender's and document's authenticity.

Online *certificate authority* (CA) providers issue digital certificates. Each CA is a trusted third party that takes responsibility for verifying the sender's identity before issuing a certificate. Every digital certificate has identical components because it is

generated using a standard, called X.509. The International Telecommunication Union coordinates this standard along with all telecommunications regulations in effect since 1865 with the invention of the telegraph.

Digital certificates typically have these components: version number, serial number, certificate algorithm identifier, issuer name, validity period, subject name, subject public key information, issuer unique identifier, subject unique identifier, extensions, and certification authority's digital signature.

Individuals and companies can purchase digital certificates from one of more than 35 online CA providers. The cost varies depending upon the desired level of data encryption, with the strongest levels recommended for financial and e-commerce

transactions. The certificates can be valid for a maximum of two years.

Digital signatures also tie the signer's identity to the contents of a specific document, but they use an algorithm to detect changes to the file. The sender encrypts the file with a private key and creates a digital signature. Then, the receiver decrypts the same file with a public key and uses the same algorithm to open the document. A symbol, such as a green check mark, often is used to indicate the document is authentic; a different symbol, such as a yellow triangle, would indicate the document has been altered.

✷ Have you ever received a document with a digital certificate or a digital signature? When might you need to generate one for your personal or professional transactions?

Hardware Theft, Vandalism, and Failure

Users rely on computers and mobile devices to create, store, and manage important information. As discussed in Chapter 3, you should take measures to protect computers and devices from theft, vandalism, and failure.

Hardware theft is the act of stealing digital equipment. Hardware vandalism involves defacing or destroying digital equipment. Hardware can fail for a variety of reasons: aging hardware, natural or man-made disasters, or random events such as electrical power problems, and even errors in programs or apps. Figure 5-14 summarizes the techniques you can use to safeguard hardware from theft, vandalism, and failure.

 BTW

LoJack
Technology Innovator:
You should be familiar with the device-tracking app, LoJack.

Hardware Theft and Vandalism Safeguards
- Physical access controls (i.e., locked doors and windows)
- Alarm system
- Physical security devices (i.e., cables and locks)
- Device-tracking app

Hardware Failure Safeguards
- Surge protector
- Uninterruptible power supply (UPS)
- Duplicate components or duplicate computers
- Fault-tolerant computer

Figure 5-14
Summary of safeguards against hardware theft, vandalism, and failure.
© Cengage Learning; © iStock-photo / Norebbo

Backing Up — The Ultimate Safeguard

To protect against data loss caused by hardware/software/information theft or system failure, users should back up computer and mobile device files regularly. As previously described, a **backup** is a duplicate of a file, program, or media that can be used if the original is lost, damaged, or destroyed. And, to **back up** a file means to make a copy of it. In the case of system failure or the discovery of corrupted files, you **restore** the files by copying the backed up files to their original location on the computer or mobile device.

If you choose to back up locally, be sure to use high-quality media. A good choice for a home user might be optical discs or an external hard disk. Keep your backup media in a fireproof and heatproof safe or vault, or offsite. *Off-site* means in a location separate from where you typically store or use your computer or mobile device. Keeping backup copies off-site minimizes the chance that a single disaster, such as a fire, would destroy both the original and the backup media. An off-site location can be a safe deposit box at a bank, a briefcase, or cloud storage (Figure 5-15). Recall that cloud storage is an Internet service that provides storage to computer users.

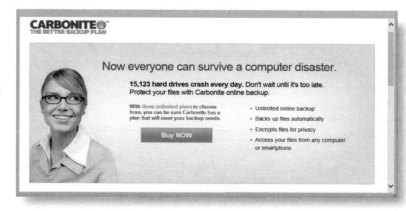

Figure 5-15 Cloud storage, such as Carbonite shown here, is a popular method for off-site backups.
Source: Carbonite, Inc.

Backup programs are available from many sources. Most operating systems include a backup program. Backup devices, such as external disk drives, also include backup programs. Numerous stand-alone backup tools exist. Cloud storage providers include backup services.

Business and home users can perform four types of backup: full, differential, incremental, or selective. A fifth type, continuous data protection, typically is used only by large enterprises. Table 5-3 on the next page summarizes the purpose, advantages, and disadvantages of each of these backup methods.

Some users implement a three-generation backup policy to preserve three copies of important files. The *grandparent* is the oldest copy of the file. The *parent* is the second oldest copy of the file. The *child* is the most recent copy of the file.

Table 5-3 Various Backup Methods

Type of Backup	Description	Advantages	Disadvantages
Full backup	Copies all of the files on media in the computer	Fastest recovery method. All files are saved.	Longest backup time.
Differential backup	Copies only the files that have changed since the last full backup	Fast backup method. Requires minimal storage space to back up.	Recovery is time-consuming because the last full backup plus the differential backup are needed.
Incremental backup	Copies only the files that have changed since the last full or incremental backup	Fastest backup method. Requires minimal storage space to back up. Only most recent changes saved.	Recovery is most time-consuming because the last full backup and all incremental backups since the last full backup are needed.
Selective backup	Users choose which folders and files to include in a backup	Fast backup method. Provides great flexibility.	Difficult to manage individual file backups. Least manageable of all the backup methods.
Continuous data protection (CDP)	All data is backed up whenever a change is made	The only real-time backup. Very fast recovery of data.	Very expensive and requires a great amount of storage.

 MINI FEATURE 5-2

Disaster Recovery

A **disaster recovery plan** is a written plan that describes the steps an organization would take to restore its computer operations in the event of a disaster. A disaster can be natural or man-made (hackers, viruses, etc.). Each company and each department or division within an organization usually has its own disaster recovery plan. The

following scenario illustrates how an organization might implement a disaster recovery plan.

Rosewood Associates is a consulting firm that helps clients use social media for marketing and customer outreach. Last week, a fire broke out in the office suite above Rosewood. The heat and smoke, along with water from the sprinkler system, caused extensive damage. As a result, Rosewood must replace all computers, servers, and storage devices. Also, the company lost all of the data that was not backed up.

Rosewood currently backs up its systems daily to an internal server and weekly to a remote cloud server. Because the internal server was damaged, the company lost several days of data. Rosewood does not have a plan for replacing hardware. Thus, they will lose several additional days of productivity while purchasing, installing, and configuring new hardware.

To minimize the chance of this type of loss in the future, the company hired you as a consultant to help create a disaster recovery plan. You first discuss the types of disasters that can strike, as shown in the table. You then explain that the goal of a disaster recovery plan is to prevent, detect, and correct system threats, and to restore the most critical systems first.

A disaster recovery plan typically contains these four components: emergency plan, backup plan, recovery plan, and test plan.

Emergency Plan: An emergency plan specifies the steps Rosewood will take as soon as a disaster strikes. The emergency plan is organized by type of disaster, such as fire, flood, or earthquake, and includes:

1. Names and phone numbers of people and organizations to notify (company management, fire and police department, clients, etc.)

2. Computer equipment procedures, such as equipment or power shutoff, and file removal; these procedures should be followed only if it is safe for an employee to do so

Considerations for Disaster Recovery

Disaster Type	What to Do First	What Might Occur	What to Include in the Plan
Natural (earthquake, hurricane, tornado, etc.)	Shut off power Evacuate, if necessary Pay attention to advisories Do not use telephone lines if lightning occurs	Power outage Phone lines down Structural damage to building Road closings, transportation interruptions Flooding Equipment damage	Generator Satellite phone, list of employee phone numbers Alternate worksite Action to be taken if employees are not able to come to work/leave the office Wet/dry vacuums Make and model numbers and vendor information to get replacements
Man-made (hazardous material spill, terrorist attacks, fire, hackers, malware, etc.)	Notify authorities (fire departments, etc.) of immediate threat Attempt to suppress fire or contain spill, if safe to do so Evacuate, if necessary	Data loss Dangerous conditions for employees Criminal activity, such as data hacking and identity theft Equipment damage	Backup data at protected site Protective equipment and an evacuation plan Contact law enforcement Make and model numbers and vendor information to obtain replacements

3. Employee evacuation procedures

4. Return procedures (who can enter the facility and what actions they are to perform)

Backup Plan: The backup plan specifies how Rosewood will use backup files and equipment to resume computer operations, and includes:

1. The location of backup data, supplies, and equipment

2. Who is responsible for gathering backup resources and transporting them to an alternate computer facility

3. The methods by which the data that is backed up on cloud storage will be restored

4. A schedule indicating the order and approximate time each application should be up and running

Recovery Plan: The recovery plan specifies the actions Rosewood will take to restore full computer operations. As with the emergency plan, the recovery plan

differs for each type of disaster. You recommend that Rosewood set up planning committees. Each committee would be responsible for different forms of recovery, such as replacing hardware or software.

Test Plan: The test plan includes simulating various levels of disasters and recording Rosewood's ability to recover. You run a test in which the employees follow the steps in the disaster recovery plan. The test uncovers a few needed recovery actions that are not specified in the plan, so you modify the plan. A few days later, you run another test without giving the employees any advance notice so that they can test the plan again.

✳ For what kind of natural and man-made disasters should a company plan? What roles can cloud storage providers play in helping to recover from a disaster? How involved should employees be in developing and testing disaster recovery plans?

© iStockphoto / Hans Laubel;
© iStockphoto / William Sen;
© Gewoldi / Photos.com

Wireless Security

Billions of home and business users have laptops, smartphones, and other mobile devices to access the Internet, send email and instant messages, chat online, or share network connections — all wirelessly. Home users set up wireless home networks. Mobile users access wireless networks in hot spots at airports, hotels, shopping malls, bookstores, restaurants, and coffee shops. Schools have wireless networks so that students can access the school network using their mobile computers and devices as they move from building to building (Figure 5-16).

Although wireless access provides many conveniences to users, it also poses additional security risks. Some perpetrators connect to other's wireless networks to gain free Internet access; others may try to access an organization's confidential data. Read Ethics & Issues 5-2 to consider issues associated with unsecured wireless networks.

Figure 5-16 Wireless access points or routers around campus allow students to access the school network wirelessly from their classrooms, the library, dorms, and other campus locations.

© Robert Kneschke / Shutterstock.com; © iStockphoto / Christopher Futcher; © Natalia Siverina / Shutterstock.com; © Jupiterimages / Photos.com; © Natalia Siverina / Shutterstock.com; © Bonnie Kamin / PhotoEdit; © Cengage Learning

✳ **ETHICS & ISSUES 5-2**

 Would You Connect to an Unsecured Wireless Network?

If you turn on your laptop and notice that you can connect to a nearby home or business's wireless network and access the Internet for free, you may find yourself in an ethical dilemma. Because they do not know how to secure a wireless network, many home and business users leave their networks open for use by anybody in their signal's range. One study found that 25 percent of wireless connections are unsecured, leaving them susceptible to hackers.

Criminals sometimes use unsecured wireless networks to cover up technology-

related crimes. Others may steal connections to avoid the costs of Internet service. In other cases, a user's laptop or mobile device may connect automatically to an open wireless network, without the user's authorization or knowledge.

The Electronic Communications Privacy Act (ECPA) states that it is not illegal "to intercept or access an electronic communication made through an electronic communication system that is configured so that such electronic communication is readily accessible to the general public." It is unclear whether this law refers to an unsecured home network

or whether it pertains only to public hot spots, such as restaurants or libraries. Some lawmakers even support punishing those who leave their networks unsecured.

Would you use your neighbor's unsecured wireless home network without permission? Why or why not? What would you do if you found out that someone was using your wireless home network? How should legal authorities address such abuse? How should violators be punished? Should those leaving their networks unsecured be punished, too? Why or why not?

To access a wireless network, the individual must be in range of the wireless network. Some intruders intercept and monitor communications as they transmit through the air. Others connect to a network through an unsecured wireless access point (WAP) or combination router/WAP (Figure 5-12). Read How To 5-2 for instructions about ways to secure a wireless network, in addition to using firewalls.

✳ **CONSIDER THIS**

Can you detect if someone is accessing your wireless home network?
If you notice the speed of your wireless connection is slower than normal, it may be a sign that someone else is accessing your network. You also may notice indicator lights on your wireless router flashing rapidly when you are not connected to your wireless network. Most wireless routers have a built-in utility that allows you to view the computers currently connected to your network. If you notice a computer that does not belong to you, consult your wireless router's documentation to determine how to remove it from the network.

⚙ **HOW TO 5-2**

Secure Your Wireless Network
When you set up a wireless network, it is important to secure the network so that only your computers and mobile devices can connect to it. Unsecured wireless networks can be seen and accessed by neighbors and others nearby, which may make it easier for them to connect to and access the data on the computers and mobile devices on your network. The following list provides suggestions for securing your wireless network.

• Immediately upon connecting your wireless access point and/or router, change the password required to access administrative features. If the password remains at its default setting, others may possibly be able to connect to and configure your wireless network settings.

• Change the *SSID* (service set identifier), which is a network name, from the default to something that uniquely identifies your network, especially if you live in close proximity to other wireless networks.

• Do not broadcast the SSID. This will make it more difficult for others to detect your wireless network. When you want to

connect a computer or mobile device to your wireless network, it will be necessary to enter the SSID manually.

• Enable an encryption method such as WPA2 (Wi-Fi Protected Access 2), and specify a password or passphrase that is difficult for others to guess. Passwords and passphrases that are more than eight characters, contain uppercase and lowercase letters, numbers, and special characters are the most secure.

• Enable and configure the MAC (Media Access Control) address control feature. A *MAC address* is a unique hardware identifier for your computer or device. The *MAC address control* feature specifies the computers and mobile devices that can connect to your network. If a computer or device is not specified, it will not be able to connect.

• Choose a secure location for your wireless router so that unauthorized people cannot access it. Someone who has physical access to a wireless router can restore factory defaults and erase your settings.

✳ In addition to safeguarding the data and information on your computers from others, why else might it be a good idea to secure your wireless network?

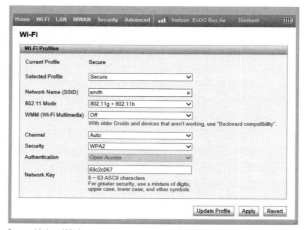

Source: Verizon Wireless

⚙ **MINI FEATURE 5-3**

Mobile Security

According to some estimates, 113 mobile phones are lost or stolen in the United States every minute. Symantec, one the world's leading online security companies, projects that only one-half of these phones eventually will be returned to their owners. Chances are that the people who find the missing phones likely will have viewed much of the content on the devices in a quest to find the owners and possibly to gain access to private information. Given the amount of storage and the variety of personal and business data stored, the

consequences of losing a smartphone or mobile device are significant.

The goal, therefore, for mobile device users is to make their data as secure as possible. Follow these steps to protect sensitive and personal data and to fight mobile cybercrime.

• **Avoid clicking unsafe links.** Nearly 40 percent of Americans are likely to click an unknown link, which often leads them to malicious websites. If you receive a text message from someone you do not know or an invitation to click a link, resist the urge to fulfill the request. Your financial institution never will send you a message requesting you to enter your account user name and password. Malicious links can inject malware on the mobile device to steal personal information or to create *toll fraud*, which secretly contacts wireless messaging services that impose steep fees on a monthly bill.

- **Be extra cautious locating and downloading apps.** Any device that connects to the Internet is susceptible to mobile malware. Cyberthieves target apps on widely used phones and tablets. Popular games are likely candidates to house malware, and it often is difficult to distinguish the legitimate apps from the fake apps. Obtain mobile device apps from well-known stores, and before downloading anything, read the descriptions and reviews. Look for misspellings and awkward sentence structure, which could be clues that the app is fake. If something looks awry, do not download. Scrutinize the number and types of permissions the app is requesting. If the list seems unreasonable in length or in the personal information needed, deny permission and uninstall the app.

- **Turn off GPS tracking.** GPS technology can track the mobile device's location as long as it is transmitting and receiving signals to and from satellites. This feature is helpful to obtain directions from your current location, view local news and weather reports, find a lost device, summon emergency personnel, and locate missing children. Serious privacy concerns can arise, however, when the technology is used in malicious ways, such as to stalk individuals

or trace their whereabouts. Unless you want to allow others to follow your locations throughout the day, disable the GPS tracking feature until needed.

- **Use mobile security software.** Enable the password feature on a mobile device as the first step in stopping prying eyes from viewing contents. More protection is necessary, however, to stop viruses and spyware and to safeguard personal and business data. Mobile security apps can allow you to lock your mobile device and SIM card remotely, erase the memory, and activate the GPS function. Other apps prevent cyberthieves from hijacking your phone and taking pictures, making recordings, placing calls to fee-imposed businesses, and sending infected messages to all individuals in your contact list. Look for security software that can back up data to an online account, set off a screeching alarm on the lost or stolen mobile device, offer live customer service, and provide theft, spam, virus, and malware protection.

✳ As the number of smartphones and mobile devices in use increases, the possibility of security breaches and lost devices increases proportionally. How can manufacturers and wireless carriers emphasize the importance of mobile security and convince users to take the precautions suggested above? What mobile security safeguards have you taken to protect your smartphone or mobile device? What steps will you take after reading this mini feature?

turn off location services until needed

© iStockphoto / Henk Badenhorst; © iStockphoto / Marcello Bortolino; © Cengage Learning

---

 NOW YOU KNOW

Be sure you understand the material presented in the sections titled Software Theft; Information Theft; Hardware Theft, Vandalism, and Failure; Backing Up – The Ultimate Safeguard; and Wireless Security as it relates to the chapter objectives. *You now should know . . .*

- What actions you are allowed according to a software license agreement (Objective 4)
- Why you would want to use encryption, digital signatures, or digital certificates (Objective 5)
- How you can protect your hardware from theft, vandalism, and failure (Objective 6)
- Which backup method is most suited to your needs (Objective 7)
- How you can protect your wireless communications (Objective 8)

🖥 Quiz Yourself Online: Check your knowledge of related content by navigating to this book's Quiz Yourself resource on Computer Concepts CourseMate and then tapping or clicking Objectives 4–8.

Ethics and Society

As with any powerful technology, computers and mobile devices can be used for both good and bad intentions. The standards that determine whether an action is good or bad are known as ethics.

Computer ethics are the moral guidelines that govern the use of computers, mobile devices, and information systems. Frequently discussed areas of computer ethics are unauthorized use of computers, mobile devices, and networks; software theft (piracy); information accuracy; intellectual property rights; codes of conduct; green computing; and information privacy. The questionnaire in Figure 5-17 raises issues in each of these areas.

Previous sections in this chapter discussed unauthorized use of computers, mobile devices and networks, and software theft (piracy). The following sections discuss issues related to information accuracy, intellectual property rights, codes of conduct, green computing, and information privacy.

Your Thoughts?

	Ethical	Unethical
1. An organization requires employees to wear badges that track their whereabouts while at work.	☐	☐
2. A supervisor reads an employee's email message.	☐	☐
3. An employee uses his computer at work to send email messages to a friend.	☐	☐
4. An employee sends an email message to several coworkers and blind copies his supervisor.	☐	☐
5. An employee forwards an email message to a third party without permission from the sender.	☐	☐
6. An employee uses her computer at work to complete a homework assignment for school.	☐	☐
7. The vice president of your Student Government Association (SGA) downloads a photo from the web and uses it in a flyer recruiting SGA members.	☐	☐
8. A student copies text from the web and uses it in a research paper for his English Composition class.	☐	☐
9. An employee sends political campaign material to individuals on her employer's mailing list.	☐	☐
10. As an employee in the registration office, you have access to student grades. You look up grades for your friends, so that they do not have to wait for grades to be posted online.	☐	☐
11. An employee makes a copy of software and installs it on her home computer. No one uses her home computer while she is at work, and she uses her home computer only to finish projects from work.	☐	☐
12. An employee who has been laid off installs a computer virus on his employer's computer.	☐	☐
13. A person designing a webpage finds one on the web similar to his requirements, copies it, modifies it, and publishes it as his own webpage.	☐	☐
14. A student researches using only the web to write a report.	☐	☐
15. In a society in which all transactions occur online (a cashless society), the government tracks every transaction you make and automatically deducts taxes from your bank account.	☐	☐
16. Someone copies a well-known novel to the web and encourages others to read it.	☐	☐
17. A person accesses an organization's network and reports to the organization any vulnerabilities discovered.	☐	☐
18. Your friend uses a neighbor's wireless network to connect to the Internet and check email.	☐	☐
19. A company uses recycled paper to print a 50-page employee benefits manual that is distributed to 425 employees.	☐	☐
20. An employee is fired based on the content of posts on his or her social networking site.	☐	☐

Figure 5-17 Indicate whether you think the situation described is ethical or unethical. Be prepared to discuss your answers.
© Cengage Learning

Information Accuracy

Information accuracy is a concern today because many users access information maintained by other people or companies, such as on the Internet. Do not assume that because the information is on the web that it is correct. As discussed in Chapter 2, users should evaluate the value of a webpage before relying on its content. Be aware that the organization providing access to the information may not be the creator of the information.

In addition to concerns about the accuracy of computer input, some individuals and organizations raise questions about the ethics of using computers to alter output, primarily graphic output such as a retouched photo. With graphics equipment and software, users easily can digitize photos and then add, change (Figure 5-18), or remove images.

Figure 5-18 This digitally edited photo shows a fruit that looks like an apple on the outside and an orange on the inside.
© Giuliano20 / Dreamstime.com

Intellectual Property Rights

Intellectual property (IP) refers to unique and original works such as ideas, inventions, art, writings, processes, company and product names, and logos. *Intellectual property rights* are the rights to which creators are entitled for their work. Certain issues arise surrounding IP today because many of these works are available digitally and easily can be redistributed or altered without the creator's permission.

A *copyright* gives authors, artists, and other creators of original work exclusive rights to duplicate, publish, and sell their materials. A copyright protects any tangible form of expression.

A common infringement of copyright is piracy, where people illegally copy software, movies, and music. Many areas are not clear-cut with respect to the law, because copyright law gives the public fair use to copyrighted material. The issues surround the phrase, fair use, which allows use for educational and critical purposes. This vague definition is subject to widespread interpretation and raises many questions:

- Should individuals be able to download contents of your website, modify it, and then put it on the web again as their own?
- Should a faculty member have the right to print material from the web and distribute it to all members of the class for teaching purposes only?
- Should someone be able to scan photos or pages from a book, publish them on the web, and allow others to download them?
- Should someone be able to put the lyrics of a song on the web?
- Should students be able to take term papers they have written and post them on the web, making it tempting for other students to download and submit them as their own work?

These issues with copyright law led to the development of *digital rights management* (DRM), a strategy designed to prevent illegal distribution of movies, music, and other digital content. Read Ethics & Issues 5-3 on the next page to consider liability issues related to copyrighted material.

Internet Research

What is meant by fair use?

Search for: fair use definition

ETHICS & ISSUES 5-3

Who Is Liable for Unauthorized Postings of Copyrighted Streaming Materials?

Websites that host user content, such as blogs and social media sites, specify guidelines about what users can and cannot post, including streaming content and links. For example, you cannot stream or post copyrighted digital content, such as music, movies, or book chapters. If a user violates these terms, is the host liable? For example, if a blogger uses a blogging platform to post copyrighted material, is the blogging platform liable?

Several proposed laws attempt to protect copyrighted material from online distribution.

For example, the United States Congress introduced the Stop Online Piracy Act (SOPA), which placed the responsibility on the hosting site to monitor all user-posted content, including links and even comments made about an article. If violations occur, this type of legislation enables judges to block access to websites and requires that advertisers, search engines, and payment services cease conducting business with the website. The movie and music businesses support this type of legislation, saying that it protects intellectual property. Opponents fear that it would shut down an entire domain, such as a blogging

website, because of content posted by a single blogger. For this reason, several websites participated in a large-scale blackout in protest of SOPA. Soon after, Congress abandoned it.

How can the government balance copyright protection with free speech? What types of websites would be affected by a law such as SOPA? Should websites that enable users to post content be liable for the content? Why or why not? Can the government require search engines to remove links to a website if it violates copyright laws? Why or why not?

Codes of Conduct

A **code of conduct** is a written guideline that helps determine whether a specificaction is ethical/unethical or allowed/not allowed. An IT code of conduct focuses on acceptable use of technology. Employers and schools often specify standards for the ethical use of technology in an IT code of conduct and then distribute these standards to employees and students (Figure 5-19). You also may find codes of conduct online that define acceptable forms of communications for websites where users post commentary or other communications such as blogs, wikis, discussion forums, and so on.

Sample IT Code of Conduct

1. Technology may not be used to harm other people.
2. Employees may not meddle in others' files.
3. Employees may use technology only for purposes in which they have been authorized.
4. Technology may not be used to steal.
5. Technology may not be used to bear false witness.
6. Employees may not copy or use software illegally.
7. Employees may not use others' technology resources without authorization.
8. Employees may not use others' intellectual property as their own.
9. Employees shall consider the social impact of programs and systems they design.
10. Employees always should use technology in a way that demonstrates consideration and respect for fellow humans.

Figure 5-19 Sample IT code of conduct employers may distribute to employees.
© Cengage Learning; © iStockphoto / Oleksiy Mark

Green Computing

People use, and often waste, resources such as electricity and paper while using technology. Recall from Chapter 1 that **green computing** involves reducing the electricity and environmental waste while using computers, mobile devices, and related technologies. Figure 5-20 summarizes measures users can take to contribute to green computing.

Personal computers, display devices, printers, and other devices should comply with guidelines of the ENERGY STAR program. The United States Department of Energy (DOE) and the United States Environmental Protection Agency (EPA) developed the *ENERGY STAR program* to help reduce the amount of electricity used by computers and related devices. This program encourages manufacturers to create energy-efficient devices. For example, many devices switch

Internet Research

Where can I recycle outdated electronics?

Search for: recycle old electronics

to sleep or power save mode after a specified number of inactive minutes or hours. Computers and devices that meet the ENERGY STAR guidelines display an ENERGY STAR label (shown in Figure 5-20).

Enterprise data centers and computer facilities consume large amounts of electricity from computer hardware and associated devices and utilities such as air conditioning, coolers, lighting, etc. Organizations can implement a variety of measures to reduce electrical waste:

- Consolidate servers by using virtualization.
- Purchase high-efficiency equipment.
- Use sleep modes and other power management features for computers and devices.
- Buy computers and devices with low power consumption processors and power supplies.
- When possible, use outside air to cool the data center or computer facility.

Some organizations continually review their *power usage effectiveness* (*PUE*), which is a ratio that measures how much power enters the computer facility or data center against the amount of power required to run the computers and devices.

Green Computing Tips

1. Conserve Energy
   a. Use computers and devices that comply with the ENERGY STAR program.
   b. Do not leave a computer or device running overnight.
   c. Turn off the monitor, printer, and other devices when not in use.

2. Reduce Environmental Waste
   a. Use paperless methods to communicate.
   b. Recycle paper and buy recycled paper.
   c. Recycle toner and ink cartridges, computers, mobile devices, printers, and other devices.
   d. Telecommute.
   e. Use videoconferencing and VoIP for meetings.

Figure 5-20 A list of suggestions to make computing healthy for the environment.
US Environmental Protection Agency, ENERGY STAR program; © Roman Sotola / Shutterstock.com; © Cengage Learning

 CONSIDER THIS

Should you save out-of-date computers and devices?
Users should not store obsolete computers and devices in their basement, storage room, attic, warehouse, or any other location. Computers, monitors, and other equipment contain toxic materials and potentially dangerous elements including lead, mercury, and flame retardants. In a landfill, these materials release into the environment. Recycling and refurbishing old equipment are much safer alternatives for the environment. Manufacturers can use the millions of pounds of recycled raw materials to make products such as outdoor furniture and automotive parts. Before recycling, refurbishing, or discarding your old computer, be sure to erase, remove, or destroy its hard disk so that the information it stored remains private.

Information Privacy

Information privacy refers to the right of individuals and companies to deny or restrict the collection, use, and dissemination of information about them. Organizations often use huge databases to store records such as employee records, medical records, financial records, and more. Much of the data is personal and confidential and should be accessible only to authorized users. Many individuals and organizations, however, question whether this data really is private. That is, some companies and individuals collect and use this information without your authorization. Websites often collect data about you, so that they can customize advertisements and send you personalized email messages. Some employers monitor your computer usage and email messages.

Figure 5-21 lists measures you can take to make your personal data more private. The following sections address techniques companies and employers use to collect your personal data.

Electronic Profiles

When you fill out a printed form, such as a magazine subscription or contest entry, or an online form to sign up for a service, create a social networking profile, or register a product warranty, the merchant that receives the form usually stores the information you provide in a database. Likewise, every time you click an advertisement on the web or perform a search online, your information and preferences enter a database. Some merchants may sell or share the contents of their databases with national marketing firms and Internet advertising

How to Safeguard Personal Information

1. Fill in only necessary information on rebate, warranty, and registration forms.

2. Do not preprint your phone number or Social Security number on personal checks.

3. Have an unlisted or unpublished phone number.

4. If you have Caller ID, find out how to block your number from displaying on the receiver's system.

5. Do not write your phone number on charge or credit receipts.

6. Ask merchants not to write credit card numbers, phone numbers, Social Security numbers, and driver's license numbers on the back of your personal checks.

7. Purchase goods with cash, rather than credit or checks.

8. Avoid shopping club and buyer cards.

9. If merchants ask personal questions, find out why they want to know before releasing the information.

10. Inform merchants that you do not want them to distribute your personal information.

11. Request, in writing, to be removed from mailing lists.

12. Obtain your credit report once a year from each of the three major credit reporting agencies (Equifax, Experian, and TransUnion) and correct any errors.

13. Request a free copy of your medical records once a year from the Medical Information Bureau.

14. Limit the amount of information you provide to websites. Fill in only required information.

15. Install a cookie manager to filter cookies.

16. Clear your history file when you are finished browsing.

17. Set up a free email account. Use this email address for merchant forms.

18. Turn off file and printer sharing on your Internet connection.

19. Install a personal firewall.

20. Sign up for email filtering through your ISP or use an anti-spam program.

21. Do not reply to spam for any reason.

22. Surf the web anonymously or through an anonymous website.

Figure 5-21 Techniques to keep personal data private.
© iStockphoto / Norebbo; © Cengage Learning

firms. By combining this data with information from public records such as driver's licenses and vehicle registrations, these firms can create an electronic profile of individuals. Electronic profiles may include personal details such as your age, address, phone number, marital status, number and ages of dependents, interests, and spending habits.

Direct marketing supporters claim that using information in this way lowers overall selling costs, which lowers product prices. Critics contend that the information in an electronic profile reveals more about an individual than anyone has a right to know. They argue that companies should inform people if they plan to provide personal information to others, and people should have the right to deny such use. Many websites allow people to specify whether they want their personal information shared or preferences retained (Figure 5-22).

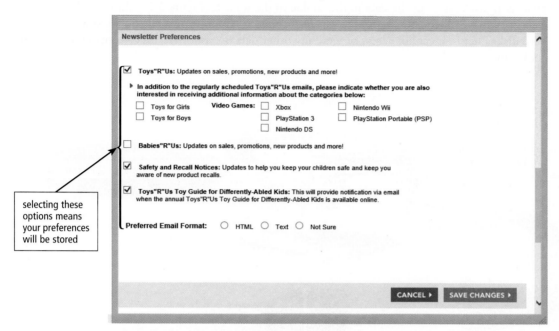

selecting these options means your preferences will be stored

Figure 5-22 Many companies, such as Toys"R"Us shown here, allow users to specify whether they want the company to retain their preferences.
Source: Geoffrey, LLC

Cookies

A **cookie** is a small text file that a web server stores on your computer. Cookie files typically contain data about you, such as your user name, postal code, or viewing preferences. Websites use cookies for a variety of purposes:

• Most websites that allow for personalization use cookies to track user preferences. These cookies may obtain their values when a user fills in an online form requesting personal information. Some websites, for example, store user names in cookies in order to display a personalized greeting that welcomes the user, by name, back to the website. Other websites allow users to customize their viewing experience with preferences such as local news headlines, the local weather forecast, or stock quotes.

• Some websites use cookies to store user names and/or passwords, so that users do not need to enter this information every time they sign in to the website.

• Online shopping sites generally use a *session cookie* to keep track of items in a user's shopping cart. This way, users can start an order during one web session and finish it on another day in another session. Session cookies usually expire after a certain time, such as a week or a month.

• Some websites use cookies to track how often users visit a site and the webpages they visit while at the website.

• Websites may use cookies to target advertisements. These websites store a user's interests and browsing habits in the cookie.

✳ CONSIDER THIS ─────────────────────────────────────

Do websites ever sell information stored in cookies?
Some websites sell or trade information stored in your cookies to advertisers — a practice many believe to be unethical. If you do not want personal information distributed, you should limit the amount of information you provide to a website or adjust how your browser handles cookies. You can set your browser to accept cookies automatically, prompt if you want to accept a cookie, or disable all cookie use. Keep in mind if you disable cookie use, you may not be able to use some e-commerce websites. As an alternative, you can purchase software that selectively blocks cookies. Read How To 5-3 on the next page for instructions about cookies and other settings you can adjust in your browser.

Many commercial websites send a cookie to your browser; your computer's hard disk then stores the cookie. The next time you visit the website, your browser retrieves the cookie from your hard disk and sends the data in the cookie to the website. Figure 5-23 illustrates how websites work with cookies. A website can read data only from its own cookie file stored on your hard disk. That is, it cannot access or view any other data on your hard disk — including another cookie file.

How Cookies Work

Step 1
When you enter the address of a website in a browser, the browser searches your hard disk for a cookie associated with the website.

http://www.omahasteaks.com/

cookies

Internet

identification number

cookie information

Step 2
If the browser finds a cookie, it sends information in the cookie file to the website.

webserver for www.omahasteaks.com

Step 3
If the website does not receive cookie information, and is expecting it, the website creates an identification number for you in its database and sends that number to your browser. The browser in turn creates a cookie file based on that number and stores the cookie file on your hard disk. The website now can update information in the cookie file whenever you access the website.

Figure 5-23 This figure shows how cookies work.
© Alex Staroseltsev / Shutterstock.com; Source: Omaha Steaks International, Inc; © iStockphoto / Norman Chan; © Cengage Learning

---

HOW TO 5-3

Secure Your Browser

Configuring the security settings in your browser can help ensure that others cannot determine the websites you have visited, your browsing habits, or any personally identifiable or confidential information you might have entered on websites. The settings for securing your browser typically are found in the browser's Settings or Preferences dialog box. The following list provides suggestions for securing a browser.

• **Clear your browsing history often.** Your *browsing history* is a list of all websites you have visited over a period of time. By default, some browsers save your browsing history for 20 days or more. Configuring your browser to clear your browsing history often will help prevent others from seeing the websites you have visited.

• **Enable private browsing.** During *private browsing*, your browser does not keep track of the websites you are visiting. Websites you visit during a private browsing session will not store files on your computer, nor will they appear in your browsing history after you end the browsing session.

• **Turn off location sharing.** *Location sharing* gives websites access to your current location. While this can be particularly useful on websites that display the weather in your current location, this information also could be misused by dishonest individuals.

• **Never store passwords.** Many browsers have the capability of storing your passwords so that you do not have to enter them each time you visit the same websites. Others with access to your computer, however, will be able to access

these secure websites using your account information with relative ease.

• **Clear cookies regularly.** Websites may store cookies and other files on your computer. These files not only take up space, but they also may be used to track your browsing habits. Regularly clear cookies and other data that websites place on your computer.

• **Avoid phishing websites.** Phishing websites often look remarkably similar to real websites and trick visitors into entering confidential information that could be used in an identity theft scam. Many browsers have a built-in feature to help identify phishing websites. Enable this feature and be cautious on websites labeled as unsafe.

※ What security settings do you currently have enabled on your browser?

Phishing

Recall from Chapter 4 that **phishing** is a scam in which a perpetrator sends an official looking email message that attempts to obtain your personal and/or financial information. These messages look legitimate and request that you update credit card numbers, Social Security numbers, bank account numbers, passwords, or other private information. Read How To 5-4 for instructions about protecting yourself from phishing scams.

Clickjacking is yet another similar scam. With *clickjacking*, an object that can be clicked on a website, such as a button, image, or link, contains a malicious program. When a user clicks the disguised object, a variety of nefarious events may occur. For example, the user may be redirected to a phony website that requests personal information, or a virus may download to the computer. Browsers typically include clickjacking protection.

 Internet Research

Which phishing scams are prevalent?

Search for: recent phishing scams

 HOW TO 5-4 ————————————————————————————————

Protect against a Phishing Scam

Phishing scams can be perpetrated via email messages, websites, and even on the phone. The following guidelines will help protect you against a phishing scam.

Phone Scams

- If you receive a phone call from someone claiming to be from a company with which you do business, record his or her name and the time of the call. Do not disclose personal or financial information to the caller. If the caller is offering a product or service and is requesting a payment, call the company back at the number you have on file, and ask to be transferred to the person who called you initially.

- Whenever possible, enter your payment information on secure websites instead of reading credit card numbers or bank account information on the phone. You never know whether the caller is recording your payment information to use later for malicious purposes.

Email Scams

- If you receive an email message from someone requesting you to verify online account or financial information, do not reply with this information.

- Never tap or click links in email messages, even if the message appears to be from someone you know. Nor should you copy and paste the link from the email message to a browser. Instead, type the link's web address into a browser's address bar manually, and make sure you type it correctly. If you are visiting your financial institution's website, make sure the web address you enter matches the web address you have on file for them.

- Do not reply to email messages asking you for financial assistance — even if the email message appears to originate from someone you know. If you receive this type of email message from someone you know, call the person to verify the message's authenticity.

Website Scams

- When visiting a website, such as your financial institution's website, that will require you to enter confidential information, be sure to type the web address correctly. Typing it incorrectly may take you to a phishing website where the information you enter can be collected by an unknown party.

- Make sure websites requiring your confidential information use the https:// protocol.

- Websites with misspellings, poor grammar, or formatting problems may indicate a phishing website. Do not enter personal or financial information on a website that looks suspicious.

- Enable the *phishing filter* in your browser that can warn or block you from potentially fraudulent or suspicious websites.

✴ Have you experienced a phishing scam? If so, how did it attempt to trick you into providing personal or financial information? How did you respond?

Spyware and Adware

Recall from Chapter 4 that **spyware** is a program placed on a computer or mobile device without the user's knowledge that secretly collects information about the user and then communicates the information it collects to some outside source while the user is online. Some vendors or employers use spyware to collect information about program usage or employees. Internet advertising firms often collect information about users' web browsing habits. Spyware can enter your computer when you install a new program, through malware, or through a graphic on a webpage or in an email message.

Adware is a program that displays an online advertisement in a banner or pop-up window on webpages, email messages, or other Internet services. Adware on mobile phones is known as *madware*, for mobile adware. Sometimes, spyware is hidden in adware.

To remove spyware and adware, you can obtain spyware removers, adware removers, or malware removers that can detect and delete spyware and adware. Some operating systems and browsers include spyware and adware removers. Read Secure IT 5-5 on the next page for tips about the types of websites that might contain spyware or other malware.

SECURE IT 5-5

Risky Business: Websites to Avoid

Browsing various websites can be a risky practice if you are unaware of the dangers that could be lurking. Specific types of websites are more likely to contain malware, spam, and links to malicious sites. They include websites with .com and .info top-level domains (TLDs) and some country code TLDs (ccTLDs). Scammers are hopeful that users browsing the web will make a typing error and arrive at their websites in error. For example, if a person carelessly types .com and omits the letter, o, the top-level domain becomes .cm, which is the ccTLD for Cameroon, one of the most prolific TLDs for malware.

According to a report by online security firm Symantec, nearly 20 percent of websites categorized as "blogs / web communications" contain malware. Other dangerous categories are "hosting / personal hosted sites; business / economy; shopping; education / reference; technology; computer and Internet; entertainment and music; automotive; and health and medicine."

Symantec reports that social media sites, especially Facebook, are popular websites for online criminals due to the millions of subscribers, many of whom share personal information freely and believe they are operating in a safe environment. For example, cybercriminals created a Dislike button and a stalking app, which claimed to allow users to view names of individuals who had been viewing their profile. In reality, the Dislike button and stalking apps were rogue applications with deceitful intentions such as capturing personal information, sending or posting spam messages, or tricking users into agreeing to charges for phone or online services.

The cybercriminals obtain their website registration from companies with low fees, minimal registration documentation requirements, and volume discounts. These companies often respond to complaints slowly, if at all.

☀ Do you visit websites that fall in the categories of websites more likely to contain malware? If so, what precautions will you take the next time you view these websites?

Social Engineering

As related to the use of technology, **social engineering** is defined as gaining unauthorized access to or obtaining confidential information by taking advantage of the trusting human nature of some victims and the naivety of others. Some social engineers trick their victims into revealing confidential information such as user names and passwords on the phone, in person, or on the Internet. Techniques they use include pretending to be an administrator or other authoritative figure, feigning an emergency situation, or impersonating an acquaintance. Social engineers also obtain information from users who do not destroy or conceal information properly. These perpetrators sift through company dumpsters, watch or film people dialing phone numbers or using ATMs, and snoop around computers or mobile devices looking for openly displayed confidential information.

To protect yourself from social engineering scams, follow these tips:

- Verify the identity of any person or organization requesting personal or confidential information.
- When relaying personal or confidential information, ensure that only authorized people can hear your conversation.
- When personal or confidential information appears on a computer or mobile device, ensure that only authorized people can see your screen.
- Shred all sensitive or confidential documents.
- After using a public computer, clear the cache in its browser.
- Avoid using public computers to conduct banking or other sensitive transactions.

Privacy Laws

The concern about privacy has led to the enactment of federal and state laws regarding the storage and disclosure of personal data, some of which are shown in Table 5-4. Common points in some of these laws are as follows:

1. Information collected and stored about individuals should be limited to what is necessary to carry out the function of the business or government agency collecting the data.
2. Once collected, provisions should be made to protect the data so that only those employees within the organization who need access to it to perform their job duties have access to it.

3. Personal information should be released outside the organization collecting the data only when the person has agreed to its disclosure.

4. When information is collected about an individual, the individual should know that the data is being collected and have the opportunity to determine the accuracy of the data.

Table 5-4 Major U.S. Government Laws Concerning Privacy	
Law	**Purpose**
Children's Internet Protection Act	Protects minors from inappropriate content when accessing the Internet in schools and libraries
Children's Online Privacy Protection Act (COPPA)	Requires websites to protect personal information of children under 13 years of age
Computer Abuse Amendments Act	Outlaws transmission of harmful computer code such as viruses
Digital Millennium Copyright Act (DMCA)	Makes it illegal to circumvent antipiracy schemes in commercial software; outlaws sale of devices that copy software illegally
Electronic Communications Privacy Act (ECPA)	Provides the same right of privacy protection of the postal delivery service and telephone companies to various forms of electronic communications, such as voice mail, email, and mobile phones
Financial Modernization Act	Protects consumers from disclosure of their personal financial information and requires institutions to alert customers of information disclosure policies
Freedom of Information Act (FOIA)	Enables public access to most government records
HIPAA (Health Insurance Portability and Accountability Act)	Protects individuals against the wrongful disclosure of their health information
PATRIOT (Provide Appropriate Tools Required to Intercept and Obstruct Terrorism)	Gives law enforcement the right to monitor people's activities, including web and email habits
Privacy Act	Forbids federal agencies from allowing information to be used for a reason other than that for which it was collected

Employee Monitoring

Employee monitoring involves the use of computers, mobile devices, or cameras to observe, record, and review an employee's use of a technology, including communications such as email messages, keyboard activity (used to measure productivity), and websites visited. Many programs exist that easily allow employers to monitor employees. Further, it is legal for employers to use these programs.

 BTW

Computer Vision
Innovative Computing: You should be familiar with computer vision and how it helps to increase security.

✷ **CONSIDER THIS**

Do employers have the right to read employee email messages?
Actual policies vary widely. Some organizations declare that they will review email messages regularly, and others state that email messages are private. In some states, if a company does not have a formal email policy, it can read email messages without employee notification.

Content Filtering

One of the more controversial issues that surround the Internet is its widespread availability of objectionable material, such as prejudiced literature, violence, and obscene pictures. Some believe that such materials should be banned. Others believe that the materials should be filtered, that is, restricted.

Content filtering is the process of restricting access to certain material. Many businesses use content filtering to limit employees' web access. These businesses argue that employees are unproductive when visiting inappropriate or objectionable websites. Some schools, libraries, and parents use content filtering to restrict access to minors. Content filtering opponents argue that banning any materials violates constitutional guarantees of free speech and personal rights. Read Ethics & Issues 5-4 to consider whether content filtering violates first amendment rights.

Web filtering software is a program that restricts access to specified websites. Some also filter sites that use specific words (Figure 5-24). Others allow you to filter email messages, chat rooms, and programs. Many Internet security programs include a firewall, antivirus program, and filtering capabilities combined. Browsers also often include content filtering capabilities.

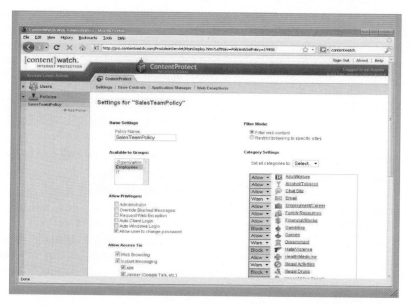

Figure 5-24 Web filtering software restricts access to specified websites.
Courtesy of ContentWatch, Inc.

ETHICS & ISSUES 5-4

Does Content Filtering in a Public Library Violate First Amendment Rights?
Among the resources libraries offer are Internet-enabled computers, which allow patrons to read the news, perform research, and more. The use of content filtering software on library computers controls the type of information a patron can access. Free speech advocates argue that this violates the First Amendment because it restricts library patrons from viewing certain websites and content.

The Children's Internet Protection Act (CIPA) requires that schools and libraries use content filtering software in order to receive certain federal funds. Proponents of CIPA claim it is necessary to protect children. CIPA does allow libraries to turn off the filters, if requested by an adult patron. Some libraries use content filtering software on computers used only by children.

Critics of content filtering software argue that the programs do not always work as intended. They can overfilter content, blocking information or education websites based on a single word; conversely, they can under filter content, which could result in access to webpages with inappropriate media.

Libraries typically have a policy stating acceptable use of the Internet, which outlines appropriate content. In addition, existing copyright laws apply to downloading and viewing content. Libraries' policies also should state whether they use content filtering software, so that the patrons are aware that their search results may not reflect the entire scope of content available on the Internet.

Is it fair for a government to require that libraries use content filtering software? Why or why not? Is content on the Internet covered under free speech? Why or why not?

NOW YOU KNOW

Be sure you understand the material presented in the sections titled Ethics and Society, and Information Privacy as it relates to the chapter objectives.

You now should know . . .

- What issues you might encounter with respect to information accuracy, intellectual property, codes of conduct, and green computing (Objective 9)

- How you can make your personal data more private (Objective 10)

- Why your computer might have a cookie (Objective 10)

Quiz Yourself Online: Check your knowledge of related content by navigating to this book's Quiz Yourself resource on Computer Concepts CourseMate and then tapping or clicking Objectives 9–10.

Chapter Summary

This chapter presented a variety of digital security risks. You learned about cybercrime and cybercriminals. The chapter discussed risks and safeguards associated with Internet and network attacks, unauthorized access and use, software theft, information theft, and hardware theft, vandalism, and failure. It presented various backup strategies and methods of securing wireless communications. You learned about ethical issues in society and various ways to protect the privacy of personal information.

Test your knowledge of chapter material by accessing the Study Guide, Flash Cards, and Practice Test apps that run on your smartphone, tablet, laptop, or desktop.

TECHNOLOGY @ WORK

National and Local Security

Since 2001, the federal government, local governments, businesses, and individuals have been implementing aggressive new security measures because of the increase in terrorist activity. A security threat can exist anywhere, and it is nearly impossible for humans alone to protect the country. As a result, technology now assists governments, law enforcement officials, business owners, and other individuals with monitoring and maintaining security.

Advancements in computer vision enable computers to monitor indoor and outdoor areas that might be subject to a high volume of criminal activity. For example, some cities are installing cameras in problematic areas. A program analyzes the output from the camera and can determine whether two or more people in close proximity to one another might be engaged in a physical confrontation. If the computer detects suspicious behavior, it automatically notifies local law enforcement.

Computers also use facial recognition to identify individuals who do not belong in a particular area. For example, one theme park takes a picture of individuals they escort out of and ban from the park. As visitors walk from their cars to the park, surveillance cameras positioned in strategic locations scan visitors' faces and compare them with the database containing images of those who are banned from the park. If the computer finds a match, it alerts a security officer who then can investigate the situation. Thousands of people visit theme parks each day, and computers make it easier to perform the otherwise impossible task of identifying those who might be trespassing.

The federal government, particularly the Department of Homeland Security, uses a computerized No Fly List to track individuals who are not authorized to travel on commercial flights within the United States. When an individual makes a reservation, a

computer compares his or her name to the names on the No Fly List. If the computer finds a match, the individual must prove that he or she is not the person on the list before being allowed to board an aircraft.

Whether you are walking outside, visiting an attraction, or traveling, the chances are good that computers are, in some way, ensuring your safety.

In what other ways do computers and technology play a role in national and local security?

Study Guide

The Study Guide exercise reinforces material you should know for the chapter exam. You will find answers to items with the icon only in the e-book.

Access the Study Guide app that runs on your smartphone, tablet, laptop, or desktop by navigating to this book's Apps resource on Computer Concepts CourseMate.

Instructions: Answer the questions below using the format that helps you remember best or that is required by your instructor. Possible formats may include one or more of these options: write the answers; create a document that contains the answers; record answers as audio or video using a webcam, smartphone, or portable media player; post answers on a blog, wiki, or website; or highlight answers in the book/e-book.

1. Define the terms, digital security risk and cybercrime.

2. Differentiate among hackers, crackers, script kiddies, cyberextortionists, and cyberterrorists. Identify issues with punishing cybercriminals.

3. List common types of malware. A(n) _____ is the destructive event malware delivers.

4. Identify risks and safety measures when gaming.

5. Define these terms: botnet, zombie, and bot.

6. Describe the damages caused by DoS and DDoS attacks.

7. A(n) _____ allows users to bypass security controls.

8. Define the term, spoofing. List ways to protect against Internet and network attacks.

9. Explain how macros can be a security risk.

10. Define the terms, firewall and proxy server. List steps to set up a firewall.

11. 📄 Name the contributions of AVG, McAfee, and Symantec, with respect to security.

12. Give examples of unauthorized use of a computer or network.

13. Identify what an AUP should specify.

14. Explain how an organization uses access controls and audit trails.

15. Differentiate among user names, passwords, and passphrases.

16. Explain the two-step verification process.

17. Describe the purpose of a CAPTCHA.

18. PIN stands for_____.

19. Define the term, biometric device. List disadvantages of biometric devices.

20. Describe how companies use the following recognition or verification systems: face, hand, voice, signature, and iris.

21. 📄 Name the security contributions of the FBI's face recognition technology project.

22. Define the term, digital forensics. Name areas in which digital forensics are used.

23. Define the terms, keygen and software piracy. Identify methods to prevent software theft.

24. Explain the process of product activation.

25. Describe the following license agreement types: end-user, network, and site. 📄 List conditions provided in a license agreement.

26. Give examples of information theft.

27. Describe the functions of an encryption algorithm and an encryption key. Differentiate between private and public key encryption.

28. Unencrypted data is called _____ ; encrypted data is called _____.

29. Describe the purpose of a VPN.

30. Define these terms: digital signature, digital certificate, and secure site.

31. Explain how to verify a digital certificate or signature's authenticity.

32. Describe what occurs during hardware theft or vandalism.📄 Name the hardware security contributions of LoJack.

33. Define the terms, back up and restore.

34. List the five types of backups. Describe the three-generation backup policy.

35. Identify the components of a disaster recovery plan.

36. Describe security risks associated with wireless access.

37. Identify ways to secure your wireless network.

38. List guidelines to protect your mobile device data.

39. Describe information accuracy, intellectual property rights, and codes of conduct.

40. List measures users can take to contribute to green computing.

41. Define the term, copyright. Identify issues surrounding streaming copyrighted materials.

42. Explain how companies, websites, and employers might infringe on your right to information privacy.

43. Describe how the following techniques are used to collect personal data: electronic profiles, cookies, phishing, and spyware and adware.

44. List methods for securing your browser. How can you protect against phishing scams?

45. 📄 List some federal and state privacy laws that affect the storage and disclosure of data.

46. Identify methods to protect yourself from social engineering scams.

47. Describe what a company might track when monitoring employees.

48. Identify issues surrounding content filtering.

49. Give examples of how various agencies and businesses use computers to ensure security.

You should be able to define the Primary Terms and be familiar with the Secondary Terms listed below.

Key Terms

 Access the **Flash Cards** app that runs on your smartphone, tablet, laptop, or desktop by navigating to this book's Apps resource on Computer Concepts CourseMate. **View definitions** for each term by navigating to this book's Key Terms resource on Computer Concepts CourseMate. **Listen to definitions** for each term on your portable media player by navigating to this book's Audio Study Tools resource on Computer Concepts CourseMate.

Primary Terms   (shown in **bold-black** characters in the chapter)

adware (231)
back door (207)
back up (219)
backup (219)
biometric device (213)
botnet (206)
code of conduct (226)
computer crime (202)
computer ethics (224)
content filtering (234)
cookie (229)
cracker (204)
cybercrime (202)

cyberextortionist (204)
cyberterrorist (204)
decrypt (216)
denial of service attack
    (DoS attack) (206)
digital certificate (218)
digital forensics (214)
digital security risk (202)
digital signature (218)
disaster recovery plan (220)
employee monitoring (233)
encryption (216)
fingerprint reader (213)

firewall (208)
green computing (226)
hacker (204)
information privacy (227)
information theft (216)
license agreement (215)
malware (205)
online security service (208)
password (211)
personal firewall (209)
phishing (231)
PIN (213)
piracy (215)

product activation (215)
restore (219)
script kiddie (204)
secure site (218)
social engineering (232)
software piracy (215)
software theft (215)
spoofing (207)
spyware (231)
user name (211)
web filtering software (234)
zombie (206)

Secondary Terms   (shown in *italic* characters in the chapter)

acceptable use policy (AUP) (210)
access control (211)
adware (205)
asymmetric key encryption (217)
audit trail (211)
biometric payment (214)
bot (206)
browsing history (230)
*Business Software Alliance (BSA)
    (215)*
Caesar cipher (217)
CAPTCHA (212)
CERT/CC (208)
certificate authority (218)
child (219)
ciphertext (216)
clickjacking (231)
*Computer Emergency Response Team
    Coordination Center (208)*
continuous data protection (CDP) (220)
copyright (225)

crimeware (202)
cyberforensics (214)
cyberwarfare (204)
cypher (216)
differential backup (220)
digital rights management (225)
*distributed DoS attack (DDoS
    attack) (207)*
email spoofing (207)
encryption algorithm (216)
encryption key (216)
*end-user license agreement (EULA)
    (215)*
ENERGY STAR program (226)
face recognition system (213)
full backup (220)
grandparent (219)
hand geometry system (213)
incremental backup (220)
intellectual property (IP) (225)
intellectual property rights (225)

IP spoofing (207)
iris recognition system (214)
keygen (215)
location sharing (230)
MAC address (222)
MAC address control (222)
macros (208)
madware (231)
malicious software (205)
network license (216)
off-site (219)
parent (219)
passphrase (212)
payload (205)
personal identification number (213)
phishing filter (231)
plaintext (216)
power usage effectiveness (227)
private browsing (230)
private key encryption (217)
proxy server (209)

public key encryption (217)
rootkit (205)
selective backup (220)
session cookie (229)
signature verification system (214)
single-user license agreement (215)
site license (216)
spyware (205)
SSID (222)
symmetric key encryption (217)
toll fraud (223)
trojan horse (205)
unauthorized access (210)
unauthorized use (210)
user ID (211)
virtual private network (VPN) (218)
virus (205)
voice verification system (213)
worm (205)
zombie army (206)

hand geometry system (213)

Checkpoint

The Checkpoint exercises test your knowledge of the chapter concepts. The page number containing the answer appears in parentheses after each exercise. The Consider This exercises challenge your understanding of chapter concepts.

Complete the Checkpoint exercises interactively by navigating to this book's Checkpoint resource on Computer Concepts CourseMate. **Access the Test Prep app** that runs on your smartphone, tablet, laptop, or desktop by navigating to this book's Apps resource on Computer Concepts CourseMate. After successfully completing the self-assessment through the Test Prep app, **take the Practice Test** by navigating to this book's Practice Test resource on Computer Concepts Coursemate.

True/False Mark T for True and F for False.

_____ 1. Any illegal act involving the use of a computer or related devices generally is referred to as crimeware. (202)

_____ 2. Some malware contains elements of a virus, worm, and trojan horse. (205)

_____ 3. A rootkit displays an online advertisement in a banner or pop-up window on webpages, email, or other Internet services. (205)

_____ 4. An audit trail records in a file both successful and unsuccessful access attempts. (211)

_____ 5. It is good practice to change your password frequently. (211)

_____ 6. A typical license agreement allows you to rent or lease the software. (216)

_____ 7. Unencrypted, readable data is called ciphertext. (216)

_____ 8. Private key encryption also is called asymmetric key encryption. (217)

_____ 9. VPNs encrypt data to help ensure that the data is safe from being intercepted by unauthorized people. (218)

_____ 10. Although wireless access provides many conveniences to users, it also poses additional security risks. (221)

_____ 11. It is impossible to detect if someone is accessing your wireless home network. (222)

_____ 12. Before recycling, refurbishing, or discarding your old computer, you should erase, remove, or destroy its hard disk so that the information it stored remains private. (227)

Multiple Choice Select the best answer.

1. A _____ is someone who demands payment to stop an attack on an organization's technology infrastructure. (204)
   a. cyberterrorist   c. cracker
   b. script kiddie   d. cyberextortionist

2. _____ is a type of malware that is placed on a computer without the user's knowledge that secretly collects information about the user. (205)
   a. A rootkit   c. A trojan horse
   b. Spyware   d. Adware

3. An employee using an organization's computer to send personal email messages might be an example of _____. (210)
   a. cybercrime
   b. hardware vandalism
   c. intellectual property rights violation
   d. unauthorized access and use

4. A _____ is a private combination of words, often up to 100 characters in length and containing mixed capitalization and punctuation, associated with a user name that allows access to certain computer resources. (212)
   a. passphrase   c. public key
   b. private key   d. encryption algorithm

5. A(n) _____ encryption algorithm inserts characters between existing characters. (217)
   a. expansion   c. compaction
   b. transposition   d. substitution

6. A(n) _____ is a set of characters that the originator of the data uses to encrypt the text and the recipient of the data uses to decrypt the text. (217)
   a. cipher
   b. plaintext
   c. public key
   d. encryption key

7. A(n) _____ backup method is the only real-time back up, providing very fast recovery of data. (220)
   a. selective
   b. full
   c. incremental
   d. continuous data protection

8. Online shopping websites generally use a _____ to keep track of items in a user's shopping cart. (229)
   a. phishing filter
   b. session cookie
   c. location sharing algorithm
   d. keygen

Checkpoint

Matching   Match the terms with their definitions.

_____ 1. digital security risk (202)

_____ 2. bot (206)

_____ 3. zombie (206)

_____ 4. denial of service attack (206)

_____ 5. spoofing (207)

_____ 6. back door (207)

_____ 7. access control (211)

_____ 8. cyberforensics (214)

_____ 9. digital certificate (218)

_____ 10. digital rights management (225)

a. compromised computer or device whose owner is unaware the computer or device is being controlled remotely by an outsider

b. technique intruders use to make their network or Internet transmission appear legitimate to a victim computer or network

c. program that performs a repetitive task on a network

d. program or set of instructions in a program that allows users to bypass security controls when accessing a program, computer, or network

e. notice that guarantees a user or website is legitimate

f. strategy designed to prevent illegal distribution of movies, music, and other digital content

g. an assault whose purpose is to disrupt computer access to an Internet service such as the web or email

h. any event or action that could cause a loss of or damage to computer or mobile device hardware, software, data, information, or processing capability

i. security measure that defines who can access a computer, device, or network, when they can access it, and what actions they can take while accessing it

j. the discovery, collection, and analysis of evidence found on computers and networks

Short Answer   Write a brief answer to each of the following questions.

1. What is cyberwarfare? (204) Differentiate among the various categories of cybercriminals. (204)

2. Differentiate among denial of service attacks, back doors, and spoofing. (206–207) What are methods to protect computers, mobile devices, and networks from attacks? (208)

3. How does a biometric device work? (213) Explain how a biometric payment is made. (214)

4. List five backup methods and how they differ. (220) What are the four components contained in a disaster recovery plan? (220)

5. What is private browsing? (230) List ways you can secure your browser. (230)

✳ Consider This   Answer the following questions in the format specified by your instructor.

1. Answer the critical thinking questions posed at the end of these elements in this chapter: Ethics & Issues (204, 221, 226, 234), How To (210, 222, 230, 231), Mini Features (220, 222), Secure IT (206, 208, 212, 218, 232), and Technology @ Work (235).

2. What are some common digital security risks? (202)

3. How does malware deliver its payload? (205)

4. Why would a programmer or computer repair technician build a back door? (207)

5. Are passphrases more secure than passwords? Why or why not? (212)

6. How are fingerprint readers used with personal computers? (213)

7. What conditions are found in a typical single-user license agreement? (215)

8. What security protocols do secure sites use? (218)

9. What should you include in a disaster recovery plan for natural disasters? What should you include for man-made disasters? (220)

10. Is it ethical to access an unsecured wireless network without permission? Why or why not? (221)

11. How can mobile security apps protect your mobile device data? (223)

12. What are some questions that arise surrounding fair use with respect to copyrighted material? (225)

13. What role does the ENERGY STAR program play in green computing? (228)

14. For what purposes do websites use cookies? (229)

15. What is click jacking? (230)

⊛ How To: Your Turn

The How To: Your Turn exercises present general guidelines for fundamental skills when using a computer or mobile device and then require that you determine how to apply these general guidelines to a specific program or situation.

Instructions: You often can complete tasks using technology in multiple ways. Figure out how to perform the tasks described in these exercises by using one or more resources available to you (such as a computer or mobile device, articles on the web or in print, online or program help, user guides, blogs, podcasts, videos, other individuals, trial and error, etc.). Summarize your 'how to' steps, along with the resource(s) used, in the format requested by your instructor (brief report, presentation, discussion, blog post, video, or other means).

❶ Update Virus Definitions

In addition to installing an antivirus program on your computer or mobile device to keep it safe from viruses, it also is necessary to keep the virus definitions updated so that the antivirus program can search for and detect new viruses on your computer or mobile device. New virus definitions can be released as often as once per day, depending on the number of new viruses that are created. Antivirus programs either can search for and install new virus definitions automatically at specified intervals, or you can update the virus signatures manually. The following steps describe how to update the virus definitions for an antivirus program.

Source: Microsoft

Update Virus Definitions Manually

a. If necessary, establish an Internet connection so that you will be able to update the virus definitions.
b. Run an antivirus program.
c. Tap or click the button to check for updated virus definitions.
d. If new virus definitions are available for the antivirus program, tap or click the link to download the definitions to the computer or mobile device.
e. When the update is complete, tap or click the button to scan the computer or mobile device for viruses.

Configure Automatic Updates for Virus Definitions

a. If necessary, establish an Internet connection so that you will be able to update the virus definitions.
b. Run an antivirus program.
c. Tap or click the option to update virus definitions automatically.
d. Tap or click the option to display the virus definition update schedule.
e. To provide the maximum protection from viruses, configure the antivirus program to update definitions as frequently as possible.
f. After configuring the update schedule, tap or click the button to update virus definitions manually.
g. When the update is complete, tap or click the button to scan the computer or mobile device for viruses.

Exercises

1. What antivirus program, if any, currently is installed on your computer? Is it scheduled to update virus definitions automatically?
2. In addition to downloading and installing virus definitions from within the antivirus program, are other ways available to obtain the latest virus definitions?
3. In addition to keeping the antivirus program's virus definitions current, what other ways can you protect a computer or mobile device from viruses?

❷ Determine Whether a Computer or Mobile Device Is Secured Properly

Several steps are required to secure a computer or mobile device properly. In addition to installing antivirus software and updating the virus definitions regularly, you also should install and configure a firewall, keep the operating system up to date, and be careful not to open suspicious email messages, visit unsecure webpages, or download untrusted files while using the Internet. The following steps guide you through the process of making sure your computer or mobile device is secured properly by verifying antivirus software is installed and running, a firewall is enabled and configured, and the operating system is up to date.

Verify Antivirus Software

a. Use the search tool in the operating system or scan the programs on the computer or mobile device for antivirus software.

How To: Your Turn ☀

b. If you are unable to locate antivirus software on the computer or mobile device, obtain an antivirus program and install it.

c. Run the antivirus program.

d. Verify the virus definitions in the antivirus program are up to date. More information about updating virus definitions can be found in How To: Your Turn Exercise 5-1.

Verify the Firewall

a. Use the search tool in the operating system or scan the programs, apps, and settings on the computer or mobile device to access and configure the firewall.

b. If you are unable to locate a firewall on the computer or mobile device, obtain a firewall program and install it.

c. Run the firewall program.

d. View the firewall settings and verify the firewall is turned on.

e. View the list of programs, apps, and features allowed through the firewall. If you do not recognize or use one or more of the programs, apps, or features, remove them from the list of allowed programs, apps, and features.

Verify Operating System Updates

a. If necessary, establish an Internet connection.

b. Navigate to the area of the operating system where you can access the button, link, or command to search for operating system updates. For example, in Microsoft Windows, you would display the settings for Windows Update.

c. Tap or click the button, link, or command to check for updates.

d. If no updates are available, your operating system is up to date. If the operating system locates additional updates, download and install the updates. **NOTE: If the computer or mobile device you are using does not belong to you, check with its owner before downloading and installing updates for the operating system.**

Exercises

1. Before you began this exercise, was your computer or mobile device secured properly? How did you know your computer or mobile device was secured properly? If it was not, what actions did you need to perform to secure it?

2. Which programs, apps, and features do you think are safe to allow through your firewall? Which programs, apps, and features do you feel are not safe to allow through your firewall?

3. What additional ways can you properly secure your computer?

❸ Configure a Browser's Cookie Settings

As discussed in this chapter, cookies can be used for a variety of reasons. Websites can install cookies on your computer or mobile device that can store information on your computer or mobile device, or track your browsing habits. You can configure a browser's settings to disallow websites from storing and accessing cookies on your computer or mobile device. The following steps guide you through the process of configuring a browser's cookie settings.

a. Run the browser.

b. Display the browser's settings.

c. Navigate to the settings that configure the browser's cookie settings. These settings often are found in the Privacy category.

Source: Apple, Inc.

d. Configure how the browser handles first-party cookies and third-party cookies. Some users choose to reject all cookies. To function properly, however, some websites require that you accept their cookies.

e. Save the changes to the settings.

f. Restart the browser.

Exercises

1. What is the difference between first-party cookies and third-party cookies?

2. Configure the browser to deny all first-party and third-party cookies and then navigate to five websites you visit most frequently. Do the websites display any differently now that you are denying all cookies? Describe your browsing experience while the browser is configured to deny all cookies.

3. What security risks are associated with cookies?

✳ Internet Research

The Internet Research exercises broaden your understanding of chapter concepts by requiring that you search for information on the web.

Instructions: Use a search engine or another search tool to locate the information requested or answers to questions presented in the exercises. Describe your findings, along with the search term(s) you used and your web source(s), in the format requested by your instructor (brief report, presentation, discussion, blog post, video, or other means).

❶ Making Use of the Web
News, Weather, and Sports

When a major news, weather, or sports story breaks, more than 40 percent of people turn to the Internet to learn the latest details. They view video and photos from eyewitnesses and fans, read analyses from investigators and coaches, and comment on stories. Apps on tablets, smartphones, and other mobile devices are changing the delivery of the day's top stories, as both younger and older consumers are abandoning the traditional print newspaper. Men and college-educated people are the heaviest users of mobile news websites, and they are likely to read in-depth investigations and analyses. Social networking sites also are a major source of information for many people.

(a) Visit two news websites or apps and locate one national event covered in both sources. Compare the coverage of the two stories. What information is provided in addition to the text, such as video, graphics, or links to related articles? Which story offers a better analysis? Which source is easier to navigate and read? Then, using another website or app, locate and read today's top international news story. What did you learn by reading the story? Were you aware of this event prior to reading the online story? Does the coverage include videos and photos to increase your comprehension?

(b) Visit a weather website or app and obtain the five-day forecast for your hometown. Include details about information that supplements the current and forecast conditions, such as a pollen or air quality index, storm tracking, travel advisories, or season summaries.

(c) Visit a sports website or app and read the first story reported. Describe the coverage of this event. Which sources are quoted in the story? Which links are included to other stories? Describe the features provided on this website, such as the ability to chat, customize the page for your favorite teams, or share the content with media sharing sites.

❷ Social Media 📑

Sharing photos on your social media sites of yesterday's visit to the nature center might be at the top of today's to-do list, but these images might be just the clue cyberthieves need to access your account. Facebook, in particular, is one website that scammers and advertisers use to gather information regarding your whereabouts and your personal life. Their malicious attacks begin with a visit to your timeline or other record of your activities. Searching for keywords on your page, they send targeted messages appearing to originate from trusted friends. If you open their attachments or tap or click their links, you have given these unscrupulous individuals access to your account. In addition, you may think you have crafted a password no one could guess. With your page open for others to view, however, the thieves scour the contents in hopes of locating starting clues, such as children's names, anniversary dates, and pet breeds, which could be hints to cracking your password.

In the Help section of a social network site you use, search for information about changing your profile's security and privacy settings. What steps can you take to mitigate the chance of becoming the victim of a hack? For example, can you adjust the connection settings to restrict who can see stories, send friend requests and messages, or search for you by name or contact information? Can you hide certain posts or block people from posting on your page? Can you report posts if they violate the website's terms?

Internet Research ☀

3 Search Sleuth

(1) reCAPTCHA is helping to digitize old editions of which newspaper and books? (2) Which U.S. president signed into law the Electronic Signatures in Global and National Commerce (ESIGN) Act, which legalizes and enforces digital signatures, in 2000? (3) What is the name of the teenage hacker group that allegedly stole passwords and data from phone companies in the early 1990s? (4) According to the McAfee website, what are the three newest virus threats? (5) The person behind "Project Rivolta" carried out DDoS attacks on the websites of Yahoo!, CNN, eBay, Dell, and Amazon in 2000. What was his Internet alias? (6) The CERT Program is located in the Software Engineering Institute at which university? (7) Ancient Babylonians used which method to record secure business transactions? (8) What animal is the mascot for the Business Software Alliance's Play it Cyber Safe campaign? (9) What percent of Americans recognized the ENERGY STAR label when the first National Awareness survey was conducted in 2000? (10) The Internet Crime Complaint Center (IC3) is a partnership between which two organizations?

Source: Carnegie Mellon University

4 Green Computing

Energy-conserving features on your smartphone, mobile device, and computer may add a level of security to your data. Battery-operated devices may shut down (or power off), go into sleep mode, or hibernate after a period of inactivity to extend the battery charge. The power-off mode is more secure because you normally need to press a button to turn on the device. In sleep and hibernate modes, however, the device is placed in a low power-consumption state. The data remains in memory, so the device is vulnerable to the possibility of someone accessing the device remotely over a network. To enhance security, a password sometimes is required to wake the device from its sleep.

You often can specify in a settings menu which of these three modes you prefer. View the Help information for your smartphone, mobile device, or computer to read about setting the sleep and display settings. Which time options are available for turning off the display and putting the computer to sleep? Which

power settings can you change? How can you restore the default settings?

5 Security

Digital certificates and signatures detect a sender's identity and verify a document's authenticity. Secure IT 5-4 on page 218 gives details about how these certificates are issued and how encryption and algorithms identify the documents. Visit websites of at least two companies that issue digital certificates. Compare products offered, prices, and certificate features. What length of time is needed to issue a certificate? What is a green address bar, and when is one issued? What business or organization validation is required? Then, visit websites of at least two companies that provide digital signatures. Compare signing and sending requirements, types of supported signatures, and available security features. Which documents are required to obtain a digital signature? When would a business need a Class 2 rather than a Class 3 digital signature?

6 Ethics in Action

Retailers are using technology to sell their goods, unbeknownst to most shoppers. Some stores have purchased mannequins equipped with a camera in one eye to record video as input for face recognition software that can identify shoppers' age, race, and gender. The camera also is used to measure the amount of time shoppers view displays and also to search for shoplifters. In another instance, radio frequency identification (RFID) tags placed on such items as prescriptions, computer hardware, and clothing help retailers track inventory, reduce labor costs, and keep shelves stocked. Also, some malls have installed technology that monitors mobile phone signals to track shoppers' activities as they move from store to store. Privacy experts claim these security techniques invade shoppers' privacy because information about specific shoppers' habits and whereabouts are recorded. They claim law enforcement officials, lawyers, marketers, as well as thieves, could use this detailed electronic data to track people at all times of the day.

Visit websites that discuss using spy mannequins, RFID tags, and phone tracking in retail stores and malls. What are the benefits for stores to purchase this technology? What security and privacy issues arise from their use?

STUDENT ASSIGNMENTS

✳ Problem Solving

The Problem Solving exercises extend your knowledge of chapter concepts by seeking solutions to practical problems with technology that you may encounter at home, school, work, or with nonprofit organizations. The Collaboration exercise should be completed with a team.

 Challenge yourself with additional Problem Solving exercises by navigating to this book's Problem Solving resource on Computer Concepts CourseMate.

Instructions: You often can solve problems with technology in multiple ways. Determine a solution to the problems in these exercises by using one or more resources available to you (such as a computer or mobile device, articles on the web or in print, blogs, podcasts, videos, television, user guides, other individuals, electronics or computer stores, etc.). Describe your solution, along with the resource(s) used, in the format requested by your instructor (brief report, presentation, discussion, blog post, video, or other means).

Personal

1. **No Browsing History** While using the browser on your tablet, you realize that it is not keeping a history of websites you have visited. What might be wrong, and what is the first step you will take to correct this problem?

2. **Windows Updates Will Not Install** Microsoft Windows is notifying you that updates are available for your computer. You are able to download the updates to the computer, but you receive an error message each time you attempt to install the updates. What are your next steps?

3. **Suspicious File Attachment** You receive an email message that appears to be from someone you know. When you click to open the attachment, nothing happens. You attempt to open the attachment two more times without any success. Several minutes later, your computer is running slower and you are having trouble running apps. What might be wrong?

4. **Antivirus Software Outdated** After starting your computer and signing in to the operating system, a message is displayed stating that your virus definitions are out of date and need to be updated. What are your next steps?

5. **Laptop's Physical Security** You plan to start taking your laptop to school so that you can record notes in class. You want to make sure, however, that your computer is safe if you ever step away from it for a brief period of time. What steps can you take to ensure the physical security of your laptop?

© iStockphoto / Stephen Krow

Professional

6. **Corporate Firewall Interference** You installed a new browser on your work computer because you no longer wish to use the default browser provided with the operating system. When you run the new browser, an error message appears stating that a user name and password are required to configure the firewall and allow this program to access the Internet. Why has this happened?

7. **Problems with CAPTCHA** You are signing up for an account on a website and encounter a CAPTCHA. You attempt to type the characters you see on the screen, but an error message appears stating that you have entered the incorrect characters. You try two more times and get the same result. You are typing the characters to the best of your ability but think you still might be misreading at least one of the characters. What are your next steps?

8. **Unclear Acceptable Use Policy** You read your company's acceptable use policy, but it is not clear about whether you are able to use the computer in your office to visit news websites on your lunch break. How can you determine whether this type of activity is allowed?

9. **Potential Password Breach** While signing in to your office computer one morning, you suspect that one of your coworkers was looking over your shoulder when you entered your password. You use the same password to access highly sensitive information, and you fear you may lose your job if someone else accesses your account. What are your next steps?

10. **Connecting Corporate Email** You want to access your corporate email on your tablet, but your information technology department has asked you first to describe the security measures you take to protect your tablet from unauthorized use. How will you respond?

Collaboration

11. **Technology in National and Local Security** National and local security agencies often use technology to protect citizens. For example, computers are used to maintain a list of individuals not cleared to board a commercial aircraft. Form a team of three people to create a list of the various ways technology helps to keep the public safe. One team member should research how local agencies, such as police departments, use technology to ensure security. Another team member should research ways national security agencies use technology to protect the public from threats, and the last team member should research ways that private businesses use technology to enhance security. Compile these findings into a report and submit it to your instructor.

The Critical Thinking exercises challenge your assessment and decision-making skills by presenting real-world situations associated with chapter concepts. The Collaboration exercise should be completed with a team.

Critical Thinking ✷

 Challenge yourself with additional Critical Thinking exercises by navigating to this book's Critical Thinking resource on Computer Concepts CourseMate.

Instructions: Evaluate the situations below, using personal experiences and one or more resources available to you (such as articles on the web or in print, blogs, podcasts, videos, television, user guides, other individuals, electronics or computer stores, etc.). Perform the tasks requested in each exercise and share your deliverables in the format requested by your instructor (brief report, presentation, discussion, blog post, video, or other means).

1. Class Discussion

Online Gaming Safety   You and your friend frequently play a popular online role-playing game. Your friend's computer had a virus recently, which was traced back to a malware-infected website. Your friend tells you that she visited the website after clicking a link while playing the game. What risks are involved when playing online games? Use the web to find articles about incidents of malware infections associated with online gaming. Research tips for increasing security when playing online games. Did you find other threats and security tips in addition to the ones mentioned in this chapter? Have you ever downloaded updates to a game? If so, how did you ensure the updates were safe? Locate a list of games that are known to cause malware infections. Share your findings and any online gaming security problems you have experienced with the class.

2. Research and Share

Ensuring Safety and Security Online   You work in the information technology department for a large enterprise. An increasing number of users are contacting the help desk complaining about slow computer performance. Help desk representatives frequently attribute the decreased performance to malware. Although the help desk has installed security software on each computer, users also must practice safe computing. Your manager asked you to prepare information that teaches employees how to guard against malware and other security threats. Include information such as how to determine if a website is safe, how to identify spoofing schemes, guidelines for downloading programs from the Internet, email attachment safety, and how to avoid phishing scams. Create a list of how organizations use common safeguards to protect other users on the network, such as firewalls, proxy servers, user names and passwords, access controls, and audit trails. Compile your findings.

3. Case Study

Farmers' Market   You are the new manager for a group of organic farmers who have a weekly market in season. The market's board of directors asked you to develop a disaster recovery plan for its main office. The main office consists of a small storefront with two back rooms: one room is the office, with all of the electronic equipment and paper files; the other is for storage of nonelectronic equipment. The staff members — you, an administrative assistant, and an IT specialist — work in the office. The electronic equipment in the office includes two desktops, a laptop, an external hard disk for backups, a wireless router, and two printers. In addition, each staff member has a smartphone. Choose either a natural or man-made disaster. Create a disaster recovery plan that outlines emergency strategies, backup procedures, recovery steps, and a test plan. Assign staff members roles for each phase of the disaster recovery plan. Compile your findings.

Collaboration

4. Implementing Biometric Security   You are the chief technology officer of a large company. You have been reading an article about computer security. The article discussed several examples of security breaches, including thieves breaking into an office and stealing expensive equipment, and a recently terminated employee gaining access to the office after hours and corrupting data. Because of these incidents, your company would like to start using biometric devices to increase its security. Form a three-member team and research the use of biometric devices to protect equipment and data. Each member of your team should choose a different type of biometric device, such as fingerprint readers, face recognition systems, and retinal scanners. Find products for each device type, and research costs and user reviews. Search for articles by industry experts. Would you recommend using the biometric device for security purposes? Why or why not? Meet with your team, discuss and compile your findings, and then share with the class.

✴ Beyond the Book

The Beyond the Book exercises expand your understanding of chapter concepts by requiring research.

Access premium content by visiting Computer Concepts CourseMate. If you have a Computer Concepts CourseMate access code, you can reinforce and extend your learning with MindTap Reader, practice tests, video, and other premium content for Discovering Computers. To sign in to Computer Concepts CourseMate at www.cengagebrain.com, you first must create a student account and then register this book, as described at www.cengage.com/ct/studentdownload.

Part 1 Instructions: Use the web or e-book to perform the task identified for each book element below. Describe your findings, along with the search term(s) you used and your web source(s), if appropriate, in the format requested by your instructor (brief report, presentation, discussion, blog post, video, or other means).

1. **Animation** 📖 Review the animation associated with this chapter and then answer the question(s) it poses (217). What search term would you use to learn more about a specific segment of the animation?

2. **Consider This** Select a Consider This in this chapter (206, 207, 208, 211, 212, 214, 216, 217, 222, 227, 230, 233) and find a recent article that elaborates on the topic. What information did you find that was not presented in this book or e-book?

3. **Drag-and-Drop Figures** 📖 Complete the Drag-and-Drop Figure activities associated with this chapter (205, 217, 220, 230, 232). What did you learn from each of these activities?

4. **Ethics & Issues** Select an Ethics & Issues in this chapter (204, 221, 226, 234) and find a recent article that supports one view presented. Does the article change your opinion about the topic? Why or why not?

5. **Facebook & Twitter** Review a recent Discovering Computers Facebook post or Twitter Tweet and read the referenced article(s). What did you learn from the article?

6. **High-Tech Talk** 📖 Locate an article that discusses topics related to complex encryption algorithms. Would you recommend the article you found? Why or why not?

7. **How To** Select a How To in this chapter (210, 222, 230, 231) and find a recent article that elaborates on the topic. Who would benefit from the content of this article? Why?

8. **Innovative Computing** 📖 Locate two additional facts about unique Wi-Fi signal blocking innovations, computer vision, or the FBI's face recognition technology project. Do your findings change your opinion about the future of this innovation? Why or why not?

9. **Internet Research** Use the search term in an Internet Research (204, 206, 207, 215, 225, 226, 230) to answer the question posed in the element. What other search term could you use to answer the question?

10. **Mini Features** Locate an article that discusses topics related to one of the mini features in this chapter (214, 220, 222). Do you feel that the article is appropriate for this course? Why or why not?

11. **Secure IT** Select a Secure IT in this chapter (206, 208, 212, 218, 232) and find a recent article about the topic that you find interesting. How can you relate the content of the article to your everyday life?

12. **Technology @ Work** Locate three additional, unique usages of technology in the national and local security industry (235). What makes the use of these technologies unique to the national and local security industry?

13. **Technology Innovators** 📖 Locate two additional facts about AVG, McAfee, Symantec, and LoJack. Which Technology Innovator impresses you most? Why?

14. **Third-Party Links** 📖 Visit one of the third-party links identified in this chapter (204, 206, 208, 209, 212, 218, 219, 221, 226, 232, 235) and read the article or watch the video associated with the link. Would you share this link on your online social network account? Why or why not?

Part 2 Instructions: Find specific instructions for the exercises below in the e-book or on Computer Concepts CourseMate. Beside each exercise is a brief description of its online content.

1. 📖 **You Review It** Search for and review a video, podcast, or blog post about recent malware or virus outbreaks, or other tips to keep your computer or mobile device safe.

2. 📖 **Windows and Mac** Enhance your understanding and knowledge about using Windows and Mac computers by completing the Check Your Security Programs Status and Clear Your Browsing History activities.

3. 📖 **Android, iOS, and Windows Mobile** Enhance your understanding of mobile devices by completing the Set a Lock Screen on Your Device and Set Bluetooth-enabled devices to Non-discoverable activities.

4. 📖 **Exploring Computer Careers** Read about a career as a digital forensics examiner, search for related employment ads, and then answer related questions.

5. 📖 **App Adventure** Find and compare products you might purchase using retail apps on your smartphone or tablet.

Troubleshooting Computer and Mobile Device Problems

While using a computer or mobile device, at some point you probably will experience a technology problem that requires troubleshooting. Technology problems that remain unresolved may impact your ability to use your device. This Focus On section identifies some common problems you might experience with computers and mobile devices; it also includes some suggestions for correcting these problems. If the recommended solutions in the table below do not solve your problem, or you are uncomfortable performing any of the recommended actions, contact a repair professional (independent computer repair company, technical support department at your job or academic institution, or computer or mobile device manufacturer) for additional options.

This Focus On section also might assist you with completing some of the Problem Solving exercises found at the end of each chapter in this textbook. Table 1 contains possible solutions for problems that might occur on your computer or mobile device.

Note: The following steps are suggestions; they are not comprehensive solutions. When working with a computer or mobile device, follow all necessary safety precautions before implementing any of these recommended solutions. Contact a professional if you require additional information.

Table 1 Problems and Recommended Solutions

Problem	Desktop	Laptop	Tablet	Phone	Recommended Solution(s)
Computer or device does not turn on.	X	X	X		The computer might be in sleep or hibernate mode; to wake up the computer, try pressing a key on the keyboard, pressing the power button, or tapping the touch screen if applicable.
	X				Make sure power cables are plugged securely into the wall and the back of the computer.
		X	X	X	Make sure the battery is charged if the computer or device is not connected to an external power source.
					If the battery is charged, connect the external AC adapter and attempt to turn on the computer or device. If the computer or device still does not turn on, the problem may be with the computer or device.
	X	X	X	X	If none of the above options resolve the issue, the power supply or AC adapter might be experiencing problems; contact a professional for assistance.
Battery does not hold a charge.		X	X	X	Verify the AC adapter used to charge the battery is working properly. If the mobile computer or device can run from the AC adapter without a battery installed, the AC adapter most likely is working properly. If the AC adapter works, it may be time to replace the battery.
Computer issues a series of beeps when turned on.	X	X			Refer to your computer's documentation to determine what the beeps indicate, as the computer hardware may be experiencing a problem.

Problem	Desktop	Laptop	Tablet	Phone	Recommended Solution(s)
Computer or device turns on, but operating system does not run.	X	X	X	X	Disconnect all nonessential peripheral devices, remove all storage media, and then restart the computer or device.
					Restart the computer or device; if the problem persists, the operating system might need to be restored.
Monitor does not display anything.	X				Verify the monitor is turned on.
					Verify the video cable is connected securely to the computer and monitor.
					Make sure the power cables are plugged securely into the wall and the back of the monitor.
					Make sure the monitor is set to the correct input source.
					Restart the computer.
					If you have access to a spare monitor, see if that monitor will work. If so, your original monitor might be faulty. If not, the problem may be with your computer's hardware or software configuration.
Screen does not display anything.		X	X	X	Restart the device.
Keyboard or mouse does not work.	X	X	X		Verify the keyboard and mouse are connected properly to the computer or device.
					If the keyboard and mouse are wireless, make sure they are turned on and contain new batteries.
					If the keyboard and mouse are wireless, attempt to pair them again with the computer or wireless receiver. Read How To 3-3 on page 132 for more information.
					If you have access to a spare keyboard or mouse, see if it will work. If so, your original keyboard or mouse might be faulty. If not, the problem may be with your computer's hardware or software configuration.
		X			Make sure the touchpad is not disabled.
Wet keyboard no longer works.	X	X			Turn the keyboard upside down to drain the liquid, dab wet areas with a cotton swab, and allow the keyboard to dry.
Speakers do not work.	X	X	X	X	Verify that headphones or earbuds are not connected.
					Make sure the volume is not muted and is turned up on the computer or mobile device.
	X	X			Verify the speakers are turned on.
	X				Make sure the speakers are connected properly to the computer.
					If necessary, verify the speakers are plugged in to an external power source.
Hard drive makes noise.	X	X			If the computer is not positioned on a flat surface, move it to a flat surface.
					If the problem persists, contact a professional.
Fan contains built-up dust/ does not work.	X	X			If possible, open the system unit and use a can of compressed air to blow the dust from the fan and away from the system unit.
	X				Remove obvious obstructions that might be preventing the fan from functioning.
					Verify the fan is connected properly to the motherboard.
					If the fan still does not work, it may need to be replaced.

Problem	Desktop	Laptop	Tablet	Phone	Recommended Solution(s)
Computer or device is too hot.		X	X	X	Verify the fan or vents are not obstructed. If the fan or vents obstructed, use a can of compressed air to blow the dust from the fan or vent and away from the computer or device or remove other obstructions.
		X			Purchase a cooling pad that rests below the laptop and protects it from overheating.
Cannot read from optical disc.	X	X			Clean the optical disc and try reading from it again.
					Try reading from another optical disc. If the second optical disc works, the original disc is faulty.
					If the second disc does not work, the problem may be with the optical disc drive.
External drive (USB flash drive, optical drive, or external hard drive) is not recognized.	X	X	X		Remove the drive and insert it into a different USB port, if available.
					Remove the drive, restart the computer, and insert the drive again.
					Try connecting the drive to a different computer. If you still cannot read from the drive, it may be faulty.
Program or app does not run.	X	X	X	X	Restart the computer or device and try running the program or app again.
					If feasible, uninstall the program or app, reinstall it, and then try running it again. If the problem persists, the problem may be with the operating system's configuration.
Computer or device displays symptoms of a virus or other malware.	X	X	X	X	Make sure your antivirus software is up to date and then disconnect the computer or device from the network and run antivirus software to attempt to remove the malware. Continue running scans until no threats are detected and then reconnect the computer to the network.
					If you do not have antivirus software installed, obtain and install a reputable antivirus program or app and then scan your computer in an attempt to remove the malware. You should have only one antivirus program or app installed on your computer or mobile device at one time. Read How To 1-4 on page 27 for more information.
					If you are unable to remove the malware, take your computer to a professional who may be able to remove the malicious program or app.
Computer or device is experiencing slow performance.	X	X			Defragment the hard disk.
	X	X	X	X	Uninstall programs and apps that you do not need.
					Verify your computer or device meets the minimum system requirements for the operating system and software you are running.
					If possible, purchase and install additional memory (RAM).
Screen is damaged physically.		X	X	X	Contact a professional to replace the screen; if the computer or device is covered under a warranty, the repair may be free.
					Replacing a broken screen on a computer or device might be more costly than replacing the computer or device; consider your options before replacing the screen.
Touch screen does not respond.	X	X	X	X	Clean the touch screen.
					Restart the computer or device.

Problem	Desktop	Laptop	Tablet	Phone	Recommended Solution(s)
Computer or device is wet.		X	X	X	Turn off the computer or device, remove the battery, and dry off visible water with a cloth. Fill a plastic bag or box with rice, submerge the computer or device and battery into the rice so that it is surrounded completely, and then do not turn on the computer or device for at least 24 hours.
					If the computer or device does not work after it is dry, contact a professional for your options.
Computer or device does not connect to a wireless network.	X	X	X	X	Verify you are within range of a wireless access point.
					Make sure the information to connect to the wireless network is configured properly on the computer or device.
					Make sure the wireless capability on the computer or device is turned on.
Computer or device cannot synchronize with Bluetooth accessories.	X	X	X	X	Verify the Bluetooth device is turned on.
					Verify the Bluetooth functionality on your computer or device is enabled.
					Verify the computer or device has been paired properly with the accessory. Read How To 3-3 on page 132 for more information.
					Make sure the Bluetooth device is charged.
Device continuously has poor cell phone reception.			X	X	Restart the computer or device.
					If you have a protective case, remove the case to see if reception improves.
					Contact your wireless carrier for additional suggestions.

Jump Starting Your Technology Career

Nearly every job requires you to interact with technology to complete projects, exchange information with colleagues, and meet customers' needs. The technology field provides many opportunities for people of all skill levels and interests. As new technologies emerge, organizations look for potential employees who possess skills and a desire to learn and who are comfortable using all types of technology. You can use social media and job search websites both to learn about technology careers and to promote yourself to potential employers. By creating a professional online presence, hiring managers can learn more about you beyond what you can convey in a traditional one-page paper resume. This Focus On section explores current technology careers and how you can prepare for them. It also discusses social media sites and job search websites. You can use these websites as you look for the perfect job with which to begin your technology career.

Note: This Focus On section uses a variety of terms that are described throughout this book. These terms also are defined in the index at the back of this book. If you need additional information about a particular topic, refer to the appropriate chapter in this book.

Career Considerations

Many of the careers mentioned in this Focus On section did not exist a few years ago. As new technologies and trends emerge, you should stay informed about them to ensure your relevance in the technology market.

Careers in Technology

Career opportunities in the technology field are available for people with a variety of skills and talents. Most of these careers require a bachelor's or associate's degree in technology. Some, however, require only a certificate. The following sections list and describe some of the more popular technology-related careers. For a more complete list and discussion, see the Technology Careers appendix (available in the e-book).

Career Considerations

Your instructors may be helpful resources when you are looking for a job. Because of their professional experience, they may be able to connect you with potential employers, recommend classes you should take, or suggest internship opportunities.

System Development

Careers in the system development area require you to analyze or create software, apps, databases, websites and web-based development platforms, and networks. Some careers are listed in Table 1.

Table 1 System Development Jobs	
Job Title	**Job Description**
Cloud Architect	Identifies business requirements, strategies and solutions for cloud storage and services that meet a company's goals or needs
Database Designer	Specifies the structure, interface, and requirements of a large-scale database; determines security and permissions for users
Program and App Developer	Specifies, designs, implements, tests, and documents programs and apps in a variety of fields, including robotics, operating systems, animation, and applications
Systems Analyst	Works closely with users to analyze their requirements, designs and develops new information systems, and incorporates new technologies
Systems Programmer	Installs and maintains operating system software and provides technical support to the programming staff
Web Designer	Designs the layout, navigation, and overall appearance of a website with a focus on user experience; specifies a website's appearance using HTML5, JavaScript, CSS, media, and other web design technologies
Web Developer	Analyzes, develops, and supports the functionality of a website, including applications that often interact with databases or other online resources

Technology Operations

Careers in technology operations require you to have knowledge about how hardware, software, and networks function. Some careers are listed in Table 2.

Table 2 Technology Operations Jobs	
Job Title	**Job Description**
Computer Technician	Installs, maintains, and repairs hardware and servers; installs, upgrades, and configures software; troubleshoots hardware problems
Help Desk Specialist/ Help Desk Technician	Answers technology-related questions in person, on the phone, or in an online chat room
Network Administrator/ Network Engineer	Installs, configures, and maintains LANs, WANs, wireless networks, intranets, Internet systems, and network software; identifies and resolves connectivity issues
Technical Project Manager	Guides design, development, and maintenance tasks; serves as interface between programmers/developers and management

Web Marketing and Social Media

Careers in web marketing and social media require you to be knowledgeable about web-based development platforms, social media apps, and marketing strategies. Some careers are listed in Table 3.

Table 3 Web Marketing and Social Media Jobs	
Job Title	**Job Description**
Customer Relationship Management (CRM) Specialist	Integrates apps and data related to customer inquiries, purchases, support requests, and behaviors in order to provide a complete application that manages a company's relationships with its customers
Internet/Social Media Marketing Specialist	Directs and implements an organization's use of Internet and social media marketing, including Facebook pages, Twitter feeds, blogs, and online advertisements
Search Engine Optimization (SEO) Expert	Writes and develops web content and website layouts so that they will appear at the beginning of search results when users search for content
User Experience (UX) Designer	Plans and designs software and apps that consider a user's reaction to a program and its interface, including its efficiency, its effectiveness, and its ease of use

App Development and Mobile Technologies

Careers in app development and mobile technologies require you to have knowledge about trends in the desktop and mobile app market, as well as the ability to develop secure apps for a variety of computers and mobile devices. Some careers are listed in Table 4.

Table 4 App Development and Mobile Technologies Jobs	
Job Title	**Job Description**
Desktop or Mobile Application Programmer/ Developer	Converts the system design into the appropriate application development language, such as Visual Basic, Java, C#, and Objective C, and the toolkits from various platforms
Games Designer/ Programmer	Designs games and translates designs into a program or app using an appropriate application development language
Mobile Strategist	Integrates and expands the company's initiatives for mobile users
Mobile Technology Expert	Develops and directs an organization's mobile strategy, including marketing and app development

Data Storage, Retrieval, and Analysis

Careers in data storage and analysis require you to be knowledgeable about collecting, analyzing, and reporting data from databases or the web. Some careers are listed in Table 5.

Table 5 Data Storage, Retrieval, and Analysis Jobs	
Job Title	**Job Description**
Data Scientist	Uses analytics and other Big Data tools to determine statistics on data that an organization can use to plan product development or create strategies for marketing
Database Analyst	Uses data modeling techniques and tools to analyze and specify data usage
Digital Forensics Examiner	Collects and analyzes evidence found on computers, networks, mobile devices, and databases
Web Analytics Expert	Collects and measures Internet data, such as website traffic patterns and advertising, and develops reports that recommend strategies to maximize an organization's web presence

Information and Systems Security

Careers in information and systems security require you to be knowledgeable about potential threats to a device or network, including viruses and hacking. Security specialists need to know the tools and techniques to protect against threats. Some careers are listed in Table 6 on the next page.

Table 6 Information and Systems Security Jobs	
Job Title	**Job Description**
Computer Security Specialist/ Mobile Security Specialist	Responsible for the security of data and information stored on computers and mobile devices within an organization
Network Security Administrator	Configures routers and firewalls; specifies web protocols and enterprise technologies
Security Analyst	Implements security procedures and methods, looks for flaws in security of a company's devices and networks, works with and trains employees at all levels, and assigns permissions and network settings
Security System Project Manager	Develops and maintains programs and tools designed to provide security to a network
Digital Forensics Analyst	Inspect electronic data to recover documents and files from data storage devices that may have been damaged or deleted, in order to use them as evidence in a crime investigation

Technology Certifications

A certification demonstrates your knowledge in a specific area to employers or potential employers. Organizations often require certification to ensure quality standards and to confirm their workforce remains up to date with respect to technology. Technology certifications are available in many areas, including:

- Applications
- Database systems
- Digital forensics
- Hardware
- The Internet
- Networking
- Operating systems
- Programming
- Security

Career Considerations

When taking a certification exam, read the instructions provided by the testing center to ensure you bring all necessary supplies, equipment, or technology. Print a copy of the directions in case your GPS device or app fails. Arrive early and silence or turn off your mobile devices. Know approximately how long the exam will take so that you can use your time wisely.

To assist you in preparing for a certification exam, training options are available to suit every learning style: self-study, online training, instructor-led training, and web resources. Authorized testing centers provide most certification exams for a fee. The exam sponsor's website typically lists testing centers near you. On the website, you can schedule and pay for your exam. At a testing center, you may use a computer to take the examination, or mark your answers on a scannable answer form. You likely will know before you leave the testing center whether you pass the examination. Some tests are in a multiple-choice format. Others are skill based. If you do not pass an exam, you may have to pay the fee again to retake it.

Obtaining a certification requires time and money. Certifications demonstrate your commitment to your chosen area. When deciding whether to obtain a certification, consider your long-term career goals, as well as your current experience. Read evaluations of the certification to determine its value in the industry you have chosen. Examine employment projections and available job opportunities to determine if it is worth obtaining the certification.

Start Your Job Search Online

Begin your job search by reviewing the information on social networking sites, job search websites, and organizations' websites. On these websites, you can learn about career opportunities and prepare for an interview. You also can follow an organization's activity on Facebook, Twitter, LinkedIn, and other social media channels. Researching a company's online activity helps you become familiar with some of the products, services, and opportunities that they provide.

Many colleges and universities have career services departments. Career services websites often contain information about career fairs, resume planning workshops, and campus recruitment activities. For example, the career services website shown in Figure A identifies career events on campus, featured jobs, interviewing tips, and targeted information for students with different majors. These websites can be a valuable tool in your career planning process.

Career Considerations

If your school has a career center or alumni network, take advantage of these valuable resources. Career counselors and experienced alumni can help you prepare for and secure an interview in your chosen field. They also might provide references to potential employers.

blogs for different majors provide students with pertinent information for their areas of study

career services offices often hold special events with visiting employers

career services websites often feature jobs and companies that hire graduating students

blog posts provide insights that help students prepare for their careers

Figure A A college or university career services website provides helpful career planning information.
Mark Frydenberg, Bentley University

Whether you are seeking a new job or are currently employed, you may find a career planning website useful (Figure B on the next page). These websites offer information about available jobs and local salaries. You also can use them to research corporate work environments, technology news, and opportunities for professional networking.

Figure B Career planning websites, such as GlassCeiling, Dice, and LinkedIn, provide career information, job listings, and resume posting services.
© GlassCeiling.com; Dice.com; LinkedIn.com

Many of the career planning websites shown in Table 7 also offer mobile apps. Use a search engine to locate these career planning websites and their mobile apps.

Table 7 Career Planning Websites	
Website Name	**Description**
CareerBuilder	Allows you to post your resume online for potential employers to review and offers a searchable database by company or industry; enables you to set up alerts to be notified when jobs that match your interests, skills, or salary requirements are posted
Dice	Features news, career advice, and salary surveys of interest to professionals, companies, and recruiters seeking or hiring for technology jobs
GlassCeiling	Provides stories of women succeeding in business, a job board, career planning information, and information about starting your own company
Indeed	Offers a job search engine, which presents job listings from job search websites, as well as individual employers' websites. Jobs are searchable by job title, company, salary, or location
LinkedIn	Manages your network of professional contacts and allows you to search for others with similar career interests and goals
Mashable Jobs	Focuses on jobs related to web technologies and social media trends; features a job board providing listings for web and social media opportunities, employer directory, and resume resources
Monster	Allows you to post your resume online for potential employers to review; also offers a searchable job database, career advice, company profiles, and salary information

Career Considerations

Before distributing or uploading your resume, ask at least two people to proofread it for any spelling and grammar mistakes. Keep the language professional. Use bullets and formatting to make it easy to read.

Career planning websites often allow you to post your resume online for potential employers to review. To do so, create your resume using a word processing program. Save the resume file in PDF format. Files in the PDF format have a consistent appearance when viewed on a variety of computers or mobile devices. You may attach your resume file saved in the PDF format to an email message that you send to a potential employer. You also can upload it to a job search website when applying for a job online. Alternatively, some websites allow you to enter resume information using a form displayed in a browser and then the information is saved to the site's resume database.

Maintain Your Professional Online Presence

In addition to the information provided in a job application and resume, many employers will search the web to learn more about job candidates. For this reason, it is important to have a professional online presence that positively conveys your accomplishments, skills, interests, and personality. Many beginning and established technology professionals promote themselves online. Providing links to a blog, online portfolio, or website can present your qualifications, skills, and interests. These online resume supplements may include digital media or other content that offers potential employers a more complete picture of you beyond what can be conveyed in a resume.

Tips for Creating a Professional Online Presence

An understanding of the web, digital media, and social networking sites is beneficial in creating your online presence. A professional online presence is one of the ways to present yourself to potential employers. Consider one or more of the following strategies:

- Register a form of your name as a domain name and host a blog or website at that web address. If your name is not available or you do not wish to host a blog or website on a server, include your name as part of the web address for your website on a free service, such as Blogger or WordPress.
- Include a photo of yourself.
- Use a webcam to create a 30-second video in which you introduce yourself. In the video, summarize your skills and professional interests. Post the video on YouTube or another video sharing site.
- Upload the PDF file of your resume, and include a link to it on your blog or website.
- Include links to your profiles on LinkedIn and Twitter on your blog or website.
- Include links to any other publications, articles, videos, or digital content you have created.
- Create accounts on social media sites, such as Facebook, LinkedIn, Twitter, Skype, or Google+. Use a consistent user name so that you will be easy to find on many channels. If you use Twitter primarily for personal purposes, consider creating a separate account for professional use. Adjust the privacy settings social networking sites on which you have personal content. Ensure that only those you specify can view your profile and information.
- Follow people who share your personal or professional interests, or those who you might want as a follower. Following others and adding followers helps you to build your own professional network on social networking sites.
- Post appropriate content to your blog, website, or social networking sites regularly.
- Share items of professional interest with your followers on Twitter. If you write blog posts regularly, Tweet about your new blog post and provide a link that will lead your followers to read the post.

Career Considerations
Social networking sites revise their privacy settings often. Periodically revisit your privacy settings on all personal social media accounts to ensure you have chosen the most current options that will secure your privacy.

Career Considerations
Present your best self in any photos you post online that potential employers might view. Avoid informal or humorous names for your account profiles, blog title, or domain name.

Career Considerations
Blogging or posting links to current trends in your technology career shows employers and networking contacts that you keep current with the latest developments in your field.

Creating a Professional Presence on LinkedIn

LinkedIn is a social networking site where professionals can connect with coworkers and industry colleagues. LinkedIn uses the term, contacts, to describe the individuals in your professional network, and also stores your relationship with each contact in your network. Many people use LinkedIn to stay in touch with current and former coworkers. In addition, companies may use LinkedIn as a recruiting tool for finding potential employees.

Upon joining LinkedIn, you specify a profile that allows contacts, prospective contacts, and others to learn about you. Your profile contains your name. It also may contain a photo, your current and previous work experience, and your education. Include any publications, and the web address of your website or blog. Ask other members to provide recommendations about your skills. When you look at another LinkedIn user's profile page, you also can see names of others with similar characteristics, along with the people in your network who connect you to that particular user. Figure C shows how the profile page of LinkedIn founder Reid Hoffman appears when you view it.

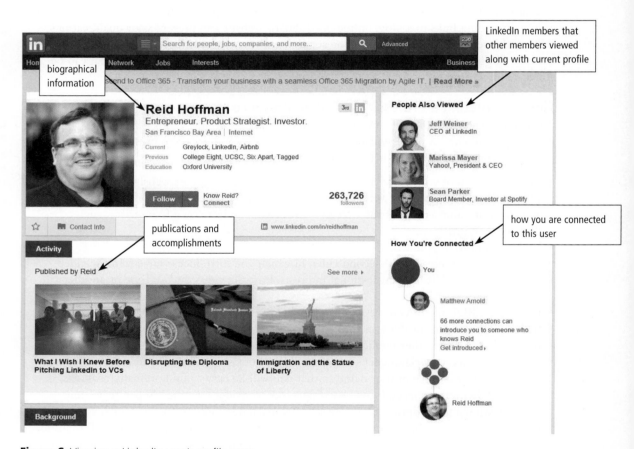

Figure C Viewing a LinkedIn user's profile page.
LinkedIn.com

Building a professional network on LinkedIn can help you locate professionals who can introduce you to employees at companies where you might like to work. You build your network on LinkedIn by finding other LinkedIn members to add to your network. To see if any of your current acquaintances are on LinkedIn, you can import email addresses from your email address book or import profiles of friends from your other social networking sites. LinkedIn also suggests people who you might know because you share common profile information. For example, LinkedIn will suggest members who have attended the same school or worked at the same company.

Your extended contacts include the network of your contacts' contacts. Extended contacts may be especially important when using social networking sites for job seeking or to find people with specific knowledge or skills that could be helpful to you. By completing your profile and participating regularly online in blogs and on social networking sites, you become easy to locate by others who are looking for people with your skills.

When you search LinkedIn's employment database to learn about career opportunities, search results may contain jobs posted by contacts who are in your extended network. For each job listing found, LinkedIn displays the name of the person who posted the job. LinkedIn also will display connections between you and those members you might want to contact in order to learn about a company or about career information or open jobs.

On LinkedIn, you also can join groups of people with similar interests or experiences. For example, if your school has an alumni group on LinkedIn, you might connect with some of the members. Through these relationships, you can become familiar with the companies that hire students from your school. These members also might be able to assist you as you prepare for a job search. Other examples of LinkedIn groups include people who work at the same company, people looking to share experiences they had when starting their own businesses, and people who use specific apps who are willing to share their expertise.

Interviewing Online

Many companies will offer to interview prospective employees or those seeking career information online. These interviews use free web-based videoconferencing services, such as Skype or Google+. Online interviews save both the employer and the prospective candidate time and money, as travel is not required for either party (Figure D). If mutual interest exists after the online interview, the employer may schedule an in-person interview with the candidate.

You should prepare for an online interview just as if it were an in-person interview. Preparation includes:

- Research the company and job for which you are applying.
- Be sure to dress appropriately.
- Select a location for the video call that has a neutral background and is free from distractions.
- Use a professional-looking photo for your videoconferencing app profile.
- Make sure that you have exchanged contact information with the person with whom you will be speaking. Share your user profile names for the videoconferencing app.
- Know how to initiate or receive a video call.
- Keep your eyes focused on the webcam so that you will appear attentive to your interviewer(s).

Career Considerations

If you invite an extended contact to connect, be sure to include a note that introduces yourself and indicates your professional reason for connecting.

Career Considerations

Before an interview, research the company online. Be prepared to discuss the company's mission, products, and accomplishments. You also should be familiar with current industry trends and news.

Career Considerations

Before an interview, silence or turn off your cell phone and any other mobile devices. Do not check any incoming text messages or notifications until after you have completed the video call.

Figure D Virtual remote interviews are becoming common as the first form of contact between jobseekers and their potential employers
Source: Albuquerque Journal/ZUMAPRESS.com

Career Considerations

Although each interview is different, most include standard questions. Search online for lists of common interview questions, and practice your answers with a friend.

Career Considerations

After an interview, consider sending handwritten thank you notes to each person who interviewed you. Mention something specific you discussed. Include at least one detail you learned that makes you a suitable candidate for the job. If a career counselor or alumnus from your school helped you obtain the interview, send him or her a thank you note, as well.

You should prepare the computer or mobile device you will use for the interview. Preparation includes:

- Plug in the computer or device. It is preferable to plug the computer or device into a wall outlet rather than relying on battery power when holding a videoconference. If you must use battery power, be sure that the battery is fully charged.
- Use a wired Internet connection, rather than connecting to a wireless network, to minimize the risk of losing Internet connectivity during the interview.
- Exit your email, chat, and other unnecessary applications during the interview so that you are not distracted or interrupted by alerts and notification messages.
- Test the videoconferencing software with a friend beforehand to ensure your configuration works.
- Adjust the microphone, webcam, and speakers before the actual interview. This enables you to configure optimum call quality. If your sound quality is poor, try wearing a headset with a microphone to minimize feedback.
- Check the webcam settings to ensure that your image is clear and that the place you will be sitting for the interview has sufficient light.
- Practice switching between the videoconferencing app's chat window and your desktop or a browser window, in case you want to share a link, file, or instant message with your interviewer during the interview.

Summary

Preparing for a technology career involves many steps, including education and obtaining degrees and certifications. Many career paths exist in the technology field, including (but not limited to): system development; technology operations; web marketing and social media; app development and mobile technologies; data storage, retrieval, and analysis; and information and systems security. Passing a certification exam demonstrates ability in a particular area to potential employers.

You can use the web to locate resources that will help you find jobs. Following a company's online presence, such as social media sites and the company's website, helps you learn about the company's current focuses and successes. Your school may have a career services website that offers resources specific to your location and area of study. When searching for a job, you should create a professional online presence in order to secure an interview. Career planning websites, such as LinkedIn, enable you to establish a professional online presence. Some companies may use web-based videoconferencing technologies to conduct online interviews. Preparation for an online interview includes not only researching the company and the job for which you are applying, but also familiarizing yourself with the technology you will use for the online interview.

Workbook

Please contact your instructor for the solutions.

Chapter One Crossword

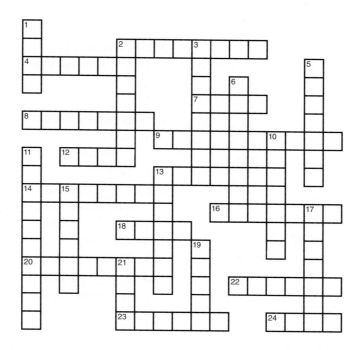

Across

2. Allow you to hear audio
4. Thin, lighterweight mobile computer that has a touch screen
7. Informal website consisting of time-stamped articles in a diary format
8. Output device that visually conveys text, graphics, and video information
9. Internet-capable phone
12. Named collection of stored data, instructions, or information
13. Recorded media that users can download or stream to a computer
14. Device that can accept data, process data, produce info, and store info
16. Electronic document on the web
18. Built-in connection to other documents, graphics, webpages, or websites
20. The electric, electronic, and mechanical components contained in computers
22. Duplicate of content on a storage medium
23. Computer dedicated to providing services to other computers on a network
24. One who interacts with a computer or utilizes the information it generates

Down

1. Collection of unprocessed items
2. Holds data, instructions, and information for future use
3. Contains keys you press to enter data and instructions into a computer
5. Input device that converts printed text into a form a computer can process
6. Instructions that tell a computer tasks to perform and how to perform them
10. Wireless network that provides Internet connections to mobile devices
11. Input device that enables you to speak into a computer or mobile device
13. Output device that produces text and graphics on a physical medium
15. Stores instructions waiting to be executed and data needed by those instructions
17. Motion made on a touch screen with tip of fingers or hand
19. Pointing device that fits under the palm of your hand comfortably
21. Programs on a smartphone

Chapter One Practice Test

1. Electronic components in computers process data using ____, which are the steps that tell the computer how to perform a particular task.
   a. information
   b. instructions
   c. tags
   d. links

2. A mobile computer is a ____.
   a. personal computer you can carry from place to place
   b. computing device small enough to hold in your hand
   c. tall and narrow tower, which can sit on the floor vertically
   d. mobile device on which you can store, organize, and play digital media

3. A notebook computer is also called a ____.
   a. handheld computer
   b. mainframe computer
   c. desktop computer
   d. laptop computer

4. A ____ is a collection of computers and devices connected together, often wirelessly.
   a. webpage
   b. website
   c. server
   d. network

5. A(n) ____ is a short note, typically fewer than 300 characters, sent to or from a smartphone or other mobile device.
   a. text message
   b. picture message
   c. video message
   d. instant message

6. A(n) ____ is an electronic version of a printed book, readable on computers and other digital devices.
   a. virtual book
   b. online book
   c. e-book
   d. i-book

7. Four widely used input devices are the keyboard, mouse, microphone, and ____.
   a. scanner
   b. printer
   c. speakers
   d. monitor

8. ____ consists of electronic components that store instructions waiting to be executed and the data needed by those instructions.
   a. Networking
   b. Data
   c. Memory
   d. Storage

9. A ____ is a named collection of stored data, instructions, or information and can contain text, images, audio, and video.
   a. link
   b. tag
   c. memory disk
   d. file

10. By subscribing to a(n) ____, you can connect to the Internet through your computers and mobile devices.
    a. CSS
    b. VoIP
    c. ISP
    d. FTP

11. A website is a collection of related webpages, which are stored on a web ____.
    a. connection
    b. network
    c. server
    d. cloud

12. A(n) ____ is software that finds websites, webpages, images, videos, news, maps, and other information related to a specific topic.
    a. query app
    b. browser
    c. online social network
    d. search engine

13. With ____, users can transfer items to and from other computers on the Internet.
    a. FTP
    b. IM
    c. VoIP
    d. ISP

14. Two behavioral health risks are computer addiction and ____.
    a. technology overload
    b. carpal tunnel syndrome
    c. computer vision syndrome
    d. repetitive stress

15. ____ consists of programs designed to make users more productive and/or assist them with personal tasks.
    a. Operating systems
    b. Application software
    c. System software
    d. Utility programs

16. A widely used communications device is a ____.
    a. scanner
    b. modem
    c. microphone
    d. motherboard

Chapter Two Crossword

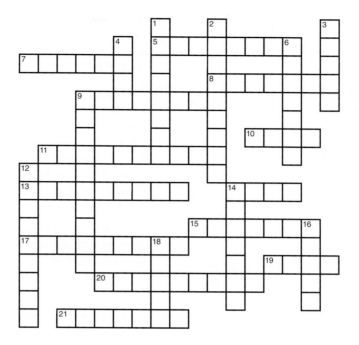

Across

5. Connects millions of businesses, educational institutions, and individuals

7. Website that offers many Internet services from a single, convenient location

8. Holds data, instructions, and information for future use

9. Equal to approximately one million characters

10. Enables users to speak to other users via their Internet connection

11. Code of acceptable behaviors users should follow while on the Internet

13. Appearance of motion created by displaying a series of still images in sequence

14. Website that allows users to create, modify, or delete content via a browser

15. Each electronic document on the web

17. Organization that sells and manages domain names

19. Real-time typed conversation that takes place with many other online users

20. Represents the amount of data that travels over a network

21. Wireless network that provides Internet connections to mobile computers

Down

1. Equal to approximately one billion characters

2. Computer that delivers requested webpages to your computer or mobile device

3. Consists of images displayed in motion

4. Informal website consisting of time-stamped articles in a diary/journal format

6. Communications activity

9. Refers to any application that combines text with media

12. Links to preferred websites

14. Collection of related webpages and associated items

16. Transmission of messages and files via a computer network

18. Includes music, speech, or any other sound

Chapter Two Practice Test

1. The web, email, and _____ are three of the more widely used Internet services.
   a. TIFF   c. ISP
   b. VoIP   d. PDF

2. A host, more commonly known today as a _____, is any computer that provides services and connections to other computers on a network.
   a. client   c. terminal
   b. net   d. server

3. Fixed wireless provides high-speed Internet connections using a dish-shaped antenna on a building to communicate with a tower location via _____.
   a. DSL   c. ISDN
   b. radio signals   d. satellite

4. A(n) _____ is a business that provides individuals and organizations access to the Internet free or for a fee.
   a. VoIP   c. FTP
   b. IP   d. ISP

5. A(n) _____ address is a sequence of numbers that uniquely identifies the location of each computer or device connected to the Internet.
   a. Internet Protocol
   b. File Transfer Protocol
   c. Voice over Internet Protocol
   d. Hypertext Transfer Protocol

6. The organization that approves and controls top-level domains is the _____.
   a. World Wide Web Consortium (W3C)
   b. Internet Society (IS)
   c. Uniform Resource Locator (URL)
   d. Internet Corporation for Assigned Names and Numbers (ICANN)

7. The domain name system (DNS) is the method that the Internet uses to store domain names and their corresponding _____.
   a. IP addresses
   b. uniform resource locators (URLs)
   c. hyper text transfer protocols (https)
   d. TCP addresses

8. A web _____ is a computer that delivers requested webpages to your computer or mobile device.
   a. browser   c. server
   b. network   d. search engine

9. A webpage has a unique address, called a web address or _____.
   a. DNS   c. HTML
   b. HTTP   d. URL

10. Some _____, such as Bing and Google, are helpful in locating information on the web for which you do not know an exact web address or are not seeking a specific website.
    a. social networks
    b. message boards
    c. search engines
    d. email programs

11. Depending on your search text, search engines may respond with thousands to billions of search results, sometimes called _____.
    a. hits   c. flames
    b. links   d. tags

12. A(n) _____ website offers exciting, challenging avenues for formal and informal teaching and learning.
    a. news   c. educational
    b. informational   d. online social network

13. The term _____ refers to the worldwide collection of blogs.
    a. W3C   c. blogworld
    b. blogosphere   d. blog portal

14. _____ e-commerce occurs when one consumer sells directly to another, such as in an online auction.
    a. Business-to-business (B2B)
    b. Business-to-consumer (B2C)
    c. Consumer-to-consumer (C2C)
    d. Consumer-to-business (C2B)

15. The first step in web publishing is to _____.
    a. deploy a website
    b. create a website
    c. plan a website
    d. analyze and design a website

16. Of the graphics formats for displaying images on the web, the JPEG and _____ formats are more common.
    a. GIF   c. TIFF
    b. BMP   d. PNG

Chapter Three Crossword

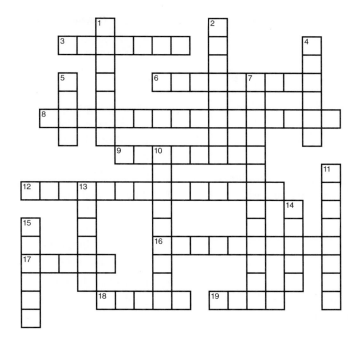

Across

3. Device that combines features of a smartphone with a tablet
6. Component that interprets and carries out instructions that operate a computer
8. Computer small enough to fit in one hand
9. Can accept and process data and produce and store information for future use
12. Practice of sharing or pooling computing resources, such as servers
16. Number of horizontal and vertical pixels in a display device
17. Smallest element in an electronic image
18. Frame that houses the system unit on a desktop
19. Point at which a peripheral device attaches to a computer

Down

1. Small speakers that rest inside each ear canal
2. Complete power failure
4. Computer dedicated to providing services to other computers on a network
5. Unsolicited email messages
7. Fastest, most powerful computer
10. Powerful server that can handle thousands of connected users simultaneously
11. Prolonged (more than a minute) undervoltage
13. Thin, lightweight mobile computer that has a touch screen
14. Momentary overvoltage
15. Lightweight mobile computer with a screen in its lid and a keyboard in its base

Chapter Three Practice Test

1. Types of ____ include desktops, laptops, and tablets.
   a. embedded computers
   b. personal computers
   c. supercomputers
   d. microcomputers

2. Two main components on the motherboard are the ____ and memory.
   a. server   c. processor
   b. modem   d. computer chip

3. A laptop, also called a ____, is a thin, lightweight mobile computer with a screen in its lid and a keyboard in its base.
   a. desktop computer
   b. notebook computer
   c. phablet
   d. convertible computer

4. A ____ is a tablet that has a screen it its lid and a keyboard in its base, with the lid and base connected by a swivel-type hinge.
   a. phablet   c. convertible tablet
   b. slate tablet   d. supertablet

5. A ____ server is a server that is housed in a slot on a metal frame.
   a. tower   c. rack
   b. bay   d. blade

6. ____ is the practice of sharing or pooling computing resources, such as servers and storage devices.
   a. Virtualization   c. Tethering
   b. Streaming   d. Converging

7. A self-service ____ is a freestanding terminal that usually has a touch screen for user interaction.
   a. kiosk   c. rack server
   b. phablet   d. thin client

8. Popular types of ____ are smartphones, digital cameras, portable media players, and e-book readers.
   a. mobile devices   c. laptops
   b. phablet   d. processors

9. A(n) ____ keyboard, which is a full-sized keyboard that communicates with a smartphone via a dock, cables, or wirelessly.
   a. on-screen   c. virtual
   b. tower   d. portable

10. ____ is the number of horizontal and vertical pixels in a display device.
    a. Resolution   c. Clarity
    b. Conversion   d. Virtualization

11. A(n) ____ is a mobile device that is used primarily for reading digital publications.
    a. virtual reader
    b. e-book reader
    c. i-media player
    d. cloud player

12. The general price range for a supercomputer is ____.
    a. several hundred to several thousand dollars
    b. several hundred dollars or less
    c. several hundred to several million dollars
    d. half a million to several billion dollars

13. Instead of the term, port, the term, ____, sometimes is used to identify audio and video ports.
    a. hub   c. bud
    b. spike   d. jack

14. Devices that connect to a ____ include the following: card reader, digital camera, external hard disk, modem, mouse, printer, scanner, smartphone, speakers, USB flash drive, and webcam.
    a. server farm   c. thin client
    b. USB port   d. mainframe

15. A USB ____ is a device that plugs in a USB port on the computer or mobile device and contains multiple USB ports, into which you plug cables from USB devices.
    a. hub   c. center
    b. farm   d. link

16. A ____ is a complete power failure.
    a. brownout   c. power surge
    b. blackout   d. whiteout

Chapter Four Crossword

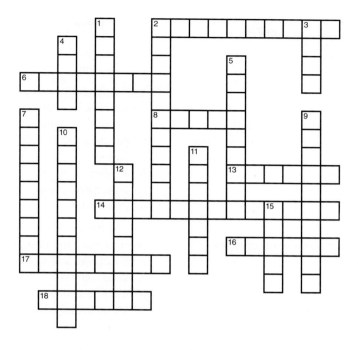

Across

2. To unzip or expand
6. Predefined formula that performs common calculations
8. Frame that houses the system unit on a desktop
13. Displays an online advertisement in a banner/pop-up window on Internet services
14. Reorganizing a hard disk so that the files are stored in contiguous sectors
16. Small text file that a web server stores on your computer
17. Collection of data organized to allow access, retrieval, and use of that data
18. Specific named location on a storage medium that contains related documents

Down

1. Another term for a program
2. Tool that removes a program
3. Unsolicited email message sent to many recipients at once
4. Name assigned to a specific design of characters
5. Copyrighted software that is distributed at no cost for a trial period
7. Temporary storage location
9. Area of a hard disk that holds infected files until the infection can be removed
10. Program designed to make users more productive and assist with personal tasks
11. Instructions that tell a computer tasks to perform and how to perform them
12. Software provided at no cost by an individual who retains rights to the software
15. Enable you to perform maintenance-type tasks

Chapter Four Practice Test

1. A(n) _____ consists of a series of related instructions, organized for a common purpose, that tells the computer what tasks to perform and how to perform them.
   a. operating system
   b. program
   c. suite
   d. media library

2. To use applications, such as a browser or email program on a personal computer, your computer must be running a(n) _____.
   a. productivity software suite
   b. operating system
   c. server
   d. utility

3. A(n) _____ gives authors, artists, and other creators of original work exclusive rights to duplicate, publish, and sell their materials.
   a. registration
   b. agreement
   c. license agreement
   d. copyright

4. _____ is copyrighted software that is distributed at no cost for a trial period.
   a. Freeware
   b. Public-domain
   c. Shareware
   d. Custom

5. A(n) _____ is the right to use a program or app.
   a. copyright
   b. product activation agreement
   c. license agreement
   d. software registration

6. A single _____ is about 1/72 of an inch in height.
   a. byte
   b. point
   c. pixel
   d. bit

7. A _____ is information that exists on a physical medium, such as paper.
   a. handout
   b. presentation
   c. print out
   d. hard copy

8. A feature, called _____, allows users to type words in a paragraph continually without pressing the ENTER key at the end of each line.
   a. wrapping
   b. e-wrap
   c. autowrap
   d. wordwrap

9. _____ software is an application that allows users to organize data in rows and columns and perform calculations on the data.
   a. Personal finance
   b. Database
   c. Tax preparation
   d. Spreadsheet

10. A software _____ is a collection of individual applications available together as a unit.
    a. package
    b. collection
    c. suite
    d. series

11. _____ software provides standard contracts and documents associated with buying, selling, and renting property; estate planning; marriage and divorce; and preparing a will or living trust.
    a. Legal
    b. Project management
    c. Enterprise computing
    d. Note taking

12. _____ software is a type of application that assists professionals and designers in creating engineering, architectural, and scientific designs and models.
    a. Desktop publishing
    b. Computer-aided design
    c. Paint/image editing
    d. Multimedia

13. Illustration software is another name for _____ software.
    a. desktop publishing
    b. paint
    c. image editing
    d. computer-aided design

14. _____ software allows users to combine text, graphics, audio, video, and animation in an interactive application.
    a. Desktop publishing
    b. Video editing
    c. Computer-aided design
    d. Multimedia authoring

15. A _____ resides in active memory and replicates itself over a network to infect computers and devices, using up the system resources and possibly shutting down the system.
    a. cookie
    b. rootkit
    c. worm
    d. trojan horse

16. A(n) _____ protects a computer against viruses by identifying and removing any computer viruses found in memory, on storage media, or on incoming files.
    a. virus blocker
    b. quarantine
    c. antivirus program
    d. trojan horse

Chapter Five Crossword

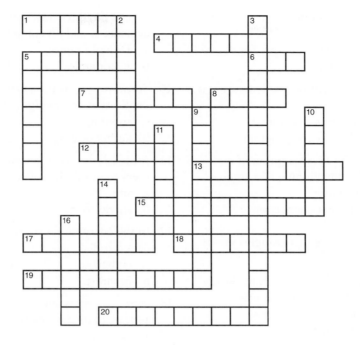

Across

1. Duplicate that can be used if the original is lost, damaged, or destroyed
4. Unauthorized and illegal duplication of copyrighted software
5. Useful to record, save, and execute keystrokes and instructions repeatedly
6. Program that performs a repetitive task on a network
7. Displays an online ads in a banner or pop-up window on webpages
8. Program that copies itself repeatedly
12. Consists of images displayed in motion
13. Technique used to make network or Internet transmissions appear legitimate
15. The encrypted (scrambled) data in the encryption process
17. Program that hides in a computer and allows someone to take control of it
18. Destructive event or prank
19. Online or Internet-based illegal acts
20. The unencrypted, readable data in the encryption process

Down

2. Private combination of characters associated with the user name
3. Demands payment to stop an attack on an organization's technology infrastructure
5. Programs that act without a user's knowledge and alter computer operations
9. Private combination of words associated with a user name
10. Compromised computers connected to a network and used to attack other networks
11. Small text file that a web server stores on your computer
14. Someone who accesses a computer or network illegally
16. Compromised computer or device

Chapter Five Practice Test

1. Today, combating cybercrime is one of the _____'s top priorities.
   a. CIA
   b. CTS
   c. FTC
   d. FBI

2. The _____ is the destructive event or prank malware is intended to deliver.
   a. virus hoax
   b. payload
   c. virus signature
   d. antivirus program

3. Which of the following is NOT a symptom of a computer or mobile device functioning as a zombie?
   a. Unusually high disk activity
   b. Slower than normal Internet connection
   c. Low audio quality
   d. Connected devices becoming increasingly unresponsive

4. Programmers often build _____ into programs during system development in order to bypass security controls while writing and testing programs.
   a. zombies
   b. back doors
   c. macros
   d. botnets

5. Some viruses are hidden in _____, which are instructions saved in software such as a word processing program or spreadsheet program.
   a. macros
   b. Trojan horses
   c. cascade style sheets
   d. menus

6. An organization's _____ should specify the acceptable use of technology by employees for personal reasons.
   a. PGP
   b. AUP
   c. TLS
   d. BSA

7. A(n) _____ is a private combination of characters associated with the user name that allows access to certain computer resources.
   a. password
   b. user name
   c. digital signature
   d. access control

8. Any item that you must carry to gain access to a computer or computer facility is called a _____.
   a. biometric device
   b. personal identification number (PIN)
   c. possessed object
   d. callback system

9. _____ is the discovery, collection, and analysis of evidence found on computers and networks.
   a. Digital forensics
   b. Ergonomics
   c. Computer crime
   d. Malware

10. Software _____ is the unauthorized and illegal duplication of copyrighted software.
    a. spoofing
    b. authenticating
    c. phishing
    d. piracy

11. A(n) _____ license is a legal agreement that permits users to install the software on multiple computers.
    a. site
    b. single-user
    c. network
    d. end-user

12. In the encryption process, the encrypted (scrambled) data is called _____.
    a. ciphertext
    b. hashtext
    c. plaintext
    d. keytext

13. A(n) _____ encryption algorithm removes characters and stores them elsewhere.
    a. expansion
    b. compaction
    c. substitution
    d. transposition

14. Web addresses of _____ sites often begin with https instead of http.
    a. secure
    b. encrypted
    c. authorized
    d. acceptable use

15. Some users implement a(n) _____ policy to preserve three copies of important files.
    a. three-generation backup
    b. full backup
    c. selective backup
    d. online backup

16. A wireless network should be configured so that it does not broadcast a network name, known as a(n) _____.
    a. SSL
    b. VPN
    c. RSI
    d. SSID

Index

3-D graphics, 170

A

academic apps, 177

acceptable use policy (AUP): Outlines the activities for which a computer and network may and may not be used. 210

access control: A security measure that defines who can access a computer, device, or network, when they can access it, and what actions they can take while accessing it. 211

accessibility, website guidelines, 80

accessories, gaming, 10–11

accounting software: An application that helps businesses of all sizes record and report their financial transactions. 164, 168

accuracy of information, 225

acronym reference, APP 1–2

add-ons, 83

address book scans, 70

Adobe Reader, 83, 167

Advanced Research Projects Agency (ARPANET), 54

adware: A program that displays an online advertisement in a banner or pop-up window on webpages, email, or other Internet services. 182, 205, 231

adware remover: A program that detects and deletes adware. 182

air gestures, 10

all-in-one desktop: Desktop that does not have a tower and instead houses the screen and system unit in the same case. 107, 108

Amazon's storefront, 75

animation: The appearance of motion created by displaying a series of still images in sequence. 81

anonymous FTP: File transfer method whereby anyone can transfer some, if not all, available files. 88

Anticybersquatting Consumer Protection Act (ACPA): Legislation whose goal is to protect trademark owners from being forced to pay a cybersquatter for a domain name that includes their trademark. ACPA for short. 60

anti-spam program: A filtering program that attempts to remove spam before it reaches your inbox or forum. 183

antivirus program: Software that protects a computer against viruses by identifying and removing any computer viruses found in memory, on storage media, or on incoming files. 23, 107, 108, 181–182, 208

app: Program designed to make users more productive and/or assist them with personal tasks. 26, 152. *See also* **application**; a**pplication software**

Apple computers, 25

Apple's iOS, 25

Apple's Mac OS, 25

application: Programs designed to make users more productive and/or assist them with personal tasks. 26, 152. *See also* **app**

application software: Program designed to make users more productive and/or assist them with personal tasks. *See also* **app**; **application**

application server, 111

applications

  categories of (table), 26, 153

  developing, 28

  downloading safely, 157

  graphics and media, 170–176

  help systems, 176

  installing, securing, 27–28

  vs. software suites, 164

  tracking your location, 66

apps

  fitness videos, apps as medical advice, 126

  fraudulent, 165

  help systems, 176

  payment, 168

  and programs, 25–28

  removing, 185

  security, 222–223

ARPANET: Agency of the U.S. Department of Defense whose goal was to build a network that (1) allowed scientists at different physical locations to share information and work together on military and scientific projects and (2) could function even if part of the